State and Local Politics

GOVERNMENT BY THE PEOPLE

TWELFTH EDITION

State and Local Politics

GOVERNMENT BY THE PEOPLE

David B. Magleby
Brigham Young University

David M. O'Brien
University of Virginia

Paul C. Light
New York University

James MacGregor Burns
University of Maryland, College Park
and Williams College

J.W. Peltason
University of California

Thomas E. Cronin
Whitman College

PEARSON

Prentice
Hall

Upper Saddle River, NJ 07458

Library of Congress Cataloging-in-Publication Data
State and local politics : government by the people / David B. Magleby
. . . [et al.].—12th ed.
p. cm.
Includes bibliographical references and index.
ISBN 0-13-199231-7
1. State governments—United States.   2. Local government—United
States.   I. Magleby, David B.
JK2408.S79 2006
320.973—dc22

2005034610

Editor-in-Chief: Charlyce Jones Owen
Associate Editor: Rob DeGeorge
Editorial Assistant: Jennifer Murphy
Developmental Editor: Betty Gatewood
Marketing Manager: Emily Cleary
Managing Editor: Lisa Iarkowski
Production Liaison: Joe Scordato
Prepress and Manufacturing Manager:
Nick Sklitsis
Prepress and Manufacturing Buyer:
Mary Ann Gloriande
Interior Design: Carmen DiBartolomeo
and TechBooks

Manager, Cover Visual Research &
Permissions: Karen Sanatar
Cover Design: Bruce Kenselaar
Cover Photo: Don Farrall / Photodisc /
Getty Images, Inc.
Illustrations: Mirella Signoretto
Composition/Full-Service Management:
TechBooks/Karen Ettinger
Printer/Binder: R. R. Donnelley &
Sons, Inc.
Cover Printer: Phoenix Color Corp.
Text: Utopia 9/12

Credits and acknowledgments borrowed from other sources and reproduced, with
permission, in this textbook appear on appropriate page within text.

Pearson Education LTD.
Pearson Education Singapore, Pte. Ltd
Pearson Education, Canada, Ltd
Pearson Education—Japan

Pearson Education Australia PTY, Limited
Pearson Education North Asia Ltd
Pearson Education de Mexico, S.A. de C.V.
Pearson Education Malaysia, Pte. Ltd

10 9 8 7 6 5 4 3 2 1
ISBN 0-13-199231-7

CONTENTS

PREFACE

State and local governments remain vital and important. When natural disasters, like Hurricane Katrina, or terrorist attacks occur, citizens expect their governments to respond quickly and effectively. The urgent needs of people are more important than which part of government responds or who has jurisdiction. The failure of government to meet these expectations in recent years has focused attention on how our federal system of government functions. What are the appropriate roles for municipal, county, state, and federal government agencies? While the scale of some problems may prompt the intervention of the federal government, there is also a longstanding preference for local autonomy. Additionally, there is a deeply held fear of the possible abuse of concentrated power, and dividing power among municipal, state, and federal governments may alleviate some of this concern.

This book is about the institutions and political forces that shape policy making and policy outcomes in state and local communities. To those of us who are students of American politics, states and their local government subdivisions are fascinating political laboratories that allow comparisons among different political systems and traditions. States vary in the powers given to governors, how their legislatures are structured, how judges are selected and reviewed, and how they operate in a host of policy areas, including how they impose taxes. The party system is much weaker in some regions of the country than in others. State legislatures in some of the smaller or rural states meet for just a few months a year, whereas in other states, they meet all year. The importance of interest groups and the media varies from state to state and from city to city. Generalizations are sometimes difficult, yet we try in this book to summarize what political scientists know about state and local politics and government.

State and local government and politics remain important not only to the residents of a particular state but to all Americans. A tax-cutting ballot initiative can spawn scores of similar votes in other states just as successful bonds to pay for highways and education can do the same. And as we learned form welfare reform, states can be catalysts for change on the national level and then central to its implementation.

Those who want better government in their communities and states will be more likely to achieve it by doing something to make it happen. If government by the people is to be more than just rhetoric, citizens must understand state and local politics and be willing to form political alliances, respect and protect the rights of those with whom they differ, and be willing to serve as citizen leaders and citizen politicians. We hope this book will motivate you to appreciate that every person can make a difference, and that we should each work toward this end.

For the Instructor

Instructor's Resource Manual with Test Item File This supplement provides the following resources for each chapter of the text: summary, review of major concepts, lecture suggestions and topic outlines, suggestions for classroom discussions, a content outline for lecture planning, and test questions. Contact your local representative for a copy of the manual.

Acknowledgments

We have had the benefit of useful criticisms and suggestions from Professors Thad Beyle, University of North Carolina at Chapel Hill; Gary C. Cornia, Brigham Young University; Yoram Haftel, Ohio State University; and Gary Moncrief, Boise State University.

   We would be pleased to hear from our readers with any reactions or suggestions. Write to us at our college addresses or in care of the Political Science Editor, Prentice Hall, Upper Saddle River, New Jersey 07458. Thanks.

David B. Magleby   Distinguished Professor of Political Science and Dean of FHSS, Brigham Young University, Provo, UT 84602 david_magleby@byu.edu

David M. O'Brien   Leone Reaves and George W. Spicer Professor, Department of Government and Foreign Affairs, University of Virginia, Charlottesville, VA 22903 dmo2y@virginia.edu

Paul C. Light   Paulette Goddard Professor of Public Service at New York University paul.light@nyu.edu

James MacGregor Burns   Academy of Leadership, University of Maryland, College Park, MD 20742

J. W. Peltason   School of Social Sciences, University of California, Irvine, CA 92717-5700 jwpeltas@uci.edu

Thomas E. Cronin   Office of the President, Whitman College, Walla Walla, WA 99362 cronin@whitman.edu

State and Local Politics

GOVERNMENT BY THE PEOPLE

STATE AND LOCAL POLITICS
WHO GOVERNS?

Many of the most critical domestic and economic issues facing the United States are decided by our state and local officials. Elected and appointed officials in our states and localities decide how our schools are run, how welfare policy is shaped, who goes to prison or gets probation, and how much property and sales taxes we pay. Such challenging responsibilities as overseeing the transition from welfare to work, maintaining prisons and jails (over 90 percent of the people incarcerated in America are in state and local facilities, not federal prisons), and bringing the residents of the inner cities in our large metropolitan areas into the economic mainstream require leadership and thoughtful public policy making at the state and local levels of government as well as in Washington, D.C.

State and local governments are beginning to recover from the economic downturn of the early 2000s. States had to raise income and sales taxes as well as fees on all kinds of services, from fishing and marriage licenses to divorce filings and college tuition fees. Over a three-year period, the University of Arizona, the University of Virginia, and the California State University system, for example, all increased tuition by over 30 percent.[1] States also had to make deep cuts in spending on health care and other programs, along with turning to one-time gimmicks such as borrowing against pension funds.[2] The budget crisis in California led to the recall of Governor Gray Davis and the election of Arnold Schwarzenegger, who vowed not to raise taxes, proposing instead a referendum to authorize a $15 billion bond sale order to deal with the state's $14 billion shortfall.

State and local governments flourished long before there was a national government. Indeed, the framers of our Constitution shaped the national government largely according to their practical experience with colonial and state governments. What happens today in state and local governments continues to influence the policies of the national government. The reverse, of course, is also true: The national government and its policies have an important impact on local and state government. The national government's activities—such as the war against international terrorism, key Supreme Court decisions, and major congressional investigations and legislation—receive such great publicity that we often overlook the countless ways governments closer to home affect our lives.

Studying state and local governments to find out how they operate and who governs them is also a challenge. It is one thing to study our national system, vast and complex as it is; it is something else to study 50 separate state governments, each with its own legislature, executive, and judiciary and each with its own intricate politics and political traditions. Moreover, state and local governments are only part of a much larger picture. To discuss the government of the state of Mississippi or the city of Detroit without mentioning race, the government of New York City or Los Angeles without noting the politics of ethnic groups, or the government of Texas without referring to the cattle and oil industries would be to ignore the real dynamics of the political process. State and local governments, like the national government, are more than organizational charts. They are systems of politics and people with their own unique histories that affect how and what public policies are enacted. The great variations among the states and localities—in population, economic resources, and environment—make comparisons and generalizations difficult.

Still, every government system is part of a larger social system. A government is a structure and a process that resolves, or at least manages, conflicts. It regulates, distributes, and sometimes redistributes property and wealth. It is also a means for achieving certain goals and performing services desired both by those who govern and by the governed. It operates in the context of an economic system, class structure, and lifestyle that are often more important than the structure of the government itself or even the nature of its political processes. The interrelations among the economic, social, and political systems are complex and difficult to unscramble, and it is hard to decide which is cause and which is effect.[3]

This already complex picture is complicated further by the fact that almost 88,000 cities, counties, towns, villages, school districts, water control districts, and other governmental units are piled one on top of another within the states.[4] If all states or cities or towns were alike, the task might be manageable. But of course they are not. Each city, like each state, has distinct characteristics.

WHO HAS THE POWER?

How can we grasp the operations and problems of state and local government without becoming bogged down in endless detail? We can do so by focusing on the core components of democratic governance: citizen participation, liberty, constitutional checks and balances, representation, and responsible leadership. Further, we can address several questions that throw light on all these problems: Who governs? How much influence or control is in the hands of the business community? Does political power tend to gravitate toward a relatively small number of people? If so, who are these people? Do they work closely together, or do they oppose each other? Do the same people or factions shape the agenda for public debate and dominate all decision making? Or do some sets of leaders decide certain questions and leave other questions to other leaders or simply to chance?

In 1924, two sociologists from Columbia University, Robert and Helen Lynd, decided to study a typical American city as though they were anthropologists investigating a tribe in Africa or Indonesia. For two years, they lived in Muncie, Indiana—at that time a city of 38,000 residents—asking questions and watching how people made their living, raised their children, used their leisure time, and joined in civic and social associations. The Lynds reported that despite the appearance of democratic rule, a social and economic elite actually ran things.[5] Their work stimulated studies in all kinds of communities to find out whether power is concentrated in the hands of the few, is dispersed among the many, or operates in some other way.

Relying on a mix of research methods, social scientists since the Lynds' time have studied patterns of power in communities and arrived at a variety of findings. Floyd Hunter, a sociologist who analyzed Atlanta in the 1950s, found a relatively small and stable group of top policy makers drawn largely from the business class. This elite operated through secondary leaders who sometimes modified policy, but the power of the elite was almost always important.[6] In contrast, Robert Dahl and his graduate students at Yale studied New Haven at the same time and concluded that although some people had a great deal of influence, there was no permanent elite. Instead, there were shifting coalitions of leaders who sometimes disagreed among themselves but who always had to keep in mind what the public would accept when making decisions.[7]

Rule by a Few or Rule by the Many?

One group of investigators, chiefly sociologists such as Hunter, have been concerned with **social stratification** in the political system—how politics is affected by divisions among socioeconomic groups or classes in a community. These social scientists assume that political influence is a function of social stratification. They try to find out who governs particular communities by asking various citizens to identify the people who are most influential. Then they study those influential people to determine their social characteristics, their roles in decision making, and the interrelations among them and between them and the rest of the citizens. Using this technique, they find that the upper socioeconomic groups make up the *power elite,* that elected political leaders are subordinate to that elite, and that the major conflicts within the community are between the upper and the lower socioeconomic classes.

Other investigators question these findings and raise objections to the research techniques used. They contend that the evidence in social stratification studies does not support the conclusion that communities are run by a power elite. Rather, the notion of a power elite is merely a reflection of the techniques used and the assumptions made by stratification theorists. Instead of studying the activities of those who are thought to have "clout," these researchers insist, one should study how decisions are actually made.

Researchers conducting *community power* studies analyzing the making of decisions usually find a relatively open, pluralistic power structure. Some people do have more influence than others, but that influence is shared among many people and tends to be limited to particular issues and areas. For example, those who decide how the public schools are run may have little influence over other economic policies. In many communities and for many issues, there is no identifiable group of influential people. Policies emerge not from the actions of a small group but rather from the unplanned and unanticipated consequences of the behavior of a relatively large number of people, especially from the countless contending groups that form and win access to those who make the important decisions. According to community power theorists, the social structure of the community is certainly one factor, but not the determining factor in how goods and services are distributed.

Comparing power elite and community power studies highlights the fact that how we ask questions often influences the answers we get. If we ask highly visible and actively involved citizens for their opinions of who is powerful, we find that they name a relatively small number of people as the real brokers of power. But if we study dozens of local events and decisions, we find that a variety of people are actually involved—different people in different policy areas.

Other studies of local politics suggest that local values, traditions, and the structure of governmental organizations also determine which issues get on the local agenda.[8] Thus tobacco, mining, or steel interests may be so dominant in some areas that tax, regulation, or job safety policies are kept off the local policy agenda for fear of offending the "powers that be." Those "powers" may indeed go to great lengths to prevent what they deem to be adverse policies. This type of research alerts us to weigh carefully the possibility that defenders of the status quo can mobilize power resources in such a way that nondecisions may be more important than decisions. In effect, these researchers tell us not only to study who governs but also to study the procedures and rules of the game. They urge us to determine which groups or interests would gain and which would lose by political decisions.[9]

On many economic policy matters, local corporations and business elites are involved. Studies of cities in Michigan and of Atlanta employing refined and contextual analysis of political decision making concluded that business elites are indeed important, but they are not necessarily the controlling factor in city governance:

> There is, then, no controlling hand in community politics. No conspiracy of business and government exists. Business interests do not invariably dominate government policy even where a single industry dominates the community. However, the giant industrial companies do provide the backdrop against which the public policy process operates in the industrial city. They are always there, seldom intervening in specific policy matters but never far from the calculations of policy makers.[10]

Studies of states and communities have now produced enough findings that we can see how formal government institutions, social structure, economic factors, and other variables interact in a working political system.

THE STAKES IN THE POLITICAL STRUGGLE

The national government has become the driving force behind the nation's economic strength and security. It assumes major responsibility for protecting civil rights, fighting inflation and unemployment, regulating sectors with great economic power, and subsidizing weaker sectors of the economy—not to mention matters of war and peace. State and local governments cannot claim so central a role. Yet the role of states and localities is increasing over a range of domestic policies, even though they diverge in their priorities and policies as a result of the maze of interests in each state. In response to health concerns and budget deficits, for example, seven states charge more than $1 per pack of cigarettes in taxes, while about half charge just 33 cents or less, and some cities, like New York, impose additional taxes both to discourage smoking and to raise revenue.

Since World War II, state and local government activities have increased much faster than the nondefense activities of the federal government. In the past decade, the federal government has been downsizing while state and local governments have been growing. About six times as many people work for state and local governments—15 million—than work for the federal government, which has fewer than 3 million civilian employees.[11] Most state and local employees work in education (8.2 million), hospitals (917,000), law enforcement (887,000), and corrections (702,000).[12]

State and local governments deal more directly with the average person than the national government does, because neighborhood, school, and housing problems are closely regulated at the state and local levels. States have had to assume greater responsibilities for raising taxes, setting economic and social priorities, and administering most welfare and job creation programs as a result of cutbacks in federal funds and devolution of responsibilities to the states.

The points at which people come into contact with government services and officials most often concern schools, streets and highways, parks and playgrounds, police and fire protection, zoning, and health care. But even in these areas, the mix of national, state, and local programs and responsibilities is such that it is often hard to isolate which level of government does what to or for whom. Also, there are some national-to-individual relationships that bypass state and local governments altogether, such as the Internal Revenue Service, the U.S. Postal Service, and Social Security.

The Maze of Interests

Special-interest groups can be found in varying forms in every state and locality. For example, industrial Rhode Island has farm organizations, and rural Wyoming has trade unions. Influential economic pressure groups and political action committees, organized to raise and disburse campaign funds to candidates for public office, operate in the states much as they do nationally. They try to build up the membership of their organizations, they lobby the state capitals and city halls, they educate and organize the voters, and they support their political friends in office and oppose their enemies. They also face the same internal problems all groups face: maintaining unity, dealing with subgroups that break off in response to special needs, and balancing democracy with discipline.

One great difference, however, is that group interests can be concentrated and highly influential in states and localities, whereas their strength tends to be diluted in the national government. Big business does not really run things in Washington, D.C., any more than Wall Street, the Catholic Church, or the American Legion does. But in some states and localities, certain interests clearly dominate because they represent the social and economic majorities of the area. Few politicians in Wisconsin will attack dairy farmers, few candidates for office in Florida will oppose benefits for senior citizens, and few officeholders in Idaho will support gun control. In other areas, industries such as timber or energy are influential because of their role in the local economy.

It is the range and variety of these local groups that give American politics its special flavor, excitement, and challenge: auto unions and manufacturers in Michigan, corn and hog farmers in Iowa, gas and oil dealers in Texas, gun owners in New Hampshire and Idaho, tobacco farmers in North Carolina and Virginia, poultry growers in Arkansas, Boeing and Microsoft in the Seattle area, coal miners in West Virginia, and sheep ranchers in Utah. However, the power of these groups should not be exaggerated.

We have to be cautious about lumping all workers, all businesspeople, all teachers, all Hispanics, or all African Americans together. The union movement is sometimes sharply divided among the truckers, building trades, machinists, auto workers, and so on. The business community is often divided between big industrial, banking, and commercial firms on the one hand and small merchants on the other. In New England, Irish and Italian fraternal societies express the opinions of their respective groups on public issues; other organizations speak for people of French Canadian or Polish descent. New England politicians fear the power of ethnic groups to influence elections, especially primaries, yet there are plenty of examples of "Yankees" winning in heavily ethnic areas. Similarly, Asian American, Latino, and African American communities are playing an increasingly important role in elections in states such as California, Florida, and Texas.

Compared to the other considerations affecting voters' choices, the ethnic factor may be small. Still, even a small percentage of the populace voting according to their ethnic interests can have a decisive effect on an election. Much depends on the character of the candidates and their personal appeal. Any group, no matter how strong, must cope with a variety of cross pressures, including a general sense that the voter does not vote for "one of our own" on that ground alone.

Other interests that are more specialized may also have a close relationship with local government. Many businesspeople sell products to the state or perform services for it: milk dealers, printers, contractors, parking meter manufacturers, computer and communications technology firms, makers of playground equipment, textbook publishers, and so on. They often organize formally or informally to improve their relations with purchasing officials. At the local level, developers and home builders and their lawyers press for zoning and planning commission action. Millions of dollars are often at stake, and the resulting action or inaction frequently shapes both the economic growth and the environmental quality of a community.

Business interests are inevitably involved in city and county politics and policy making. As one study of Atlanta found, the business elite is rarely a passive or reluctant partner in setting local priorities. "Atlanta's postwar political experience is a story of active business-elite efforts to make the most of their economic and organizational resources in setting the terms on which civic cooperation occurs."[13] Businesses everywhere depend on local governments for parking,

TOP TEN ISSUES FACING STATE LEGISLATURES

State legislatures are confronting a range of controversial issues. The top ten state legislative issues are:

- Dealing with budget shortfalls
- Providing for health coverage
- Raising educational standards
- Lowering the cost of prescription drugs
- Providing tax incentives for attracting and retaining businesses
- Reforming tax laws
- Regulating energy production and delivery
- Addressing the rising cost of medical malpractice liabilities and insurance premiums
- Improving air quality
- Deciding whether to recognize same-sex marriages

SOURCE: Melissa Conradi, "Ten Issues to Watch," *Governing* (January 2004), available at www.governing.com/articles/1issues.htm © 2004 Congressional Quarterly Inc. All rights reserved. Reprinted with permission.

good roads and transportation, safety, urban renovations, and much more. Business elites get involved in long-range community planning, are keenly interested in who gets elected, and are ever watchful of changes in taxation structures.

Another type of interest group intimately concerned with public policy is the professional association. States license barbers, beauticians, architects, lawyers, doctors, teachers, accountants, dentists, and many other occupational groups. You will find representatives from the Beauticians Aid Association, the Funeral Directors and Embalmers Association, the Institute of Dry Cleaning, and the Association of Private Driver-Training Schools lobbying at the statehouse. Associations representing such groups are concerned with the nature of the regulatory laws and the makeup of the boards that do the regulating. They are especially concerned about the rules for admission to their profession or trade and about the way in which professional misconduct is defined and punished. Stiffening licensing requirements for physicians will decrease the supply of new doctors, for example, and thereby raise the incomes of those in practice. Bar associations, for the same reason, closely monitor licensing standards for the legal profession and the appointment of state and local judges.

Today, other groups of citizens are also likely to organize to influence decisions in the state capital: those who are pro-life and those who are pro-choice, those who want stiffer sentences for drunken driving, and those who favor three-strikes-and-you're-out legislation to send repeat criminals to jail for life. Right to Life groups, Planned Parenthood, antismoking groups, animal rights activists, and prison guards are also well organized. Increasingly significant are environmental groups such as the Sierra Club, both in forging public policies and as forces in election contests.

Lobbyists at the Statehouse

Many businesses, especially larger corporations, employ lobbyists, public relations specialists, political consultants, or law firms to represent them.[14] One of the growth businesses in state politics is consulting, usually by specialized lawyers or former state legislators. For a fee, lobbyists push desired bills through the legislature or block unwanted ones. This kind of activity again raises the question of who has clout or who governs. Clearly, those who can hire skilled lobbyists and other experts to shape the public agenda often wield more influence than unorganized citizens, who rarely even follow state and regional governmental decision making.

Lobbyists are present in every state capital, and they are there to guide through the legislature a small handful of bills their organization wants passed or to stop those their organization wants defeated.[15] Legislators process hundreds or even thousands of bills each year, in addition to doing casework on behalf of constituents and worrying about reelections. Shrewd lobbyists usually get a chance—sometimes several chances—to influence the fate of their few bills.

There is a widespread impression that lobbyists have freer rein in state legislatures than they do in the U.S. Congress and, what is more, that bribes or informal payoffs by lobbyists are cruder and more obvious in state legislatures. Certainly lobbying restrictions in the states are more relaxed than at the federal level, although in some of the larger states they may be even more stringent. There is less media coverage of state politics in many states than is focused on national politics in Washington, D.C. Corruption of legislators and state officials is usually hard to prove. Exposure of scandals in several

CHANGING FACE OF AMERICAN POLITICS

THE GROWING DIVERSITY OF STATE POPULATIONS

The 2000 Census showed significant changes in both the number and location of minority Americans. The percentage of whites declined from 76 percent of the population in 1990 to 69 percent in 2000, while the percentage of Hispanics increased from 9 percent to 12.5 percent, blacks from 11.7 percent to 12.1 percent, and Asian-Pacific Islanders from 2.8 percent to 3.7 percent.

America's growing minority population is not equally distributed across the states and cities, however. Roughly three-quarters of all Hispanics live in the West or South, accounting for a quarter of the population in the West and 12 percent of the population in the South. In turn, just over half of all blacks live in the South, making up 20 percent of the total population; while half of the Asian-Pacific Islander population live in just three states, California, New York, and Hawaii; and two-fifths of all Native Americans live in the West.

Although Hispanics are counted as a single minority group, almost 60 percent of Hispanics actually identified themselves in the 2000 Census as Mexican, another 10 percent as Puerto Rican, and 4 percent as Cuban. Similarly, the Asian-Pacific Islander population includes Asian Indians, Chinese, Filipinos, Japanese, Koreans, Native Hawaiians, and Samoans; while Native Americans include members of six American Indian tribes—Cherokee, Navajo, Latin American Indian, Choctaw, Sioux, and Chippewa—as well as Eskimo.

By 2025, the U.S. Census Bureau predicts that the percentage of white Americans will decline to 62 percent. By then, four states and the District of Columbia will be "majority minority," and several others will be closing in on the 50 percent mark.

Top Ten States by Minority Population in 2000	Top Ten States by Minority Population Projected in 2025
District of Columbia 72%	Hawaii 77%
Hawaii 71	District of Columbia 74
New Mexico 52	California 66
California 50	New Mexico 60
Texas 44	Texas 54
Mississippi 38	New York 47
Louisiana 36	Maryland 46
Maryland 35	New Jersey 45
New York 35	Alaska 43
Georgia 33	Louisiana 43

SOURCE: U.S. Census Bureau, "State Projections by Single Year of Age, Sex, Race, and Hispanic Origin, 1995–2025," accessed online at www.census.gov/population/www/projections/stproj.html on February 15, 2004.

states pushed many legislatures to curb election abuses and pass ethics codes with stringent conflict-of-interest provisions.[16] Several legislatures have enacted comprehensive financial disclosure laws, and today most state governments are more open, professional, and accountable than in the past.[17] Former President Jimmy Carter, who served in the Georgia Senate and then became governor, recalled that only a "tiny portion" of the 259 members of the Georgia legislature were not good or honest people. But Carter found that "it is difficult for the common good to prevail against the intense concentration of those who have a special interest, especially if the decisions are made behind locked doors."[18]

In a few states, one corporation or organization may exercise considerable influence; in others, a "big three" or "big four" dominate politics. But in most states, there is competition among organizations; no single group or coalition of groups stands out. In no state does only one organization control legislative politics, although the powerful Anaconda Company once came close in Montana. For example, some 400 lobbyists are registered in Arkansas. Of these, 125 represent utilities; more than 200 represent individual businesses, industry, or professions; nine represent labor interests; eight work on behalf of senior citizens; and three lobby for environmental interests. The Arkansas Power and Light Company, the railroads, the poultry and trucking industries, the teachers, and the state Chamber of Commerce are the most effective lobbyists. "It is still true that ordinarily those with greater economic resources, greater numbers, and higher status have far more impact than those who lack these attributes," writes political scientist Diane Blair. "Nevertheless, an increasingly complex economy has produced many more actors in the political system, and especially when there is division among the economic elite, some of the lesser voices can be heard."[19]

In Michigan, about 1,250 lobbyists are registered with the state, including representatives of the "big three" automakers, the United Auto Workers, the AFL-CIO, the Michigan Education Association, the Michigan Manufacturers Association, the city of Detroit, the Michigan Chamber of Commerce, certain conservation and environmental groups, and various antitax groups.[20]

As a result of the influence and growing number of lobbyists, states have adopted ethics laws that regulate their activities. Seven states completely ban lobbyists from contributing to campaign contributions at any time, for instance; 23 states prohibit lobbyists from making contributions during a legislative session. Half of the states restrict the monetary value of gifts that public employees may receive.

Not to be overlooked are the growing number of groups and media outlets that view themselves as "watchdogs" of the public policy process. Groups such as the League of Women Voters, Common Cause, and various citizens' groups regularly monitor state politics for questionable fund-raising or lobbying practices. Their "watchdog" efforts are sometimes aided by reporters who cover state capitals.

PARTICIPATION PATTERNS IN SMALL- AND MEDIUM-SIZED CITIES

Although it is widely believed that citizens feel "closer" to city and county governments than they do to the more remote national government in Washington, D.C., citizens generally take less interest in, vote less often in, and are less informed about their local governments than they are about the national government. There are understandable reasons for the lower involvement in local government. Although issues about where to locate a garbage dump or a prison or how to deal with police brutality can arouse considerable heat, most of the time local governments are preoccupied with relatively noncontroversial routine matters, such as keeping the roads in shape, providing fire and police service, attracting businesses that can create more jobs, or applying for state and federal financial assistance.

Local communities want to keep their tax rates down and promote their cities as "nice places" in which to live, work, and raise families. Mayors and city officials generally try to avoid controversy and the kind of criticism that will divide a community. Although they do not always succeed, they go to considerable lengths to be reasonable and work for the good of the community. Few aggressively seek to alter the status quo. They do not, as a rule, try to promote equality by redistributing various resources to needier citizens. **Redistributive policies** are programs to shift wealth or benefits from one segment of the population to another, usually from the rich to the poor. Local officials tend to believe that this is the task of the national or state authorities—if they think it should be done at all. Typically, they say their communities do not have the funds for such programs. They might add, "Go see the governor" or "Go talk to your member of Congress." This may be good advice, because various programs (educational loans, unemployment compensation, disability assistance, and so on) explicitly designed to help the less fortunate are administered at the state or federal level.

Neighborhood groups sometimes become involved in protecting their neighborhoods and petitioning for improvements. One concern that often activates neighborhood groups is the possibility that "undesirable" facilities might be located in their neighborhood, such as drug rehabilitation clinics, prisons, dumps, or homeless shelters. Although attendance at local government meetings is usually low, the announcement of a landfill area or a prison construction project often stimulates the reaction that local officials call NIMBY, an acronym for "Not In My Back Yard!"

The Role of Local Media

Most communities have only one newspaper, and in small communities it is often a weekly. Some newspapers and local radio and television stations do a good job of covering city and county politics, but this is the exception rather than the rule. Reporters assigned to cover local politics are often inexperienced beginners, yet they provide the only news that citizens get about their city council or zoning board. Even the best of them have difficulty conveying the full complexities of what is going on in a column or two of newsprint.

Some local newspapers enjoy a cozy relationship with elected local officials. Sometimes the owners or editors are social friends or golfing buddies of local officials. Friendships and mutual interests develop, and close scrutiny of what goes on in city hall takes a back seat to city boosterism. In effect, "newspapers boost their hometown, knowing that its prosperity and expansion aid their own. Harping on local faults, investigating dirty politics, revealing unsavory scandals, and stressing governmental inefficiencies only provide readily available documentary material to competing cities."[21]

Editors and station managers recognize that their readers or listeners are more interested in state or national news, and especially in sports, than in what is going on at municipal planning meetings or county commission sessions. Much of what takes place in local government is rather dull. It may be important to some people, yet it strikes the average person as decidedly less exciting than what goes on at the White House or whether Congress has finally solved the Social Security problem or whether their stocks have gone up or down or whether the New York Jets or the Los Angeles Lakers won last night. We have dozens of ways to find out about Congress and the White House, but we usually have only one source for stories about the mayor or sheriff or school board. Of course, we could attend board meetings or even talk with our mayor, but that is not what most people are likely to do.

Apathy in Grassroots America

Voter apathy in local elections is summed up in the bumper sticker "DON'T VOTE. IT ONLY ENCOURAGES THEM." Many important political and economic transactions in communities are ignored by the press and citizens. Charter revision and taxation often galvanize only those directly affected by the new taxes or regulations. Even New England town meetings have difficulty getting people to participate—despite the fact that decisions made at these meetings have major consequences for local tax rates and the quality of the schools, the police force, and the parks and recreational areas. Thomas Jefferson once proclaimed the town meeting to be the noblest, wisest instrument yet devised for the conduct of public affairs, but today most towns find that only about 2 or 3 percent of the population cares enough to come.[22]

The major reason for grassroots apathy is that local politics simply does not interest the average person. Most people are content to leave politics and political responsibilities to a relatively small number of activists while they pursue their own private concerns—their bowling leagues, their children's Little League or soccer games, golf, or fishing. In a healthy democracy, we can expect that most people will be involved with their families and jobs; other than voting occasionally, they tend to leave civic responsibilities to a relatively small number of their fellow citizens. This is probably a reasonable choice. It may also be an indication of satisfaction with the state of the community.

Cynicism about the effectiveness and fairness of local political processes is sometimes reflected in the politics of protest—mass demonstrations, economic boycotts, even civil disorders—to make demands on government. When certain issues become intense, people become politically active. African Americans, Hispanics, gays, and others form political organizations to present their grievances and marshal votes. Neighborhood organizations work for better housing and enforcement of inspection ordinances and to prevent crime and drug dealing.

Civic Initiatives in Local Governments

Just as there will always be indifference toward politics and apathy about government, so too will there always be creative, entrepreneurial people who are willing to step forward and find new ways of solving problems. States such as Oregon and Minnesota seem to encourage a climate of innovation and civic enterprise, and a wider look at the United States finds buoyant, optimistic, creative problem solvers in nearly every corner of the nation.

Enterprising local activists have advocated and implemented cost-saving energy programs, environmental cleanup campaigns, recycling and solar energy initiatives, job training centers, AIDS prevention efforts, housing for the elderly, tutoring for the illiterate, housing for the poor, and hundreds of other problem-solving and opportunity-enhancing community efforts.[23] In almost every case, they create partnerships with elected officials at city hall, sometimes with the Urban League or Chamber of Commerce, and often with local foundations and business corporations.

Sometimes it takes a tragedy to get community groups mobilized. Such a tragic event happened in Boston when gang members burst into the funeral of a young man.

"In the presence of the mourners, the gang killed one of those in attendance," writes the Reverend Eugene Rivers of the Azusa Christian Community:

> That brazen act told us we had to do more. Now. That young man's death galvanized us, and soon the Ten Point Coalition was reaching out to at-risk youth. Our mission was to pair the holy and the secular, to do whatever it took to save our kids. The black churches worked hand-in-hand with the schools, courts, police, and social service agencies. We called on anyone and everyone who had the means to help our children. We formed programs for teens, neighborhood watches, and patrols. . . . We established ourselves in the neighborhood, standing on the same street corner where the drug dealers once stood. We tracked down the thieves, dealers, and gangs. We tried to give people a chance, but if they wouldn't take it, we staked our claim and ran them out of our neighborhood.[24]

There are persistent debates about how to solve social, economic, and racial problems in our large metropolitan areas. Some people contend that government can't undertake this task and that private initiatives can be more effective. Others insist that state and local governments are best suited to deal with these challenges. Still others contend that imaginative public–private collaboration is needed to fashion the strategies and mobilize the resources to revive our cities and bring about greater opportunity. Whatever the merits of such contending interpretations, it is clear that neighborhood organizations and spirited civic renewal are critical to the vitality of local government.[25]

CHALLENGES FOR STATE AND LOCAL GOVERNMENTS

Most states and communities are confronting testing times. Virtually all of the states and major cities face serious budget problems and increasing demands for services. People don't like tax increases, but they want better schools, a clean environment, and safe roads. About one-third of our inner-city governments and school systems are in financial distress. The cycle of poverty in the inner cities remains one of the greatest threats to the economic health of the country. Cities, though, often cannot raise enough funds through local taxes to create jobs and to provide adequate educational opportunities and housing. Federal and state initiatives have attempted to create economic opportunities for inner-city residents. Community development banks, "empowerment zones," Head Start, charter schools, and national service (Americorp) programs have all been tried in an attempt to bring residents of depressed inner cities into the economic mainstream. But these efforts have been inadequate and must compete with other demands on financially pressed states and localities.

The following central issues in the states and local communities command the attention of the country. They vary depending on location, of course, yet these urgent challenges are part of the unfinished business of a government by the people:

- *People want more services yet at the same time would like to see their taxes cut.* City and state officials are constantly trying to do more with less and introduce efficiencies into city and state operations. Voters in many communities have enacted spending limits that constrain growth in public budgets.

- *Racism still exists in many communities.* As our nation has become more diverse, most Americans have learned to appreciate the strength that comes from multiple cultures and races. Yet racist groups still thrive in some areas, and bigotry and discrimination persist.

■ *Drugs, gangs, and drug-related crime impose tough policy challenges.* The costs of corrections and prisons have skyrocketed in recent years, yet gangs, drugs, and crime are still a menace in some urban and even rural areas.

■ *The costs of Homeland Security.* Due to the continuing threat of international terrorism, states and localities must assume a greater role in safeguarding airports and other public places, as well as assume the role of "first responders" in the event of an attack. Mayors of major cities and some governors, however, complain that the national government has failed to provide and deliver the funding necessary for these expanded responsibilities.

■ *Poverty in the inner cities persists.* We have extremes of rich and poor within metropolitan regions, and often the wealthier suburbs turn their backs on the problems and poverty of the older cities. Indifference to these inequalities and lack of opportunities may undermine a sense of community and fairness in America.

■ *We need to guarantee the best possible education for all our young people.* Parents are demanding better education and more parental involvement. Communities have been experimenting with educational choice and competition, school vouchers, and charter schools. Improving the public schools is necessary, but their resources and the salaries of teachers are often too low to attract and retain the best-qualified teachers. State and local governments have the responsibility to pay for public education, so educational reform and the search for excellent teachers and learning processes will remain a top state and local priority. Many states, though, object to the Bush administration's push for national standards, under its No Child Left Behind program, as an intrusion on the states and too costly in the current economic environment. Utah decided to forgo federal funds and declined to participate in the program, and some other states may do likewise.

■ *Environmental regulation, land use, and recycling are also major challenges at the local level.* Every city and state wants economic growth and economic opportunities for its workers and businesses, but many forms of economic development impose costs in terms of the quality of air, water, landscapes, and health. Local officials face tough decisions about the need to balance economic and environmental concerns.

■ *Health care costs and delivery are challenges to all levels of government.* Health care reform has been an important policy issue for many years. Some states, like Maine, have experimented with universal health care; others have worked to control costs. Many of the uninsured end up obtaining health care in emergency rooms in local public hospitals, which in turn seek funding from the local and state governments.

For more information on these and other issues confronting state and local governments, go to our home page at www.prenhall.com/burns, or to the Web site of the Council of State Governments at www.csg.org, or that of the National Conference of State Legislatures at www.ncsl.org.

S U M M A R Y

1. Many of the most critical domestic and economic issues facing the United States today are decided at the state and local levels of government.

2. Studies of states and communities have investigated how formal government institutions, social structure, economic factors, and local traditions interact to create a working political system. Some studies find that a power elite dominates, whereas community power studies find pluralism and diverse interest groups competing for influence over a range of policy areas. Special-interest groups operate in every state and locality, but their influence varies.

3. Although it is widely believed that local governments are "closer to the people" than the national government, voting and other forms of participation at the local level are low.

4. Innovative programs at the local level address problems in education, the environment, crime and violence, and ways to improve community life. Local civil action is one of the most important forms of citizen participation in politics.

F U R T H E R   R E A D I N G

JOHN R. BAKER, ED., *The Lanahan Readings on State and Local Government* (Lanahan Press, 2001).

THAD L. BEYLE, ED., *State Government: CQ's Guide to Current Issues and Activities, 2004–2005* (CQ Press, 2004).

BUZZ BISSINGER, *A Prayer for the City* (Random House, 1997).

ALLAN CIGLER AND BURDETT LOOMIS, EDS., *Interest Group Politics*, 6th ed. (CQ Press, 2002).

FRANK J. COPPA, *County Government* (Praeger, 2000).

THOMAS E. CRONIN AND ROBERT D. LOEVY, *Colorado Politics and Government: Governing the Centennial State* (University of Nebraska Press, 1993).

E. J. DIONNE JR., ED., *Community Works: The Revival of Civil Society in America* (Brookings Institution Press, 1998).

THOMAS D. DYE AND SUSAN A. MACMANUS, *Politics in States and Communities*, 11th ed. (Prentice Hall, 2003).

ROBERT S. ERIKSON, GERALD C. WRIGHT, AND JOHN P. MCIVER, *Statehouse Democracy: Public Opinion and Policy in the American States* (Cambridge University Press, 1993).

STEPHEN GOLDSMITH, *The Twenty-First Century City* (Regnery, 1997).

VIRGINIA GRAY, RUSSELL HANSON, AND HERBERT JACOB, EDS., *Politics in the American States*, 8th ed. (CQ Press, 2003).

VALERIE C. JOHNSON, *Black Power in the Suburbs* (State University of New York Press, 2002).

DANIEL KEMMIS, *The Good City and the Good Life* (Houghton Mifflin, 1995).

MADELEINE KUNIN, *Living a Political Life* (Vintage, 1995).

JOHN O. NORQUIST, *The Wealth of Cities* (Addison-Wesley, 1998).

DOUGLAS W. RAE, *City: Urbanism and Its End* (Yale University Press, 2003).

ALAN ROSENTHAL, *The Third House: Lobbyists and Lobbying in the States*, 2d ed. (CQ Press, 2001).

JON C. TEAFORD, *The Rise of the States* (Johns Hopkins University Press, 2002).

JOSEPH F. ZIMMERMAN, *The New England Town Meeting: Democracy in Action* (Praeger, 1999).

See also the *State Politics and Policy Quarterly* and the Web site of the Council of State Governments at www.csg.org.

AMERICAN FEDERALISM

Responding to opposition to the Massachusetts supreme court's ruling that its state constitution forbids discrimination against same-sex couples seeking to marry, President George W. Bush said "if necessary" he would "support a constitutional amendment which would honor marriage between a man and a woman." But he added that the issue was basically a state matter, not a federal one, and he would not oppose "whatever legal arrangements people want to make."[1] That disappointed some of his conservative supporters because Vermont and California already recognize "civil unions" and "domestic partnerships" that confer the same legal benefits—health, insurance, and death benefits—for gay couples as for heterosexuals.

Although the Massachusetts court's decision may be overridden by a proposed state constitutional amendment in 2006, it renewed a national debate over the U.S. Constitution's full faith and credit clause. In 1996, Congress passed and President Bill Clinton signed the Defense of Marriage Act (DOMA), which relieves states of any obligation to recognize same-sex marriages even if they are recognized in other states and stipulates that the national government only recognizes heterosexual marriages for federal benefits such as Social Security.[2] Supporters of the law argue that the Constitution gives Congress the responsibility for prescribing the manner in which states are to comply with the full faith and credit clause. But the DOMA is likely to be challenged in the courts for going beyond the power of Congress to provide states with an exemption from their constitutional obligation under the full faith and credit clause.

The Supreme Court has not addressed the issue squarely and precedents provide no clear answer. The Court has held that states must comply with other states' judicial decisions, but not necessarily with their other laws or administrative decisions. In light of recent Court rulings tilting toward states' rights and, as one scholar argues, "the fact that marriage has traditionally been an almost exclusive sphere of state authority, the Court would likely maintain the noncentralized and dual nature of American domestic relations that exist today, and allow the states to decide whether to recognize same-sex marriages."[3] However, similar DOMA laws in 38 states are likely to be challenged as well,[4] in light of the ruling in *Lawrence* v. *Texas*[5] invalidating state laws criminalizing homosexual sodomy, dissenting Justice Antonin Scalia has warned that states may no longer be able to ban same-sex marriages.

The controversy over same-sex marriages underscores the continuing debate over federalism. How do states interact with each other and with the national government? What is the proper balance of power between the national government and the states on providing homeland security, combating illegal immigration, improving education, and fighting corporate corruption and environmental pollution?

Since the founding of the Republic, Americans have debated the relationship of the national government to the states.[6] In 1787, the Federalists defended the creation of a strong national government, whereas the Antifederalists warned that a strong national government would overshadow the states. More recently, Republicans have led the charge against big government, urging the return of many functions to the states—a **devolution revolution**[7]—and they have had some success, such as when President Bill Clinton agreed to turn over more responsibilities for welfare to the states.

Federalism has recently emerged as a hot topic in other countries as well. Western European countries have formed the European Union (EU), with member nations giving up considerable authority over the regulation of businesses and labor, adopting a common monetary policy and currency (the euro), the addition in 2004 of ten Central and Eastern European countries, and debates over the ratification of a Treaty Establishing a Constitution for Europe.[8]

Heightened interest in federalism also comes from demands for greater autonomy for ethnic nationalities. The Canadian federal system strains under the demands of the French-speaking province of Quebec for special status and even independence. In the United Kingdom, devolution has occurred with Scotland, Northern Ireland, and Wales gaining their own parliaments or assemblies with considerable authority and, in the case of Scotland, limited power to tax. Belgium, Italy, and Spain have been devolving powers from their central governments to regional governments.

In contrast to some countries, the United States has had a relatively peaceful experience with the shifting balances of power under federalism. Since the New Deal in the 1930s, power and responsibility have drifted from the states to the national government. Although presidents from Richard Nixon to Bill Clinton slowed the growth of the national government, it was not until the late 1990s that the Republican-controlled Congress sought major reforms that heated the debate over federalism. As with welfare reform in 1996, Congress promoted decentralization in education with the Educational Flexibility Partnership Demonstration Act of 1999, authorizing the secretary of education to grant states waivers from federal rules setting educational goals. Still, in spite of such moves toward decentralization, Congress continues to expand federal law by making such offenses as the burning of churches, carjacking, and acts of terrorism federal crimes, even though they are already state and local crimes.

After more than half a century, the Supreme Court has placed some constraints on congressional powers in the name of federalism.[9] Like Congress, however, the Court's recent record on federalism is mixed. In spite of recent rulings holding that Congress exceeded its powers and may not authorize individuals to sue states to enforce federal laws,[10] the Court nevertheless ruled that state welfare programs may not restrict benefits to new residents to what they would have received in the states from which they moved[11] and that Congress may restrict states from selling drivers' personal information.[12]

Debates over federalism resemble those over whether "the glass is half-empty or half-full."[13] People who think they can get more of what they want from the national government usually advocate national action. Those who view states as more responsive and accountable argue for decentralization. Although Republicans generally favor action at the state level and Democrats tend to support action by the national government, neither party is consistent in its positions on the balance of power between the national government and the states. It depends on the issue at stake.

In this chapter, we first define federalism and its advantages. We then look at the constitutional basis for our federal system and how court decisions and political developments have shaped, and continue to shape, federalism in the United States.

DEFINING FEDERALISM

Scholars argue and wars (including our own Civil War) have been fought over what federalism means. One scholar counted 267 definitions.[14]

Federalism, as we define it, is a form of government in which a constitution distributes powers between a central government and subdivisional governments— usually called states, provinces, or republics—giving to both the national government and the regional governments substantial responsibilities and powers, including the power to collect taxes and to pass and enforce laws regulating the conduct of individuals.

The mere existence of both national and state governments does not make a system federal. What is important is that a *constitution divides governmental powers between the national government and the subdivisional governments,* giving clearly defined functions to each. Neither the central nor the subdivisional government receives its powers from the other; both derive them from a common source—the Constitution. No ordinary act of legislation at either the national or the state level can change this constitutional distribution of powers. Both levels of government operate through their own agents and exercise power directly over individuals.

Our definition of federalism is broad enough to include competing visions of it and the range of federal systems around the world. The following are some of the leading visions of federalism.

■ *Dual federalism* views the Constitution as giving a limited list of powers— primarily foreign policy and national defense—to the national government, leaving the rest to sovereign states. Each level of government is dominant within its own sphere. The Supreme Court serves as the umpire between the national government and the states in disputes over which level of government has responsibility for a particular activity. During our first hundred years, dual federalism was the favored interpretation given by the Supreme Court.

- *Cooperative federalism* stresses federalism as a system of intergovernmental relations in delivering governmental goods and services to the people and calls for cooperation among various levels of government.

- *Marble cake federalism,* a term coined by political scientist Morton Grodzins, conceives of federalism as a marble cake in which all levels of government are involved in a variety of issues and programs, rather than a layer cake, or dual federalism, with fixed divisions between layers or levels of government.[15]

- *Competitive federalism,* a term first used by political scientist Thomas R. Dye, views the national government, 50 states, and thousands of other units as competing with each other over ways to put together packages of services and taxes. Applying the analogy of the marketplace, Dye emphasizes that at the state and local levels, we have some choice about which state and city we want to "use," just as we have choices about what kind of automobile we drive.[16]

- *Permissive federalism* implies that although federalism provides "a sharing of power and authority between the national and state government, the states' share rests upon the permission and permissiveness of the national government."[17]

- *"Our federalism,"* championed by Ronald Reagan, Justices Sandra Day O'Connor, Antonin Scalia, and Clarence Thomas, along with Chief Justice William Rehnquist, presumes that the power of the federal government is limited in favor of the broad powers reserved to the states.

Federal nations are diverse and include Australia, Canada, Germany, Russia, and Switzerland. Although their number is not large, they "cover more than half of the land surface of the globe and include almost half of the world's population."[18] Federalism thus appears well suited for large countries with large populations, even though only 21 of the world's approximately 185 nation-states claim to be federal.

Constitutionally, the federal system of the United States consists of only the national government and the 50 states. "Cities are not," the Supreme Court reminded us, "sovereign entities." But in a practical sense, we are a nation of almost 88,000 governmental units, from the national government to the school board district. This does not make for a tidy, efficient, easy-to-understand system; yet, as we shall see, it has its virtues.

Alternatives to Federalism

Among the alternatives to federalism are **unitary systems** of government, in which a constitution vests all governmental power in the central government. The central government, if it so chooses, may delegate authority to constituent units, but what it delegates it may take away. France, Israel, and the Philippines have unitary governments. In the United States, state constitutions usually create this kind of relationship between the state and its local governments.

At the other extreme from unitary governments are **confederations,** in which sovereign nations, through a constitutional compact, create a central government but carefully limit the power of the central government and do not give it the power to regulate the conduct of individuals directly. The central government makes regulations for the constituent governments, but it exists and operates only at their direction. The 13 states under the Articles of Confederation operated in this manner (see Figure 2–1), as did the

Government Under the Articles of Confederation, 1781–1788

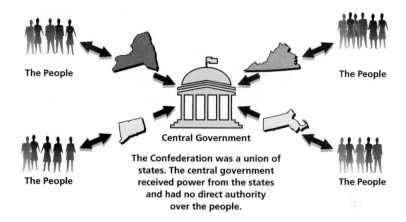

The People

The People

The People

The People

Central Government

The Confederation was a union of states. The central government received power from the states and had no direct authority over the people.

Government Under the U.S. Constitution (Federation) Since 1789

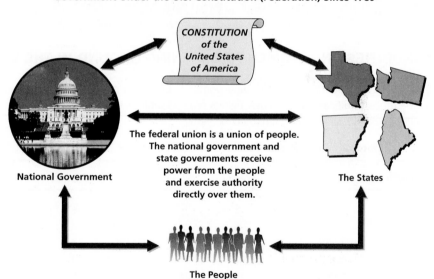

CONSTITUTION of the United States of America

National Government

The federal union is a union of people. The national government and state governments receive power from the people and exercise authority directly over them.

The States

The People

FIGURE 2–1 A Comparison of Federalism and Confederation.

southern Confederacy during the Civil War. The European Union is another example, though debates over its integration continue.[19]

Why Federalism?

In 1787, federalism was an obvious choice. Confederation had been tried but proved unsuccessful. A unitary system was out of the question because most people were too deeply attached to their state governments to permit subordination to central rule. Federalism was, and still is, thought to be ideally suited to the needs of a heterogeneous people spread over a large continent, suspicious of concentrated power, and desiring unity but not uniformity. Federalism offered, and still offers, many advantages for such a people.

FEDERALISM CHECKS THE GROWTH OF TYRANNY   Although in the rest of the world, federal forms have not always been notably successful in preventing tyranny, and many unitary governments are democratic, Americans tend to associate freedom with federalism.[20] As James Madison pointed out in *The Federalist,* No. 10: If "factious leaders . . . kindle a flame within their particular states," national leaders can check the spread of the "conflagration through the other states." Moreover, when one political party loses control of the national government, it is still likely to hold office in a number of states. It can then regroup, develop new policies and new leaders, and continue to challenge the party in power at the national level.

Such diffusion of power creates its own problems. It makes it difficult for a national majority to carry out a program of action, and it permits those who control state governments to frustrate the policies enacted by Congress and administered by federal

CHANGING FACE OF AMERICAN POLITICS

MINORITIES AND WOMEN ARE GAINING GROUND IN THE WORKFORCE

In the last few decades minorities and women have made significant gains in prestigious professions, especially as physicians and lawyers, but white males still dominate in certain highly visible occupations like police and firefighters.

Civil Workforce by Gender and Race—As a Percentage of Total Occupation

Occupation	Year	Men	Women	White	Black	Hispanic	Other	Total
Lawyers	1980	86%	14%	95%	3%	2%	1%	468,378
	1990	76	24	93	3	2	1	697,272
	2000	71	29	89	4	3	2	871,115
Physicians	1980	87	13	83	3	4	10	421,985
	1990	79	21	81	4	5	11	571,319
	2000	73	27	74	4	5	17	705,960
Firefighters	1980	99	1	89	6	4	1	186,867
	1990	97	3	84	9	5	2	216,914
	2000	96	4	82	8	6	3	242,395
Police Officers	1980	93	7	85	9	4	1	379,758
	1990	87	13	79	12	7	2	492,107
	2000	87	13	76	12	9	4	597,925

SOURCE: Census Bureau, 2000 Census; D'Vera Cohn and Sarah Cohen, "Minorities, Women Gain Professionally," *The Washington Post* A1 (December 30, 2003).

agencies. To the framers, these obstacles were an advantage. They feared that a single interest group might capture the national government and suppress the interests of others. Of course, the size of the nation and the many interests within it are the greatest obstacles to the formation of a single-interest majority—a point often overlooked today but emphasized by Madison in *The Federalist*, No. 10. If such a majority were to occur, having to work through a federal system would check its power.

FEDERALISM ALLOWS UNITY WITHOUT UNIFORMITY   National politicians and parties do not have to iron out every difference on every issue that divides us, whether it be abortion, same-sex marriage, gun control, capital punishment, welfare financing, or assisted suicide. Instead, these issues are debated in state legislatures, county courthouses, and city halls. But this advantage of federalism is becoming less significant as many local issues become national ones and as events in one state immediately affect policy debates at the national level.

FEDERALISM ENCOURAGES EXPERIMENTATION   Supreme Court Justice Louis Brandeis pointed out that state governments provide great "laboratories" for public policy experimentation; states may serve as proving grounds. If they adopt programs that fail, the negative effects are limited; if programs succeed, they can be adopted by other states and by the national government. Georgia, for example, was the first state to permit 18-year-olds to vote; Wisconsin experimented with putting welfare recipients to work; California pioneered air pollution control programs; Oregon and Hawaii created new systems for the delivery of health care. Nevada is the only state, so far, to legalize statewide gambling, but aspects of legalized casino gambling are now found in more than half the states. Not all innovations, even those considered successful, become widely adopted. Nebraska is the only state to have a unicameral legislature, although in recent years both Minnesota and California considered adopting one.

NUMBER OF GOVERNMENTS IN THE UNITED STATES

National	1
States	50
Counties	3,034
Municipalities	19,431
Townships or towns	16,506
School districts	13,522
Special districts	35,356
Total	87,900

Source: U.S. Bureau of the Census, *Statistical Abstract of the United States*, available at http://www.census.gov/prod/2003pubs/02statab/stlocgov.pdf.

FEDERALISM KEEPS GOVERNMENT CLOSER TO THE PEOPLE
By providing numerous arenas for decision making, federalism involves many people and helps keep government closer to the people. Every day, thousands of Americans are busy serving on city councils, school boards, neighborhood associations, and planning commissions. Since they are close to the issues and have firsthand knowledge of what needs to be done, they may be more responsive to problems than the experts in Washington.

We should be cautious, however, about generalizing that state and local governments are necessarily closer to the people than the national government. True, more people are involved in local and state politics than in national affairs, and confidence in state governments has increased while respect for national agencies has diminished. A majority of the public often appears dissatisfied with the federal government. Yet national and international affairs are on people's minds more often than state or local politics. And fewer voters participate in state and local elections than in congressional and presidential elections.

THE CONSTITUTIONAL STRUCTURE OF AMERICAN FEDERALISM

Dividing powers and responsibilities between the national and state governments has resulted in thousands of court decisions, hundreds of books, and endless speeches to explain them—and even then the division lacks precise definition. Nonetheless, a basic understanding of how the Constitution divides these powers and responsibilities and of what obligations are imposed on each level of government is helpful (see Table 2–1).

The formal constitutional framework of our federal system may be stated relatively simply:

1. The national government has only those powers delegated to it by the Constitution (with the important exception of the inherent power over foreign affairs).

2. Within the scope of its operations, the national government is supreme.

3. The state governments have the powers not delegated to the central government, except those denied to them by the Constitution and their state constitutions.

4. Some powers are specifically denied to both the national and state governments; others are specifically denied only to the states; still others are denied to the national government but not the states.

Powers of the National Government

The Constitution, chiefly in the first three articles, delegates legislative, executive, and judicial powers to the national government. In addition to these **express powers,** such as the power to regulate interstate commerce and to appropriate funds, Congress has

TABLE 2–1   THE FEDERAL DIVISION OF POWERS

Powers Delegated to the National Government	*Some Powers Reserved for the States*	*Some Concurrent Powers Shared by the National and State Governments*
• Express powers stated in the Constitution	• To create a republican form of government	• To tax citizens and businesses
• Implied powers that may be inferred from the express powers	• To charter local governments	• To borrow and spend money
• Inherent powers that allow the nation to present a united front to foreign powers	• To conduct elections	• To establish courts
	• To exercise all powers not delegated to the national government or denied to the states by the Constitution	• To pass and enforce laws
		• To protect civil rights

assumed constitutionally **implied powers,** such as the power to create banks, which are inferred from the express powers. The constitutional basis for the implied powers of Congress is the **necessary and proper clause** (Article I, Section 8, Clause 18). This clause gives Congress the right "to make all Laws which shall be necessary and proper for carrying into Execution the foregoing Powers, and all other Powers vested . . . in the Government of the United States."

In the field of foreign affairs, the Constitution gives the national government **inherent powers.** The national government has the same authority to deal with other nations as if it were the central government in a unitary system. Such inherent powers do not depend on specific constitutional provisions. For example, the government of the United States may acquire territory by purchase or by discovery and occupation, though no specific clause in the Constitution allows such acquisition. Even if the Constitution were silent about foreign affairs—which it is not—the national government would still have the power to declare war, make treaties, and appoint and receive ambassadors.

Together, these express, implied, and inherent powers create a flexible system that allows the Supreme Court, Congress, the president, and the people to expand the central government's powers to meet the needs of a modern nation in a global economy and confronting threats of international terrorism. This expansion of central government functions rests on four constitutional pillars.

These four constitutional pillars—the *national supremacy article,* the *war power,* the *commerce clause,* and most especially, the *power to tax and spend* for the general welfare—have permitted a tremendous expansion of the functions of the national government, so much so that despite the Supreme Court's recent declaration that some national laws exceed Congress's constitutional powers, the national government has, in effect, almost full power to enact any legislation that Congress deems necessary, so long as it does not conflict with the provisions of the Constitution designed to protect individual rights and the powers of the states.

THE NATIONAL SUPREMACY ARTICLE One of the most important pillars is found in Article VI of the Constitution: "This Constitution, and the Laws of the United States which shall be made in Pursuance thereof; and all Treaties made . . . under the Authority of the United States, shall be the supreme Law of the Land; and the Judges in every State shall be bound thereby; any Thing in the Constitution or Laws of any State to the Contrary notwithstanding." All officials, state as well as national, swear an oath to support the Constitution of the United States. States may not override national policies; this restriction also applies to local units of government, since they are agents of the states. National laws and regulations of federal agencies *preempt* the field so that conflicting state and local regulations are unenforceable.

THE WAR POWER The national government is responsible for protecting the nation from external aggression, whether from other nations or international terrorism. The government's power to protect national security includes the power to wage war. In today's world, military strength depends not only on troops in the field but also on the ability to mobilize the nation's industrial might as well as to apply scientific and technological knowledge to the tasks of defense. The national government has the power to do whatever is necessary and proper to wage war successfully. Thus the national government has the power to do almost anything not in direct conflict with constitutional guarantees.

THE POWER TO REGULATE INTERSTATE AND FOREIGN COMMERCE   Congressional authority extends to all commerce that affects more than one state. Commerce includes the production, buying, selling, renting, and transporting of goods, services, and properties. The **commerce clause** (Article I, Section 8, Clause 3) packs a tremendous constitutional punch; it gives Congress the power "to regulate Commerce with foreign Nations, and among the several States, and with the Indian Tribes." In these few words, the national government has been able to find constitutional justification for regulating a wide range of human activity, since very few aspects of our economy today affect commerce in only one state and are thus outside the scope of the national government's constitutional authority.[21]

The broad authority of Congress over interstate commerce was affirmed in the landmark ruling of *Gibbons* v. *Ogden* in 1824. There, in interpreting the commerce clause, Chief Justice John Marshall asserted national interests over those of the states and laid the basis for the subsequent growth in congressional power over commerce and activities that affect interstate commerce.

AN EXPANDING NATION

A great advantage of federalism—and part of the genius and flexibility of our constitutional system—has been the way in which we acquired territory and extended rights and guarantees by means of statehood, commonwealth, or territorial status, and thus grew from 13 to 50 states, plus territories.

Louisiana Purchase	1803
Florida	1819
Texas	1845
Oregon	1846
Mexican Cession	1848
Gadsden Purchase	1853
Alaska	1867
Hawaii	1898
Philippines	1898–1946
Puerto Rico	1899
Guam	1899
American Samoa	1900
Canal Zone	1904–2000
U.S. Virgin Islands	1917
Pacific Islands Trust Territory	1947

Gibbons v. *Ogden* arose from a dispute over a monopoly to operate steamboats in New York waters that was granted to Robert Livingston and Robert Fulton. They in turn licensed Aaron Ogden to exclusively operate steamboats between New York and ports in New Jersey. Ogden sued to stop Thomas Gibbons from running a competing ferry. Gibbons countered that his boats were licensed under a 1793 act of Congress governing vessels "in the coasting trade and fisheries." New York courts sided with Ogden in holding that both Congress and the states may regulate commerce, just as each has the power to tax. Congress, therefore, had not preempted New York from granting the monopoly. Gibbons appealed to the Supreme Court.

The stakes were high in *Gibbons* v. *Ogden,* for at issue was the very concept of "interstate commerce." May both Congress and the states regulate interstate commerce? And when conflicts arise between national and state regulations, which prevails?

Chief Justice Marshall asserted that national interests prevail and astutely defined "interstate commerce" as "intercourse that affects more states than one." Unlike the power of taxation, Congress's power over interstate commerce is complete and overrides conflicting state laws.[22]

Gibbons v. *Ogden* was immediately heralded for promoting a national economic common market in holding that states may not discriminate against interstate transportation and out-of-state commerce. Chief Justice Marshall's brilliant definition of "commerce" as *intercourse among the states* provided the basis clause for national regulation of an expanding range of economic activities, from the sale of lottery tickets[23] to prostitution[24] to radio and television broadcasts,[25] and telecommunications and the Internet.

The commerce clause has also been used to sustain legislation that goes beyond commercial matters. When the Supreme Court upheld the Civil Rights Act of 1964, forbidding discrimination because of race, religion, gender, or national origin in places of public accommodation, it said: "Congress's action in removing the disruptive effect which it found racial discrimination has on interstate travel is not invalidated because Congress was also legislating against what it considers to be moral wrongs."[26] Discrimination restricts the flow of interstate commerce; therefore, Congress could legislate against discrimination. Moreover, the law applies even to local places of public accommodation because local incidents of discrimination have a substantial and harmful impact on interstate commerce. The Court, however, has recently limited congressional power to address some other similar harms because it did not find a substantial connection with interstate commerce.[27]

THE POWER TO TAX AND SPEND   Congress lacks constitutional authority to pass laws solely on the grounds that they will promote the general welfare, but it may raise taxes and spend money for this purpose. For example, Congress lacks the power to regulate education or agriculture directly, yet it does have the power to appropriate money to support education or to pay farm subsidies. By attaching conditions to its grants of money, Congress may thus regulate what it cannot directly control by law.

When Congress puts up the money, it determines how the money will be spent. By withholding or threatening to withhold funds, the national government can influence or control state operations and regulate individual conduct. For example, Congress has stipulated that federal funds should be withdrawn from any program in which any person is denied benefits because of race, color, national origin, sex, or physical handicap. Congress also used its power of the purse to force states to raise the drinking age to 21 by tying such a condition to federal dollars for highways.

Congress frequently requires states to do certain things—for example, provide services to indigent mothers and clean up the air and water. These requirements are called **federal mandates.** Often Congress does not supply the funds required to carry out these mandates—called "unfunded mandates"—and its failure to do so has become an important issue as states face growing expenditures with limited resources. The Supreme Court has also ruled that Congress may not compel states through "unfunded mandates" to enact particular laws or require state officials to enforce federal laws, such as, requiring checks on the backgrounds of handgun purchasers.[28]

Powers of the States

The Constitution *reserves for the states all powers not granted to the national government,* subject only to the limitations of the Constitution. Powers not given exclusively to the national government by provisions of the Constitution or by judicial interpretation may be exercised concurrently by the states, as long as there is no conflict with national law. Such **concurrent powers** with the national government include the power to levy taxes and regulate commerce internal to each state.

In general, a state may levy a tax on the same item as the national government does, but a state cannot, by a tax, "unduly burden" commerce among the states, interfere with a function of the national government, complicate the operation of a national law, or abridge the terms of a treaty of the United States. Where Congress has not preempted the field, states may regulate interstate businesses, provided that these regulations do not cover matters requiring uniform national treatment or unduly burden interstate commerce.

Who decides what matters require "uniform national treatment" or what actions might place an "undue burden" on interstate commerce? Congress does, subject to final review by the Supreme Court. When Congress is silent or does not clearly state its intent, the courts—ultimately, the Supreme Court—decide if there is a conflict with the national Constitution or if there has been federal preemption by law or regulation.

Constitutional Limits and Obligations

In order to ensure that federalism works, the Constitution imposes certain restraints on both the national and the state governments. States are prohibited from:

1. Making treaties with foreign governments
2. Authorizing private persons to prey on the shipping and commerce of other nations
3. Coining money, issuing bills of credit, or making anything but gold and silver coin legal tender in payment of debts
4. Taxing imports or exports
5. Taxing foreign ships
6. Keeping troops or ships in time of peace (except the state militia, now called the National Guard)
7. Engaging in war, unless invaded or in such imminent danger as will not admit of delay

The national government, in turn, is required by the Constitution to refrain from exercising its powers, especially its powers to tax and to regulate interstate commerce, in such a way as to interfere substantially with the states' abilities to perform their responsibilities. Today, the protection states have from intrusions by the national government comes primarily from the political process because senators and representatives elected from the states participate in the decisions of Congress. However, the Court has held that Congress may not command states to enact laws to comply with or order state employees to enforce unfunded federal mandates; for example, as noted earlier, Congress may not require local law enforcement officials to make background checks prior to handgun sales.[29] It has also ruled that the Eleventh Amendment's guarantee of states' sovereign immunity from lawsuits forbids state employees from suing states in federal and state courts in order to force state compliance with federal employment laws.[30] Although Congress may not use those sticks, it may offer the carrot of federal funding if states comply with national policies, such as establishing a minimum drinking age.

The Constitution also requires the national government to guarantee to each state a "republican form of government." The framers used this term to distinguish a republic from a monarchy, on the one side, and from a pure, direct democracy, on the other. Congress, not the courts, enforces this guarantee and determines what is or is not a republican form of government. By permitting the congressional delegation of a state to be seated in Congress, Congress acknowledges that the state has the republican form of government guaranteed by the Constitution.

In addition, the national government is obliged by the Constitution to protect states against *domestic insurrection.* Congress has delegated to the president the authority to dispatch troops to put down such insurrections when so requested by the proper state authorities. If there are contesting state authorities, the president decides which is the proper one. The president does not have to wait, however, for a request from state authorities to send federal troops into a state to enforce federal laws.

Interstate Relations

Three clauses in the Constitution, taken from the Articles of Confederation, require states to give full faith and credit to each other's public acts, records, and judicial proceedings; to extend to each other's citizens the privileges and immunities of their own citizens; and to return persons who are fleeing from justice.

FULL FAITH AND CREDIT   The **full faith and credit clause** (Article IV, Section 1), one of the more technical provisions of the Constitution, requires state courts to enforce the civil judgments of the courts of other states and accept their public records and acts as valid.[31] It does not require states to enforce the criminal laws or legislation and administrative acts of other states; in most cases, for one state to enforce the criminal laws of another would raise constitutional issues. The clause applies especially to enforcement of judicial settlements and court awards.

INTERSTATE PRIVILEGES AND IMMUNITIES   Under Article IV, Section 2, states must extend to citizens of other states the privileges and immunities granted to their own citizens, including the protection of the laws, the right to engage in peaceful occupations, access to the courts, and freedom from discriminatory taxes. Because of this clause, states may not impose unreasonable residency requirements, that is, withhold rights to American citizens who have recently moved to the state and thereby have become citizens of that state. For example, a state may not set unreasonable time limits to withhold state-funded medical benefits from new citizens or to keep them from voting. How long a residency requirement may a state impose? A day seems about as long as the Supreme Court will tolerate to withhold welfare payments or medical care, 50 days or so for voting privileges, and one year for eligibility for in-state tuition for state-supported colleges and universities.

Financially independent adults who move into a state just before enrolling in a state-supported university or college may be required to prove that they have become citizens of that state and intend to remain after finishing their schooling by supplying such evidence of citizenship as tax payments, a driver's license, car registration, voter registration, and a continuous, year-round off-campus residence. Students who are financially dependent on their parents remain citizens of the state of their parents.

EXTRADITION   In Article IV, Section 2, the Constitution asserts that when individuals charged with crimes have fled from one state to another, the state to which they have fled is to deliver them to the proper officials upon the demand of the executive authority of the state from which they fled. This process is called **extradition.** "The obvious objective of the Extradition Clause," the courts have claimed, "is that no State should become a safe haven for the fugitives from a sister State's criminal justice system."[32] Congress has supplemented this constitutional provision by making the governor of the state to which fugitives have fled responsible for returning them. Despite their constitutional obligation, governors of asylum states have on occasion refused to honor a request for extradition.

INTERSTATE COMPACTS   The Constitution also requires states to settle disputes with one another without the use of force. States may carry their legal disputes to the Supreme Court, or they may negotiate **interstate compacts.** Interstate compacts often establish interstate agencies to handle problems affecting an entire region. Before most interstate compacts become effective, congressional approval is required. After a compact has been signed and approved by Congress, it becomes binding on all signatory states, and its terms are enforceable by the federal judiciary. A typical state may belong to 20 compacts dealing with such subjects as environmental protection, crime control, water rights, and higher education exchanges.[33]

THE ROLE OF THE FEDERAL COURTS: UMPIRES OF FEDERALISM

Although the political process ultimately decides how power will be divided between the national and the state governments, the federal courts—and especially the Supreme Court—are often called on to umpire the ongoing debate about which level of government should do what, for whom, and to whom. This role for the courts was claimed in the celebrated case of *McCulloch* v. *Maryland.*

McCulloch Versus *Maryland*

In *McCulloch* v. *Maryland* (1819), the Supreme Court had the first of many chances to define the division of power between the national and state governments.[34] Congress established the Bank of the United States, but Maryland opposed any national bank and levied a $10,000 tax on any bank not incorporated within the state. James William McCulloch, the cashier of the bank, refused to pay on the grounds that a state could not tax an instrument of the national government.

Maryland was represented before the Court by some of the country's most distinguished lawyers, including Luther Martin, who had been a delegate to the Constitutional Convention. Martin said that the power to incorporate a bank was not expressly delegated to the national government in the Constitution. He maintained that the necessary and proper clause gives Congress only the power to choose those means and to pass those laws absolutely essential to the execution of its expressly granted powers. Because a bank is not absolutely necessary to the exercise of its delegated powers, he argued, Congress had no authority to establish it. As for Maryland's right to tax the bank, the power to tax is one of the powers reserved to the states; they may use it as they see fit.

The national government was represented as well by distinguished counsel, including Daniel Webster. Webster conceded that the power to create a bank is not one of the express powers of the national government. However, the power to pass laws necessary and proper to carry out Congress's express powers is specifically delegated to Congress. Therefore, Congress may incorporate a bank as an appropriate, convenient, and useful means of exercising the granted powers of collecting taxes, borrowing money, and caring for the property of the United States. Although the power to tax is reserved to the states, Webster argued that states cannot interfere with the operations of the national government. The Constitution leaves no room for doubt; in cases of conflict between the national and state governments, the national government is supreme.

Speaking for a unanimous Court, Chief Justice John Marshall rejected every one of Maryland's contentions. He summarized his views on the powers of the national government in these now-famous words: "Let the end be legitimate, let it be within the scope of the Constitution, and all means which are appropriate, which are plainly adapted to that end, which are not prohibited, but consist with the letter and spirit of the constitution, are constitutional." Having thus established the doctrine of *implied national powers,* Marshall set forth the doctrine of **national supremacy.** No state, he said, can use its taxing powers to tax a national instrument. "The power to tax involves the power to destroy. . . . If the right of the States to tax the means employed by the general government be conceded, the declaration that the Constitution, and the laws made in pursuance thereof, shall be the supreme law of the land, is empty and unmeaning declamation."

The long-range significance of *McCulloch* v. *Maryland* in providing support for the developing forces of nationalism and a unified economy cannot be overstated. The contrary arguments in favor of the states, if they had been accepted, would have strapped the national government in a constitutional straitjacket and denied it powers needed to deal with the problems of an expanding nation.

Federal Courts and the Role of the States

The authority of federal judges to review the activities of state and local governments has expanded dramatically in recent decades because of modern judicial interpretations of the Fourteenth Amendment, which forbids states from depriving any person of life, liberty, or property without *due process of the law.* States may not deny any person the *equal protection of the laws,* including congressional legislation enacted to implement the Fourteenth Amendment. Almost every action by state and local officials is now subject to challenge before a federal judge as a violation of the Constitution or of federal law.

Preemption occurs when a federal law or regulation takes precedence over enforcement of a state or local law or regulation. State and local laws are preempted not only when they conflict directly with federal laws and regulations but also if they touch a field in which the "federal interest is so dominant that the federal system will be assumed to preclude enforcement of state laws on the same subject."[35] Examples of federal preemption include laws regulating hazardous substances, water quality, clean air standards and many civil rights acts, especially the Civil Rights Act of 1964 and the Voting Rights Act of 1965.

Over the years, federal judges, under the leadership of the Supreme Court, have generally favored the powers of the federal government over the states. In spite of the Supreme Court's recent bias in favor of state over national authority, few would deny the Supreme Court the power to review and set aside state actions. As Justice Oliver Wendell Holmes of the Supreme Court once remarked: "I do not think the United States would come to an end if we lost our power to declare an Act of Congress void. I do think the Union would be imperiled if we could not make that declaration as to the laws of the several States."[36]

The Great Debate: Centralists Versus Decentralists

From the beginning of the Republic, there has been an ongoing debate about the "proper" distribution of powers, functions, and responsibilities between the national government and the states. Did the national government have the authority to outlaw slavery in the territories? Did the states have the authority to operate racially segregated schools? Could Congress regulate labor relations? Does Congress have the power to regulate the sale and use of firearms? Does Congress have the right to tell states how to clean up air and water pollution? Even today, as in the past, such debates are frequently phrased in constitutional language, with appeals to the great principles of federalism. But there are also arguments over who gets what, where, when, and how.

During the Great Depression of the 1930s, the nation debated whether Congress had the constitutional authority to enact legislation on agriculture, labor, education, housing, and welfare. Only 40 years ago, some legislators and public officials—as well as some scholars—questioned the constitutional authority of Congress to legislate against racial discrimination. The debate continues between **centralists,** who favor national action, and **decentralists,** who defend the powers of the states and favor action at the state and local levels.

THE DECENTRALIST POSITION　Among Americans favoring the decentralist or **states' rights** interpretation were the Antifederalists, Thomas Jefferson, John C. Calhoun, the Supreme Court from the 1920s to 1937, and more recently, Presidents Ronald Reagan and George H.W. Bush, the Republican leaders of Congress, Chief Justice William H. Rehnquist, and Justices Sandra Day O'Connor, Antonin Scalia, and Clarence Thomas.

Most decentralists contend that the Constitution is basically a compact among sovereign states that created the central government and gave it very limited authority. As Justice Clarence Thomas, an ardent advocate of states' rights, wrote in a dissenting opinion supporting the argument that a state has the power to impose term limits on members of Congress, "The ultimate source of the Constitution's authority is the consent of the people of each individual State, not the consent of the undifferentiated people of the Nation as a whole."[37] Thus the national government is little more than an agent of the states, and every one of its powers should be narrowly defined. Any question about whether the states have given a particular function to the central government or have reserved it for themselves should be resolved in favor of the states.

Decentralists hold that the national government should not interfere with activities reserved for the states. The Tenth Amendment, they claim, makes this clear: "The powers not delegated to the United States by the Constitution, nor prohibited by it to the States, are reserved to the States respectively, or to the people." Decentralists insist that state governments are closer to the people and reflect the people's wishes more accurately than the national government does. The national government, they add, is inherently heavy-handed and bureaucratic; to preserve our federal system and our liberties, central authority must be kept under control.

THE CENTRALIST POSITION　The centralist position has been supported by Chief Justice John Marshall, Presidents Abraham Lincoln, Theodore Roosevelt, and Franklin Roosevelt, and throughout most of our history, the Supreme Court.

Centralists reject the whole idea of the Constitution as an interstate compact. Rather, they view the Constitution as a supreme law established by the people. The national government is an agent of the people, not of the states, because it was the people who drew up the Constitution and created the national government. They intended that the central government's powers should be defined by the national political process and is denied authority only when the Constitution clearly prohibits it from acting.

Centralists argue that the national government is a government of all the people, whereas each state speaks only for some of the people. Although the Tenth Amendment clearly reserves powers for the states, it does not deny the national government the authority to exercise, to the fullest extent, all of its powers. Moreover, the supremacy of the national government restricts the states, because governments representing part of the people cannot be allowed to interfere with a government representing all of them.

The Supreme Court and the Role of Congress

From 1937 until the 1990s, the Supreme Court essentially removed federal courts from what had been their role of protecting states from acts of Congress. The Supreme Court broadly interpreted the commerce clause to allow Congress to do whatever Congress thought necessary and proper to promote the common good, even if the federal laws and regulations infringed on the activities of state and local governments. The Court went so far as to tell the states that they should look to the political process to protect their interests, not to the federal courts.[38]

In the past decade, however, a bare majority of the Supreme Court has signaled that federal courts should no longer remain passive in resolving federalism issues.[39] The Court declared that a state could not impose term limits on its members of Congress, but it did so only by a 5 to 4 vote. Justice John Paul Stevens, writing for the majority, built his argument on the concept of the federal union as espoused by the great Chief Justice John Marshall, as a compact among the people, with the national government serving as the people's agent. By contrast, Justice Clarence Thomas, writing for the dissenters, espoused a view of federalism not heard from a justice of the Supreme Court since prior to the New Deal. He interpreted the Tenth Amendment as requiring the national government to justify its actions in terms of an enumerated power and granting to the states all other powers not expressly given to the national government.[40]

The Court also declared that the clause in the Constitution empowering Congress to regulate commerce with the Indian tribes did not give Congress the power to authorize federal courts to hear suits against a state brought by Indian tribes.[41] Unless states consent to such suits, they enjoy "sovereign immunity" under the Eleventh Amendment. The effect of this decision goes beyond Indian tribes. As a result, except to enforce rights stemming from the Fourteenth Amendment, which the Court explicitly acknowledged to be within Congress's power, Congress may no longer authorize individuals to bring legal actions against states in order to force their compliance with federal law in either federal or state courts.[42]

Building on those rulings, the Court continues to press ahead with its "constitutional counterrevolution"[43] in returning to an older vision of federalism not embraced since the constitutional crisis over the New Deal in the 1930s. Among other recent rulings, the Court struck down the Violence Against Women Act, which had given women who are victims of violence the right to sue their attackers for damages.[44] Congress had found that violence against women annually costs the national economy $3 billion, but the Court held that Congress exceeded its powers in enacting the law and intruded on the powers of the states.

These Supreme Court decisions—most of which split the Court 5 to 4 along ideological lines, with the conservative justices favoring states' rights—may signal a major shift in the Court's interpretation of the constitutional nature of our federal system.

Chief Justice Rehnquist, joined by Justices Scalia, Thomas, O'Connor, and frequently Justice Anthony M. Kennedy, have pushed the Court back to a decentralist position. President Clinton's two appointees, Justices Ruth Bader Ginsburg and Stephen Breyer, joined by Justices David Souter and John Paul Stevens, are resisting this movement back to a states' rights interpretation of our federal system. Consequently, federalism issues are likely to come up in future Supreme Court confirmation hearings, and the outcome of presidential elections—which greatly influence who gets appointed to the Supreme Court—could well determine how these and other federalism issues will be decided.

REGULATORY FEDERALISM: GRANTS, MANDATES, AND NEW TECHNIQUES OF CONTROL

Congress authorizes programs, establishes general rules for how the programs will operate, and decides whether and how much room should be left for state or local discretion. Most important, Congress appropriates the funds for these programs and generally has deeper pockets than even the richest states. One of Congress's most potent tools for influencing policy at the state and local levels has been federal grants.

Federal grants serve four purposes, the most important of which is the fourth:

1. To supply state and local governments with revenue.
2. To establish minimum national standards for such things as highways and clean air.
3. To equalize resources among the states by taking money from people with high incomes through federal taxes and spending it, through grants, in states where the poor live.
4. To attack national problems yet minimize the growth of federal agencies.

Types of Federal Grants

Three types of federal grants are currently being administered: *categorical-formula grants, project grants,* and *block grants* (sometimes called *flexible grants*). From 1972 to 1987, there was also *revenue sharing*—federal grants to state and local governments to be used at their discretion and subject only to very general conditions. But when budget deficits soared in the second Reagan administration (1985–1989) and there was no revenue to share, revenue sharing was terminated—to the states in 1986 and to local governments in 1987.

CATEGORICAL-FORMULA GRANTS   Congress appropriates funds for specific purposes, such as school lunches or the building of airports and highways. These funds are allocated by formula and are subject to detailed federal conditions, often on a matching basis; that is, the local government receiving the federal funds must put up some of its own dollars. Categorical grants, in addition, provide federal supervision to ensure that the federal dollars are spent as Congress wants. There are hundreds of grant programs, but two dozen, including Medicaid, account for more than half of total spending for categoricals.

PROJECT GRANTS   Congress appropriates a certain sum, which is allocated to state and local units and sometimes to nongovernmental agencies, based on applications from those who wish to participate. Examples are grants by the National Science Foundation to universities and research institutes to support the work of scientists or grants to states and localities to support training and employment programs.

BLOCK GRANTS   These are broad grants to states for prescribed activities—welfare, child care, education, social services, preventive health care, and health services—with only a few strings attached. States have great flexibility in deciding how to spend block grant dollars, but when the federal funds for any fiscal year are gone, there are no more matching federal dollars.

The Politics of Federal Grants

Republicans "have consistently favored fewer strings, less federal supervision, and the delegation of spending discretion to the state and local governments."[45] Democrats have generally been less supportive of broad discretionary block grants, favoring instead more detailed, federally supervised spending. The Republican-controlled Congress in the 1990s gave high priority to the creation of block grants, but it ran into trouble by trying to lump together welfare, school lunch and breakfast programs, prenatal nutrition programs, and child protection programs in one block grant.

Republicans, however, with President Clinton's support, succeeded in making a major change in federal-state relations—a devolution of responsibility for welfare from the national government to the states. The Personal Responsibility and Work Opportunity Reconciliation Act of 1996 put an end to the 61-year-old program of Aid to Families with Dependent Children (AFDC), a federal guarantee of welfare checks for all eligible mothers and children. The 1996 act substituted for AFDC a welfare block grant to each state, with caps on the amount of federal dollars that the state will receive. It also put another big federal child care program into another block grant—the Child Care and Development Block Grant (CCDBG).

Welfare block grants give states flexibility in how they provide for welfare, but no federal funds can be used to cover recipients who do not go to work within two years, and no one can receive federally supported benefits for more than five years. In order to slow down the "race to the bottom" in which states may try to make themselves "the least attractive state in which to be poor,"[46] Congress also stipulated that in order for states to receive their full share of federal dollars, they must continue to spend at least 75 percent of what they had been spending on welfare.

The battle over the appropriate level of government to control funding and to exercise principal responsibility for social programs tends to be cyclical. As one scholar of federalism explains, "Complaints about excessive federal control tend to be followed by proposals to shift more power to state and local governments. Then, when problems arise in state and local administration—and problems inevitably arise when any organization tries to administer anything—demands for closer federal supervision and tighter federal controls follow."[47]

Federal Mandates

Fewer federal dollars do not necessarily mean fewer federal controls. On the contrary, the federal government has imposed mandates on states and local governments, often without providing federal funds. State and local officials complained, and protests from state and local officials against unfunded federal mandates were effective. The Unfunded Mandates Reform Act of 1995 requires the Congressional Budget Office (CBO) and federal agencies to issue reports about the impact of unfunded mandates. The act also imposed some mild constraints on Congress itself. A congressional committee that approves any legislation containing a federal mandate must draw attention to the mandate in its report and describe its cost to state and local governments. If the committee intends any mandate to be partially unfunded, it must explain why it is appropriate for the cost to be borne by state and local governments.

Whether the Unfunded Mandates Reform Act significantly slows down federal mandates remains to be seen. So far, it has had little effect. The Americans with Disabilities Act (1990), for example, called on state and local governments to build ramps and alter curbs—renovations that are costing millions of dollars. Environmental Protection Agency regulations require states to build automobile pollution-testing stations and take other actions to reduce pollution, but without corresponding federal dollars. Still, state officials praise the law for increasing congressional awareness of unfunded mandates. It has forced members of Congress to take into account how a bill would affect state and local governments.[48]

New Techniques of Federal Control

In recent decades, Congress has used several other techniques in establishing federal regulations, including *direct orders, cross-cutting requirements, crossover sanctions*, and *total and partial preemption.*

DIRECT ORDERS   In a few instances, federal regulation takes the form of direct orders that must be complied with under threat of criminal or civil sanction. An example is the Equal Employment Opportunity Act of 1972, barring job discrimination by state and local governments on the basis of race, color, religion, sex, and national origin.

CROSS-CUTTING REQUIREMENTS   Federal grants may establish certain conditions that extend to all activities supported by federal funds, regardless of their source. The first and most famous of these is Title VI of the 1964 Civil Rights Act, which holds that in the use of federal funds, no person may be discriminated against on the basis of race, color, or national origin. Other laws extend these protections to persons because of gender or disability status. More than 60 cross-cutting requirements concern such matters as the environment, historic preservation, contract wage rates, access to government information, the care of experimental animals, and the treatment of human subjects in research projects.

CROSSOVER SANCTIONS   These sanctions permit the use of federal money in one program to influence state and local policy in another. For example, a 1984 act reduced federal highway aid by up to 15 percent for any state that failed to adopt a minimum drinking age of 21.

TOTAL AND PARTIAL PREEMPTION   Total preemption rests on the national government's power under the supremacy and commerce clauses to preempt conflicting state and local activities. Building on this constitutional authority, federal law in certain areas entirely preempts state and local governments from the field.[49] Sometimes federal law provides for partial preemption in establishing basic policies but requiring states to administer them. Some programs give states an option not to participate, but if a state chooses not to do so, the national government steps in and runs the program. Even worse from the states' point of view is *mandatory partial preemption,* in which the national government requires states to act on peril of losing other funds but provides no funds to support state action. The Clean Air Act of 1990 is an example of mandatory partial preemption; the federal government set national air quality standards and required states to devise plans and pay for their implementation.[50] Homeland security legislation is another example of the national government providing some funds but requiring states to provide services as "first responders" that cost more than federal funds cover.

THE POLITICS OF FEDERALISM

The formal structures of our federal system have not changed much since 1787, but the political realities, especially during the past half-century, have greatly altered how federalism works. To understand these changes, we need to look at some of the trends that continue to fuel the debate about the meaning of federalism.

The Growth of Big Government

Over the past two centuries, power has accrued to the national government. "No one planned the growth, but everyone played a part in it."[51] How did this shift come about? For a variety of reasons. One is that many of our problems have become national in scope. Much that was local in 1789, in 1860, or in 1930 is now national, even global. State governments could supervise the relations between small merchants and their few employees, but only the national government can supervise relations between multinational corporations and their thousands of employees, many of which are organized in national unions.

As industrialization proceeded, powerful interests made demands on the national government. Business groups called on the government for aid in the form of tariffs, a national banking system, subsidies to railroads and the merchant marine, and uniform rules relating to the environment. Farmers learned that the national government could give more aid than the states, and they too began to demand help. By the beginning of the twentieth century, urban groups in general and organized labor in particular pressed their claims. Big business, big agriculture, and big labor all added up to big government.

The growth of the national economy and the creation of national transportation and communications networks altered people's attitudes toward the national government. Before the Civil War, the national government was viewed as a distant, even foreign, government. Today, in part because of television and the Internet, most people know more about Washington than they know about their state capitals. People are apt to know more about the president than about their governor and more about their national senators and representatives than about their state legislators or even about the local officials who run their cities and schools.

The Great Depression of the 1930s stimulated extensive national action on welfare, unemployment, and farm surpluses. World War II brought federal regulation of wages, prices, and employment, as well as national efforts to allocate resources, train personnel, and support engineering and inventions. After the war, the national government helped veterans obtain college degrees and inaugurated a vast system of support for university research. The United States became the most powerful leader of the free world, maintaining substantial military forces even in times of peace. The Great Society programs of the 1960s poured out grants-in-aid to states and localities. City dwellers who had migrated from the rural South to northern cities began to seek federal funds for—at the very least—housing, education, and mass transportation.

Although economic and social conditions created many of the pressures for expansion of the national government, so did political claims. Until federal budget deficits became a hot issue in the 1980s and early 1990s, members of Congress, presidents, federal judges, and federal administrators actively promoted federal initiatives. Even with the return of deficit spending in the 2000s, Congress appears willing to actively promote some federal programs, at least in the areas of homeland security and prescription drug coverage. True, when there is widespread conflict about what to do—how to reduce the federal deficit, adopt a national energy policy, reform Social Security, provide health care for the indigent—Congress waits for a national consensus. But when an organized constituency wants something and there is no counterpressure, Congress "responds often to everyone, and with great vigor."[52] Once established, federal programs generate groups with vested interests in promoting, defending, and expanding them. Associations are formed and alliances are made. "In a word, the growth of government has created a constituency of, by, and for government."[53]

The politics of federalism are changing, however, and Congress is being pressured to reduce the size and scope of national programs, but at the same time to deal with the demands for homeland security. Meanwhile, the cost of entitlement programs such as Social Security and Medicare are going up because there are more older people and they are living longer. These programs have widespread public support, and to cut them is politically risky. "With all other options disappearing, it is politically tempting to finance tax cuts by turning over to the states many of the social programs . . . that have become the responsibility of the national government."[54]

The Devolution Revolution: Rhetoric Versus Reality

Recent Congresses, like their predecessors, have increased the authority of the national government in many areas. To be sure, the Republican-controlled Congress in the 1990s returned some functions, especially welfare, to the states. President Clinton also proclaimed, "The era of big government is over," though he tempered his comments by saying, "But we cannot go back to the time when our citizens were left to fend for themselves." Congress and the president came together for a major overhaul of welfare and, to a lesser degree, education. Congress also freed the states to set their own highway speed limits, changed the Safe Drinking Water Act to allow states to operate certain programs, and gave states a greater role over how federal rural development funds may be used.

In the aftermath of the attacks on the World Trade Center and the Pentagon and in confronting the continuing threats of terrorism, the role of the federal government in defending homeland security has expanded. Congress also established national criteria for state-issued drivers' licenses, forbade states from selling drivers' personal information, ended state regulation of mutual funds, nullified state laws restricting telecommunications competition, and made a host of offenses federal crimes, including carjacking and acts of terrorism. Appropriation bills pressured states to keep criminals behind bars by threatening to take grants away from states that fail to meet federal standards. Indeed, the only two major achievements of the devolution revolution remain the 1996 reform of welfare and the repeal of a national speed limit.[55] As one reporter concluded, "The 'devolution' promised by Congressional Republicans . . . has mostly fizzled. Instead of handing over authority to state and local governments, they're taking it away."[56]

THE FUTURE OF FEDERALISM

In 1933, during the Great Depression, with state governments helpless, one writer stated, "I do not predict that the states will go, but affirm that they have gone."[57] Such prophets of doom were wrong; the states are stronger than ever. During recent decades, state governments have undergone a major transformation. Most have improved their governmental structures, taken on greater roles in funding education and welfare, launched programs to help distressed cities, expanded their tax bases, and are assuming greater roles in maintaining homeland security and fighting corporate corruption. Able men and women have been attracted to the governorship. "Today, states, in formal representational, policy making, and implementation terms at least, are more representative, more responsive, more activist, and more professional in their operations than they ever have been. They face their expanded roles better equipped to assume and fulfill them."[58]

After the civil rights revolution of the 1960s, segregationists feared that national officials would work for racial integration. Thus they praised local government, emphasized the dangers of centralization, and argued that the protection of civil rights was not a proper function of the national government. As one political scientist observed, "Federalism has a dark history to overcome. For nearly two hundred years, states' rights have been asserted to protect slavery, segregation, and discrimination."[59]

Today the politics of federalism, even with respect to civil rights, is more complicated than in the past. The national government is not necessarily more favorable to the claims of minorities than state or city governments are. Rulings on same-sex marriages and "civil unions" by state courts interpreting their state constitutions have extended more protection for these rights than has the Supreme Court's interpretation of the U.S. Constitution. Other states, however, are passing legislation that would eliminate such protections, and opponents are pressing for a constitutional amendment to bar same-sex marriages.

States are also increasingly aggressive in addressing economic and environmental matters. State attorneys general are prosecuting anticompetitive business practices, as they did in joining the suit against Microsoft and, more recently, as New York attorney general Eliot Spitzer did in suing the mutual fund industry and spammers. After the Bush administration abandoned 50 investigations into violations of the Clean Air Act and changed policy on the regulation of power plants, Spitzer and several other state attorneys general sued the Bush administration and power plant companies to force them to make pollution-control improvements.[60] Business interests have argued that conflicting state regulations unduly burden interstate commerce and have sought broader preemptive federal regulation in order to save them not only from stringent state regulations but also from the uncertainties of complying with 50 different state laws. As a lawyer representing trade groups in the food and medical devices industries observed: "One national dumb rule is better than 50 inconsistent rules of any kind."[61]

The national government is not likely to retreat to a pre-1930 posture or even a pre-1960 one. Indeed, the underlying economic and social conditions that generated the demand for federal action have been altered substantially by international terrorism, the war in Afghanistan and Iraq, and rising deficits. In addition to such traditional issues as helping people find jobs and preventing inflation and depressions—which still require national action—countless new issues have been added to the national agenda by the growth of a global economy based on the information explosion, e-commerce, advancing technologies, and combating international terrorism.

Most Americans have strong attachments to our federal system—in the abstract. They remain loyal to their states and show a growing skepticism about the national government. Yet, evidence suggests the anti-Washington sentiment "is 3,000 miles wide but only a few miles deep."[62] The fact is that Americans are pragmatists: We appear to prefer federal-state-local power sharing[63] and are prepared to use whatever level of government necessary to meet our needs and new challenges.

S U M M A R Y

1. A federal system is one in which the constitution divides powers between the central government and subdivisional governments—states or provinces. Alternatives to federalism are unitary systems, in which all constitutional power is vested in the central government, and confederations, which are loose compacts among sovereign states.

2. Federal systems check the growth of tyranny, allow unity without uniformity, encourage state experimentation, permit power sharing between the national government and the states, and keep government closer to the people.

3. The national government has the constitutional authority, stemming primarily from the national supremacy clause, the war powers, and its powers to regulate commerce among the states to tax and spend, to do what Congress thinks is necessary and proper to promote the general welfare and to provide for the common defense. These constitutional pillars have permitted tremendous expansion of the functions of the federal government.

4. States must give full faith and credit to each other's public acts, records, and judicial proceedings; extend to each others' citizens the privileges and immunities it gives its own; and return fugitives from justice.

5. The federal courts umpire the division of power between the national and state governments. The Marshall Court, in decisions such as *Gibbons* v. *Ogden* and *McCulloch* v. *Maryland,* asserted the power of the national government over the states and promoted a national economic common market. These decisions also reinforced the supremacy of the national government over the states.

6. Today, debates about federalism are less often about its constitutional structure than about whether action should come from the national or state and local levels. Recent Supreme Court decisions favor a decentralist position and signal shifts in the Court's interpretation of the constitutional nature of our federal system.

7. The major instruments of federal intervention in state programs have been various kinds of financial grants-in-aid, of which the most prominent are categorical-formula grants, project grants, and block grants. The national government also imposes federal mandates and controls some activities of state and local governments by other means.

8. Over the past 218 years, power has accrued to the national government, but recently Congress has been pressured to reduce the size and scope of national programs and to shift some existing programs back to the states. Although responsibility for welfare has been turned over to the states, the authority of the national government has increased in many other areas.

FURTHER READING

SAMUEL H. BEER, *To Make a Nation: The Rediscovery of American Federalism* (Harvard University Press, 1993).

CENTER FOR THE STUDY OF FEDERALISM, *The Federalism Report* (published quarterly by Temple University; this publication notes research, books and articles, and scholarly conferences).

CENTER FOR THE STUDY OF FEDERALISM, *Publius: The Journal of Federalism* (published quarterly by Temple University; one issue each year is an "Annual Review of the State of American Federalism"; and has a Web site at www.lafayette.edu/~publius).

TIMOTHY J. CONLAN, *From New Federalism to Devolution: Twenty-Five Years of Intergovernmental Reforms* (Brookings Institution, 1998).

DANIEL J. ELAZER AND JOHN KINCAID, *The Covenant Connection: From Federal Theology to Modern Federalism* (Lexington Books, 2000).

JOHN FEREJOHN AND BARRY WEINGAST, *The New Federalism: Can the States Be Trusted?* (Hoover Institute Press, 1998).

FRANK GOODMAN, ED., *The Supreme Court's Federalism: Real or Imagined?* (Sage, 2001).

NEIL C. MCCABE, ED., *Comparative Federalism in the Devolution Era* (Rowman & Littlefield, 2002).

FORREST MCDONALD, *States' Rights and the Union: Imperim in Imperio, 1776–1876* (Univeristy Press of Kansas, 2000).

KALYPSO NICOLAIDIS AND ROBERT HOWSE, EDS., *The Federal Vision: Legitimacy and Levels of Governance in the United States and the European Union* (Oxford University Press, 2001).

JOHN T. NOONAN, *Narrowing the Nation's Power: The Supreme Court Sides with the States* (University of California Press, 2002).

DAVID M. O'BRIEN, *Constitutional Law and Politics: Struggles for Power and Governmental Accountability,* 6th ed. (Norton, 2005).

LAURENCE J. O'TOOLE JR., *American Intergovernmental Relations,* 3rd ed. (CQ Press, 2000).

PAUL J. POSNER, *The Politics of Unfunded Mandates: Whither Federalism?* (Georgetown University Press, 1998).

WILLIAM H. RIKER, *The Development of American Federalism* (Academic, 1987).

STATE
CONSTITUTIONS
CHARTERS OR STRAITJACKETS?

In response to the Massachusetts supreme court's ruling that discriminating against same-sex marriages violated the state constitution, the
legislature convened in 2004 a convention to propose an amendment
banning same-sex marriages. The convention met in February and
again in March to approve an amendment barring same-sex marriages, but
recognizing "civil unions" that confer the same benefits, rights, and privileges
on same-sex couples that legally married couples enjoy. But under Massachusetts's constitution, the amendment must be resubmitted in the next legislative session for its approval, and then submitted to the voters for
ratification in a statewide vote. The matter will therefore not come before
voters until November 2006.

Massachusetts is not alone in considering constitutional reforms growing out of
the controversy over same-sex marriages. In response to similar state supreme court
decisions, Alaska, Hawaii, Nebraska, and Nevada adopted constitutional amendments
prohibiting the marriage of same-sex couples. Constitutional amendments are likewise
now under consideration in more than a dozen other states.[1]

Constitutional conventions are nonetheless rarely successful, and constitutional
amendments in most (though not all) states are often very difficult to achieve. New York,
for example, has had only four constitutions since 1777. Yet, by constitutional mandate,
every 20 years the people of New York are asked on a general election ballot if they want
to convene a constitutional convention to propose a new constitution. In addition, the
legislature—with the concurrence of the governor—put the question before the voters

in 1965; the voters approved, and a convention was held in 1967, but its work was rejected. When voters were asked in 1977 if they wanted to convene another convention, they said no. The question came before them again in 1997, as it will in 2017.

In preparation for the 1997 vote, the Temporary Commission on Constitutional Revision was set up to identify issues and to inform voters about the need for a new constitution. The commission called for a convention of ordinary citizens and suggested that New Yorkers take advantage of new technology such as cable television and electronic town meetings to observe convention proceedings. The commission targeted the budget process, state–local relations, education, and public safety as being of special importance.[2] A constitutional convention, commission members argued, could then write a new constitution in clear English, simplify voter registration, improve voting rules and ballot access, regulate campaign finance and lobbying, reform the legislative process, restore confidence in the courts, reform the tax structure, and improve protection for the environment.[3]

But opposed to calling a constitutional convention were the American Federation of Labor–Congress of Industrial Organizations (AFL-CIO), the Conservative party, the Sierra Club, the National Abortion Rights Action League (NARAL), some antitax groups, and some legislative leaders from both parties. They saw a convention as a threat to their right to organize; trial lawyers worried about limits on lawsuits; environmentalists feared that a convention might jeopardize provisions protecting open spaces; some women's groups were fearful that the convention might restrict abortion rights; and some conservatives feared that liberal interests would control the convention.

There was little public interest in the campaign for a constitutional convention, however. Two weeks before the election, polls indicated that voters, upset by the apparent inability of the state government to get anything done, were overwhelmingly in favor of calling for a constitutional convention to make government work better. But opponents of constitutional revision got busy. Unions and other anticonvention groups launched television advertisements, direct-mail operations, and phone banks, arguing that the convention was a waste of money and would open the door to dangerous changes. On November 5, 1997, 62 percent of New York voters rejected the call for the convention.[4]

New York's experience is not unusual. In recent years, voters in several states have rejected calls for a constitutional convention. For example, in 1994 Michigan voters rejected the call for a convention by almost 3 to 1 in all 183 counties; Arkansas voters in December 1995 rejected the call by 4 to 1 in all 75 counties.[5] No constitutional conventions have been held since Rhode Island had one in 1986, and it won approval of the voters for only eight of 14 proposed revisions.

Now, you might give some thought to your own state constitution. Like the U.S. Constitution, state constitutions are both instruments of government and limitations on government. Unlike the federal constitution, however, state constitutions are not popular symbols. On a trip to your state capitol, you are unlikely to find the state constitution "displayed [like] the federal Constitution, in a setting similar to a Shinto shrine."[6]

In this chapter, we examine the roots of state constitutions and some of the ways we work around constitutional rigidity. Then we look at methods of amending state constitutions, ending with a few case studies of states that have tried, for the most part unsuccessfully, to adopt new constitutions.

THE ROOTS OF STATE CONSTITUTIONS

The first state constitutions were outgrowths of colonial charters. Massachusetts and New Hampshire can boast of charters still in effect that are older than the federal Constitution. Virginia added a bill of rights to its constitution in 1776—13 years before the national one was proposed by Congress. In 1787, the framers of the U.S. Constitution drew heavily on their experience with these state charters. "What is the Constitution of the United States but that of Massachusetts, New York, and Maryland!" remarked John Adams. "There is not a feature in it," he said, "which cannot be found in one or the other."[7]

Subject only to the broad limitations of the U.S. Constitution, the people of each state are free to create whatever kind of republican government they wish. All state constitutions are similar in general outline (see Figure 3–1). A state constitution typically

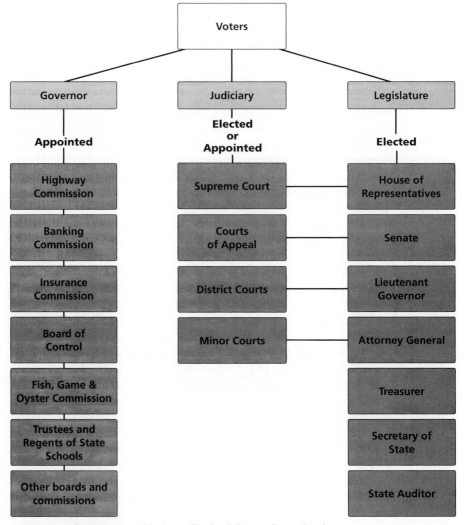

FIGURE 3–1 Government Under a Typical State Constitution.

consists of a preamble, a bill of rights, articles providing for the separation of powers (although the supreme court of Rhode Island ruled that there is no separation of powers in that state),[8] a two-house legislature, an executive branch, an independent judiciary with the power of judicial review, a description of the form and powers of local units of government, an article on how to amend the constitution, and miscellaneous provisions dealing with election procedures, corporations, railroads, finances, education, and other specific topics.

The bills of rights in state constitutions are, in general, similar to the federal Bill of Rights, although they sometimes use different language and cover different rights. For example, "Twenty-seven states have speech and press guarantees quite different from the First Amendment's, thirty-eight have equality guarantees dissimilar to the equal protection clause, and thirty-nine have guarantees of a separation of church and state that differ from the federal establishment clause."[9] Fourteen states adopted the Equal Rights Amendment even though it was never ratified to become part of the U.S. Constitution.

Constitutional Rigidity and Evasion

State constitutions contain more details than the U.S. Constitution does. They are longer and less flexible, and they require more frequent amendment[10] (see Figure 3–2). Louisiana has had 11 constitutions; Georgia has had ten; South Carolina, seven; and Alabama, Florida, and Virginia, six.[11] Only 29 states have their original constitution. The average state constitution is over 100 years old and has been amended about 120 times.[12]

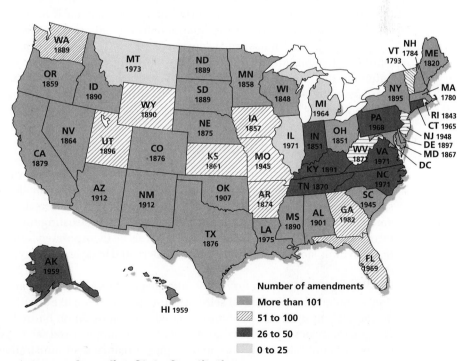

FIGURE 3–2 Amending State Constitutions.

State constitutions vary in length—from the 8,295 words of Vermont's (the only state constitution shorter than the Constitution of the United States as amended) to the longest, the 310,296 words of Alabama's. Alabama's constitution is almost 40 times as long as the U.S. Constitution, which has only 7,400 words; most state constitutions have around 26,000.[13]

Although most state constitutional provisions deal with matters of significance, some also deal with seemingly trivial subjects. California's much-amended constitution (over 500 amendments since it was adopted in 1879) goes into great detail about the taxation of fish and the internal organization of various departments.[14] The Oklahoma constitution proclaims, "Until changed by the Legislature, the flash test for all kerosene oil for illuminating purposes shall be 115 degrees Fahrenheit; and the specific gravity test for all such oil shall be 40 degrees."[15] The South Dakota constitution declares that providing hail insurance is a public purpose and authorizes the legislature to levy a tax to provide for it.[16] The Alabama constitution authorizes the legislature to indemnify peanut farmers for losses incurred as a result of *Aspergillus flavus* (a fungus) and freeze damage in peanuts.[17] In 2000, Florida voters approved an amendment declaring the development of high-speed ground transportation in the public interest of reducing traffic congestion. And in 2003 Wisconsin voters approved one guaranteeing the people's right to fish, hunt, trap, and take game.

In addition to the inclusion of these statute-like details, state constitutions and their more frequently adopted amendments tend to be longer than the U.S. Constitution because their bills of rights cover, in addition to the traditional rights, more recently emerging protections, such as the right to an equal public education and the rights of victims of crimes. Finally, state constitutions have to deal with a much wider range of functions, educational provisions, and criminal codes than the U.S. Constitution, which created a national government of intentionally limited powers to deal with a limited range of functions.[18] It has long been asserted that the length and detail of state constitutions account for the fact that many of them have not had the longevity of the national Constitution. However, a careful empirical study shows that "longer and more detailed design of state constitutions actually enhances rather than reduces their longevity."[19]

Constitutions as Roadblocks

The earliest state constitutions granted authority to the legislatures without much restriction on how their powers should be exercised. But after many legislatures gave special privileges to railroads, canal builders, and other interests, constitutional amendments were adopted to prevent such abuses. Distrusting the legislatures, reform groups began to insist that certain controls be incorporated into state constitutions. In time, state constitutions became encrusted in layer upon layer of procedural detail.

What does this mean for democratic government? It means that state constitutions—intended as charters of self-government—are often like straitjackets imposed on the present by the past. Some outdated provisions do no harm, but more often they are roadblocks to effective government. For example, fixed salaries do not reflect changing economic conditions, and a rigidly organized administrative structure is incapable of adjusting to new needs. When a constitution allocates revenues, elected officials are deprived of discretion to deal with budget difficulties as they arise. Under such conditions, the legislature cannot act, and voters then turn to constitutional amendments.

Getting Around the Constitution

Can state constitutions forever prevent the wishes of the people from being carried out? Not necessarily. The constitutional system of the states, like that of the national government, includes more than the formal written document. Unwritten rules, practices, political parties, and interest groups also shape events. When people see a need for change, they usually find ways to overcome formal barriers.

One device for constitutional change is **judicial interpretation,** whereby judges modify a constitutional provision by a new interpretation of its meaning. The more complex and detailed the constitution, the easier it is for judges to redefine meanings. Actually, one reason for the growing length of some constitutions is that amendments are often required to reverse judicial interpretations. In addition, some sections of state constitutions have been invalidated by federal action, especially in the area of civil rights and suffrage.

The New Judicial Federalism

In what is called **new judicial federalism,** state constitutions have taken on greater importance. For decades, state judges tended to look only to the U.S. Constitution and Bill of Rights and how these were interpreted by the U.S. Supreme Court. But since the 1970s, as the Supreme Court has become more conservative, some state supreme courts have been relying on their own state constitutions and state bills of rights in overruling state laws and the actions of state and local officials. In recent years, state supreme courts have refused to follow the U.S. Supreme Court's rulings and on the basis of their state constitutions have held unconstitutional sobriety checkpoints for drivers,[20] the random drug testing of public employees,[21] and restrictions on minors who seek abortions.[22]

This trend takes its inspiration from the U.S. Supreme Court, which sent clear messages to state supreme court judges that they are free to interpret their own state constitutions to impose greater restraints than the U.S. Constitution does. The U.S. Supreme Court and the U.S. Constitution set the floor, not the ceiling, for the protection of rights.[23] As a result, some state judges are now using their constitutions to require state legislatures to provide better schools for children living in poor neighborhoods, build low-income housing, provide public financing of abortions for poor women, and regulate business enterprises to protect the environment.[24]

When state judges rely on their own state constitutions to protect rights beyond those required by the U.S. Constitution, they do so at some political peril, since most judges are dependent on voter approval to keep their office. This risk has increased now that the Supreme Court requires state judges who wish to escape a review of their decisions by the Supreme Court to make it clear they have decided a case on adequate and independent state constitutional grounds.[25]

CHANGING FACE OF AMERICAN POLITICS

SAME-SEX MARRIAGES AND STATE CONSTITUTIONS

State legislatures around the country are considering proposed amendments to their state constitutions that would ban same-sex marriages. The firestorm was set off by the Massachusetts supreme court's ruling that its state constitution forbids discrimination against same-sex marriages. Subsequently, local government officials, from New Paltz, New York, to San Francisco, California, and Portland, Oregon, issued thousands of marriage licenses to same-sex couples, in some cases in violation of state law.

Thirty-nine states already prohibit same-sex marriages with state laws modeled after the federal Defense of Marriage Act of 1996, which bars federal recognition of same-sex marriages and permits states to ignore those marriages performed in other states. But in New York, Washington, and elsewhere, the constitutionality of those laws is being challenged in courts. Only four states—Alaska, Hawaii, Nebraska, and Nevada—have already amended their constitutions to bar same-sex marriages.

In the November 2004 elections, voters in 11 states adopted ballot initiatives that define marriage as a union between a man and a woman: Arkansas, Georgia, Kentucky, Michigan, Mississippi, Montana, North Dakota, Ohio, Oklahoma, Oregon, and Utah.

Several states, though, have enacted laws, not constitutional amendments, that confer health, inheritance, and other benefits on same-sex couples. In response to a decision of its state supreme court, in 2000 Vermont enacted a law recognizing "civil unions" and providing same-sex couples with state-level marriage benefits. California, Hawaii, and New Jersey recognize "domestic partnerships" that confer most benefits of marriage. Bills to recognize same-sex marriages have also been introduced in the legislatures of Connecticut and New York.

AMENDING STATE CONSTITUTIONS

Amendments may be proposed by the state legislature, citizen-initiated ballot petitions, or constitutional conventions. After an amendment has been proposed, it must be ratified. In all states except Delaware, where the legislature can ratify as well as propose amendments, ratification is by the voters. In most states, an amendment becomes part of the constitution when approved by a majority of those voting on the amendment. In a 2003 special election in New Mexico, voters approved constitutional amendments that created a cabinet-level secretary of education and authorized more spending for public education by just 195 votes (92,198 to 92,003).[26] In some other states—such as Minnesota—approval by a majority of all those voting in the election is required. This provision makes ratification difficult, because some people who vote for candidates do not vote on amendments. Slightly more than three-quarters of all constitutional amendments proposed by legislatures have been adopted in recent years.[27]

Legislative Proposals

All states permit their legislature to propose amendments; in fact, this is the most commonly used method. Although provisions vary, the general practice is to require the approval by two-thirds of each chamber of the legislature. Some states, however, permit proposal of an amendment by a simple majority in two successive legislatures.

A legislature may appoint a **revision commission** to make recommendations for constitutional change that, except in Florida, have no force until acted on by the legislature and approved by the voters. The legislature creates a commission of a relatively small number of people—some selected by the governor and some by the legislature—and charges it with presenting proposals for constitutional revision. A commission is less expensive than a full-blown constitutional convention, does not require initial voter approval, and gives the legislature final control of what is presented to the electorate.

California, for instance, turned to a revision commission to overcome its budgetary gridlock after its senate rejected a 1992 proposal asking voters if they wanted a constitutional convention (the first in 113 years). California's constitution has been so frequently amended that about 85 percent of the state's annual revenues are allocated before the governor and legislature even start working on the budget! Eventually, *all* state revenues could be allocated constitutionally if the trend continued, and there would be no state funds available for programs such as higher education and health care. A 23-member revision commission was created in 1993 to examine the budget process and the configuration of state and local duties. Two years later, the commission made its recommendations. But the legislature failed to act on any of them, in part because it was an election year. Also, because the state senate was Democratic and the state assembly Republican, it proved impossible to work out any compromise.

Constitutional commissions are in fact infrequently used. The recommendations of revision commissions are also seldom implemented quickly, perhaps because the commissioners have not been responsive to political currents or are not representative of broad enough interests. Still, a commission may provide less partisan consideration of amendments and be more resistant to single-interest groups than either the legislature or a convention. Mississippi has tried, so far unsuccessfully, to use a commission for changing its 1890 constitution, which was designed to keep African Americans out of the political process.[28]

Nonetheless, Florida, Virginia, and Louisiana have used the commission procedure to bring about significant constitutional change. Utah's Constitutional Revision Commission is a permanent body, required by law to submit recommendations for constitutional revision to the legislature 60 days before each regular session.[29] It has initiated revisions relating to the rights of crime victims as well as to changes in revenue and taxation. Florida has a Taxation and Budget Reform Commission that is called into session every ten years. Unlike other such commissions, in addition to making recommendations to the legislature, it may propose constitutional amendments directly to the voters. In 1998, the commission recommended nine amendments; Florida voters approved eight of them.

Initiative Petitions

At the end of the nineteenth century, revelations of corruption diminished the prestige of state governments, especially state legislatures. Out of this disillusionment came a variety of reforms as part of the Progressive movement. Among them was the **constitutional initiative petition,** a device that permits voters to place specific constitutional amendments on the ballot by petition. Eighteen states allow amendments to their constitutions to be proposed by initiative petitions.

The number of signatures required on petitions varies from 4 to 15 percent of either the total electorate or the number of voters who voted in the last election.[30] Although it takes more signatures to propose a constitutional amendment than to place other kinds of initiatives on the ballot, "the higher threshold is no longer a significant impediment to well-financed special-interest groups."[31]

Once the appropriate state official (attorney general or secretary of state) approves the precise wording of a petition, the amendment is placed on the ballot at the next general election. (California allows initiatives to appear even on primary election ballots.) The number of votes required to approve a constitutional amendment is typically a majority vote, although a few states have a more demanding requirement. Illinois requires a majority of those voting in the election or three-fifths of those voting on the amendment, and Nevada requires a majority vote on the same measure in two successive elections.

In some states, initiative proposals are limited to *amending* the state constitution, not to *revising* it. The distinction between revision and amendment is that revision refers to a comprehensive change to the basic governmental plan, a substantial alteration in the basic governmental framework, or a substantial alteration of the entire constitution, rather than to a less extensive change in one or more of its provisions.[32] Some states exclude certain subjects from amendment by initiative. Massachusetts, for example, does not allow amendments by popular initiative that concern religion, the judiciary, or judicial decisions; that are restricted to a particular town, city, or political division; that appropriate money from the state treasury; or that restrict rights such as freedom of speech.

In recent years, voters have approved about 50 percent of amendments proposed by initiative petitions. This figure compares with a slightly more than 75 percent approval rate for amendments proposed by state legislatures.[33] A variety of factors may account for the lower adoption rate of initiative measures. Initiatives tend to be used for controversial issues that have already been rejected by the legislature and engender an organized opposition. Initiatives are also often proposed by narrow-based groups or by reform-minded elites who lack broad support for their views. Sometimes initiatives are proposed in order to launch educational campaigns rather than to actually win adoption.

People anxious to limit the power of state and local governments are using the initiative process in more states. Since California in 1978 adopted Proposition 13, which limited the state government's right to raise property taxes, other states have followed suit. In addition, these "new reformers" have produced "a series of state constitutional amendments that, taken together, fundamentally altered the character and powers of state governments by limiting the tenure of governmental officials, reducing their powers, and transferring policy making responsibilities to the people."[34] In addition, "the focus of constitutional initiatives . . . has shifted from questions of governmental structure . . . to questions of substantive policy," such as initiatives on tort liability, the rights of gays, affirmative action, and the rights of immigrants.[35]

Constitutional Conventions

Americans love constitutional conventions (or at least we used to); we have had 233 of them—144 in the nineteenth century but only 63 in the twentieth century.[36] One scholar noted that calling conventions of the people is a uniquely American idea, emphasizing that legislators cannot be trusted and that the supreme power belongs to the people.[37]

Forty-one state constitutions authorize their legislature to submit the calling of a convention to the voters; the other states assume that the legislature has the power to do so. Fourteen state constitutions require the legislature to question voters about a convention at fixed intervals, varying from every 9 to every 20 years. For example, Missouri is required to submit the question to the voters every 20 years; Hawaii raises the issue every 9 years; Michigan, every 16 years.

If the voters approve, the next step is to elect delegates to a convention. Some state constitutions contain elaborate procedures governing the number of delegates, the method of election, and the time and place of the convention. Others leave the details to the legislature. The way convention delegates are selected seems to affect the kind of document the convention proposes. Selection by nonpartisan, multimember districts is more likely to result in a reform convention that makes major changes than one in which political parties play a major role.[38]

After delegates have been chosen, they usually assemble at the state capital. When the convention has prepared a draft of the new constitution, the document is submitted to the voters. But first the convention delegates have to make a difficult choice: Should the voters be asked to accept or reject the new constitution as a whole? Or should they vote on each section separately?

The advantage of the first method is that each provision of a constitution ties in with another, and to secure all the advantages of revision, the entire constitution should be adopted. The disadvantage is that those who oppose a particular provision may vote against the entire constitution. When convention delegates know that a particular provision is controversial, they may decide to submit that provision separately. Whichever method they choose, the supporters of change must rally their forces to gain voter approval of their work.

THE POLITICS OF CONSTITUTIONAL REVISION

Constitutions are not a neutral set of rules perched above the world of everyday politics. Rather, they significantly affect who gets what from government. Therefore, how a constitution is changed can help or hinder various groups.

Although recently there have been campaigns for constitutional reform under way in Alabama, Oklahoma, and Texas, most people simply do not care.[39] It is difficult to work up enthusiasm for revising a state constitution except among people with special interests, and they are more likely to oppose than to favor adoption. Supporters of the status quo thus have a built-in advantage, which, combined with obstacles to the amending process in the constitution, helps explain the lack of action. "Revision is time-consuming, requiring sophisticated legal and drafting skills of the highest order, and involves negotiation and compromise. To be successful, revision requires gubernatorial as well as legislative leadership. . . . An effective political campaign is essential. . . . Success at the polls is not assured. Constitutional revision can be a high-risk endeavor and will continue to be."[40] Following are some case studies that illustrate the risky nature of constitutional revision.

Rhode Island Amends Its Constitution

Rhode Island's constitutional convention produced 14 separate propositions for amending its 1843 constitution. On November 4, 1986, voters approved eight of the 14 provisions, rejecting attempts to increase compensation of state legislators, to provide for merit selection of judges, and to create a "paramount right to life without regard to age, health, function, or condition of dependency," which would have banned abortions or public funding of them. The voters approved provisions strengthening free speech, due process, equal protection rights, and expanding fishing rights and access to the shore, as well as a statement that the rights protected by the Rhode Island constitution "stand independent of the U.S. Constitution."

The Rhode Island constitution calls for voters to be asked every ten years if they want to convene a constitutional convention. In November 1994, the voters rejected a convention by a vote of 173,693 to 118,545.[41] There nonetheless remained considerable public pressure in the form of a 2-to-1 vote in November 2001 in favor of a nonbinding ballot question for a constitutional convention focused on separation of powers issues in order to reverse a decision of the Rhode Island supreme court to the effect that the Rhode Island constitution allows the state legislature to both make and execute state laws. After years of debate and continued pressure from Common Cause and 30 other organizations, in 2003 Rhode Island's legislature approved a constitutional amendment strengthening the separation of powers and placed it on the 2004 ballot for voters' approval.[42]

Louisiana Revises Its Constitution

The Louisiana Constitutional Revision Commission set out during 1973 and 1974 to write a streamlined "people's constitution"—one the average person could understand.[43] The AFL-CIO, National Association for the Advancement of Colored People, League of Women Voters, Committee for a Better Louisiana, National Municipal League, and many other lobbying groups became involved in shaping the new constitution. It took well over a year to write, and it cost the taxpayers approximately $4 million. In the end, a readable 26,000-word document replaced the existing 265,000-word document that contained some 536 amendments. In April 1974, Louisiana voters approved the new charter by a large margin.

The Louisiana constitution can no longer be cited as the prime example of an unworkable state constitution, although over 100 amendments have been added since 1974 and the length has inched back up to about 54,112 words. "Indeed," according to one commentator, constitutional amendment in Louisiana is "sufficiently continuous to justify including it with Mardi Gras, football, and corruption as one of the premier components of state culture."[44]

Changing the Hawaii Constitution

More than 800 proposals for constitutional changes were submitted to the Hawaii state constitutional convention of 1978. The League of Women Voters and other groups conducted extensive information and discussion meetings, and the convention held many public hearings on key issues. The 102 delegates to the convention met for nearly three months. After extensive debate, the convention narrowed the proposals to 34 questions to be placed on the fall ballot. Convention delegates rejected proposals for the initiative, referendum, and recall; for a unicameral legislature; and for an elected (instead of an appointed) attorney general.

The delegates were not opposed to all government reforms, for they endorsed a two-term limit for governor and lieutenant governor, moved to make Hawaii party primaries more open by allowing voters to cast ballots without declaring party preference, and authorized the state legislature to provide partial public funding for election campaigns and establish spending limits. The convention reflected concern over government spending by setting tougher overall debt and spending limits for the state. It also strengthened environmental safeguards and gave further constitutional and financial protection to the special status of native Hawaiians. In November 1978, 74 percent of the voters went to the polls; all 34 amendments were adopted; 20 percent of the voters had accepted the amendments as a package.

However, in 1986, Hawaiians rejected the periodic question of whether to call a convention by a vote of 173,977 to 139,236. Again in 1996, the question of calling a convention was put to the voters, and the vote was 163,869 in favor and 160,153 against, but 45,245 people left the question unanswered. Blank ballots were tallied as a no, in response to a decision of the state supreme court that the Hawaii constitution required approval by a majority of all ballots cast. The Ninth U.S. Circuit Court of Appeals, which refused to order a new election, sustained this decision.

Other proposals for a convention had been backed by several interests, including those who wanted to overturn a decision of the Hawaii supreme court favoring the legalization of same-sex marriages, by those who wanted to impose term limits, and by those who wanted to limit the power of state courts to restrict police searches.

Hawaii's experiences with the revision process are reminders that constitution making is not just an exercise in abstract argument or logical reasoning but flows directly from a state's political life.

Texas Keeps Its Old Constitution

Texas has a lengthy constitution. Adopted in 1876, it has been amended more than 370 times. The most recent effort to thoroughly revise it was in 1972, after political scandals brought in a new governor, Dolph Briscoe, and a reform-oriented state legislature. After pushing through a variety of reforms dealing with the ethics of officeholders, campaign practices, and registration of lobbyists, the legislature did an unconventional thing by calling into being a constitutional convention consisting of members of the legislature rather than a specially elected body.

After working for 17 months, the legislator-delegates came up with a much revised and shortened document intended to modernize many obsolete governmental practices. The convention deadlocked, however, over whether to give constitutional status to the state's right-to-work law, which prohibits labor contracts that require union membership as a condition of employment, so this issue was referred to the voters. In the end, neither the AFL-CIO nor Governor Briscoe supported all of the convention's recommendations. The governor was especially opposed to the proposal that legislative sessions be held annually, rather than every two years, which he argued would cause higher taxes. Advocates of the revised constitution tried to salvage their work by offering substantial parts of the new charter to the voters as amendments to the existing constitution.

Conservatives praised the old constitution, claiming it had served Texas well for 100 years. Progressives complained that the old constitution was elitist, permitted only the narrowest governmental objectives, and made real change nearly impossible. In November 1975, amid charges and countercharges, Texas voters rejected the amendments by a 2-to-1 margin.[45] Since then, Texans have approved 143 amendments and rejected 33 but have not held another convention.

The Arkansas Constitution

Arkansas's eighth constitutional convention was a protracted affair. The 100 delegates who were elected in 1978 held their organizational session in the winter of that year but did not get down to work until the spring of 1979. Having reconvened in June 1980 to revise the final draft, they submitted the proposed constitution to the voters in November 1980.

Opposition developed to a provision in the new constitution allowing the legislature, by a two-thirds vote, to set interest rates rather than limit them, as in the current constitution. Other groups opposed a provision enlarging the taxing powers of local governments. Even though then Governor Bill Clinton, the Democratic party, and the Arkansas Education Association endorsed the new constitution, the voters rejected it, 2 to 1.

The question of a constitutional convention was again put to Arkansas voters in December 1995. Those planning the 1995 convention structured the convention call in such a way that the convention would avoid addressing "issues which were not critical to state government but which would inflame folks" and would concentrate on "issues of pure governance."[46] Nonetheless, the call for the convention was decisively rejected.

Alabama Considers a New Constitution

Alabama has had six constitutions. The most recent, written in 1901 and adopted in 1902, was "a document of the Old South,"[47] unashamedly and openly designed to keep African Americans segregated in public schools and from voting or participating in governmental matters.[48] It has been amended more than 740 times and there have been many unsuccessful attempts to modernize and replace it.

The issue of constitutional reform remains on Alabama's agenda. A 21-member, independent commission called the Alabama Citizens for Constitutional Reform has been pushing the idea for years.[49] It proposed that the legislature put the issue of whether a constitutional convention should be held to a statewide vote and if voters approved, they would select in a special election delegates from each of the 105 House districts, who would convene to propose a new constitution, which then would be presented to the people for approval or rejection. One poll showed that 61 percent of the state's residents favored constitutional reform.[50]

The proposal for putting the issue of calling a constitutional convention before the voters in November 2002 was nonetheless defeated in the House of Representatives by a vote of 33 to 105.[51] However, both of the Democratic and Republican candidates for governor supported constitutional reforms and a statewide vote on the matter, though Republican candidate Bob Riley opposed holding a citizens' constitutional convention. Shortly after his inauguration as governor in 2003, Riley instead addressed the matter by establishing a 35-member Alabama Citizens' Constitutional Commission to propose constitutional reforms in five areas: strengthening the governor's line-item veto power, giving more home rule back to counties, requiring more than a simple majority of the legislature to raise taxes, changing provisions that earmark 90 percent of all tax revenues for specific purposes, and studying how the constitution might be shortened and reformed. The commission's recommendations went to the legislature for approval and they must be ratified by the voters. The legislature proposed amendments eliminating language in the constitution that requires segregated schools and poll taxes, which remain even though they were invalidated by federal courts over forty years ago.[52] But in 2004 voters defeated that amendment by just 1850 votes out of the more than 1.3 million cast.

S U M M A R Y

1. State constitutions spell out the fundamental laws of the states. Although they vary considerably in detail, each outlines the organizational framework of the state, vesting powers in the legislature and other departments. Each includes a bill of rights, sets procedures for holding elections, provides for local governments, and contains a variety of provisions dealing with finances, education, and other state issues.

2. Most state constitutions are cumbersome documents containing much more detail than the U.S. Constitution. Although reformers may have introduced such detail to prevent abuse, most constitutional scholars believe such matters are better left to statutory law.

3. In the past 20 years, there has been a flurry of renewed interest in state constitutions as they have been discovered to be additional instruments for protecting and expanding rights in what is known as the new judicial federalism.

4. State constitutions can be amended by ratification by the voters of proposals submitted by the legislature, by popular initiative petitions, or by constitutional conventions. Conventions tend to revise the entire constitution rather than just amend portions of it.

5. In recent decades, there has been an expanded use of the initiative process in several states to bring about narrowly targeted constitutional reforms.

6. Despite the considerable constitutional change brought about during the last half-century through amendments, voters have often been resistant to sweeping constitutional revision.

F U R T H E R   R E A D I N G

The Greenwood Publishing Group has commissioned reference guides for the constitution of each state, written by an expert on the state. As of 2004, guides for 38 states have been published, including Alabama, Alaska, Arizona, Arkansas, California, Colorado, Connecticut, Delaware, Florida, Hawaii, Idaho, Indiana, Iowa, Kansas, Kentucky, Louisiana, Maine, Michigan, Minnesota, Mississippi, Montana, Nebraska, Nevada, New Hampshire, New Jersey, New Mexico, New York, North Carolina, North Dakota, Oklahoma, Tennessee, Texas, Utah, Vermont, Washington, Wisconsin, West Virginia, and Wyoming.

WILLI PAUL ADAMS, *The First American Constitutions: Republican Ideology and the Making of State Constitutions in the Revolutionary Era* (Rowman & Littlefield, 2001).

PAUL FINKELMAN AND STEPHEN E. GOTTLIEB, EDS., *Toward a Usable Past: Liberty Under State Constitutions* (University of Georgia Press, 1991).

RICHARD J. ELLIS, *Democratic Delusions: The Initiative Process in America* (University Press of Kansas, 2003).

JENNIFER FREISEN, *State Constitutional Law* (Michie, 1996).

SANFORD LEVINSON, ED., *Responding to Imperfection: The Theory and Practice of Constitutional Amendment* (Princeton University Press, 1995).

CHARLES LOPEMAN, *The Activist Advocate: Policy Making in State Supreme Courts* (Praeger, 1999).

ROBERT L. MADDEX, *State Constitutions of the United States* (CQ Press, 1998).

JAMES T. McHUGH, *Ex Uno Plura: State Constitutions and Their Political Cultures* (State University of New York, 2003).

LAURA J. SCALIA, *America's Jeffersonian Experiment: Remaking State Constitutions, 1820–1850* (Northern Illinois University Press, 1999).

G. ALAN TARR, *Understanding State Constitutions* (Princeton University Press, 2000).

ROBERT F. WILLIAMS, *State Constitutional Law: Cases and Materials* (Michie, 1993).

See also the quarterly review *State Constitutional Commentaries and Notes,* published by the Edward McNail Burns Center for State Constitutional Studies at Rutgers University.

PARTIES AND ELECTIONS IN THE STATES

The chaos in the counting of ballots in Florida in the 2000 election surprised many Americans, who assumed that vote counting is simple and precise. They were wrong. The problems were not isolated to Florida's clogged voting machines, defective punch cards, and inconsistent standards for dealing with problems. Ballots were misplaced in New Mexico; voting machines broke down in several states; people's names were incorrectly purged from voting lists; and long lines of people waiting to vote led to court challenges in many states. In the weeks and months following the election, at least half the states launched efforts to study the problems and propose solutions; in addition, national commissions, advisory groups, and experts undertook extensive analyses of our voting procedures.

Most people agree that many communities need new voting equipment and that the antiquated and flawed punch-card technology used by "roughly 30 percent of the nation's voters" needed to be replaced.[1] As a result of the widespread problems in election administration in 2000, Congress passed the Help America Vote Act (HAVA) in 2002. HAVA provides federal funds to help states replace antiquated punch-card and lever voting machines. By accepting the funding, states were to have these new machines in place by the November 2004 election or apply for a waiver to delay implementation until 2006. In as many as 42 states, new voting machines were in place in 2004. Nevertheless, of the 30 states that applied for federal funds to replace punch-card and/or lever voting machines, 24 applied for a waiver."[2] Despite widespread concerns before the election, there were no major problems with voting technology in the 2004 election. Had the election been closer in any one of several states, then more concerns would likely have surfaced.

Some of this technology prompted debates about the accuracy of computerized voting machines, especially if the machines were paperless and did not allow voters to know if their votes had been tallied correctly. Those working the polls in 2004 were required by the 2002 legislation to demand identification from first-time voters who registered by mail but did not provide identification with their registration.

The National Association of Secretaries of State—the state officials charged with election administration—issued recommendations that included better pay for poll workers; aggressive voter education on matters like how to ask for a second ballot if the first is spoiled; equal access to balloting for minorities, the poor, and elderly voters; maintaining up-to-date voter lists; ensuring the integrity of absentee ballots; and providing federal money to local communities to upgrade their voting systems.[3] The 2002 elections saw no repeats of the troubled recounts in Florida in 2000. There was, however, some controversy in South Dakota about the registration drives among Native Americans. Charges of fraud in Native American voter registration surfaced before the election but were dismissed by the South Dakota attorney general. The 2000 election and its aftermath taught us to not take election administration for granted. The states have the responsibility to manage elections and to ensure the right of participation to every citizen. The central role of states in our electoral democracy is the subject of this chapter.

ELECTORAL POLITICS IN THE STATES AND LOCALITIES

The U.S. Constitution provides only the most general guidelines to the states concerning the regulation of elections for members of the U.S. Congress. Article I, Section 4, says, "The Times, Places and Manner of holding Elections for Senators and Representatives shall be prescribed in each State by the Legislature thereof; but the Congress may at any time by Law make or alter such Regulations, except as to the Places of choosing Senators." The constitutional language regarding presidential elections also defers to state law: "Each State shall appoint, in such Manner as the Legislature thereof may direct, a Number of Electors."

Amendments to the U.S. Constitution relating to elections do not alter the central role of state constitutions and state law regarding voting rights. Rather, these amendments expressly forbid the states to restrict the right to vote in any election, for state and local as well as for national offices, to certain kinds of people. States cannot deny the franchise on the basis of "race, color, or previous condition of servitude" (Fifteenth Amendment), gender (Nineteenth Amendment), failure to pay a poll tax (Twenty-Fourth Amendment), or age for persons over age 18 (Twenty-Sixth Amendment).

Federalism and Elections

Political federalism in this country is noteworthy. Most elected officials, including even the president, are elected in a process that reinforces the importance of states. State identities are important to both politicians and voters. We think of ourselves as citizens of a particular state as well as of the United States. States have distinctive political traditions and political cultures. Because of these strong state identities and differences between the states in laws and practices, it should not be surprising that state parties are in many ways more important than national parties. Indeed, national parties, aside from their congressional campaign committees, are largely federations of state parties. And since our national parties as electoral organizations have never been strong, the activities they undertake usually end up being carried out by the state parties. The independence of state parties also helps explain why, for instance, Democratic voters in one state can be so different from those in another and why Republicans from different states can come down on opposite sides of some major issues.

The electoral process in the United States is *decentralized* in its rules and administration. Elections in the United States are administered by state and local governments, not by the national government. Even the president is chosen in state elections conducted according to state rules. Because of the electoral college and the winner-take-all system, presidential politics focuses not on getting the most popular votes but instead on getting a plurality of votes in as many states as possible. State elections also determine who will serve as members of Congress, as governor, and as other statewide officials like attorney general, as well as the outcome of many ballot measures.

Most states prescribe the organization of the state parties, the means by which their officers are elected, and the nomination process for president and other offices.[4] In states that have some form of public financing of elections or parties, such as Maine and Arizona, the state also regulates the distribution of public funds to the parties and the reporting of how those funds are spent.

States differ in the hours the polls are open, how close to the voting place campaigning may be conducted, and whether they require voter registration. Largely because of overriding federal legislation, differences between the states in how long you must have lived in the state before voting and how you may register to vote have diminished in recent years.

As we learned in the 2000 presidential election in Florida, there is great variation in the way people vote, even from county to county. Some Florida counties used ballots read by optical scanners, and others used punch-card ballots. Other states use these same types of ballots as well as paper ballots, voting machines, and even the Internet. Following the 2000 election, Florida mandated that voting in statewide elections be by computerized touch screens or ballots read by optical scanning machines.[5] Some of these devices malfunctioned in the 2002 Florida primary election. Despite these mishaps, a substantial amount of variation in voting systems continued through the 2004 election. In nearly half of the states (22), some voters continued to have punch card ballots, for example.[6] Delays in funding the 2002 legislation delayed implementation of new voting technologies in 2004 in many states. For a state by state summary of election reforms, see www.electionline.org.

Along with the variation in ballots, we have many types of elections, including *general elections* to determine who holds office and *primary elections* to determine who will run in the general elections. Most statewide elections are partisan, whereas most local elections for school boards, water districts, and city governments are nonpartisan. State legislative elections are partisan except in Nebraska, where the legislature is nonpartisan. Voters in all states but Delaware must ratify changes to the state constitution in a referendum. Roughly half of the states allow votes on initiatives and referendums put on the ballot by petition. The initiative and referendum are also found in many local governments.

THE ROLE OF POLITICAL PARTIES

Although political parties are not mentioned in the U.S. Constitution, they are vital not only to our national government but also to the functioning of the electoral system within the states. Parties organize the competition by recruiting and nominating candidates, function as the loyal opposition when out of power, unify and organize the electorate, and provide a link between the people and their government. The existence of political parties is acknowledged in many state constitutions.

Election rules in general favor the two major parties over minor parties. The Republican and Democratic parties have a "preferred position"—that is, their candidates will definitely be placed on the ballot. Ballot access for minor party and independent candidates is less certain. State laws typically require minor parties to garner a minimum number of votes in the previous election or submit a prescribed number of signatures of registered voters in order to appear on the ballot. States vary in the difficulty of ballot access for minor parties, depending on three factors: the number of signatures required, the time allowed to collect them, and whether signatures must be distributed across several counties.

State election ballots are of two kinds. The **party column ballot** (also known as the *Indiana ballot*), which encourages party-line voting, is organized by parties, with the party name and symbol at the top of a column that lists all the party's candidates running for offices in that election (see Figure 4–1). Typically, there is an option at the top of the ballot column that allows voters to cast votes for all candidates of that party. When voters choose such an option, they cast a **straight ticket** vote. Voters may also have to work their way through state constitutional amendments, referendums, and initiatives on the ballot.

CHANGING FACE OF AMERICAN POLITICS

A DEMOGRAPHIC PROFILE OF LOCAL GOVERNMENT OFFICIALS

Number of Local Elected Officials   **494,093**

Gender	
Male	76.3%
Female	23.7

Race	
White	96.7
Black	2.8
American Indian or Alaskan Native	0.4
Asian or Pacific Islander	0.1
Hispanic	1.4

SOURCE: U.S. Bureau of the Census, "Popularly Elected Officials in 1992," *1992 Census of Governments* (U.S. Government Printing Office, 1992). Note: This is the most recent census of elected officials and these proportions may have changed somewhat since the data were collected.

Official Ballot for Piute County, Utah, November 2, 2004

REPUBLICAN	DEMOCRATIC	CONSTITUTION	GREEN PARTY	LIBERTARIAN	PERSONAL CHOICE
For PRESIDENT OF THE UNITED STATES GEORGE W. BUSH For VICE-PRESIDENT OF THE UNITED STATES DICK CHENEY	For PRESIDENT OF THE UNITED STATES JOHN F. KERRY For VICE-PRESIDENT OF THE UNITED STATES JOHN EDWARDS	For PRESIDENT OF THE UNITED STATES MICHAEL ANTHONY PEROUTKA For VICE-PRESIDENT OF THE UNITED STATES CHUCK BALDWIN	For PRESIDENT OF THE UNITED STATES For VICE-PRESIDENT OF THE UNITED STATES	For PRESIDENT OF THE UNITED STATES MICHAEL BADNARIK For VICE-PRESIDENT OF THE UNITED STATES RICHARD V. CAMPAGNA	For PRESIDENT OF THE UNITED STATES CHARLES JAY For VICE-PRESIDENT OF THE UNITED STATES MARILYN CHAMBERS TAYLOR
For U.S. SENATOR ROBERT F. BENNETT	For U.S. SENATOR R. PAUL VAN DAM	For U.S. SENATOR GARY R. VAN HORN	For U.S. SENATOR	For U.S. SENATOR	For U.S. SENATOR JOE LABONTE
For U.S. REPRESENTATIVE, District #2 JOHN SWALLOW	For U.S. REPRESENTATIVE, District #2 JIM MATHESON	For U.S. REPRESENTATIVE, District #2 JEREMY PAUL PETERSEN	For U.S. REPRESENTATIVE, District #2 PATRICK S. DIEHL	For U.S. REPRESENTATIVE, District #2	For U.S. REPRESENTATIVE, District #2 RONALD R. AMOS
For GOVERNOR JON M. HUNTSMAN, JR.	For GOVERNOR SCOTT M. MATHESON, JR.	For GOVERNOR	For GOVERNOR	For GOVERNOR	For GOVERNOR KEN LARSEN
For LIEUTENANT GOVERNOR GARY R. HERBERT	For LIEUTENANT GOVERNOR KAREN HALE	For LIEUTENANT GOVERNOR	For LIEUTENANT GOVERNOR	For LIEUTENANT GOVERNOR	For LIEUTENANT GOVERNOR TALEA SHADOWIND
For ATTORNEY GENERAL MARK L. SHURTLEFF	For ATTORNEY GENERAL GREGORY G. SKORDAS	For ATTORNEY GENERAL	For ATTORNEY GENERAL	For ATTORNEY GENERAL W. ANDREW McCULLOUGH	For ATTORNEY GENERAL
For STATE AUDITOR AUSTON G. JOHNSON	For STATE AUDITOR CARLOS VASQUEZ	For STATE AUDITOR	For STATE AUDITOR	For STATE AUDITOR MIKE STODDARD	For STATE AUDITOR VALERIE S. LARSEN
For STATE TREASURER EDWARD T. ALTER	For STATE TREASURER DEBBIE HANSEN	For STATE TREASURER	For STATE TREASURER	For STATE TREASURER JIM ELWELL	For STATE TREASURER MARY A. PETERSEN
For STATE SENATOR, District #24 LEONARD M. BLACKHAM	For STATE SENATOR, District #24 JAMES PARKER	For STATE SENATOR, District #24 FRANK CROWTHER	For STATE SENATOR, District #24	For STATE SENATOR, District #24	For STATE SENATOR, District #24
For STATE REPRESENTATIVE, District #73 MIKE NOEL	For STATE REPRESENTATIVE, District #73	For STATE REPRESENTATIVE, District #73	For STATE REPRESENTATIVE, District #73 VICTORIA WOODARD	For STATE REPRESENTATIVE, District #73	For STATE REPRESENTATIVE, District #73
For COUNTY COMMISSIONER W. KAY BLACKWELL	For COUNTY COMMISSIONER	For COUNTY COMMISSIONER	For COUNTY COMMISSIONER	For COUNTY COMMISSIONER	For COUNTY COMMISSIONER

FIGURE 4–1 A Sample Party Column Ballot.

Partly to discourage straight ticket voting, some states use the **office block ballot** (also known as the *Massachusetts ballot*), which lists all the candidates running for an office together in one block or on one screen, all those running for another office in another block/screen, and so on (see Figure 4–2). If voters want to cast a straight ticket vote, they have to hunt through each block/screen for their preferred candidate. Office block ballots encourage **split ticket** voting, or voting for candidates from more than one party. One consequence of computerized ballots will be a shift to office block formats.

Party Organization and Officers

AN EARLIER ERA: MACHINES AND BOSSES   In the nineteenth century, political *machines* became established in a number of American cities. Typically, these were organizations in which one political party dominated the political life of the city, often by recruiting new immigrants as supporters and voters by offering them patronage jobs and social welfare benefits. For many years, the epitome of a political machine in the United States was Tammany Hall, the building where the Tammany Society (named after a Delaware Indian chief) met and ran New York City politics. Tammany Hall was closely identified with Democrats and was ruled by William Tweed, the boss of New York City politics.

A *boss* is a party leader who uses patronage, government contracts, and access to power to dictate policy. Some bosses, like Tweed, were never elected to office but were powers behind the scene who told the mayor and other city officials what to do. Party bosses were common after the Civil War and well into the twentieth century. Other cities

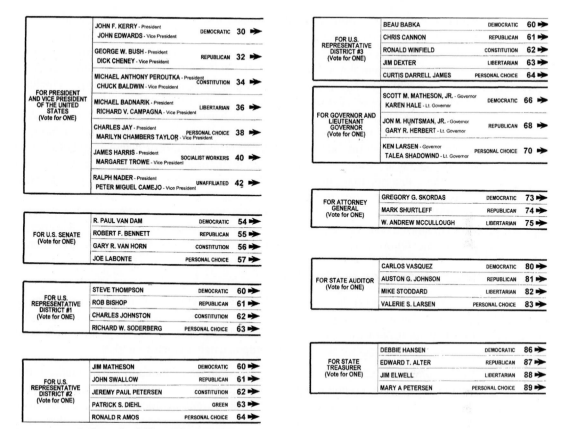

FIGURE 4–2 A Sample Office Block Ballot.

with powerful political machines were Chicago, Los Angeles, Boston, Pittsburgh, Cincinnati, Philadelphia, Indianapolis, San Francisco, and Baltimore.

The principal objective of the urban reform movement in the early twentieth century was to overthrow the bosses and the political machines. Reformers advocated nonpartisan local elections, competitive bids for projects, and civil service in place of patronage. They achieved most of their goals, although it is not clear whether the power of political machines was reduced by these reforms or by other social and economic forces.

PARTY ORGANIZATIONS TODAY   Although state party organizations are not all alike, most organize themselves along the same lines as the national parties. In all states, there is a *party chair* who is elected by the party's central committee or delegates to a party convention. Other statewide party officers include the *vice chair,* who by state law or party bylaws often must be of the opposite gender from the party chair,[7] plus officers like treasurer and secretary. Party leaders generally answer to a *central committee,* which consists of 20 or more persons who are elected or otherwise chosen for specified terms.

The state party chair is the spokesperson for the party, especially when the party does not control the governorship. He or she raises money for the party and its candidates. When the party controls the governorship, the central committee defers to the governor in the selection of the chair. Because overt expressions of partisanship are thought to be unbecoming of elected officials, it is often the party chair who defends the party and, when necessary, goes on the offensive against the opposition party.

The day-to-day operations of the party are usually carried out by the party's *executive director,* a full-time employee who oversees the staff, assists the chair, and coordinates the work of the central committee and other party officials. The executive director schedules functions and serves as a liaison with the national organizations.

At the local level, political parties generally have a structure patterned after the state party organization. In some counties, party organizations are fully staffed and functioning, but in most counties, they are run by volunteers and are mostly inactive until just before an election. Local parties provide opportunities for ordinary citizens to become involved in politics, a first step that can eventually lead to running for office. Some states, like Minnesota, have congressional district parties as well.[8]

Although party bosses and strong party machines are a thing of the past, local politics is still organized on a partisan basis in many of our largest cities. More typically, as noted, local politics is nonpartisan with three-quarters of U.S. cities having nonpartisan elections.[9]

Party Activities in Elections

American politics is candidate-centered. Candidates create their own campaign organizations. Yet parties serve important secondary roles in elections. They provide the structure for elections; in some places, they recruit candidates, register voters, mobilize voters on election day, and supply resources and campaign help to their candidates.

STRUCTURE FOR ELECTIONS   Our election system would function in a dramatically different way if we had no political parties to organize the competition. Parties narrow the field of candidates through a primary election or convention process, providing voters with relatively few choices in the general election. Candidates, to one degree or another, must secure the support of fellow partisans to win a place on the ballot as the party's nominees for the offices they are seeking.

CANDIDATE RECRUITMENT   Party officials often seek out candidates to run for office, help train them in how to run, and occasionally provide modest financial support. One sign of the weakness of our parties is that many offices go uncontested, including some members of Congress. The number of unopposed candidates increases as you go down the ballot. To be sure, some incumbents have done such a good job that to oppose them would be an exercise in futility. Yet lack of competition in elections violates American assumptions about democracy and is reminiscent of politics in the former communist states, where party officers ran unopposed. One important characteristic of American parties at all levels is that they are extremely open to would-be candidates. Virtually anybody can run for the state legislature. Generally speaking, the greater the likelihood that a party nomination will help with winning the general election, the more competition there is for that nomination.

VOTER REGISTRATION   All states except North Dakota require citizens to register before permitting them to vote. In California, you can register online, at www.ss.ca.gov/elections/elections.htm, and some states, like Wisconsin, allow registration at the polls on election day. Voter registration became easier when Congress passed the National Voter Registration, or Motor Voter, Act in 1993. People are now able to register to vote when they apply for or renew their driver's license or visit certain public agencies. The half-dozen states that permit election day registration or do not require voter registration are exempt from the law. The idea behind Motor Voter is to ease the registration process, thereby increasing the number of registered voters and turnout.

What difference has Motor Voter made? During the 2002 election cycle, over 16 million people were added to the voter registration rolls via the Motor Voter, or just under 43 percent of all new registrants.[10] Many of the new Motor Voter registrants are registering as Independents. In terms of party balance, Motor Voter does not appear to have made much difference, contrary to expectations that it would result in a bias in favor of Democrats.[11]

At the time of registration, some states ask voters to register with a political party; in other states, party registration is optional. Most states do not register voters by party. To see what your state requires, visit the voter registration section of the Federal Election Commission Web site at www.fec.gov. Even in states that require party registration, voters have the option to decline to state their party at the time of registration. For example, in California in 2002, 15 percent of the registered voters declined to state their party preference.[12] Opting out of party registration often means voters may not vote in a party primary, which in some states may be the election that effectively decides the officeholder. An excellent data bank on voter registration and turnout is maintained by the National Conference of State Legislatures at www.ncsl.org.

Helping register sympathetic voters is important to candidates, parties, and interest groups. These efforts are typically aimed at citizens they anticipate will vote for their party's candidate. Voter registration drives targeted at African Americans helped Democrats in key states and congressional districts. Both parties worked to register Hispanic voters in 2002. Interest groups with active voter registration efforts include organized labor, business groups, and groups concerned about the environment and abortion.

Political parties favor laws requiring voters to disclose their party preference at the time they register. First, this requirement permits parties to limit participation in their primaries to registered party members in states that have a closed primary system. Second, party registration creates voter registration lists, which parties find extremely useful for campaigning and fund raising. In addition, *list vending*—selling voter lists with addresses, phone numbers, and party preferences—is a multimillion-dollar industry. Third, voter registration helps the parties in the redistricting process because state legislators, using party registration, voting, and other data, can draw new congressional and state legislative district boundaries in ways that give their party an advantage. Examples of states where partisanship was a major factor in the 2001–2002 redistricting are Georgia for the Democrats and Utah for the Republicans.[13]

VOTER MOBILIZATION   Just over three-quarters of eligible voters are registered, and of that number, only about two-thirds vote in presidential elections, meaning that *only half the voting-age population bothers to vote* in a presidential election and fewer still in a midterm election.[14] Get-out-the-vote drives are therefore a major activity of candidates and parties. Elections are often decided by which party does better at turning out its supporters. Party workers, through telephone or door-to-door canvassing, identify registered voters who are likely to support their party and then contact those voters personally on election day, perhaps more than once, to encourage them to go to the polls. Where resources permit, the parties may even provide transportation to the polls or baby-sitting services.[15]

In states that permit registration by mail or by roving registrars, volunteers register voters at the same time they find voters who will support their party's candidates in the election. When absentee or mail ballots are options, voter mobilization efforts help voters fill out the form requesting an absentee ballot and then mail the form for them. A few weeks later, a party volunteer checks to make sure a ballot has arrived and has been filled out and returned. Because most voters prefer one party over another, it makes sense for candidates from the same party to consolidate their efforts.

CAMPAIGN RESOURCES   American political parties, with some notable exceptions, are organizationally weak. In better-organized states, parties often provide campaign funds and campaign help. They raise funds for their party organization and finance voter registration and mobilization efforts, often with the help of national parties. As at the national level, control of the governorship helps in fund raising because interest groups are much more likely to contribute to the governor's party. Texas Governor George W. Bush not only tapped into his base of affluent Texans but also won the support of other governors to finance much of his 2000 presidential campaign. He built on this network to raise record-setting amounts as a candidate in his 2004 reelection campaign.

In states with well-organized parties, the parties train the candidates they have recruited. Wisconsin and New York have strong state legislative campaign committees that distribute resources to candidates, as the national party committee does to congressional candidates.[16] Sometimes the state parties provide polling data to state and local candidates, help establish campaign themes, or prepare generic advertising that can be used in several state legislative districts.

Until 2004, parties also channeled money from the national congressional and senatorial campaign committees to local candidates for U.S. Senate or U.S. House involved in competitive races. This **soft money,** which could come in disclosed but unlimited amounts, was banned at the national level by the Bipartisan Campaign Reform Act (BCRA) in 2002.[17] State parties operate under their own rules, and all but Connecticut permit soft money for state and local candidates. Moreover, the 2002 reforms permit limited amounts of soft money, $10,000, to go to state and local parties for voter registration and mobilization.[18] Between 1996 and 2002, Republican and Democratic national party committees, including the congressional and senatorial campaign committees, raised and distributed large amounts of soft money. Because state parties largely spend the soft money for the national parties, this expenditure has not generally made state parties stronger.

One reason parties raised soft money was to respond to **issue advocacy,** in which an interest group attacks some political candidates or supports others but carefully avoids specifically telling voters to vote for or against that individual. Though much of the soft money and issue advocacy advertising focuses on presidential and congressional elections, both parties have also devoted these resources to gubernatorial, judicial,[19] and state legislative races.[20]

Issue advocacy, which aims to defeat or elect a particular candidate, has been important since the 1996 elections and was again significant in 2002.[21] One notable example was again the pharmaceutical industry, which in 2000 provided substantial funding for a group named Citizens for Better Medicare. In 2002, their money was directed to another group—United Seniors. In both instances, the issue advocacy was important in reshaping the debate on the prescription drug issue for senior citizens. The pharmaceutical industry did not mount major issue ads in 2004. Tort reform was a more important topic for issue ads in 2004.

Voting Choices

Voters generally base their election decisions on three factors, listed in decreasing order of importance: political party identification, candidate appeal, and issues. But in many local elections, since party labels are absent from the ballot, voters rely more on candidate appeal, issues, and factors like incumbency, media endorsements, and name recognition.

PARTY IDENTIFICATION   Party identification is the most important predictor of voting behavior. Parties provide a party label that guides voters in making their decisions. Party labels are especially important in elections in which voters have little information about candidates, as in contests for attorney general, state senator, state representative, or county commissioner. The simplifying device of party labels helps voters sort through the many candidate choices they encounter on election day.

People who identify themselves as strong Democrats and strong Republicans are remarkably loyal to their party when voting for governor and other state and local offices. Independent-leaners have clear partisan preferences in the direction of one party or the other. Pure Independents have no party preference and are most inclined to vote for one party and then another with changing circumstances, but there are few Pure Independents in the total electorate.[22]

CANDIDATE APPEAL   Although party identification is important, it is not decisive. Candidate appeal can be crucial. For example, in the 2003 California recall election, voters not only viewed governor Gray Davis negatively,[23] they were positive about Arnold Schwarzenegger's success in business, his independence from special interests because of his personal wealth, and his sponsorship of a ballot initiative that provided for after-school programs.[24] In some respects the 2003 California recall election resembled the 1998 Minnesota gubernatorial election, in which Reform party candidate Jesse Ventura was elected largely because his style and approach generated interest among voters, and a plurality preferred him over the established candidates in the major parties. Minnesota's system of public financing helped Ventura become visible, and he worked hard to become credible. In the end, he won in a stunning upset. As governor, he remained unconventional, abandoned the Reform Party for the Independent party, found working with the state legislature difficult, and took exception to media scrutiny of his family.[25] He decided not to run for reelection in 2002.

In state and local elections, name identification and the advantages of incumbency are important. Incumbents generally have an advantage in candidate appeal because of greater name recognition and access to campaign resources. Candidates sometimes use creative means to generate positive name recognition. For example, when Bob Graham was governor of Florida, he often worked one day a week in different jobs around the state to demonstrate his desire to relate to his constituents.

ISSUE VOTING   Issues can be very important to the outcome of elections. Economic conditions are an important factor in state and local elections, as they are in national ones. William Weld, a Republican, was able to win his first Massachusetts gubernatorial election in 1990, despite the fact that Massachusetts is a very strong Democratic state, because the economy was so bad. Former New Jersey Governor Christine Todd Whitman won election in part because her incumbent opponent had raised state taxes and she promised a 30 percent tax cut. Mitt Romney campaigned successfully in 2002 for governor of Massachusetts on the theme of an outsider being able to restore economic growth and fiscal discipline. His success as a businessman and as head of the 2002 Salt Lake City Winter Olympics reinforced this message. Democratic candidate Kathleen Sebelius won her 2002 gubernatorial election in a heavily Republican state by emphasizing her support for public education and her opponent's view that schools in Kansas "can make it with 1 or 2 or 3%" less funding. "Sebelius' stance on this issue appealed to enough moderate Republicans to win her the election."[26] Although issues are important in state and local elections, it is fair to say that they are probably less important than at the national level.[27]

JUDICIAL ELECTIONS   Judicial elections in some states are partisan and resemble campaigns for other offices in intensity. In 2000, the Michigan Democratic party ran ads attacking incumbent candidates for the Michigan supreme court who had been appointed by a former Republican governor. One of the ads showed an insurance executive sitting at his desk searching through papers and asking the secretary, "Where are my judges?" She replies, "Just where they've always been, right in your pocket." The executive looks in his suit coat pocket to see three justices frolicking in handfuls of money. Three pictures appear on the screen and a voice says, "Justices Markman, Taylor, and Young have accepted hundreds of thousands from insurance and big business. Justice should not be for sale."[28]

Ads attacking judicial candidates like this were not unique to Michigan in 2000. Ohio, Illinois, Alabama, and Idaho had races in which similar ads were used by political parties or interest groups[29]; this occurred again in several states in 2002. A 2002 Supreme Court decision, *Republican Party of Minnesota* v. *White,* allowes judicial candidates to state their views on disputed legal and political issues. One potential consequence of this will be more position taking on issues by judicial candidates. Substantial spending by political parties and interest groups in judicial elections has prompted criticism by good-government groups and led the American Bar Association to form a task force on this topic.

NONPARTISAN LOCAL ELECTIONS   Nonpartisan elections were intended to weaken political parties in local elections, and they have been successful. Arguing that political parties had little to contribute to the administration of local government, reformers during the first half of the twentieth century introduced nonpartisan elections. The two parties were, in effect, blocked from exerting an open influence on local politics.

Some observers contend that nonpartisan local elections make it more difficult for poor persons, minorities, and the less educated to participate effectively. For such people, the party label serves to identify politicians who share their values and perspectives on government. Well-educated and wealthy voters know more about who is running and what they stand for, even without party labels. Nonpartisan elections sometimes help Republican candidates, especially in cities with populations of more than 50,000, because Republican voters tend to vote more in low-turnout elections and are more likely to know which candidates are Republicans.[30] Others have found that there is not generally an advantage to Republican candidates in nonpartisan elections.[31]

Parties in State Government

PARTIES IN THE EXECUTIVE BRANCH   Just as winning the presidency is the big prize at the national level, so is winning the governorship at the state level. The party that controls the governorship has the power to appoint executive department officials and some state judges. Governors are usually perceived as the leaders of their party, and they establish the political agenda and help define the party for their state. They customarily win office with the help of fellow partisans, and they know from the day they take office that the other party is planning ways to defeat them and their party in the next election.

Governors often assist in recruiting candidates for the state legislature; they usually campaign on behalf of their party, even when they are not on the ballot for reelection. Presidential candidates often seek the help of governors. Governors raise money for campaigns as well as for the state party. They have wide latitude in appointing boards, commissions, judges, and state administrators, and they almost always take party affiliation and activity into account when making appointments.

PARTIES IN THE LEGISLATURE Like Congress, state legislatures (excluding Nebraska, which is nonpartisan) are organized largely along party lines. The *speaker of the house or assembly* and the *president of the senate* are elected by the majority party in most states. They preside over floor proceedings and make key assignments to standing committees and study committees. Most state legislatures have floor leaders, called *majority leaders* and *minority leaders* and majority and minority *whips.*

In most states, parties sit on different sides of the aisle in the legislative chambers and are separated in committee meetings as well. Committee chairs in most state legislatures go to members from the majority party in that chamber, with the leaders of the majority party wielding great power in the final decision. The **party caucus** is often important in state legislatures. The caucus is a meeting of party leaders and legislators to discuss party policy. Because some state legislatures meet for only a few months a year, the party caucus can help hammer out agreements rapidly.

One area in which legislatures are predictably partisan is **redistricting.** Each decade, following the national census, state legislatures are constitutionally required to realign congressional and state legislative district boundaries to make them equal in population and reflect population changes. The 2001–2002 redistricting was especially important because the two parties were so evenly divided in numbers of legislative chambers controlled. Going into the 2004 elections, the Democrats controlled 43 chambers, the Republicans 51, and three were tied.[32]

How district lines are drawn can help or hurt a party. Where one party controls both houses and the governorship or has a veto-proof majority in the legislature, the majority party can do pretty much what it wants with district boundaries, so long as it keeps the districts equal in population and respects the rights of racial minorities. Where power is divided between the parties, the result is often a redistricting that protects incumbents.

Typically, after redistricting occurs, several U.S. House incumbents retire rather than face the uncertainty of an election in a newly drawn district or the prospect of running against another incumbent. This was less the case in 2002 because to a very large extent, state legislatures drew district boundaries to protect incumbents. California, with its 53 congressional districts, emerged from redistricting with only one or two districts considered competitive in 2002 and 2004. Three notable exceptions to this are the partisan gerrymandering carried out in Utah and Texas by Republicans and in Georgia by Democrats. In these cases, the parties controlled the process and sought to create districts more favorable to their party, even if it gave incumbents from their party districts that were less safely partisan.

In five states, commissions rather than the legislature do the redistricting. Commissions tend to be more neutral and often create more competitive districts. This was the case in Arizona with the last redistricting. Arizona's new congressional district, the First District, had nearly equal numbers of registered Democrats and Republicans and was seen as a toss-up by political prognosticators.

Parties in Local Government

Political parties are still important in the politics of many cities, especially the larger ones, although they are in a much weaker position now than they were 25 or 50 years ago. Mayors often lead city party organizations and play a role in the campaigns of presidents, senators, and governors. The mayor's office is sometimes a stepping-stone to other offices. Former Governor Jesse Ventura began his political career as mayor of Brooklyn Park, Minnesota; U.S. Senator Richard Lugar was once mayor of Indianapolis; George Voinovich was mayor of Cleveland and became governor of Ohio before going on to the U.S. Senate; and U.S. Senator Dianne Feinstein was mayor of San Francisco. In 2002, former St. Paul mayor Norm Coleman was elected to the U.S. Senate from Minnesota.

Parties rarely get involved in initiative and referendum elections at the local or state level, but some nonpartisan local elections have partisan overtones as candidates may be identified with the parties, or the parties may want to advance the career of a local nonpartisan candidate.

PARTY BALANCE AND IMBALANCE

State politics may be classified according to how the parties share public offices. In a **two-party state,** the Republican and Democratic parties regularly assemble winning majorities. Two-party states include Indiana, Illinois, and Missouri. In a **one-party state,** one party wins all or nearly all the offices, and the second party usually receives only one-third or less of the popular vote. One-party Republican states currently include Utah, Idaho, and Kansas. Massachusetts is an example of a Democratic one-party state. Democrats occasionally win in Utah, and the same is true for Republicans in Massachusetts, but the more predictable tendency is to support the predominant party.

Since the end of World War II, there has been an accelerating trend toward two-party politics. The Democratic party lost its previously solid support in the South as more and more white southerners moved over to the Republican party. At first, Republican resurgence in the South was mainly evident in presidential and congressional elections, but in recent years, Republicans have regularly been elected to southern state legislatures. Since the mid-1970s, the number of Republicans in southern state legislatures has increased from about 12 percent to near parity.[33]

Republican gains have also been evident in contests for governor. Since 1966, all southern states have at least once elected a Republican governor, and in 2005, seven southern states were led by Republican governors. In terms of the popular vote for president, the South has voted more Republican than the country as a whole in nine of the last 11 presidential elections.[34] In 2004, all eleven former confederate states went to George W. Bush. Even with southerner Al Gore on the ballot, the Democrats carried no southern state in 2000.

Outside the South, there has also been a gradual spread of two-party politics, with the rise of Democratic strength in the formerly solid Republican states of Iowa, Maine, and New Hampshire. Democrats have lost strength in parts of the Rocky Mountain area; however, the Democratic party has been gaining loyalists in the Northeast and Pacific Coast states.

What are the consequences of party balance? When parties and their candidates compete on an equal basis, they are more likely to be sensitive to public opinion, for the loss of even a fraction of the voters can tip the scales to the other side in the next election. Party competition tends to push leaders within each party to work together, at least as elections draw near. Any defection may throw a race to the opponents, so competition generally produces more teamwork and efficiency in government. It may also generate more service to constituents by legislators.

In a one-party state, party imbalance may have a serious effect on the accountability that is part of electoral competition. Competition that otherwise would occur *between* the major parties occurs *within* the majority party. The most important contests in some states like Massachusetts are generally not between Democrats and Republicans but among Democrats in the primary; the same is true for Republicans in Utah. In these intraparty fights, personalities dominate the campaign. Voters do not participate as much as they do in two-party contests.

If party imbalance disorganizes the dominant party, it pulverizes the minority party. With faint hope of winning, minority party leaders do not put up much of a fight. They find it difficult to raise money for campaigns and to persuade people to become candidates. They have no state or local patronage to give out. Volunteers are slow to come forward. Young people wishing to succeed in politics drift into the dominant party. The second party is likely to be concerned only with national politics, where it may win an election, and the patronage that could come its way if its candidate wins the White House.

Party imbalance can be found in more extreme forms in cities and towns than at the state level. Republicans hardly ever carry Chicago, Boston, Washington, Baltimore, Albany, Hartford, Pittsburgh, and many other cities throughout the industrial North. But party balance is not always a determining factor. In heavily Democratic New York City, for example, voters elected a Republican, Michael Bloomberg, as mayor in 2001. Bloomberg had been a Democrat but ran for mayor as a Republican with the strong endorsement of outgoing Republican mayor Rudolph Giuliani.

ELECTIONS AT THE STATE AND LOCAL LEVELS

Each year, there are thousands of state and local elections. Europeans, who are used to voting for one or two candidates at the national and local levels and voting only once every two or three years, are flabbergasted to learn that we engage in elections almost continuously. Selection of town and local officials in the late winter may be followed in the spring by primaries to choose delegates to conventions, then primaries to choose party candidates, then general elections in the fall in which the actual officeholders are chosen—all interspersed with special elections, special town or state referendums, and even, in some states, recall elections to throw officials out of office as happened in California in 2003 when voters removed Gray Davis from the governorship and replaced him with Arnold Schwarzenegger.

Even more bewildering to some is the number of offices we vote on, from president to probate judge, from senator to sheriff, from governor to library board member. This is the *long ballot*. Europeans are more accustomed to electing a handful of key officials, who in turn appoint career officials. Given this volume of election activity, it is fair to conclude that Americans like elections, even though most of them choose not to vote in most of those elections.

Differences in Who May Vote

Subject to constitutional constraint, states can regulate who may vote. Most, for example, do not permit prison inmates to vote. If a state wanted to permit 16-year-olds to vote, it could do so. Voter registration rules can discourage people from participating in elections. States differ in the length of their residency requirement, as well as in whether they permit roving registrars, postcard registration, online registration, or election day registration. Most states require a periodic purge of the voter registration list to remove people who have moved or died.

A common reason why people do not register is that they have moved and have not registered at their new address. Fifteen percent of Americans change their residence every year.[35] After moving, they may not realize that they need to register at their new address until only a few days before the election, and then it is too late. Maryland, North Carolina, and the District of Columbia allow college students who have moved within a city or county to vote without registering if they notify election officials of their move. All told, a state's registration rules can lower turnout by as much as 9 percent.[36]

Differences in How We Vote

Although millions of Americans carry cell phones, own computers, and shop on the Internet, as a nation we still vote in an antiquated way. One of the surprises of the 2000 presidential election was the extent to which we are still using outdated technology. Nearly one in five counties in the United States use punch-card ballots, which are subject to problems like dangling or dimpled chads that do not clearly indicate the voter's intent. Another two in five communities use optically scannable ballots on which the voter uses a pencil to mark the ballot and a scanner records the vote.[37] Although much more reliable than punch cards, scanned ballots are also subject to problems if voters mark outside the box or do not use a pencil.

Voting machines with levers are used in 15 percent of counties, and paper ballots are used in 12 percent. Unlike punch cards, optical scanners, and paper ballots, voting machines do not permit an audit of the vote.[38]

Surprisingly, fewer than 10 percent of counties use electronic or computer voting systems. Such voting could be facilitated by the fact that many high school computer labs are connected to the Internet and could provide voting locations for those that do not have Internet access at home. The costs for these types of reforms are estimated to be around $3.5 billion over five years.[39] One concern will be the secrecy of voting by computer, and another will be how to do a recount. The issue of some audit device, perhaps a paper printout of each person's vote, was seen by some as a necessary precauton in the move to electronic voting. Most observers agree that voting processes and machinery are in need of an overhaul. Despite these concerns, significant changes in how we vote are certain to occur.

The biggest voting problem in 2004 was long lines in several states. This was more the result of insufficient voting machines and booths than a breakdown in voting technology. The margin of victory for President Bush was large enough that the process was not as contested as in 2000.

Voting by Mail and by Absentee Ballot

Modern technology makes it possible to vote by other means than appearing in person at a voting place on election day. Cities like San Diego, Berkeley, and Vancouver first experimented with holding *elections by mail.* Voters are mailed a pamphlet that describes the questions to be decided in the election and gives instructions on how to complete the ballot and return it by mail. Voters sign the return envelope, and their signature is compared against their signature on the voter registration form. There have been no major problems in administering these local mail ballot elections, and the response has been considerably higher than the norm for in-person special elections.[40]

In January 1996, Oregon voters elected a U.S. senator in a special election through the mail rather than in person. Oregonians had 20 days from the date the ballots were mailed to return them to county clerks, and two-thirds of those who received ballots returned them. Now all Oregon elections are conducted through the mail, including the 2000 and 2002 general elections. There appear to have been few instances of fraud, and the Oregon election officials are strong advocates of vote-by-mail elections in the future.

Opponents of the vote-by-mail system worry about fraud and that voters might be pressured to vote a certain way. A husband might press his wife to vote a certain way, or parents might try and direct the vote of their young adult children still living at home. Another problem might be if supporters of a candidate might visit voters at home soon after the ballots are delivered and pressure people to vote on the spot, perhaps offering to mail the ballot. Supporters point to the higher turnout and lower costs in administering vote-by-mail elections. They also point to the absence of fraud or abuse in the vote-by-mail elections.

A less dramatic reform of election laws is the *absentee ballot.* In most of the country, voters may request a ballot by mail, often without having to state a reason for doing so.[41] Absentee balloting is especially useful for initiative measures. In states like California or Washington, where voters may face 20 or more complicated ballot questions, those who vote by absentee ballot can take their time researching and pondering how they are going to vote and do not have to decide within the few minutes they would have in a voting booth.

Increased ease in obtaining ballots has significantly expanded the rate of absentee voting in California. It has been used especially by Republicans to activate retirees and other voters who find it difficult to get from their homes to the polling places. Absentee ballots made up nearly half of all ballots in Washington in 1998.[42] Other states have also liberalized their absentee voting provisions. Oklahoma and Texas, for instance, have *early voting,* whereby voters may vote for several days before an election at several locations in each county.

Absentee ballots also figured in the controversy in the Florida 2000 presidential voting. In two counties, absentee ballot request forms had incorrect voter identification numbers, but the county clerk permitted the Republican party to correct the mistake after the forms were returned to the county. In other Florida counties, some absentee ballots from military personnel did not have postmark dates or were otherwise technically not in compliance with the law. Initially, some counties did not count these ballots, but eventually, most military ballots were counted.

Differences in Nomination Processes

State law establishes the process by which party nominees are selected. Most states use a *primary election,* but some permit the parties to nominate their candidates through a *caucus* or *convention.* In the caucus system, party delegates who are elected in local voting district meetings decide on the party nominee. In some states, a convention narrows the field to two candidates if no candidate gets a set percentage of delegate votes at the party convention.

The dynamics of winning a nomination in states with a caucus system are different from those in states with a primary. In a caucus system, having a grassroots organization that can mobilize voters to attend a neighborhood meeting is essential for candidates. The state best known for the caucus system is Iowa, whose party caucuses yield the first decision in our presidential election system and are covered extensively by the media. Some form of the caucus or convention system is used in about a dozen states.

There are two kinds of party primaries, closed and open. In a **closed primary,** only voters registered in a party may vote in that party's primary. Such a primary discourages **crossover voting**—allowing voters from outside the party to help determine the party's nominee—which is why partisans prefer closed primaries. In an **open primary,** any voter can participate in any party's primary. Wisconsin has long had open primaries.

Some states, like Montana, Washington, and California, allowed voters to vote for more than one party in the same primary election; this is called a **blanket primary.** Thus a voter could choose a Democratic nominee for governor and Republican nominees for U.S. senator and attorney general. The blanket primary, according to those who advocated it, encouraged voters to select the best nominees regardless of party and was thought to help moderate candidates. Opponents said it further weakened parties, made our system even more candidate-driven, and gave voters from one party the opportunity to choose the weakest candidate from the opposing party. However, research shows that less than 5 percent of voters actually vote for the weakest candidate from the opposing party.[43] In July 2000, the Supreme Court ruled that blanket primaries are unconstitutional because they violate the right to political association under the First Amendment.[44]

In a primary election, when all the candidates are from the same party, voters make their choices based on candidate appeal and issues. They may also vote for the candidate they perceive has the best chance of winning the general election.[45] California voters rejected an initiative to establish an open primary in 2004.

Louisiana has a unique system. All candidates, regardless of party, run in a single election. If no candidate gets a majority of the votes, there is a runoff election to determine the winner. It is not uncommon for both candidates in a runoff to be from the same party.

Differences in Timing and Frequency of Elections

Federal law sets the date of the presidential election as "the Tuesday next after the first Monday in November, in every fourth year," with similar language applying to elections for the House and Senate. States are free to determine the dates of all other elections, but for ease of administration, they usually consolidate gubernatorial and state general elections on the first Tuesday after the first Monday in November. Two states elect their governor every two years. Five states conduct their elections (primary and general) for governor, other state officials, and the state legislature in odd-numbered years, leaving the even-numbered years for federal elections. Two-thirds of the states (including the two-year states) elect governors in presidential midterm years, halfway between presidential elections.

Separating state elections from presidential or federal elections permits voters to focus more closely on state issues than if they had to vote for state and federal candidates at the same time. Separating elections also means that state and local officials are not as likely to be hurt by an unpopular presidential candidate at the top of the ticket. The passage of campaign finance reform at the federal level may prompt some states to consider off-year state elections. Having state elections in a different year from federal elections may reduce federal oversight and encourage soft money donors to contribute more to state parties.

Some states hold their primaries in late spring, others in mid-September. Primary elections are under the control of state law. Some states have two primaries in presidential years, one for the presidency in the spring and one for other contests in the fall.

State law establishes the rules for local elections but often allows cities and towns some discretion in setting the dates of elections. Many municipal elections are held in the spring of odd-numbered years, again to avoid any positive or negative carryover from candidates running for federal or statewide office. Counties usually conduct their elections at the same time state officials are elected.

State governments can also hold *special elections* to vote on a ballot initiative, a statewide constitutional change, or even a whole new constitution or to replace a U.S. senator who has died or resigned. Participation in special elections varies greatly, depending on what is being decided, but turnout is generally lower than in midterm general elections. Before states hold special elections to fill a vacated U.S. Senate seat, they often have a special primary election to determine the party nominees for that election. In these primaries, turnout is even lower than in the special general election.

The frequency of our elections and the range of choices sometimes make it hard for voters to pay enough attention to cast informed votes. For this reason, some reformers have proposed consolidating elections to once or twice every couple of years.

Participation

What are the consequences of holding so many elections at so many different times? One is that Americans pick and choose which elections, if any, they participate in. States vary significantly in their rate of **turnout,** the proportion of the voting-age public that votes. Note that political scientists do not calculate turnout on the basis of voter registration because there is such variability in state registration rules that it is unfair to compare the turnout in a state with difficult registration laws with the turnout in a state whose laws make voting registration much more accessible. Rather, turnout is calculated on the Census Bureau's estimate of the voting-age population in each state.

Primaries usually draw fewer voters than general elections, and sometimes the turnout is quite low. Low turnout raises concerns about whether voters in primary elections reflect the general public. Primary voters are generally better educated, earn more money, and are more likely to be white than voters in general elections, who themselves are not representative of the voting-age population.[46] Primary election turnout is also related to strength of partisan identification, ease of voter registration, and the issues in the campaign.

Campaign Finance

In the early 1970s, many states enacted campaign finance disclosure laws, a few instituted partial public financing of elections, and others provided partial underwriting of the costs of parties. **Disclosure** is a common element of campaign finance legislation at the state and local levels. Candidates are typically asked to file disclosure statements specifying where the money came from to finance their campaign. Interest groups are often required to file reports on how they distribute their campaign contributions. Once elected, most state and local officials are required to file a different kind of disclosure form, one that indicates their personal wealth, investments, and other financial matters that may reveal conflicts of interest.

Roughly three-fourths of the states have enacted campaign finance reforms that limit individual contributions, and several states provide some form of public financing. State laws are often patterned after federal law, but states have experimented with lower contribution limits than those allowed in federal elections.[47] Other states have experimented with tax credits to encourage small contributions. In 1996, Maine voters passed a ballot initiative that provided what supporters call a "clean money" option of public financing.[48] Under this system, candidates who agree to raise a limited amount of private money and accept spending limits receive public funds for their campaigns.

Voting on Ballot Questions

Voting on ballot questions is heavily influenced by campaign spending. Presumably, greater expenditures make the most difference when there is a low level of information, as is the case with many ballot propositions. And opinions on ballot propositions are more volatile because voters' views on such matters are not deeply rooted in party affiliation, feelings toward an incumbent, or party appeal.[49]

Because many initiatives are supported by well-funded interests and because a vote in one state can start a national movement on an issue, initiative campaigns can attract large sums of money. Some examples of heavy spending include a 1988 election in Maryland in which the National Rifle Association and other groups spent a record $6.8 million in an unsuccessful attempt to defeat a handgun registration referendum. The tobacco industry spent more than $21 million in California in 1988 to defeat an initiative raising the cigarette tax. More than $101 million was spent in California in that year on five initiatives that dealt with automobile insurance reform. A decade later, in what remains one of the most expensive initiative battles in U.S. history, over $92 million was spent for and against a successful initiative to permit casinos on Native American lands in California.[50]

Voting on ballot questions is different from voting for candidates because voters do not have such simplifying factors as party identification and candidate appeal to rely on. More people vote for candidates than vote on ballot questions. Voters who are confused tend to vote no. "Ballot fatigue," tiring from too many contests and questions on the ballot, also makes people more likely to vote no.[51]

Voting in Recall Elections

Recall elections permit citizens to attempt to remove elected public officials from office before the end of their term of office. As with initiatives and referendums, recalls require sufficient petition signatures from registered voters to meet a preestablished threshold. Recall elections have been relatively rare at the statewide level. For example, before the successful 2003 recall of Governor Gray Davis there had been 31 unsuccessful attempts started to recall California governors, none of which made it to the ballot.[52] Only two governors in American history have ever been recalled, including Davis.[53] Some argue that Davis was recalled largely because of his failing political character, which resulted in a lack of goodwill and trust with voters.[54]

The 2003 California recall ballot consisted of two questions: the first asking whether or not to remove Governor Davis from office, and the second asking who should replace Davis if he were recalled.[55] If a majority had voted no on the first question, the results of the second question would not have mattered. Because a majority voted yes on the first question, the person who got the most votes on the second question became the new governor. Other states divide the questions, first having an election to decide whether to recall the official and if a majority votes yes, a second election to determine the replacement.

Recall elections have been more common at the local level, including elections for school board.

THE FUTURE OF GRASSROOTS DEMOCRACY

Political parties are vital to the operation of our democracy. Many political scientists believe that our system would be strengthened if we had stronger political parties. The first step in the renewal of the parties would be to change their negative image and persuade citizens that political activity is essential to a healthy constitutional democracy. The next would be to give people who support parties a greater say in choosing the candidates who run under their party's label. Although our candidate-centered tradition will certainly remain, it is important to moderate it with strengthened parties that can discipline candidates, at least by withholding resources that candidates cannot easily acquire elsewhere. We would do well to make ballots and elections more voter-friendly. The proliferation of elections, including special elections, turns off even the most committed citizens. Why not, many reformers argue, consolidate elections so that voters might exercise their vote only once or twice, rather than three or four times, a year?

Getting qualified people to run for office is another challenge. The spiraling cost of campaigns and the advantages enjoyed by incumbents have deterred many good potential candidates. Others are repelled by the nasty and negative tone of recent elections. But unless a democracy produces able citizens who are willing to run for office, it loses its ability to hold incumbents accountable.

One of the advantages of 50 states and thousands of communities is that they afford citizens a multitude of opportunities for participation, making involvement less intimidating. The fact that our states do not all have the same approach to elections, parties, or voting also provides valuable data for states considering changing their process. One disadvantage of so many governmental units and so many different elected officials is that they make politics seem more complicated. Citizens willing to become involved, however, often find they can have more influence than they expected.

S U M M A R Y

1. In the United States, there are no national elections, only state elections. Even the presidential election is really a set of 51 different elections to choose electors who will in turn cast their ballots for president. Elections for U.S. senators and representatives are conducted largely under state law.

2. Political parties are essential to the functioning of democracy at all levels, but they are principally organized at the state, congressional district, or county levels. This arrangement makes state parties vitally important. Routinely, they are patterned after the national party organization and include a chair, a vice chair, and a central committee. State parties are often run by full-time party administrators called executive directors.

3. Political parties play important roles in candidate recruitment, voter registration, voter mobilization, and fund raising, and they provide a link between people and government. Parties are also important to the operation of most state legislatures. The governor is the head of his or her party. Governors consider party loyalty when appointing people to executive and judicial openings.

4. Voters usually vote along party lines in state and local elections, although candidate appeal and issues can also influence them.

5. Political parties were once strong and well organized at the local level; in some cities, these organizations were called machines and were led by party bosses. Reaction to the abuses of these machines led to reform efforts. One of these reforms was to make most local politics officially nonpartisan.

6. States vary in whether the two parties are competitive. In one-party states, elections are generally won by one party, while in two-party states, the parties alternate in holding power.

7. State election law is important in defining who may vote, when elections will be held, how party nominees are chosen, and which candidates will appear on the ballot. State election law also establishes a framework for ensuring fair elections.

8. State registration laws make voting more or less difficult, depending on their requirements. States may require persons to register by party to vote in primary elections; when voting is thus limited, the primaries are called closed primaries. Over the course of U.S. history, states have gradually eased registration requirements.

9. Turnout varies by type of election; it is higher in general than primary elections and higher in presidential than midterm elections. Turnout is higher in state than local elections, and regularly scheduled elections typically have higher turnout than special elections. Turnout in vote-by-mail elections is also higher than in in-person elections in most cases. More people vote for major candidate races than vote on ballot questions.

F U R T H E R   R E A D I N G

BRUCE E. CAIN and ELISABETH R. GERBER, EDS., *Voting at the Political Fault Line: California's Experiment with the Blanket Primary* (University of California Press, 2002).

THOMAS M. CARSEY, *Campaign Dynamics: The Race for Governor* (University of Michigan Press, 2000).

THOMAS E. CRONIN, *Direct Democracy: The Politics of Initiative, Referendum, and Recall* (Replica Books, 2000).

PAUL S. HERRNSON, *Party Campaigning in the 1980s* (Harvard University Press, 1988).

MALCOLM E. JEWELL and SARAH M. MOREHOUSE, *Political Parties and Elections in American States*, 4th ed. (CQ Press, 2001).

V. O. KEY, JR., *American State Politics: An Introduction* (Knopf, 1956).

NORMAN R. LUTTBEG, *The Grassroots of Democracy* (Lexington Books, 1999).

DAVID B. MAGLEBY, *Direct Legislation: Voting on Ballot Propositions in the United States* (Johns Hopkins University Press, 1984).

L. SANDY MAISEL AND KARA Z. BUCKLEY, *Parties and Elections in America: The Electoral Process,* 4th ed. (Rowman & Littlefield, 2005).

A. JAMES REICHLEY, ED., *Elections American Style* (Brookings Institution Press, 1987).

ALAN ROSENTHAl, *Governors and Legislators: Contending Powers* (CQ Press, 1990).

ALAN ROSENTHAL, *Legislative Life: People, Process, and Performance in the States* (Harper & Row, 1981).

BYRON E. SHAFER, *The Two Majorities and The Puzzle of Modern American Politics* (University Press of Kansas, 2003).

LINDA WITT, KAREN M. PAGET, AND GLENNA MATTHEWS, *Running as a Woman: Gender and Politics in American Politics* (Free Press, 1994).

JOSEPH FRANCIS ZIMMERMAN, *The Initiative: Citizen Lawmaking* (Greenwood Press, 1999).

STATE
LEGISLATURES

S tate legislatures existed long before the Continental Congress was formed in 1776 and exerted great power under the Articles of Confederation. Having existed as the primary form of government even under British colonial rule, state legislatures were reluctant to give up their power to either the national government or their own governors. Most states had relatively weak executives, and several had no executive at all. Indeed, the creation of the Constitution was in part a reaction against the excessive power of the state legislatures, which is why the framers of the Constitution imposed limits on the powers of the state legislatures (see especially Article I, Section 9).

The Tenth Amendment to the U.S. Constitution makes it clear that any power not given to the national government or denied to the states lies with the states or with the people. State constitutions, in turn, give some of this reserved power exclusively to nonlegislative agencies and specifically deny some to the legislature. What is left is inherited by the state legislatures.

Although state legislatures today do not dominate state policy making the way they did in 1787, they do play a vital role in state politics and policy. State legislators strive to solve problems and provide services—and do so, whenever possible, without raising taxes or creating larger bureaucracies. Legislators these days seek to make the legislature a counterbalance to powerful governors and powerful state bureaucracies.

In recent years, legislatures have been involved in a remarkable variety of activities:

- Colorado's legislature adopted stronger gun control legislation.
- New Hampshire legislators voted to prevent the use of death penalty sentencing.
- Vermont voted to recognize "civil unions" between same-sex couples, granting them virtually all the benefits, protections, and responsibilities given to married couples.
- Mississippi legislators overrode their governor's veto of a major Medicaid program.
- South Carolina legislators voted, by a narrow margin, to remove the Confederate flag over their statehouse dome but allowed it to fly over a monument on the capitol grounds.
- Hawaii's legislature approved the medical use of marijuana.
- The Tennessee legislature overrode the governor's veto and enacted an $18.3 billion budget without a state income tax their governor had demanded.
- New York adopted legislation banning hand-held cell phone use while driving.
- By enacting large penalties for "excessive prices," Maine has attempted to force down drug prices.
- Many states have adopted some form of election reform, including new ballots, a ban on punch cards, and new computer voting systems.
- Many states launched new homeland security programs in the wake of September 11.

In short, legislatures everywhere make or modify policies on all kinds of issues by balancing conflicting political pressures, while facilitating compromises between political factions or different parts of the state. They also make laws and modify and approve budgets. Legislatures perform countless constituency services and, along with the governor and the courts, help keep state agencies accountable to both the laws and the citizens. Legislators must constantly reconcile pressures among competing interest groups. Representing local views at the state level, they dramatize issues and bring them into the open. A state legislature serves as a lightning rod to which most of the conflicting pressures of American society are drawn.

This chapter will examine state legislatures in greater detail by asking what they do, how they are organized, and how they have adapted to a much more complex world. As they have grown into more professional bodies, state legislatures are claiming a greater role in how government works and are important partners in both state policy and federal action.

THE LEGISLATIVE BRANCH

The 50 state legislatures share many characteristics—all states except Nebraska have a two-house **bicameral legislature.** Nebraska has a one-house **unicameral legislature.**[1] The larger chamber is generally called the house of representatives. (In a few states, it is called the assembly or house of delegates.) It contains from as few as 40 members in

Alaska and 41 in Delaware to as many as 400 members in New Hampshire and 203 in Pennsylvania; the average number is around 100. In all but five states, representatives serve two-year terms; in Alabama, Louisiana, Maryland, Mississippi, and North Dakota, representatives serve for four years. The smaller chamber, known as the Senate, is typically composed of about 40 members. State senators serve four-year terms in most states.

But state legislatures also differ in important ways, not the least of which is their basic level of professionalism, generally defined as having full-time legislators, more staff, and higher pay, which in turn may draw more ambitious candidates for office and longer service.

How Do Legislatures Compare?

Legislative professionalism sometimes, but not always, correlates with the number of seats in the legislature. The professional nature of state legislatures is in part a product of population but also a product of how many representatives the state has chosen to have. Certain states, such as New Hampshire and Wyoming, have part-time "citizen legislatures," whereas New York and California are sometimes characterized as full-time professional legislatures.

In the New Hampshire House of Representatives, for example, legislators are essentially volunteers. These "citizen-legislators" represent districts of about 3,000 people. They earn just $200 for the two-year term and meet for no more than 45 days a year. In contrast, the California Assembly has 80 members, each representing a district of about 450,000 people. California legislators earn $99,000 a year in addition to expense allowances, meet nearly all year long, and consider their legislative work a full-time occupation (see Table 5–1).

Legislative salaries are most often set by the legislature. Most legislators are reluctant to increase their salaries, and as a result, lawmakers' salaries lag well behind the rate of inflation and increases in the cost of living. Most people run for the legislature for reasons other than compensation. "No one goes into politics to get rich," notes Massachusetts state Senator Tom Birmingham. "But you can't have a system where only the rich get into politics."[2]

Legislatures also differ by the level of activity. Forty-three state legislatures meet every year from January through May or June. Legislatures in seven states, including Arkansas, Montana, Nevada, and Texas, meet only every other year. Some state constitutions limit their legislatures to regular sessions of a fixed number of days, usually 60 or 90. Such restrictions reflect distrust of government and the feeling that "the faster we get it over with, the better." *Special sessions* have been developed to get around these limitations. The governor has the power to call the legislature into special session and in some states to determine the issues that may be discussed in the special session—a power governors frequently use. The trend in many states has been to somewhat longer annual legislative sessions and higher salaries.

How Are Legislatures Organized?

State legislatures look very very much like the United States Congress, or vice versa. A *speaker,* usually chosen by the majority party, presides over the lower house. In many states, speakers have more power to control proceedings than their national counterpart has. For example, most state speakers have the right to appoint committees and thus

TABLE 5–1   THE DIVERSITY OF STATE LEGISLATURES

State legislatures across the country vary greatly in many respects. The National Conference of State Legislatures grouped them into three types based on their length of session.

RED: Full- or Near-Full-Time, High-Pay, Large-Staff "Professional Legislatures"

Alaska	New York
California	New Jersey
Florida	Ohio
Illinois	Pennsylvania
Massachusetts	Wisconsin
Michigan	

WHITE: In-Between Hybrid

Alabama	Minnesota
Arkansas	Missouri
Arizona	Nebraska
Colorado	North Carolina
Connecticut	Oklahoma
Delaware	Oregon
Hawaii	South Carolina
Iowa	Tennessee
Kansas	Texas
Kentucky	Virginia
Louisiana	Washington
Maryland	

BLUE: Part-Time, Low-Pay, Small-Staff "Citizen Legislatures"

Georgia	New Mexico
Idaho	North Dakota
Indiana	Rhode Island
Maine	South Dakota
Mississippi	Utah
Montana	Vermont
Nevada	West Virginia
New Hampshire	Wyoming

SOURCE: National Conference of State Legislatures, "Full-Time and Part-Time Legislatures," www.ncsl.org/programs/legman/about/partfulllegis.htm, accessed April 27, 2004.

play a key role in determining policy. But the power of speakers varies greatly: Speakers have great powers in West Virginia, New Hampshire, and Arizona but minimal powers in Alaska, Mississippi, Hawaii, and Wyoming.[3] In 26 states, lieutenant governors preside over the senate, though they are usually mere figureheads; in other states, the presiding officer is chosen by the majority party in the senate.[4]

As in the U.S. Congress, the committee system prevails. In several states, such as Maine and Massachusetts, *joint committees* are used to speed up legislative action.

However, state legislative committees usually do not have the same power over bills as their national counterparts: Some still lack adequate professional assistance, the seniority system is not as closely followed as in Congress, and membership turnover is somewhat higher, especially where term limits have taken effect.

Every legislature has committees on education, transportation, agriculture, and energy or natural resources. Most also have important committees on rules, appropriations, and taxes (sometimes called the Ways and Means Committee). Legislators generally specialize and become experts on one or two substantive matters, such as education, crime, taxation, or the budget process. As in any organization or large assembly, an individual earns respect and influence primarily by developing specialized knowledge about either policy or procedural matters.

Once again, however, there are striking differences among state legislatures. Some have excellent staff and splendid information technology and are well-run professional organizations. The New York legislature has nearly 3,100 permanent staffers, for example, Pennsylvania has nearly 3,000, and California has 2,300. Others have not changed in decades.[5] North Dakota has just 31 permanent staff for the entire legislature, for example, while New Mexico has 49, Idaho has 75, and Delaware has 84. These and other differences sometimes stem from historical or ethnic traditions. They can also arise from urban-rural or east-west factional splits and sometimes from regional differences, as is the case with the "Hill people" versus the "Delta people" in Mississippi. Here is how one expert on state politics viewed some of the more distinctive characteristics shaping state politics in the United States:

> In New York professional politics, political wheeling and dealing and frantic activity are characteristic. In Virginia, one gets a sense of tradition, conservatism, and gentility. . . . Louisiana's politics are wild and flamboyant. By contrast, moderation and caution are features of Iowa. A strong disposition of compromise pervades Oregon, with politicians disposed to act as brokers and deal pragmatically rather than dogmatically. In Kansas, hard work, respect for authority, fiscal prudence, and a general conservatism and resistance to rapid social change are pervasive features of the state environment. Indiana is intensely partisan. Wyoming is mainly individualistic, and Ohio is fundamentally conservative. In Hawaii, the relatively recent political dominance of Japanese and the secondary status of Chinese, native Hawaiians, and Haoles (whites) makes for tough ethnic politics. Yankee Republicans used to run Massachusetts, but now the Irish dominate. Their personalized style, which blends gregariousness and political loyalty, results in a politics of the clan. Mormonism of course dominates Utah.[6]

Who Serves in the State Legislature?

Like members of the U.S. Congress, the vast majority of state legislators run for reelection and win. Indeed, about one-third of state legislative elections are uncontested; this is especially true in smaller, one-party states and in the South.[7]

An incumbent seeking reelection has many advantages over a challenger: name recognition, better access to campaign funds, experience in running campaigns, and a record of helping with constituent problems. Also like members of the U.S. Congress, few legislators feel politically secure, even when they have not been opposed in the last election.

In an incumbent's mind, there is seldom such a thing as a "safe district" and a sure reelection. "Whatever their margins of victory in prior elections, however 'safe' their district may appear to the analyst, incumbents know that lightning can strike. . . . They have seen colleagues relax their efforts and subsequently lose their seats. They live in perpetual danger of casting a roll-call vote that upsets their constituency or mobilizes a key interest group to seek their defeat."[8] Incumbents also worry about scandals in their party or having to run with an unpopular candidate at or near the top of their party ticket.

THE DEMOGRAPHIC PROFILE   The typical American state legislator is a 48-year-old white male, well educated and well off, often a businessman or lawyer of Anglo-Saxon origin who has had some type of previous political experience—not always elective— at the city or county level. Some have worked as a staff member in the legislature or in state government.[9] Most state legislators have held some type of local party position and have been active in political campaigns. Surprisingly, about one-third were born in some other state, a reflection of our increasingly mobile population.

State legislators tend to have more education and higher incomes than other citizens in their states. They are usually hardworking, public-spirited citizens who believe being in the legislature is a good opportunity for service. Yet state legislators enjoy less prestige than members of Congress, especially in states that have large legislatures. Discouraged by modest salaries and long hours, many serve a few terms and then either retire voluntarily or run for higher office. Some leave after just a couple of terms because they get bored listening to matters that do not interest them. As one one-termer explained, "A great deal in the political process does not—repeat, does not—involve the glamorous policy issues. Most of the work is sheer routine and hardly awe-inspiring."[10] And, of course, some are now leaving because of term limits in their states that prevent more than two or three terms.

PARTY AFFILIATION   At the start of 2004, the state legislatures were almost evenly divided between the two parties. Democrats occupied 2,676 of the 5,411 House seats, while Republicans occupied 2,715; similarly, Democrats held 950 of the 1,971 Senate seats, while Republicans held 969. Only 70 of the nation's state legislators consider themselves Independents or nonpartisan, including all 49 members of Nebraska's unicameral legislature.[11] Given these margins, a change of just three seats would alter party control of 25 legislative chambers, House or Senate, in 22 states.

Party control was even tighter following the 2004 elections. Democrats picked up one legislature, giving them a 20 to 20 tie with Republicans, with 10 states divided.

OCCUPATION   Lawyers continue to be the largest occupational group in most state legislatures, yet the percentage of attorneys has leveled off; today attorneys constitute only about 17 percent of state legislators nationwide. There has been an increase in those who consider themselves full-time legislators, and there has been a slight increase as well of teachers, homemakers, retirees, and students.[12] Real estate and insurance dealers and sales representatives are also commonly found in legislatures (see Figure 5–1).

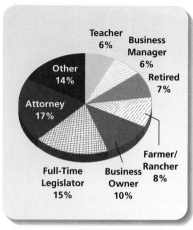

FIGURE 5–1 A Profile of State Legislators.
Source: National Conference of State Legislatures.

CHANGING FACE OF AMERICAN POLITICS

WOMEN IN THE STATEHOUSE

In the late 1960s, state legislatures were dominated by men and often had the look of a "good old boys' club." This has changed in recent years as more women have been elected, bringing the national average up from just 4.5 percent in 1971 to 22 percent in 2004. Thirty-nine percent of the Washington State legislative seats are occupied by women, followed by Colorado at 34 percent, Maryland at 33 percent, New Mexico at 31 percent, and California at 30 percent. In South Carolina, by contrast, only 9 percent of the lawmakers are women.

As women have won more legislative seats, their influence has grown, particularly as more women win election to key legislative posts. In addition, women increasingly occupy key committee positions and often meet to plan strategies on women's issues.

It is not clear if the election of women to state legislatures has made a significant difference in how women are represented. Although some an-alysts believe female legislators are more likely to offer leadership on women, family, and children's policy issues,[*] other scholars have found little or no difference in how men and women deal with gender policy issues.[†]

Although more women and African Americans are winning election to state legislatures, both groups are still notably in the minority. Of the 7,382 state legislators in 2004, 22 percent were women, 9 percent were African American, and just 3 percent were Hispanic.

[*]See Sue Thomas, *How Women Legislate* (Oxford University Press, 1996). See also Kathleen Bratton and Kerry L. Haynie, "Agenda Setting and Legislative Success in State Legislatures: The Effects of Gender and Race," *Journal of Politics* 61 (August 1999), pp. 658–679.
[†]Beth Reingold, *Representing Women: Sex, Gender, and Legislative Behavior in Arizona and California* (University of North Carolina Press, 2000).

SOURCE: National Conference of State Legislatures, "Legislator Demographics," www.ncsl.org/programs/legman/about/demographic_overview.htm, accessed April 27, 2004.

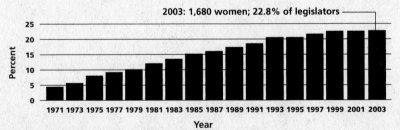

2003: 1,680 women; 22.8% of legislators

Current Percentage of Women in State Legislatures.
SOURCE: Center for (per Google) American Women and Politics; reprinted from *The New York Times*, January 4, 1999, p. A18. Updated by the authors.

The number of farmers continues to fall as redistricting continues to shift power away from rural areas and as the number of farms declines. Moreover, longer sessions of the legislatures make it less possible to be both a farmer and a legislator. When legislatures used to meet for just a few months in winter, farmers were able to fit their schedules to the legislative cycle.

Because legislators must have flexible schedules, the job often attracts retired people and those whose businesses or professional practices have been so successful that they can afford to take time off. Legislators used to identify themselves by their occupations outside the legislature, but this is less the case now; many refer to their occupation as legislator.

What State Legislators Do

The nation's 7,382 state legislators engage in many of the same lawmaking and oversight activities as members of the U.S. Congress: They enact laws that create state parks; specify salaries for state officials; draw up rules governing state elections; fix state tax rates; set workers' compensation policies; determine the quantity and quality of state correctional, mental health, and educational institutions; and oversee welfare programs. State legislators approve all appropriations and thereby confirm or modify a governor's proposed budget. Legislators in most states are also responsible for overseeing the administration of public policy. Although they do not administer programs directly, legislators can and do determine whether programs are being carried out according to legislative intentions through hearings, investigations, audits, and the budgetary process. Bill passage rate varies greatly from state to state, depending on a variety of factors, including procedural necessities, constitutional requirements, and local culture. Figure 5–2 outlines the steps involved in passing state laws.

State legislatures perform various functions within the larger federal system, such as ratifying proposed amendments to the U.S. Constitution, exercising the right to petition Congress to call for a constitutional convention in order to propose an amendment to the U.S. Constitution, and approving interstate compacts on matters affecting state policies and their implementation. The national government has recently turned back many health and welfare responsibilities to the states.

Each state's constitution prescribes the procedures its legislatures must follow and sets limits on the rate of taxation, the kinds of taxes, the subjects that may be taxed, and the purposes of taxation. State legislatures participate in amending their states' constitutions by proposing amendments for voter ratification. Legislatures also have authority to impeach and try state officials, and they also are involved in the appointive process.

State legislators help translate public wants and aspirations into laws and regulations. In addition to their lawmaking functions, they also try to be ombudsmen—to listen, learn, and find solutions to problems. Invariably, state legislators wind up doing a lot of favors: getting a merchant a license to sell lottery tickets, persuading some state agency to look into safety standards at the local hospital, pushing for funds to repair county roads, arranging for a campaign supporter to be appointed to the state labor commission, and so on. State legislators are accessible. Citizens and students can nearly always contact their legislators directly and communicate with them in person, by telephone, or via e-mail.

With the growth of state functions, legislators are spending increasing amounts of time on casework or constituency services. Constituent relations are often the most time-consuming aspect of a legislator's job. Local city and school officials always need the help of legislators, and interest groups back home are always pressing their views. Legislators usually try hard to perform constituent casework because they recognize its political value. The more help they give to home-district citizens and businesses, they reason, the more they will earn respect, win reelection, or perhaps gather support for election to higher office.

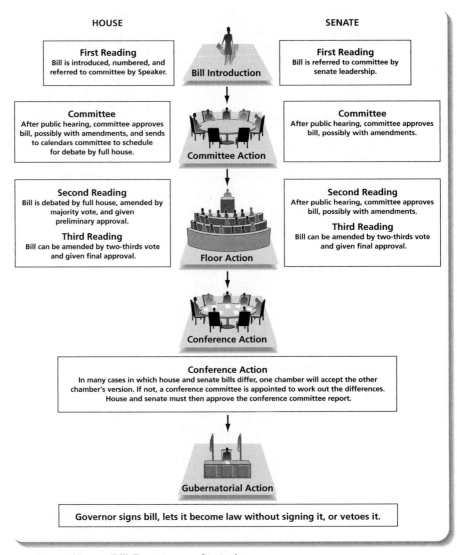

HOUSE

SENATE

First Reading
Bill is introduced, numbered, and referred to committee by Speaker.

First Reading
Bill is referred to committee by senate leadership.

Bill Introduction

Committee
After public hearing, committee approves bill, possibly with amendments, and sends to calendars committee to schedule for debate by full house.

Committee
After public hearing, committee approves bill, possibly with amendments.

Committee Action

Second Reading
Bill is debated by full house, amended by majority vote, and given preliminary approval.

Third Reading
Bill can be amended by two-thirds vote and given final approval.

Second Reading
After public hearing, committee approves bill, possibly with amendments.

Third Reading
Bill can be amended by two-thirds vote and given final approval.

Floor Action

Conference Action

Conference Action
In many cases in which house and senate bills differ, one chamber will accept the other chamber's version. If not, a conference committee is appointed to work out the differences. House and senate must then approve the conference committee report.

Gubernatorial Action

Governor signs bill, lets it become law without signing it, or vetoes it.

FIGURE 5–2 How a Bill Becomes a State Law.

What Legislative Committees Do

A legislative committee is where bills get drafted, hearings are held, and the general policy making and preliminary lawmaking takes place. Committees vary in power and influence from state to state. In general, however, the influence of committees has increased in recent decades. They used to be pale shadows of their counterparts in the U.S. Congress, and they often still are in the less populous states because of short sessions, limited staffing, and turnover of both staff and legislators. Still, legislative committees process and shape hundreds or even thousands of bills and resolutions every year.[13]

Committees do the legislature's work. They consider and amend legislation, oversee the implementation of the laws, interview judges, and serve as the major access point for citizens, interest groups, and lobbyists. The functions of a legislative committee are advisory; all of its proposals are subject to review, approval, or rejection by the legislative body of which it is a part.

Some of the functions of standing committees or interim committees include:

- Studying pending legislation
- Conducting public hearings on proposed bills and resolutions
- Debating and modifying initial proposals
- Grading legislation in terms of desirability
- Screening, eliminating, or burying undesirable legislation
- Confirming key administrative personnel
- Monitoring or overseeing administrative practices and regulations

The committee system allows members to concentrate their energies on specific areas of governmental operations. Over time, legislative committees and their members develop extensive knowledge about particular activities and provide greatly valued information about the content and desirability of proposed bills to their colleagues. Since it is impossible for everybody to be an expert on all aspects of state government, properly staffed and run committees can evaluate the merits and faults of a proposed law more effectively than any individual legislator can.

How State Legislators Decide

State legislators are influenced by many of the same factors that affect members of the U.S. Congress, including personal ideology and policy positions. For part-time, less professionalized legislatures, however, party membership and interest group pressure are much more important to legislative outcomes.

POLITICAL PARTIES   Except in Nebraska, candidates for state legislatures are nominated by political parties in primaries or by party conventions and caucuses, and they are elected *as party members.* Although the official party organization is sometimes not a dominant influence in recruiting state legislative candidates, a candidate nonetheless has to go through the party to gain the nomination. Figure 5–3 shows the current party control of the state legislatures.

The role of political parties in the governance of legislatures and in policy making varies widely from state to state. In nearly half the states—especially in the urban, industrialized states and in the Northeast—the political party is a key factor in decision making. In other states—in the Southwest, for example—parties appear less significant. Coalitions there tend to form along rural-urban, conservative-liberal, or regional lines.

Parties in most states are less influential than they used to be. Candidates welcome what help they can get from the parties, but that is often not much. However, in some states, party leaders in the legislature raise and allocate campaign contributions that prove helpful to those running for the first or second time, particularly in competitive races. Party organizations and political action committees are major sources of money for many legislative candidates. Still, legislative candidates almost always have to form

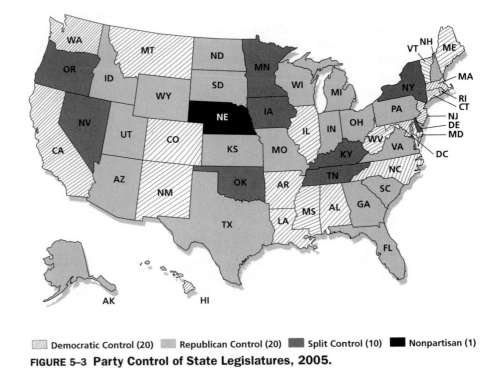

Democratic Control (20)   Republican Control (20)   Split Control (10)   Nonpartisan (1)

FIGURE 5–3 Party Control of State Legislatures, 2005.

their own personal organization, separate from the local party apparatus, to wage a winning campaign.

In nearly every state where there are two active parties, the political party selects legislative leaders and assigns members to committees. Party leaders in many state legislatures distribute sought-after perks, ranging from committee assignments to parking spaces. **Party caucuses**—meetings of all the members of one party in the chamber—also distribute campaign funds to their members and to specifically targeted districts.

Party unity on policy matters is typically found in states with a highly competitive two-party system. In those states, party caucuses develop party positions, and party members are expected to support them in the legislative chambers. In a few states, binding votes in party caucuses virtually (although not legally) force party members to vote as a unified bloc on the floor of their chamber. Binding caucus votes are taken on relatively few issues, however. Voting regularly with the party and being a member of the majority party can help legislators win discretionary grants or other favors for their districts.

The party caucus is a principal instrument for legislative decision making in about half the states, including Colorado, Delaware, Idaho, Montana, California, and Utah. In states where a party holds a slim majority of the seats in a legislative chamber, representatives are more likely to feel pressure to "toe the party line" than where a party commands a large majority.[14] Similarly, legislators are more likely to vote with their party in states where the political party plays an important role in recruiting and nominating candidates.

In legislatures in which a single party has had long-standing dominance or control, as used to be in some southern states, parties are less important in conducting and shaping legislative business. Because of the recent rise of the Republican party in the South and Southwest, however, parties and partisanship are gradually increasing in strength in such states as Florida, Texas, and North Carolina. A rebirth of partisanship and growing attention to elections of legislators are apparently making the parties more important than they have been in the past.

INTEREST GROUPS   Interest groups are a significant and growing source of influence on state legislatures. Teacher organizations, trade associations, labor groups, trial attorneys, taxpayer associations, insurance, mining, real estate, road builders, and banking interests are often the most visible single-interest groups. In states with an obvious major economic interest, such as agriculture, mining, lumbering, or fishing, legislators pay close attention to the needs of that interest, regardless of whether the group employs lobbyists. The legislatures in these states seldom pass legislation hostile to their own state's principal economic interests.

Most state interest groups use lobbying as a major tool of influence. **Lobbying** is attempting to influence the decisions of public officials, especially legislators. The right to lobby is secured by the First and Fourteenth Amendments to the Constitution, which protect the right of the people to petition the government for redress of grievances. State constitutions provide similar protections.

Anyone can try to influence how a state legislator votes. States usually define a professional **lobbyist** as someone who is paid to influence legislators on behalf of a client or clients. States now require lobbyists to register annually, either with the secretary of state's office or with an election or lobbyist commission. In most states, lobbyists must pay a fee for lobbying. In Texas, for example, professional lobbyists pay a $300 fee, although lobbyists for tax-exempt public interest groups pay only $100.

Hundreds of lobbyists openly ply their trade in the committee rooms and corridors of the state capitols. The more populated states register thousands of lobbyists. In one recent year, Texas and New York each registered as many as 1,800 professional lobbyists. At least 1,200 lobbyists work the state capitol in California. Even less-populated Vermont had more than 600 lobbyists registered with the secretary of state.

Most lobbyists are regular employees of corporations, unions, or trade associations. Many are members of law firms; others are former state employees. Effective lobbyists are specialists in both subject matter and legislative procedure. Lobbyists for organized interests know the schedule of general hearings, committee meetings, floor debates, and social events. They also know as much as possible about the legislators, their electoral support, their values, their hobbies, and who has their "ear." They are present and prepared when their interests are affected. Veteran lobbyists know how to influence legislators. Lobbyists live by two important rules: First, it's a lot easier to kill a bill than to pass it. And second, work in such a way that you have no permanent allies and no permanent enemies. Today's opponent may be your supporter on the next issue for which you are lobbying.[15]

Some of the most effective lobbyists are retired state legislators. They not only have good contacts with their former colleagues, they know where the leverage points are in the legislative process. "If you happen to know the four people on a certain senate committee," said one Colorado legislator, "it's pretty damn easy to kill a bill."[16]

Lobbyists have two sources of influence: (1) information and (2) campaign support. Information is usually the key ingredient in gaining or losing a vote. Lobbyists are useful providers of such information to anyone who can influence state policy making. "Lobbyists are strategists, tacticians, builders of coalitions among groups, experts and communicators. They testify in committees, buttonhole lawmakers one-on-one, organize meetings between their members and legislators, stage rallies and demonstrations, and try to put a favorable 'spin' on media coverage of their issues."[17] Plainly, however, lobbyists recognize that information and statistics are malleable and can be used to either support or oppose a bill.

In addition, interest groups are usually the major financial backers of incumbent legislators, and in return the lobbyists for those groups get unusual access. As the costs of state legislative races climb, so does the dependence of legislators, legislative leaders, and political parties on organized interests.[18]

Illegal use of lobbying techniques, primarily bribery, has been found in some states. Scandals have been exposed in Arkansas, Arizona, Kentucky, Massachusetts, New Mexico, and South Carolina, among others, in recent years.

Still, bribery is not a widespread problem in most states. Writing about his own experiences in the Vermont Senate, Frank Smallwood observed that as a general rule, most of the lobbyists "were articulate, hard-working, and extremely well informed in their particular areas of expertise. This last attribute—information—represented their chief weapon and gave them real clout. As far as I could find out, the lobbyists didn't offer legislators any money or other direct inducements, at least, they never offered me anything, not even a sociable drink. Instead they relied on information."[19]

In recent years, states have sought to regulate lobbying activities, conflicts of interest, and the financing of political campaigns. Wisconsin and Minnesota ban such favors as buying meals for a legislator. In the wake of a 1992 Federal Bureau of Investigation sting, lawmakers in Kentucky are now barred from taking anything from a lobbyist except $100 per year in meals and drinks. State senators in New York voluntarily declined the meals and gifts worth more than $25 that interest groups had routinely lavished on them.[20]

Not all these reforms have been easy to implement, nor have they all worked according to the original intentions. Laws that control lobbying and regulate how much individuals may spend to influence either elections or the legislative process are difficult to enforce. It is sometimes unclear, too, whether they infringe on the constitutional right of persons to petition their government and to spend their own money for political purposes.[21]

OTHER INFLUENCES ON STATE LEGISLATORS   A legislator's personality, leadership style, and conception of responsibilities influence how he or she will vote and perform constituent service.

Much as they promise to clean up state government and cut wasteful spending, many legislators fight hard to see that their own district gets a fair share of state government construction projects and subsidies. Voting for one's home district makes sense to many legislators. Former state legislator John E. Brandl writes that state legislators understand that on election day, their constituents who are grateful for favors received "are more apt to express positive sentiments on the ballot than those not receiving benefits from the capitol. . . . A former colleague of mine in the Minnesota House of Representatives seemed bewildered when he heard the suggestion that his first responsibility as a legislator might not be to look out for his district but rather to be concerned for the good of the whole state. 'Nobody who thinks like that could ever get elected from my district,' he maintained."[22]

But if state legislators are elected to represent the people and their views at the statehouse, few lawmakers think they should merely mirror or "re-present" the views of their district's constituents. Most legislators like to consider themselves **trustees** of their constituents, claiming to rely on their own conscience or on their considered judgments in making decisions. Legislators who view themselves as **delegates,** by contrast, adhere more closely to instructions from their constituents. Not surprisingly, the trustee role is not only more popular but also easier and more realistic to practice. Given the complexity of government and the difficulty of finding out where citizens stand on a wide variety of issues, the trustee role is a more workable one in the day-to-day decision making of a legislator during legislative sessions.

Views of constituents back home are influential on matters such as taxes and major construction on highway projects, yet on most issues, the people back home have little direct influence on lawmaking. On issues that are of keen local interest, legislators certainly do take their constituents into account when they vote. In other words, state lawmakers act as trustees on some issues and delegates on others. Yet conscience and personal philosophy are seldom the only, or even the most important, guide. Colleagues, committee recommendations, party leadership, staff counsel, and lobbying by the affected interests are also influential.

Newly elected legislators soon learn it makes sense to depend on friendly colleagues to inform them about issues. According to a Pennsylvania legislator, "Very early in the session, you try to find other representatives who sit on other committees and who are similar to you in their outlook politically. When a bill comes to the floor for a vote, you have to look to that person, you have to trust him."[23]

Another aspect of state politics that often fuels legislation is action taken by other states. Legislators frequently ask their staffs, "What is California, Minnesota, or Oregon doing on this problem?" Legislators are always on the lookout for innovative tax, educational, or welfare policies implemented elsewhere. Legislators are keenly interested in how their state compares to others in certain areas—on sales taxes, for example, high school dropouts, clean air, or federal moneys coming to the state. The press often uses such rankings in headlines and editorials.

The National Conference of State Legislatures, a nonpartisan professional organization funded by all 50 state legislatures, acts as an effective clearinghouse for new ideas (www.ncsl.org). With about 180 staff members located mainly in Denver, Colorado, it distributes studies to legislators across the country. A rival yet smaller and more conservative group, the American Legislative Exchange Council, has developed in recent years (www.alec.org). The Council of State Governments (www.csg.org) and the State Legislative Leaders Foundation (www.sllf.org) are two groups that also help serve state legislative leaders.

Actions taken by the federal government also influence state laws and regulations. Over the past 30 years, state legislatures have been burdened by **federal mandates,** which require states to allocate state funds to match federally stipulated programs such as Medicare. Funding for federal mandates was often the fastest-growing part of a state's budget, a sore point with state legislators. In the 1990s, Congress began to place some mild restraints on the growth of federal mandates.

MODERNIZATION AND REFORM

As states are asked to take on increasing responsibility, their legislatures face greater pressure to modernize: Lobbying is more intense than ever, campaign costs have increased, and fewer members follow the old folkways that used to make for an almost clubhouse collegiality in most legislatures. The greater participation of women, minorities, and more independent-minded legislators has meant a broader mix of agendas and ideas. The influence of legislative leaders has decreased, and that of the media and staff has grown.[24] According to state legislative scholar Alan Rosenthal, "Earlier, leaders were truly in command, and power was tightly held. Partly as a consequence of modernization and reform, legislatures have been democratized. Resources are more broadly distributed, and the gap between leaders and other legislators is narrower."[25]

State legislatures in the past were criticized as inefficient, ineffective, poorly staffed, boss-ridden, secretive, sexist, unrepresentative, and often dominated by rural interests. Most legislatures had little or no staff and high rates of turnover among members. Legislators had to rely primarily on information that came to them from lobbyists or the governor's office. Legislatures were often run by factions that could not be held accountable, and parliamentary procedures and inadequate committee systems either prevented action or served narrow or specially favored interests.

> Given the goals of members, the demands of groups, and the heavy workload, deliberation gives way to expediency. Members frequently are unwilling to say no to their colleagues, lest their colleagues say no to them. They also are averse to saying no to constituents, lest their constituents withdraw support. The process has become porous; much seeps through that probably should not. Standing committees do not screen the wheat from the chaff as diligently as they might.[26]

Most state legislatures have adopted internal reforms to address these perceived shortcomings. Thus most legislatures now have longer annual sessions, expanded and more competent staffs, more effective committee systems, streamlined procedures such as automated bill status and statute retrieval systems, higher salaries, and modern information systems.[27] In 1979, for example, state legislatures had 16,930 permanent staffers; by 2003, the number had climbed to 28,067.

Legislatures have also become more sensitive to new technologies. Every legislature now has a colorful Web site with detailed information about the workings of the lawmaking body. Hawaii has a fully equipped and staffed "public access room," making it easy for citizens to lobby their state legislators.[28] Virginia is considered a leader in e-government technology for its commitment to citizen–legislator communication through e-mail.[29] And most important, prodded by federal court rulings, legislative districts are now approximately equal in population and thus more representative of the people.

In short, the largely amateur, part-time state legislatures are a thing of the past in most states. The new professionalism reflects a determination on the part of most legislators—especially the leaders—to take charge of their own branch as major players in shaping state public policy.

The movement to encourage full-time professional legislatures with substantial staffs, however, has not been universally praised. In fact, in recent years, some political scientists and some citizens have contended that we were better off when we had part-time citizen-legislators. The groundswell in the early 1990s to enact term limits was in many ways a voters' protest against professionalized legislators who appeared to be making their job of representation into a career.

Legislative Term Limits: Problem or Solution?

Although the complexity of state problems may well require professional legislators who devote full-time attention to legislative issues, this professionalism "runs counter to the traditional theory of American politics in which citizens come together, conduct the public's business and return to their other occupations."[30] In the 33 states where there are no term limits, many legislators are now viewed as career politicians—and hence less like the people they represent.

Term limits were the most talked-about legislative "reform" in the 1990s. It began in 1990 when voters in California, Colorado, and Oklahoma approved the first term-limit restrictions through citizen-instigated ballot initiatives. Two years later, another 11 states enacted voter initiatives along the same lines. Several more approved term-limit provisions of some type for their constitutions, while voters in three states rejected them. In addition, state legislators in Utah and Louisiana voted to impose term limits on themselves. State supreme courts in four states—Massachusetts, Nebraska, Oregon, and Washington—have struck down term limits as unconstitutional. Note, however, that Nebraska voters in 2000, four years after their court nullified voter-approved limits, voted to reinstate them.

There is some evidence that the term-limit movement has run out of energy. In 2002, Idaho legislators voted to repeal term-limit provisions that had been approved on several occasions by Idaho voters. Term-limit supporters complained that this legislative repeal constituted "a slap in the face to all Idaho voters. The arrogance of the Legislature to repeal an issue that has been supported by four separate votes is unconscionable."[31] But Idaho legislative leader Bruce Newcomb responded that term limits won approval only because out-of-state money influenced the votes: "We were a cheap state to buy; it was not in the public interest. . . . There was never a real debate. . . . They had no opposition."[32] In 2003, the Utah legislature followed suit, repealing the limits it had imposed on itself only five years earlier.[33]

Nevertheless, term-limit provisions exist in 17 states (see Table 5–2). These provisions limit state legislators to legislative service of six to twelve years. In some states, lawmakers are barred from serving in the same office beyond a set number of years. In 11 other states, they must skip one term (more in some states) before running again for office. In 2002, for example, 71 percent of Michigan's legislators were forced out of office under term limits.

Voters in California went even further and enacted a measure that slashed legislative staffs and curbed legislative pension benefits as well as limited the number of terms legislators could serve. This citizen-sponsored and citizen-enacted law also prohibited legislators from ever running again for the legislature.

Voters can, of course, dispatch legislators from office by voting for challengers. But voters seem to want the added constitutional device of doing for them what most voters do not do themselves—throw the rascals out! All the drama about term limits diverts attention from other serious problems, including weak parties, too many safe-seat districts where one party virtually always wins, and neglect of educational investment and economic development in the states.

Term limits have serious consequences for state legislative activity. In California, novice lawmakers now chair committees and hold leadership positions, and there are signs in California and elsewhere that term limits discourage legislative cooperation, decrease institutional expertise, and generally weaken legislatures relative to governors, bureaucrats, and lobbyists.

TABLE 5–2   TERM LIMITS IN THE STATES

State	Year Enacted	House Limit (years)	House Year of Impact	Senate Limit (years)	Senate Year of Impact	Popular Vote in Favor
Maine	1993	8	1996	8	1996	67.6%
California	1990	6	1996	8	1998	52.2
Colorado	1990	8	1998	8	1998	71.0
Arkansas	1992	6	1998	8	2000	59.9
Michigan	1992	6	1998	8	2002	58.8
Florida	1992	8	2000	8	2000	76.8
Missouri*	1992	8	2002	8	2002	75.0
Ohio	1992	8	2000	8	2000	68.4
South Dakota	1992	8	2000	8	2000	63.5
Montana	1992	8	2000	8	2000	67.0
Arizona	1992	8	2000	8	2000	74.2
Oklahoma	1990	12	2004	12	2004	67.3
Nevada	1996	12	2008	12	2008	70.4
Utah	1994	12	2006	12	2006	—†
Wyoming	1992	12	2006	12	2006	77.2
Louisiana	1995	12	2007	12	2007	76.0
Nebraska†	2000	8	2008	—	—	55.8

SOURCE: National Conference of State Legislatures, "The Term Limited States," www.ncsl.org/programs/legman/about/states.htm, accessed April 27, 2004.

*Because of special elections, term limits became effective in 2000 for eight current members of the House and one senator in 1998.
†Passed by the legislature.
†Nebraska has a unicameral legislature.

However, term limits thus far have changed the general profile of state legislators.[34] Indeed, opponents contend correctly, it takes several years for new legislators to become acquainted with rules, procedures, and regulations; therefore, to jettison politicians just as they begin to feel comfortable, confident, and knowledgeable is to lose a wealth of accumulated experience.

THE POLITICS OF DRAWING LEGISLATIVE DISTRICT LINES

State legislatures are required by their state constitutions, by federal laws, and by court rulings to draw district boundaries for both their state legislature and U.S. House of Representative seats after each population census. The 2000 census once again triggered redistricting of congressional and state legislative lines.

Redistricting is the action of a state legislature or other body in redrawing legislative electoral district lines. About a dozen states delegate these responsibilities to independent redistricting or reapportionment commissions. In Alaska, the governor's office draws the legislative districts. Most legislatures, however, consider these once-a-decade responsibilities so important that they are unwilling to turn control of this task over to anybody else.

The drawing of legislative district boundaries has always been controversial, in large part because redistricting decisions are made by partisan majorities in legislatures. The highly political nature of the undertaking is usually reflected in the results. "Redistricting is the political equivalent," says one observer, "of moving the left field fence for a right-handed pull hitter. By changing the boundaries, redistricting helps some, hurts others—and leaves just about everyone else scrambling."[35]

The politics and debate about redistricting are most intense in the years immediately after a census is taken. Drawing district boundaries to benefit a party, group, or incumbent is called **gerrymandering.** The term was first used in 1811 to describe a strange, salamander-shaped legislative district drawn in northeastern Massachusetts when Elbridge Gerry was governor. A district does not need to be odd in shape, however, to be gerrymandered.

As a result of huge differences in population among the districts, state legislative districts used to face problems of **malapportionment.** State legislatures for decades had given rural and small-town voters more votes in the legislature than they were entitled to on the basis of their declining share of the population. In Georgia, for instance, the 1960 reapportionment gave the largest county, with 556,326 inhabitants, no more representation than the three smallest counties, whose combined population was 6,980.[36] City officials complained bitterly that small-town and farmland-dominated legislators were unsympathetic to their problems and had different legislative priorities.

But no matter how much they protested, people who were underrepresented in the state legislatures made little progress. Legislators from small towns and farm areas naturally did not wish to reapportion themselves out of jobs, and their constituents did not wish to lose their influence. Even though the failure of state legislatures to reapportion often violated express provisions of state constitutions and raised serious questions under the U.S. Constitution, state and federal judges took the position that issues having to do with legislative districting were "political questions" and outside the scope of judicial authority.

Finally, the U.S. Supreme Court stepped in. In 1962, in *Baker* v. *Carr,* the Court held that voters do have standing to challenge legislative apportionment and that such questions should be considered by the federal courts. Arbitrary and capriciously drawn districts deprive people of their constitutional rights of representation, and federal judges may take jurisdiction over such cases.[37]

One Person, One Vote

In *Wesberry* v. *Sanders* (1964), the U.S. Supreme Court announced that as far as congressional representation is concerned, "as nearly as practicable one man's vote in a congressional election is to be worth as much as another's."[38] The Court extended this principle to representation in the state legislatures, although it subsequently modified this decision allowing for somewhat more population discrepancies among state legislative districts than for congressional districts.

In *Reynolds* v. *Sims* (1964), the Court held that "the fundamental principle of representative government in this country is one of equal representation for equal numbers of people, without regard to race, sex, economic status, or place of residence within a state." In the Court's view, this principle applied not only to the more numerous house of the state legislature, which was usually based on population, but also to the state senate, where representation was often based on area, such as the county or some other governmental unit. Defenders of this pattern had argued that as long as the more numerous chamber represented population, the senate could represent geographical units. Look at the federal system embodied in the U.S. Constitution, they said. Isn't representation in the U.S. Senate based on area? Although many thought this a compelling argument, a majority of the Court did not. Chief Justice Earl Warren explained: "Legislators represent people, not trees or acres. Legislators are elected by voters, not farms or cities or economic interests. . . . The right to elect legislators in a free unimpaired fashion is a bedrock of our political system."[39] The U.S. Senate analogy, in short, did not hold.

The Supreme Court has been especially strict about how states draw districts for the U.S. House of Representatives. A state legislature must justify any variance from mathematical equality by showing it made a good-faith effort to come as close as possible to the standard. The Supreme Court is, however, less insistent on absolute equality for state legislative districts. Thus the Court in 1983 upheld a Wyoming plan that allocated at least one state legislative seat per county, saying that Wyoming's policy was rational and appropriate to the special needs of that sparsely populated state.[40] This ruling was a rare exception to the general principle of allowing at most a 10 percent deviation between state legislative districts. Nevertheless, the requirement that the districts be established in accordance with the one-person, one-vote principle still remains.

New Rules for Redrawing the Districts

Even though the one-person, one-vote principle is firmly established, many issues affecting the nature of legislative representation continue to be hotly debated. In northern metropolitan areas, for instance, the general pattern has been for the center city to be Democratic and the outlying suburbs Republican. If legislative district lines in these areas are drawn like spokes from the center city to the suburbs, fewer Republicans will probably be elected than if the district lines are drawn in concentric circles.

In recent decades, African Americans and Hispanics have begun to charge that state legislatures have an obligation under the Voting Rights Act of 1965 to redraw legislative districts to avoid dilution of the influence of minorities at the ballot box. They have gone to court to force legislators to create **majority-minority districts.** The U.S. Supreme Court, however, has put restraints on implementation of the act. The Court has held that although legislatures may take race into account in drawing state and federal legislative district lines and must act to avoid diluting the voting strength of minorities, a legislature violates the constitutional rights of white voters if race becomes the overriding motive.[41]

Controversy continues to surround reapportionment, no matter what processes are used. No one ever doubts the ability of incumbents in the majority to rig elections through reapportionment. In the words of the old-time politicians, "You tell me the results you want, and I'll draw the district map to do it." Today, computers are shaping the districts, and the people who control the computers, their programming, and their data can influence the outcome.

Neither the courts nor the two major parties have adequately addressed the competitive integrity of the electoral process as a constitutional issue. But a case can be made that the vast majority of state legislative elections offer little meaningful competition. Whether designed by legislative party leaders or redistricting commissioners, those who carve up legislative districts every ten years do so primarily with the intent to protect incumbents or create districts that at least leave their party no worse off than it was before.

"Real competition, where a challenger to an incumbent might have some actual chance of winning, is evident in elections that are won by margins of less than 10 percent of the vote," writes Columbia University law professor Samuel Issacharoff.[42] But this is rarely the case in state after state. The wonder is "that anyone bothers to participate at all in such hollow elections."[43] And this was, in part, the reason that the term-limit crusade gained support in the first place.

DIRECT LEGISLATION: POLICY MAKING BY THE PEOPLE?

Many states, mostly in the West, believe that citizens should have the power to create legislation through the initiative, referendum, and recall. This "direct democracy" movement began with populist reformers in Utah in 1900 and spread quickly to Oregon in 1902, Montana in 1904, Maine and Michigan in 1908, and Arizona and Colorado in 1910. Of the nearly 2,500 initiatives that the public has placed on the ballot in the 24 states that allow this form of direct democracy, more than 1,000 have been in five states: Oregon, California, Colorado, North Dakota, and Arizona.

Reformers had good reason to bypass their legislatures in the early 1900s—legislatures in several states were either incompetent or under the domination of the political machines. For example, the Southern Pacific Railroad's political machine in California had dominated the selection of state legislators, governors, and U.S. senators for years.[44] The Progressives placed enormous trust in the wisdom of the people, assuming that voters would inform themselves about issues and make responsible decisions on a variety of policy questions put before them.

Initiative

The **initiative** permits a designated minimum number of voters to propose a law or constitutional amendment by petition. It becomes law if approved by a majority of the voters at a subsequent election. Twenty-four states, mostly in the West, authorize the making of laws by means of the initiative petition (see Figure 5–4). In California, Oregon, Washington, North Dakota, Arizona, Colorado, Michigan, and Massachusetts, the initiative has become an important feature of state political life.

In some states, the *direct initiative* applies to constitutional amendments and to legislation; in others, it can be used only for one or the other. Thus in Florida, the direct initiative can be used only to change the state constitution, while in Idaho, direct initiative can be used only for statutory lawmaking. In a state that permits the direct initiative, any individual or interest group may draft a proposed law and file it with a designated state official, usually the secretary of state. Supporters have only to secure a

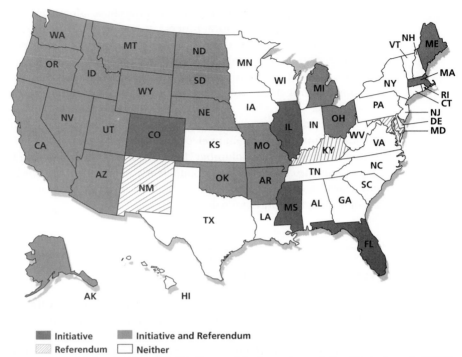

FIGURE 5–4 **Citizen-Initiated Initiative and Referendum at the State Level, 2005.**

certain number of signatures (between 2 and 15 percent of the vote in the last election) to place the measure on the next general election ballot. Only California permits initiatives on primary election ballots.

The *indirect initiative* is used in a few states, including Alaska, Maine, and Massachusetts. After a certain number of petition signatures have been collected, the state legislature is given an opportunity to act on the measure without alteration; if approved, the law simply goes into effect. If not approved, the proposed legislation is then placed on the ballot, although in some states, additional signatures are required before the proposal can be placed before the voters.

Referendum

A **referendum** permits voters to vote on, and possibly overturn, recently passed laws or legislatively proposed amendments to a state's constitution. A majority vote is required to overturn legislatively approved laws. The referendum, it should be noted, is required in every state except Delaware for the ratification of constitutional amendments.

Legislation may be subject to mandatory or optional referendums. The *mandatory referendum* calls for a waiting period, usually 60 to 90 days, before legislation goes into effect. If during this period a prescribed number of voters sign a referendum petition requesting that the act be referred to the voters, the law does not go into effect unless a majority of the voters give their approval at the next election. The *optional referendum* permits the legislature, at its discretion, to provide that a measure shall not become law until it has been approved by the voters at an election. This second kind is the more common.

Although statewide initiatives and referendums get the most attention, the same processes also flourish at the local level in many states. The annual volume of measures presented to voters in school districts, cities, and counties runs to several thousand, and covers a wide range of issues: bonds for school buildings, fluoridation of water, banning of glass bottles, restrictions on nuclear power facilities, and approval or rejection of convention facilities or sport stadiums.

Recall

Recall is the means by which voters may remove elected public officials before the end of their term. Eighteen states, mostly in the West, provide for the recall of state officers, but many others permit the recall of local officials (see Figure 5–5). Recall also requires a petition, but it needs more signatures (typically 25 percent of voters in the last election for the position in question) than the initiative or referendum.

The most famous recall in recent history involved the removal of California Governor Gray Davis and the election of former bodybuilder and movie star Arnold Schwarzenegger. In California and five other states, the recall election for the office-holder was held on the same ballot with the election of a successor—hence, the recall of Davis and election of Schwarzenegger occurred at the same time. In eight states, the recall election is held first and is followed by a special election for a successor at a later time. And in four states the recall election is held first and the successor is appointed by either a special board or the governor.

There are various kinds of recall elections. In some, the official must run and try to win reelection in a yes-or-no vote of confidence election; in others, candidates are

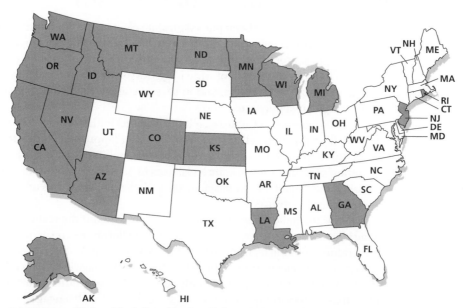

FIGURE 5–5 States That Provide for Citizen-Initiated Recall of Elected State Officials.

permitted to file and run against the incumbent, making it, in effect, a new election. If in the former case an incumbent is voted out of office, a new election is required.

Recall is akin to impeachment by the public. But unlike impeachment, formal charges of wrongdoing against the incumbent are not required. Rather, recall permits throwing people out of office merely because of policy differences. For recall, voters need only circulate petitions and obtain the required number of signatures. Recall is seldom used at the state level, although one governor and several state legislators have been recalled. Although the recall is rarely used successfully in the 18 states that now permit it, even the threat of a recall serves to remind legislators and other state officials of their obligations to the voters.

Recall is also used surprisingly often against local officials—although only 18 states allow recall of statewide officials, 36 allow recall of local officials such as mayors, county commissioners, and school board superintendents. From 1977 to 2001, nearly 10 percent of all U.S. cities held a recall election of a mayor or city council member.[45]

A few years ago, New Jersey voters were asked to approve the right to recall local, state, and federal elected officials. Taxpayer and antipolitician groups argued passionately in favor of passage. *The New York Times* vigorously opposed the recall, saying it would discourage public officials from making unpopular decisions that nevertheless bring about long-term public benefits. The *Times* also editorialized that the recall authority was unnecessary: "If voters are unhappy with someone they have elected, they can vote that person out the next time! If an official breaks the law, prosecutors can deal with it."[46] But over 70 percent of New Jersey voters voted in favor of adopting the recall.

THE DEBATE OVER DIRECT DEMOCRACY

Hundreds of issues have been placed on state election ballots by citizen initiative in recent years. Citizens have turned to the initiative process to try to regulate handguns in California, to protect the moose in Maine, to encourage the death penalty in Massachusetts, to approve the sale of wine in grocery stores in Colorado, to abolish daylight savings time in North Dakota, and in several states to allow marijuana to be used for specific medicinal purposes.

In 2004, voters in 34 states cast ballots on 163 initiatives and referendums, including $3 billion for stem cell research in California (approved), education reform in five states (three approved, two rejected), legalized gambling in Washington State (rejected), relaxation of term limits on state legislators in Arkansas and Montana (rejected), legalization of marijuana for any usage in Alaska (rejected), and bans on same-sex marriage in 11 states (all approved).

Of the 163 ballot measures, 50 were initiatives and the rest were referendums of some kind. Nebraska voters actually faced four ballot choices on gambling, including one referendum from the legislature and three initiatives from the voters (all four failed).[47]

Contrary to election-night hunches, the gay-marriage initiatives did not bring large numbers of voters to the polls in hotly contested battleground states such as Michigan and Ohio—voters in the battleground states were already engaged by the campaigns. However, the bans appear to have boosted turnout in states that were not hotly contested by the two presidential campaigns. According to an analysis by the Brookings Institution's

Michael McDonald, the same-sex marriage ban in Kentucky may have provided the margin of victory for the embattled Republican Senate incumbent, Jim Bunning.

Political scientists, law professors, and lawmakers are often critical of direct legislation.[48] Early opponents had argued that such measures would undermine the legitimacy of representative government and open the way for radical or special-interest legislation. Critics of the initiative and the referendum believe that the Progressives who advocated direct legislation were naively idealistic and that these mechanisms are more likely to be used by special interests. Only well-organized interests can gather the appropriate number of signatures and mount the required media campaigns to gain victory. Critics of direct democracy say that this is indeed what has happened in California, Oregon, and elsewhere.[49]

In addition to giving advantages to well-organized interests, direct legislation often introduces confusion because some petitions are worded not so much for clarity but to win votes. Moreover, the 30-second ads that support or oppose many initiatives also tend to confuse rather than clarify.

The results of direct democracy have been both positive and negative. Historically, direct legislation by initiative has resulted in progressive victories on many consumer and economic issues and conservative victories on social issues. Direct democracy has not weakened our legislatures; seats in state legislatures are still valued, sought after, and competed for by able citizens. However, direct democracy has clearly had a considerable impact on state taxes and spending, especially in states that have enacted budget and tax limits. These measures have pleased many conservatives, upset liberals, and made life difficult for governors and state legislators.

Another serious problem has arisen in western states. Political consulting firms, for a price, will gather signatures and put nearly anything you want on the ballot. Deceptive pitches are sometimes made to get people to sign petitions. It takes a small fortune to do this, and only well-organized, well-financed, single-interest groups can afford it.[50]

Still another problem with the initiative process is that it can be used to target minorities, as California's limitations on illegal immigrants in 1994 and affirmative action in 1996 did. Similarly, Colorado's controversial Measure 2 in 1992 targeted gays and lesbians. How far can the majority go in using the initiative process against minorities? The courts have generally reversed part or all of discriminatory initiatives that were successful at the polls, yet such reversals put the courts in the awkward position of opposing a vote of the people.

The initiative process has become a powerful tool used by interest groups, politicians, and ideologues. "A vote on an issue in a single state can propel an issue onto the national agenda because of the widespread media attention given to some controversial initiatives."[51] Interest groups have set state policy by means of the initiative and have used it to reduce local government options in taxing, zoning and planning, and related matters. "One reason for this tendency to take on matters that were previously local and decide them at the statewide level is interest group efficiency. It is easier to restrict local taxing powers, strike local rent control laws, and eliminate ordinances protecting gays and lesbians by mobilizing a single statewide vote" rather than by campaigning to reverse or defeat local initiatives.[52]

Viewed from another perspective, most of the perceived flaws of the populist processes of direct democracy are also the flaws of democracy. When we vote in an election, we often wish we had more information about issues and candidates. Delegates at constitutional conventions or national party conventions frequently have similar misgivings when they are forced to render yes-or-no votes on complicated issues. So, too, members of state legislatures—especially in those frantic days near the end of their sessions—yearn for more information, more clarity about consequences, and more discussion and compromise than time will permit.

Critics lament the rise in what they call "public policy making by bumper sticker." Opponents of direct legislation fear that the very fabric of legislative processes and representative government is at stake. To be sure, lack of faith in legislative bodies has sometimes prompted the use of direct legislation devices, but the best way to restore faith in the legislature is not to bypass it but to elect better people to it.

Supporters of populist democracy say they have not given up on the legislative process. Rather, they wish to use direct legislation primarily when legislatures prove unresponsive. If our legislature will not act, they say, give us the opportunity to debate our proposals in the open arena of election politics. Supporters further contend that the people are capable of making decisions on complex matters.

Voters throughout the country say that citizens ought to have the right, at least occasionally, to vote directly on policy issues. Surveys find that both voters and nonvoters say they would be more likely to become interested in politics and vote if some issues appeared along with candidates on their ballots.[53] Moreover, Californians, who have had to deal with more ballot issues than voters in any other state, continue to say statewide ballot propositions elections are overall "a good thing for California" (74 percent), even as they acknowledge limits to their own grasp of the process.[54]

The legislative process is never perfect. Even with larger professional staffs, hearings, new technologies, bicameralism, and other distinctive features of constitutional democracy, mistakes are made and defective bills are enacted into law in our legislatures. The Supreme Court has overturned hundreds of laws passed by state legislatures as unconstitutional, and state legislatures often spend much of their time amending or otherwise improving measures they passed in previous years. As a practical matter, however, Americans should be at least as skeptical and questioning of the initiative and referendum process as they already are of their state legislators.

S U M M A R Y

1. State legislatures were the most powerful institutions in the nation during the Revolutionary War, and remain powerful to this day. Although some state legislatures still rely on part-time legislators with little or no staff, many now elect full-time legislators who receive significant pay and staff support. In many ways, state legislatures are becoming more like the U.S. Congress every day.

2. The nation's 7,387 state legislators are called on to represent diverse views, help formulate state public policy, oversee the administration of state laws, and mediate political conflicts that arise in the state. State legislatures have become more diverse in recent decades as population changes have improved the election prospects of women and minority candidates.

3. The main influences on a state legislator's voting decisions are political parties, lobbyists and interest groups, district considerations, constituent views, colleagues, committee recommendations, the party leaders, the media, and actions taken by other states and the federal government. State legislators use many of the same tools for making decisions as members of the U.S. Congress.

4. State legislators are constantly subjected to intense lobbying by organized interests. Although lobbyists

and interest group representatives are important sources of information, legislatures have become increasingly concerned about potential conflicts of interest and ethical conduct. Many states have created special rules covering campaign contributions and lobbying activities in the wake of scandals in their own legislatures.

5. As a result of legislative reform efforts, most states now have longer annual sessions, larger and more competent staffs, open-meeting laws, and a variety of electronic-age information systems. As they have become more professionalized, they have also become more capable of producing legislative impacts in a variety of policy areas such as the environment, education, and crime control.

6. Seventeen states have limited the number of terms legislators can serve. Most state legislators and political scientists oppose term limits for a variety

of reasons, yet voters in many states have viewed them as a way of keeping their representatives accountable and encouraging the notion of citizen representation.

7. The politics of redistricting, or redrawing legislative boundaries, heats up every ten years after the census is taken. Redistricting is never easy; political careers can be ruined by redrawn boundaries. Major controversies have arisen over partisan and racially motivated drawing of legislative district lines, and the federal courts are increasingly asked to establish guidelines that will limit such outcomes.

8. Direct legislative procedures, especially the initiative petition, are a prominent part of the legislative process, particularly in the West. Other direct mechanisms, such as the referendum and the recall, are also available to voters in many states.

F U R T H E R   R E A D I N G

SHAWN BOWLER AND TODD DONOVAN, *Demanding Choices: Opinions, Voting, and Direct Democracy* (University of Michigan Press, 1998).

SHAWN BOWLER, TODD DONOVAN, AND CAROLINE J. TOLBERT, EDS., *Citizens as Legislators: Direct Democracy in the United States* (Ohio State University Press, 1998).

DAVID S. BRODER, *Democracy Derailed: Initiative Campaigns and the Power of Money* (Harcourt, 2000).

WILLIAM M. BULGER, *While the Music Lasts: My Life in Politics* (Houghton Mifflin, 1996).

BRUCE E. CAIN, *The Reapportionment Puzzle* (University of California Press, 1984).

JOHN M. CAREY, RICHARD G. NIEMI, AND LYNDA W. POWELL, *Term Limits in the State Legislatures* (University of Michigan Press, 2000).

THOMAS E. CRONIN, *Direct Democracy: The Politics of the Initiative, Referendum, and Recall* (Harvard University Press, 1989).

RICHARD J. ELLIS, *Democratic Delusions: The Initiative Process in America* (University Press of Kansas, 2002).

VIRGINIA GRAY, RUSSELL HANSON, AND HERBERT JACOB, EDS., *Politics in the American States,* 7th ed. (CQ Press, 1999).

JOHN J. KENNEDY, *The Contemporary Pennsylvania Legislature* (University Press of America, 1999).

TOM LOFTUS, *The Art of Legislative Politics* (CQ Press, 1994).

BURDETT A. LOOMIS, *A Legislative Year: Time, Politics, and Policies* (University Press of Kansas, 1994).

DAVID B. MAGLEBY, *Direct Legislation: Voting on Ballot Propositions in the United States* (Johns Hopkins University Press, 1984).

JAY MICHAEL AND DAN WALTERS, *The Third House: Lobbyists, Money, and Power in Sacramento* (Berkeley Public Policy Press, 2002).

GARY MONCRIEF, PEVERILL SQUIRE, AND MALCOLM E. JEWELL, *Who Runs for the Legislature?* (Prentice Hall, 2001).

NATIONAL CONFERENCE OF STATE LEGISLATURES AND AMERICAN SOCIETY OF LEGISLATIVE CLERKS AND SECRETARIES, *Inside the Legislative Process* (National Council of State Legislatures, 1998).

ALBERT J. NELSON, *Emerging Influentials in State Legislatures: Women, Blacks, and Hispanics* (Praeger, 1991).

BETH REINGOLD, *Representing Women: Sex, Gender, and Legislative Behavior in Arizona and California* (University of California Press, 2000).

JAMES RICHARDSON, *Willie Brown: A Biography* (University of California Press, 1996).

ALAN ROSENTHAL, *Drawing the Line: Legislative Ethics in the States* (University of Nebraska Press, 1996).

ALAN ROSENTHAL, *The Decline of Representative Democracy* (CQ Press, 1998).

PETER SCHRAG, *Paradise Lost: California's Experience, America's Future* (New Press, 1998).

FRANK SMALLWOOD, *Free and Independent: The Initiation of a College Professor into State Politics* (Stephen Greene Press, 1976).

JOHN A. STRAAYER, *The Colorado General Assembly*, 2d ed. (University Press of Colorado, 2000).

SUE THOMAS, *How Women Legislate* (Oxford University Press, 1994).

SUE THOMAS AND CLYDE WILCOX, EDS., *Women and Elective Office* (Oxford University Press, 1998).

JOEL A. THOMPSON AND GARY F. MONCRIEF, EDS., *Campaign Finance and State Legislative Elections* (CQ Press, 1998).

See *State Legislatures,* published ten times a year by the National Conference of State Legislatures. *Legislative Studies Quarterly* often has articles on state legislatures; it is published by the Legislative Studies Section of the American Political Science Association. *Governing,* published monthly by Congressional Quarterly, Inc., regularly covers state politics and state legislative issues. *Spectrum: The Journal of State Government* is a useful quarterly published by the Council of State Governments.

STATE GOVERNORS

The job of governor is one of the most important and exacting in American political life. Over the past two decades, Congress and the White House have transferred, or devolved, many activities to the states that were for a time considered national responsibilities, such as welfare assistance. This transfer has meant governors now have to be even more effective managers. They have to ask the right questions and consider the long-term implications and side effects of their policies more carefully than ever.

In good economic times, governors, with the concurrence of the state legislatures, get to spend vast sums of new money on state priorities such as education, economic development, transportation, health, and environmental protection. Such was the case during the boom times of the 1990s. Then came the recession of the early 2000s, which brought dramatic revenue shortfalls in more than 40 states. This put governors in a difficult position. To balance state budgets, they had to recommend cuts in services, project delays, state employee layoffs, pay raise postponements, and in some cases, higher taxes. In good economic times and bad, governors are invariably at the center of public policy developments.

Governors are also frequently involved in national politics and often viewed as national leaders. Seventeen governors have gone on to serve as U.S. presidents, and at least 17 members of the current U.S. Senate served earlier as governors in their states. Presidents usually pick two or three current or former governors for their cabinets, as George W. Bush did in selecting Christine Todd Whitman of New Jersey, Tom Ridge of

Pennsylvania, and Tommy Thompson of Wisconsin. Moreover, as California's 2003 recall election proved, gubernatorial campaigns can generate enormous national attention. Arnold Schwarzenegger's successful campaign to unseat Governor Gray Davis was one of the top news stories of the year.

In this chapter, we look at how governors come into and keep office, a typical governor's power and influence, efforts to bring modern management techniques to the governor's office, ways that governors interact with other elected state officials, and the rewards of being governor. But first, we examine the rising expectations we have for governors.

RISING EXPECTATIONS FOR GOVERNORS

Although the constitutional powers of governors vary from state to state, Americans evaluate and rate their governors using many of the same critieria for rating presidents.[1] Governors in the large and even medium-sized states are responsible for running complex enterprises that are at least as complicated as *Fortune* 500 corporations. Lamar Alexander, former governor of Tennessee, said that a governor needs to "see the state's few most urgent needs, develop strategies to address them, and persuade at least half the people that he or she is right."[2] An effective governor also has to perform countless symbolic and ceremonial functions and win the respect of the people and the legislature in order to exercise fully the executive functions of the office.

Today, a governor is expected to be, among other things, the state's chief policy maker, shaper of the state budget, a savvy political party leader, chief recruiter of the best available advisers and administrators, and an inspiring renewer of confidence in state programs. The governor must also champion the state's interests against the encroachments of federal or local governments and be the state's chief booster to attract business and tourism. In order to be effective, governors are expected to take trips abroad to encourage foreign investment in their states and promote their local products.[3] Thirty-eight states even operate some form of overseas office, including trade mission posts in Harare and Kuala Lumpur.[4] Governors also work with their legislatures to raise revenues for such programs as welfare, education, and economic development. Governors act as crucial links among the states and between the local and the national governments.

BECOMING AND REMAINING GOVERNOR

Each state's constitution and laws spell out the rules of eligibility, tenure, and salary for its governor. Most states require their governors to be at least 30 years of age and a state resident for at least five years immediately preceding the election. Although California, Ohio, South Dakota, Washington, and Wisconsin set the minimum age at 18, the odds against election at age 18 are staggering. In theory, any qualified voter of the state who meets a state's age qualification is eligible for the office of governor; in practice, there are well-traveled career paths to the governor's office.

Most governors are white males about 40 to 55 years old, and a substantial minority hold law degrees. As the number of women legislators has grown, so has the number of women governors. Most governors were state legislators or held statewide elective office, and some have had law enforcement experience. Of the governors in office in 2004, for example, 9 were former members of Congress, 26 had served in their state legislatures, and 10 had been mayors.

One of the most common paths upward is election to the state legislature, followed by election to a statewide office such as lieutenant governor, secretary of state, or attorney general, followed by a run for governor. Illinois Governor George Ryan spent nearly 30 years in state politics, first as a state legislator, then as Speaker of the state house, then as a two-term lieutenant governor, and finally as a two-term secretary of state before becoming governor. Mayors often run for governor; the mayors of Albuquerque; Phoenix; Indianapolis; Lincoln, Nebraska; and Las Vegas have all run for governor in their states in recent years. Former Minnesota Governor Jesse Ventura, who is remembered by many people mainly as a professional wrestler, had also served four years as mayor of a suburban community.

Although elective service is certainly helpful for building a political base, it is hardly essential. Eleven governors in 2004 had not held elected or appointed office at all, including Massachusetts Governor Mitt Romney, Mississippi Governor Haley Barbour, and Nevada Governor Kenny Guinn. Former Texas Governor George W. Bush was a businessman and baseball executive who enjoyed widespread name recognition as the son of a former president, as did his younger brother, Jeb Bush, who also went from a business career to the Florida governorship.

Two hundred years ago, most states had one- or two-year terms for their governors. Today, all states except New Hampshire and Vermont have four-year terms, and all states except Virginia allow governors to run for more than one term. Some governors, such as Jim Thompson in Illinois, Roy Romer in Colorado, Cecil Andrus in Idaho, Mario Cuomo in New York, Jim Hunt in North Carolina, and Tommy Thompson in Wisconsin, were elected to three or four terms as governors, but 37 states now have a two-term limit on governors, and Utah has a three-term limit.

Governors under Pressure

Once elected, governors enjoy high visibility in their states. Governors earn more than $100,000 in most states; salaries range from $179,000 in New York to $65,000 in Nebraska.[5] In addition, governors receive an expense allowance; all but four are provided an executive mansion; 42 of them have regular access to a state plane or helicopter or both.

But just as governors have become increasingly important in recent decades, they have also had to deal with the twin problems of rising aspirations and scarcity of resources. People want better schools, highways that do not spoil the environment, adequate welfare programs, protections for civil rights, safe streets, and clean air and water. But citizens seldom, if ever, want higher taxes.

Former New York Governor Mario Cuomo (who served from 1983 until 1995) used to say he was always running into people who wanted him to expand programs. He would look them in the eye and say, "Now what are you going to give me so that I can pay for it? Do you want to wait longer in line at the Motor Vehicle office to get your license renewed? Do we stop paving the road in front of your home? Do you mind if we plow the snow less often?" Typically, of course, he heard that the people requesting additional spending did not want to forgo any of those things, which prompted him to say, "Well, then, I don't understand. Where do I get what I need to do what you

CHANGING FACE OF AMERICAN POLITICS

WOMEN GOVERNORS

There have been only 27 women governors of the states in all of U.S. history. But of the 27, 21 were elected to office since 1975, 16 since 1990, and 9 since 2000. A tenth entered the governor's office in Connecticut after the governor resigned. As women have occupied increasingly powerful positions in state legislatures and in lower-level state-wide offices such as lieutenant governor, attorney general, and secretary of state, they have become much more visible as potential candidates for the governorship. African Americans and Hispanics have not made similar gains, however. As of 2004, there was only one Hispanic governor in office, Bill Richardson of Nevada, and no African Americans.

Women Governors Elected Since 1975

Governor	State	Term of Office	Governor	State	Term of Office
Ella Grasso	Connecticut	1975–1980	Jane Dee Hull	Arizona	1998–2002
Dixie Lee Ray	Washington	1977–1981	Judy Martz	Montana	2001–
Martha L. Collins	Kentucky	1983–1987	Ruth Ann Minner	Delaware	2001–
Madeleine Kunin	Vermont	1985–1991	Jane Swift	Massachusetts	2001–2002
Kay Orr	Nebraska	1987–1991	Janet Napolitano	Arizona	2003–
Rose Mofford	Arizona	1988–1991	Linda Lingle	Hawaii	2003–
Joan Finney	Kansas	1991–1995	Kathleen Sebelius	Kansas	2003–
Ann Richards	Texas	1991–1995	Jennifer Granholm	Michigan	2002–
Barbara Roberts	Oregon	1991–1995	Olene Walker	Utah	2003–
Christine Todd Whitman	New Jersey	1994–2001	Kathleen Blanco	Louisiana	2004–
Jeanne Shaheen	New Hampshire	1997–2002	M. Jodie Rell	Connecticut	2004–

SOURCE: National Governors Association, www.nga.org/governors, accessed on April 27, 2004.

want?" His point is simple. Given limited resources, choices must be made. Elected officials cannot afford to do everything people would like. Politicians are elected to negotiate trade-offs. You must "give to get."[6]

Governors and state legislators face the challenge of administering federally mandated welfare programs with fewer federal dollars. They have campaigned for the federal government to give more dollars to the states—without strings. The Republican-controlled U.S. Congress in the late 1990s responded by terminating some underfunded federally mandated programs and shifting a few other federal programs to the states. Governors and state legislators now face the challenge of reworking old federal welfare programs as state welfare programs with cutbacks in federal grants.

Reelection and Raising Taxes

About 75 percent of incumbent governors who run for reelection are reelected.[7] Nearly three-quarters of elections for governor are scheduled for nonpresidential or midterm election years (for example, 2006); Kentucky, Louisiana, Mississippi, New Jersey, and Virginia elect governors in odd-numbered years. Reformers have successfully argued that presidential and gubernatorial elections should be separated so that governors are not subject to the tides of national politics. In 2004, 11 governorships were up for election. (See Figure 6–1 for the party affiliations of the governors who held office in 2004.)

Incumbency is not always an advantage for reelection. Governors have to make tough decisions, which can antagonize major interests and arouse public criticism. Governors in Arizona, Alabama, Arkansas, and Oklahoma left office in recent years because of personal scandals. Governors in Oregon and Kansas left because they had such low approval ratings in the polls that they chose not to run again. Incumbents sometimes lose because of a depressed state economy or because they increased state taxes and became unpopular.

Public anger over taxes and budgets was clearly behind the 2003 Calfornia recall election. Gray Davis was widely criticized for having tripled the registration fee, or "car tax," that motorists paid on their vehicles. As future governor Arnold Schwarzenegger said repeatedly in his campaign, "I feel Californians have been punished enough. From the time they get up in the morning and flush the toilet they're taxed. When they go get a coffee they're taxed. When they get in their car they're taxed. When they go to the gas

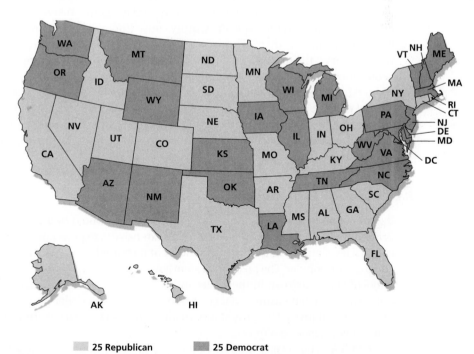

☐ 25 Republican   ■ 25 Democrat

FIGURE 6–1 Party Control of the Governor's Office, 2005.

station they're taxed. When they go to lunch they're taxed. This goes on all day long. Tax. Tax. Tax. Tax. Tax."[8]

Similarly, in New Jersey in 1993, Governor James Florio was narrowly defeated by Christine Todd Whitman due in part to a recession but mostly because Florio had recommended, and the legislature had enacted, a major tax increase. That tax increase came back to haunt Florio when he ran for U.S. senator in the New Jersey Democratic primary in 2000. His opponent, Jon Corzine, ran ads stressing Florio's role as a big spender and won the primary.

Circumstances often dictate what a governor can or cannot do. The health of the state's economy and the public's attitude toward proposed programs are critical factors. The good economic times in the late 1990s plainly helped most governors who ran for reelection while bad economic times hurt them in the early 2000s. In November 2004, only three incumbent governors won reelection, four were defeated in the primary or general election and four retired.

Some candidates for governor effectively campaign on promises to cut taxes. Republican James Gilmore in Virginia won a landslide victory in his 1998 race for governor by repeatedly saying "No Car Tax"—a reference to a highly unpopular personal property tax on cars, trucks, and motorcycles. George Pataki became governor in New York in 1994 by pledging a property tax reduction, and was reelected twice in part because he kept taxes low.[9]

Because voters reward frugality and sometimes punish elected officials for tax increases, most governors go to considerable lengths to avoid having to raise taxes, especially with an election approaching. Indeed, many politicians believe that a governor who proposes new taxes will face defeat in the next election, although some studies cast doubt on this fear.[10] Voters and legislatures often go along with governors who can make a compelling case for new revenues and new investments. When governors request a tax increase targeted for a specific worthy cause (for example, improving the schools), voters often support them. This is especially true if "political leaders are candid about why they need the money, sensible and fair in how they intend to spend it and courageous enough to lead the fight themselves. Americans are neither selfish nor short-sighted on taxes—they just want assurance that their money will be spent wisely."[11] Several governors around the country have proposed and campaigned for *investment taxes* (that is, taxes that could be invested in building better highways or increasing teachers' salaries) and became popular because of their targeted efforts to improve their state.

A GOVERNOR'S FORMAL POWERS

Before the American Revolution, royal governors, appointed by and responsible to the British crown, had broad powers, including extensive veto power over the voter-elected colonial legislatures. As anti-British sentiment increased, royal governors became more and more unpopular. The position of state governor in the new Republic was born in this atmosphere of distrust. In the 1770s and 1780s, state legislatures elected state governors, a method that ensured that governors would remain under the control of the people's representatives. The early state constitutions also limited governors to few powers and terms of just a year or two.

Gradually, however, the office of governor grew in importance. In New York, the position of chief executive was sufficiently developed and effective by 1787 that it became one of the main models for the proposed American presidency. If we compare the formal sources of authority in the U.S. Constitution and in a typical state constitution, we see significant differences. "The executive Power," says the Constitution, "shall be vested in a President of the United States of America." Compare this statement with its counterpart in a typical state constitution: "The executive department shall consist of a Governor, Lieutenant Governor, Secretary of State, Treasurer, Attorney General," and perhaps other officials. Unlike the president, the governor *shares* executive power with other elected officials. Most state constitutions go on to say, however, that "the supreme executive power shall be vested in the Governor, who shall take care that the laws be faithfully executed." Thus the public looks to the governor for law enforcement and the management of bureaucracies. In some states, the governor has been given authority to supervise the activities of local prosecutors.

Twenty-four states have strengthened the governorship by making the lieutenant governor run with the governor as a team so that the chief executive is less likely to be paired with a hostile lieutenant governor. In 39 states, the lieutenant governor, like the U.S. vice president, takes over executive office responsibilities if for any reason the governor cannot fulfill the duties of the office. Most important, in almost all states, the governor presents the state budget to the legislature and controls spending after the budget has been approved. Thus state officials must look to the governor as well as the legislature for funds.

The constitutional powers of governor vary from state to state (see Table 6–1). Yet regardless of a governor's formal constitutional authority, a governor's actual power and influence depend on his or her ability to persuade.[12] This power, in turn, usually depends on the governor's reputation, popularity, knowledge of what should be done, and, of course, ability to communicate. Governors must have political skills as well as constitutional authority if they are to provide leadership.

To supplement their formal constitutional powers, governors may hold town meetings around the state, appear on radio and television talk shows, or invite legislators and other influential party and policy leaders to the executive mansion for lobbying and consultation sessions. Remember, however, that not all states vest great constitutional power in the governor. Whether the state constitution defines a strong role is just one of the factors in determining the effectiveness of a governor.

Most governors have the following constitutional authority:

- To make appointments
- To prepare the state budget
- To veto legislation and to exercise an item veto over appropriations measures
- To issue executive orders
- To command the state National Guard
- To pardon or grant clemency
- To help establish the legislature's agenda

Appointive Power

Perhaps a governor's most important job is to recruit talented leaders and managers to head the state's departments, commissions, and agencies.[13] Through recruitment

TABLE 6–1   RANKINGS OF STATES ACCORDING TO THE FORMAL POWERS OF THE GOVERNOR

Strong

Maryland	Ohio
New Jersey	Pennsylvania
New York	Utah

Moderately Strong

Alaska	Nebraska
Colorado	North Dakota
Connecticut	South Dakota
Iowa	Tennessee
Kansas	West Virginia
Michigan	Wisconsin
Minnesota	Wyoming
Montana	

Moderate

Arizona	Louisiana
California	Maine
Delaware	Massachusetts
Florida	Missouri
Hawaii	Nevada
Idaho	New Mexico
Illinois	Oregon
Indiana	Texas
Kentucky	Virginia

Weak

Alabama	Oklahoma
Arkansas	Rhode Island
Georgia	South Carolina
Mississippi	Vermont
North Carolina	Washington
New Hampshire	

SOURCE: Adapted from Thad L. Beyle, "The Governors," in *Politics in the American States: A Comparative Analysis,* 7th ed., eds. Virginia Gray, Russell Hanson, and Herbert Jacob (CQ Press, 1999), pp. 210–211.

NOTE: Rankings are based on budget powers, appointive and organizational powers, tenure potential, veto powers, and party control.

of effective people and prudent delegation of responsibilities to them, a governor can provide direction for the state government.

In most states, the governor is one executive among many, with only limited authority over elected officials, whom the governor can neither appoint nor dismiss. And if these officials are from a different political party than the governor, they are likely to oppose the governor's recommendations. Governors have greater, yet still limited, power over officials they appoint. Some governors appoint hundreds of key officials; others, such as those in Mississippi, South Carolina, and Texas, have severe restrictions on their appointive power. Moreover, in most states, governors must share their appointive power with the state senate and may remove people only when they have violated the law or failed in their legal duties. State administrators whose programs are supported by federal funds also have a measure of independence from the governor.

But along with the appointive power comes a host of challenges. First, salaries for cabinet and agency administrators are modest in many states, especially in the smaller ones, and it is often hard to get people to leave better-paying jobs in private industry. The situation is even worse when the state capital is in a remote or rural section of the state. Second, powerful politicians may demand that their friends be appointed to certain top posts, and they may threaten to be uncooperative if the governor does not go along with their "suggestions." Finally, relatively high turnover in many state positions often hampers a governor's efforts to carry out programs.

Fiscal and Budgetary Power

A governor's financial planning and budgetary powers are key weapons in getting programs passed. Purchasing, budgeting, and personnel matters are centralized under the governor. When implemented by a strong staff and backed by a strong political base, a governor's fiscal powers are extremely important.

In almost all states, the governor has responsibility for preparing the budget and presenting it to the state legislature. This takes place every year in 30 states and every second year in 20 states. The art of budget making involves assessing requests from various departments and agencies and balancing them against available resources. Governors and their staffs have to calculate the costs of existing and newly proposed programs and weigh those costs against estimated revenues for the state.

The budget process is similar in most states. In May and June, the governor's budget office, which may be called Office of Management and Budget or Department of Administration, sends request forms to the various executive agencies. From July to October, the agencies complete their detailed requests and send them back for consideration. Their requests are invariably 10 to 15 percent higher than what is available and also much higher than the governor's proposed guidelines. The governor's budget chief evaluates all requests, sometimes holds internal administrative hearings, and then makes recommendations to the governor. Finally, the governor presents the recommendations to the legislature at the beginning of the new year.

Although the governor and chief budget officials may appear to control the budgetary process, considerable budgeting influence remains in the hands of the executive branch agencies. Further, a governor's budget reflects to a very high degree budgetary decisions made over the years (costs such as prisons or state universities that will not be shut down), so what governors end up doing in practice is tinkering or adjusting at the edges of the overall budget.

The final budget document is presented to the legislature for adoption as an *appropriations measure.* State moneys cannot be spent without legislative appropriations. Legislators can, and usually do, make a number of alterations in a governor's budget. In theory, a legislature controls all state activities through the budget process because it has the final say in approving the budget. In practice, however, most legislatures do not review every budgetary item; they merely trim or make additions at the margins. Hence budgets reflect the policy views of those responsible for their preparation—namely, the governor and the governor's budget office. A governor who has control over the budget and uses this power effectively has an important asset.

Most states spend at least 40 percent of their state's budget on education. Welfare assistance, highways, prisons and criminal justice programs, health and rehabilitation efforts, and state parks and recreation consume other large portions of the budget. Fifty percent of a state's revenue usually comes from taxes; another 20 percent comes from federal sources. When state revenues do not match expenses, governors have to cut or delay programs, since state constitutions as a rule require a balanced budget, and states cannot print money as the federal government can. In addition, states spend roughly 9 percent of their funds implementing federal mandates, such as student testing under the No Child Left Behind Act.[14]

Veto Power

Among the most useful gubernatorial powers is the **veto,** the power to conditionally reject legislative bills, especially appropriations measures. Michigan Governor Jennifer Granholm vetoed more than 30 bills in her first eighteen months in office, including one that would have banned late-term abortions, another that would have created a process for creating specialty license plates, and another that would have given suburbs more control over the Detroit Water and Sewer Board, even though the board sets their rates. Her veto activity led the *Detroit Free Press* to title a story on her tenure "Granholm stars in her own 'Kill Bill.'"[15]

In all but eight states, governors have the **item veto,** which permits them to veto individual items in an appropriations bill while signing the remainder of the bill into law. Thus they can influence the flow of funds to the executive departments and thereby attempt to control their activities. In April 2004, for example, Colorado Governor Bill Owens vetoed an 8 percent increase in college tuition as one of about 85 items he struck down in the state's $14.2 million annual budget.

In several states, a governor can reduce particular appropriations; this power is called the **reduction veto.** In 19 states, governors can exercise what is called an **amendatory veto,** which allows the governor to return a bill to the state legislature with suggested language changes, conditions, or amendments. In this last case, legislators must decide to accept the governor's recommendations or approve the bill in its original form, which in some cases requires a majority vote and in other cases a three-fifths or supermajority vote.

State legislatures can override a governor's veto; in most states, it takes a two-thirds majority of both legislative chambers. Some governors, like Wisconsin's Tommy Thompson, vetoed thousands of legislative measures. New York Governor George Pataki vetoed

1,379 provisions the legislature sent him in 1998.[16] Governors on average veto about 4 percent of the bills sent to them, but only about 2 percent of gubernatorial vetoes are overridden by legislatures.[17] Most governors believe the veto power should be used sparingly. Indeed, some observers think too frequent use of the veto is a sign of gubernatorial weakness because an effective governor usually wins battles through negotiations rather than by confronting state legislators.[18]

Legislators in several states have established a *veto session*—a short session following adjournment—so they can reconsider any measures vetoed by their governor. This is clearly an effort to reassert the legislature's check-and-balance authority in relation to the governor. Most states using veto sessions have legislatures that meet for a limited time; in full-time legislatures, a veto session would be unnecessary.

Executive Orders

One long-standing power of governors is their authority to issue **executive orders** that have the force of law. Even though executive orders differ from statutes or formal acts passed by the legislature, they have almost the same binding effect. Depending on the state, governors get their authority to issue executive orders from implied powers as chief executive, from specific constitutional grants, or from delegations of authority by their state legislatures. Executive orders supplementing a law are both more detailed and more important than the general guidelines contained in legislation. Governors have issued executive orders during such emergencies as natural disasters and energy crises, in compliance with federal rules and regulations, and to create advisory commissions. State legislators are sometimes angered by sweeping executive orders. They insist that they, not the governors or the courts, should be the primary lawmakers in a state.

In 1996, Governor Kirk Fordice of Mississippi issued an executive order banning same-sex marriages in his state. The intended effect of Fordice's executive order was to prevent county clerks from issuing marriage licenses for gays or lesbians after a similar measure had failed to win passage in the state's legislature.[19] Gay rights activists, joined by the Mississippi American Civil Liberties Union, criticized the governor, saying he was trying to circumvent the state legislature, adding that the state's constitution makes it plain that it is the legislature, not the governor, that defines the authority and duty of county clerks. In this instance, this governor's executive order brought about what the state legislature had not been able to approve.

Governors do not have to issue executive orders to make an impact on state and local government, however. Even though he opposed same-sex marriages, Governor Mitt Romney of Massachusetts reminded local officials in 2004 they had to follow the state's Supreme Judicial Court decision allowing same-sex marriage of state residents. At the same time, however, he also said he intended to use a 1913 law to prohibit the marriage of same-sex couples from other states. Such marriages would be null and void under his interpretation, he argued, thereby preventing Massachusetts from drawing same-sex couples from across the United States.[20]

Commander in Chief of the National Guard

Emergencies enhance the authority of an executive because they call for decisive action. As commander in chief of the state's National Guard when it is not in federal service, a governor may use this force when local authorities are inadequate—in case of riots, floods, and other catastrophes. The National Guard has played a role in the aftermath of floods in midwestern states, riots and earthquakes in California, fires in Florida, and hurricanes throughout the southeastern states. In most states, the state police are also available for emergencies.

Congress provides most of the money to operate the National Guard. This fact, along with the supremacy clause of the U.S. Constitution, gives Congress and the president the power to take charge of a state's National Guard even against the wishes of a governor. In 1990, the Supreme Court ruled unanimously that Congress can authorize the president to call National Guard units to active duty and send them outside the United States despite the objections of the governors, several of whom had tried to keep President Ronald Reagan from calling their respective National Guards to training exercises in Honduras.[21] States could if they wish provide and maintain from their own funds a defense force exempt from being drafted into the armed forces of the United States, but none has done so.

Although governors are technically in charge of their state's National Guard, the president can call their troops into service during national emergencies. By the spring of 2004, approximately 42 percent, or 144,000 soldiers, of the states' 345,000 Army National Guard were either deployed in Iraq or preparing for deployment. The heavy deployment was of particular concern in states such as Idaho, Montana, and Colorado, where National Guard troops play an important role in fighting summer forest fires, and in Gulf states such as Florida and Texas, where they play a critical role in disaster relief and policing in the wake of hurricanes.[22]

Pardon Power

In half the states, governors may pardon violators of state law; in the other states, they share this duty with a pardoning board. Except in cases of impeachment or certain specified crimes, the governor may pardon the offender, commute a sentence by reducing it, or grant a reprieve by delaying the punishment. The governor is normally assisted by pardon attorneys or pardon boards that hold hearings and determine whether there are sufficient reasons for a pardon.

A Tennessee governor, Ray Blanton (1975–1979), caused considerable controversy and sparked a federal investigation when he pardoned or paroled several dozen convicts just before leaving office in 1979. Critics charged that some of these convicts allegedly "purchased" their releases. Blanton's misuse of his pardon powers created such a ruckus that his elected successor, Lamar Alexander, was sworn in early and the locks to the governor's office were quickly changed so Blanton was not able to enter the office, let alone grant any additional pardons. Seldom, however, is the pardon power the subject of such controversy, because it is generally administered with appropriate care.

Similar to the governor's pardon power is the authority for a governor to grant a stay of execution in death penalty cases. This is one of the most controversial aspects of executive power in states that provide for the death penalty.[23] Texas Governor George W. Bush came under attack during the 2000 presidential campaign for allowing more than 130 executions during his time in office, in part because another Republican governor, George Ryan of Illinois, had imposed a moratorium on executions earlier in the year. Ryan had long been a death penalty supporter, but he became persuaded that too many mistakes had been made by the courts in sentencing innocent people to death row. Indeed, 13 Illinois inmates in the past generation had been exonerated. "A series in *The*

Chicago Tribune found that of 266 capital cases that had been appealed, fully half have been reversed for a new trial or sentencing hearing. In more than 30 cases, lawyers representing death row inmates were disbarred or suspended."[24] During the moratorium, Ryan established a special committee to make recommendations regarding Illinois death penalty procedures. The Ryan Commission report recommended a series of reforms aimed at creating a more just system of capital punishment.[25] Before leaving office in early 2003, Ryan commuted all Illinois death sentences to prison terms of life or less.

Policy-Making Influence

A governor's policy influence in the legislature depends in part on his or her popularity and formal powers. Obviously, governors can send detailed policy and program messages to their legislature and argue for their programs. In some states, they can trade appointive jobs for legislative support, and they can also use their veto power to trade for votes. They can attract more public attention to their views than any single legislator can. Much depends on a governor's ability, political base, and personal popularity, as well as on the political situation in which he or she operates.

Some states have a long tradition of strong executive leadership, while others give their governors relatively weak powers. On paper at least, the governors of Pennsylvania and New York, for example, have strong constitutional powers, and usually have strong party organizations behind them, which enhance close ties with followers in their respective legislatures.[26]

On paper again, the governors of Nevada and Texas have much less formal power and preside over relatively independent departments and agencies. Yet governors of rural and smaller states generally have few other competing institutions or interests when it comes time to exercise policy leadership, while governors in large states face a number of competitors. "Power governors in large urbanized states have many others with whom they must compete—heads of major industries, media personalities, mayors of large cities, and even presidents of prestigious universities," comments political scientist Thad Beyle. "There are lots of big fish in a larger pond, which can mean that a governor may not be as powerful as it might first appear."[27]

Consider these two contrasting evaluations of the governorships in New York and Mississippi:

> The office of governor of the Empire State is surely not small. On the contrary, because of substantial grants of formal power in the state constitution, the historical exercise of such power by formidable incumbents, and widespread expectations that the governor provide leadership, the New York governor is one of the strongest in the nation.[28]
>
> Mississippi's governor remained less powerful than the state legislature. The large number of independent boards and commissions and independently elected executive officials limits his ability to effectively manage the executive branch. It is easy for agency heads to "go native" and reflect the views of their co-workers and clients rather than those of the chief executive. . . . The office of governor in Mississippi has nevertheless become more influential in recent years.[29]

Balanced against a governor's formal powers are great obstacles, which may include a hostile legislature, cutbacks in federal funding, a depressed state economy, corrupt party or administrative officials, regional tensions in the state (downstate versus upstate, east versus west, urban versus rural), special interests and lobbyists, a cynical press, an indifferent or apathetic public, the sheer inertia of a vast bureaucracy, antiquated civil service systems, and the reluctance of most citizens to get involved.[30]

Some western governors complain that many of their states' problems are caused by absentee landlords or the national government, which together control much land in the West. The federal government owns 83 percent of Nevada, 68 percent of Alaska, 65 percent of Utah, and 53 percent of Oregon. This land is managed, regulated, and overseen by a score of federal agencies, such as the National Park Service, the Forest Service, the Bureau of Land Management, the Fish and Wildlife Service, and the Department of Defense. Governors of western states find they must constantly negotiate with these many federal agencies. In contrast, states east of the Rockies have only small amounts of land owned by the federal government. In Kansas and Maine, for example, less than 1 percent of the land is owned by the federal government.[31]

Governors also find they must become preoccupied with daily housekeeping tasks, and this focus often collides with their efforts to define long-range priorities. Former Vermont Governor Madeleine Kunin recalls she had to fix problems as they happened and yet simultaneously had to define her policy vision for the future. "Finding the time, energy, and perspective to carry out a dual strategy was to be the physical and mental challenge of governing."[32] Even though management duties occupy a fair amount of time, many governors consider these the least glamorous of their responsibilities (see Table 6–2).

Although governors come to office hoping to introduce new programs and reforms, they often spend most of their time raising money just to keep things going; hence some governors are viewed as merely budget balancers rather than as leaders or shapers of a

---

TABLE 6–2   HOW GOVERNORS SAY THEY SPEND THEIR TIME

Activity	*Percentage of Time Spent**
Managing state government	29%
Working with the legislature	16
Meeting the general public	14
Performing ceremonial functions	14
Working with press and media	9
Working with federal government	7
Working with local governments	7
Carrying out political activities	6[†]
Recruiting and appointing	6
Doing miscellaneous activities (staff, interstate, reading, phoning)	16

SOURCE: Thad L. Beyle, "The Governor as Chief Legislator," *State Government*, Winter 1978, p. 3.

*Totals do not add to 100 percent but are averages of the governors' estimates of the time they devoted to the particular activities. Percentages based on responses from those scheduling gubernatorial time in 40 states.
†Plainly, some governors understate time spent campaigning for reelection.

state's future. The governor's role as leader of his or her political party also has an important impact on policy. The coalitions that governors form within their political parties help them put into effect the policies they desire. A governor's power increases in a state that has a competitive two-party system. In such a state, legislators of the governor's party are likely to work more closely with the governor to produce a successful legislative record.

Recent years have witnessed the election of a new breed of well-educated and able governors who have been effective in enlarging their policy-making roles: Jennifer Granholm in Michigan, Bill Richardson in New Mexico, Frank Murkowsi in Alaska, and Jeb Bush in Florida. Because many governors come to office with impressive legislative and administrative experience, they are more likely to be real executive heads of government, not mere figureheads. Some have initiated experimental welfare and job-training programs that have become models for others to emulate. Because states are now playing a larger role in planning and administering a wide range of social and economic programs, the managerial and planning ability of a governor is clearly important.

Governors and Media Relations

Governors often attempt to shape their influence through aggressive media outreach. Many worked effectively with the media during their gubernatorial campaign and therefore understand their potential. Once in office, however, governors are thrust into a defensive role rather than the offensive role they played during the election. Instead of running aggressive advertisements for their campaign, they are now under the media's magnifying glass, subject to scrutiny and dirt digging by reporters. They are quickly evaluated in light of campaign promises and in comparison with previous governors.[33]

Past governors have been very aware of the media, with a handful having professional backgrounds in reporting or public relations. For example, former governors Tom McCall of Oregon and Thomas Kean of New Jersey both had prior experience in public relations positions—McCall as a journalist and radio announcer and Kean as a state campaign chair for President Ford and a television reporter during the Reagan campaign. Governor Kean notes the importance of communication with the media: "The most important power the governor has is the power of communicating. If that isn't done properly, you lose your power very fast."[34]

But not all governors are effective in dealing with the media, nor do they necessarily enjoy it. As Minnesota's former Governor Jesse Ventura says of the media: "The American media are suffering from very serious problems, and now I've seen them first-hand. They have the most twisted set of biases I've ever seen. As their whipping-boy-of-choice, I've been in a unique position to see what the media have become. There are a few honorable exceptions, but for the most part, they're corrupt, shameless, and irresponsible as hell."[35]

Each governor tends to have a personal style in dealing with the media. Some are very vocal, preferring to host daily radio or television talk shows, while others prefer to avoid the spotlight unless necessary. To capitalize on the media's ability to disseminate information, governors have been known to request special time on television attempting to explain and make an argument for policy changes, especially tax increases. Others become visible by attending community functions such as building dedications or opening ceremonies or even crowning beauty queens. It is especially important for governors to be publicly active as a calming influence during an emergency situation.

During a disaster, such as an earthquake, hurricane, or terrorist action, governors have the ability to call out the National Guard and organize official aid groups. To visit, show concern for, and help ameliorate the suffering of involved families can do wonders for a governor's public opinion ratings. Governors must face public scrutiny, yet they can use the media to set and gain support for the state's agenda.[36]

MANAGING THE STATE

Governors and their senior staffs are also responsible for managing their state's executive branch, whether by providing strategic planning and vision, initiating policy, settling disputes among different agencies, promoting the state (attracting tourism, exports, and investment), recruiting top state administrative and judicial officials, developing the budget, or negotiating disputes with the federal government and with nearby states.

Much recent federal legislation turning programs over to the states specifically designates the governor as the chief planning and administrative officer. This role has given governors both more flexibility and more headaches. On one hand, governors can now dispense federal funds as a form of patronage, supporting services and programs for influential professional and local communities. On the other hand, this new intergovernmental relations role requires more time, more staff, and constant negotiations both with the "feds" and with local interest group leaders vying for the money or services involved.

Some reformers have suggested that all state agencies should be accountable to the governor all the time, but others believe politics should be kept out of the day-to-day operations of a state agency. For example, how much influence should a governor have over the running of the department of corrections in a state? Should public agencies respond to fluctuations in public opinion or to a governor's political mood? Which policy decisions should be made by professionals and experts, and which should be controlled by elected officials or by partisan appointees?

Modernizing State Government

Governors in recent years have had more managerial control over their states as a result of the use of modern management techniques: strategic planning, systems analysis, and sophisticated information technology and budgeting systems. In fact, a modern system of professional management has gradually replaced the old "buddy system" in which governors relied on political pals to get things done.

In urban states with competitive party systems, such as New York, Illinois, New Jersey, Pennsylvania, Washington, and California, governors have considerable formal constitutional authority to organize their administrations as they see fit. Even in more rural states, such as South Dakota, scores of agencies have been consolidated into a few comprehensive units as the result of executive orders from the governors.

A few years ago, in the wake of highly publicized scandals, the South Carolina legislature agreed to abolish 75 state boards, folding them into 17 larger executive agencies. This restructuring also gave the governor the authority to hire and fire the directors of most of these agencies.[37]

During the past several decades, various reformers have urged that the governor be made the true manager of the executive branch, whether by consolidating agencies into a smaller number of more tightly controlled departments, giving the governor greater power to hire and fire senior executives, or modernizing state government through better information technology.

However, attempts to reorganize state governments have not received universal praise. In some states, reorganization commissions have submitted reports that were filed away and forgotten. Groups that profit from the existing structure can be counted on to resist change. So, too, can officials who fear loss of job or prestige. Also, legislators are sometimes reluctant to approve recommendations that might make a governor too powerful.

Many critics oppose not so much the idea of reorganization as the basic principle of strengthening executive power and responsibility, which has dominated the reorganization movement. Often, they say, there is little evidence to support the adoption of these reforms, and there is a real danger that reorganizers are overlooking basic values in their concern with saving money. Intent on efficiency and economy, reformers often fail to foresee the risks involved in creating a powerful chief executive where no effective party or legislative opposition exists to keep a strong governor in check.

Reformers agree that no one size of reform is right for every state. However, they maintain that the basic ideas—integrated authority, centralized direction, simplified structure, clear responsibility—are sound. In fact, it is more likely that narrow special interests not responsible to the voters will take over government when the administrative structure is cumbersome, confusing, and too spread out. The legislature can more effectively supervise an administration integrated under the governor's control than one in which responsibility is split.

Effects of Reorganization

Although large savings have been realized through centralized purchasing and the adoption of modern money management practices, it is difficult to measure the results of consolidating departments, strengthening the governor's control over the executive branch, or establishing an ombudsman office to handle citizen complaints. However, the best-governed states do seem to be those in which the administrative structure has been closely integrated under the governor.

Overall formal reorganization is not the only way states modify and modernize their governmental structures. Often they change in stages, copying innovations from other states. Certain states, in fact, serve as exporters of innovations. So does the federal government. When the federal government creates, say, the Department of Housing and Urban Development, states often respond by creating similar departments; when the federal government establishes the Department of Transportation, so do several of the states; and when the federal government creates a special White House–level office for trade, many governors set up their own offices for trade and export responsibilities.

Although governors are more powerful today than they have ever been, vigorous gubernatorial direction of a state's bureaucracy is still more the exception than the rule. Some governors fail to exploit their powers of appointment or budget setting. "Governors also have other tasks than functioning as chief bureaucrat. . . . Bureaucratic complexity also discourages involvement. Given these realities, involvement with state bureaucracies is very much a matter of governors picking their spots."[38]

Several former governors, including Mario Cuomo of New York and Pete Wilson of California, experimented with private sector reforms such as total quality management

(TQM) and performance-based pay initiatives, but these reforms were opposed by public employee labor unions. Such proposals have also been viewed as impractical: "From TQM to vision statements to performance measurements to virtual organizations, the management theories and trends come thick and fast—faster than a lot of government employees can keep up with them."[39] Moreover, management reform often gets cast aside when one governor takes over from another, as when Republican Governor George Pataki replaced Democratic Governor Mario Cuomo in New York.

"Although the analogy between a governor and a private sector chief executive is apt," writes political scientist Thad Beyle, "governors have a distance to go before possessing comparable power of appointment and removal."[40] Many governors don't have the flexibility in hiring and firing personnel that business executives have, and they must share control with various boards, commissions, and elected officials.

In sum, governors can be influential in leading certain reforms and introducing management improvements, but they are rarely as influential and as effective as most citizens assume is the case. All kinds of constitutional, legal, and political restraints put brakes on their attempts to bring about fundamental change. Still, in good economic times, governors are generally able to begin new programs and improve the performance of existing state operations.

OTHER STATEWIDE ELECTED OFFICIALS

Other executive officials elected by the people in most states include the lieutenant governor, secretary of state, attorney general, treasurer, and auditor. (See Table 6–3 for an inventory of state elected officials.)

Lieutenant Governor

Forty-two states have a lieutenant governor, a post similar to vice president at the national level. In nearly half the states, the lieutenant governor is elected on the same ticket

---

TABLE 6–3   STATES WITH ELECTED OFFICIALS

Governor	50
Attorney general	44
Lieutenant governor	42*
State treasurer	40
Secretary of state	36
Superintendent of education	14
Agriculture commissioner	13
Comptroller	13
Insurance commissioner	11

*In Alaska, Hawaii, and Utah, one elected official serves as both lieutenant governor and secretary of state. In Tennessee, there is no lieutenant governor, but the Speaker of the state senate has the additional statutory title of lieutenant governor.

as the governor, and in those states, the job is indeed like that of the vice president—the job and its influence depend very much on the mood of the governor. In 26 states, the lieutenant governor presides over the state senate. In 39 states, the lieutenant governor becomes governor or acting governor in case of the death, disability, or absence of the governor from the state. Doubtless for this reason, more governors have sprung from this office than from other statewide elective offices. For example, in 2000, two lieutenant governors were elected governor: Judy Martz of Montana and Ruth Ann Minner of Delaware. And the lieutenant governor in Texas, Rick Perry, became governor there when George W. Bush moved to the White House. Perry won his own election in 2002. In 2004, Connecticut's lieutenant governor, M. Jodi Rell, became governor when Governor John Rowland resigned in the wake of allegations that he accepted special gifts from state contractors. Rowland almost certainly would have been impeached by the state legislature if he had not resigned.

In states where the governor and lieutenant governor are elected on the same ticket, the lieutenant governor is likely to be given some significant responsibilities. Still, many lieutenant governors have no statutory duties, and in some smaller states, being lieutenant governor is really a part-time job. In the states where the lieutenant governor is elected independently of the governor, the lieutenant governor can sometimes be a member of the opposition party, and he or she can become a thorn in the side of the chief executive. In states like Texas, where the lieutenant governor is elected separately, the lieutenant governor is sometimes as politically powerful as the governor.[41]

There is some reason to question whether lieutenant governors are really necessary. After all, eight states, including Arizona, Georgia, and New Jersey, run perfectly well without one. If their only job is to stand in waiting in case the governor dies, resigns, or is impeached, the replacement function could be performed by a state's attorney general, secretary of state, or the ranking member of the governor's party in the legislature.

Although the position of lieutenant governor has worked well in some states, the view persists that lieutenant governors are often in search of job assignments that make them look important. The staffs and cabinets that are currently growing up around governors make the governor's chief of staff more of a deputy governor than most lieutenant governors. Moreover, many candidates for lieutenant governor appear to seek the post primarily for the name recognition and statewide experience to advance their political careers. In sum, the value to the state of the often obscure office of lieutenant governor is debatable.[42]

Attorney General

The attorney general—the state's chief lawyer—gives advice to state officials, represents the state before the courts, and in some states supervises local prosecutors. Some state attorneys general have real authority over local prosecutors and may prosecute cases on their own initiative, although in most states, criminal prosecution remains under the control of the local county prosecutor. In many states, attorneys general have taken the lead as champions of the consumer and protectors of the environment. They have launched major investigations into the insurance industry and into business practices. They have also led the fight against the tobacco companies and have waged antitrust investigations against corporations such as Microsoft.[43] New York State's attorney general, Eliot Spitzer, became a nationally recognized figure and *Time* magazine's 2002 Crusader of the Year through his investigations of Wall Street fraud, and he used that visibility to build a formidable campaign for governor in 2006.

An additional power of the attorney general is to make sure the state's laws are implemented properly. Attorneys general work in narcotics enforcement, investigate illegal activities, and often concentrate on laws that affect public safety. For example, Florida's attorney general, Bob Butterworth, recently set up a hot line to help eliminate Medicaid fraud.[44] In California, due to power companies' recent noncompliance with laws and allegations of gouging of California citizens, Attorney General Bill Lockyer has filed complaints against four major power companies.[45]

Disputes between attorneys general and governors can be partisan if they belong to different parties or have conflicting ambitions, but disputes can also be issue-oriented. Thus governors in many states have their own staff lawyers to represent them in contests with attorneys general. The office is sometimes a stepping-stone to the governorship—indeed, the acronym AG is often said to stand for both Attorney General and Almost Governor.

Secretary of State

The secretary of state publishes the laws, supervises elections, and issues certificates of incorporation. In some states, the secretary issues automobile licenses and registers corporate securities. Voters in 36 states elect secretaries of state. In eight states, governors appoint people to this position. In three states, secretaries of state are elected by the legislature. And three states don't have this position at all.

Although all secretaries of state have some election function, their responsibilities differ greatly from state to state. However, all share a general commitment to increasing voter education and turnout. In 1998, the National Association of Secretaries of State launched the "New Millennium Project" to encourage greater participation among young Americans. Several states now send birthday cards with voter registration forms to every 18-year-old, while others have created challenges that pit colleges against each other in registration contests.

Treasurer and Auditor

The treasurer is the guardian of the state's money. Although in some states the job is largely ministerial, state treasurers generally have the responsibility of ensuring that cash is available to meet the obligations of the state and that all available funds are invested to maximize interest return.

The auditor in most states has two major jobs: to authorize payments from the state treasury and to make periodic audits of officials who handle state money. In Montana, the state auditor serves as insurance commissioner. Before money can be spent, the auditor must sign a *warrant* certifying that the expenditure is authorized by law and that the money is available in the treasury. This job is more accurately called the *preaudit* and is increasingly being assigned to a comptroller appointed by and responsible to the governor. Auditing *after* money has been spent, however, is a job most observers believe should be given to an officer responsible to the legislature. Even advocates of much more centralized administration believe that the auditor should not be responsible to the governor.

Other Officials

Such positions as superintendent of public education, agriculture commissioner, public utilities commissioner, comptroller, and insurance commissioner are less likely to be elected than treasurers or auditors. Putting positions like these on the ballot results in a longer ballot and voter fatigue; in one election, fully half the people who went to the polls failed to vote for superintendent of public instruction. The proliferation of elected officials also makes it more difficult for governors to manage and lead state government.

As part of the trend toward integrated administration, the duties of elected state officials have generally been limited to those specified in the state constitution. Some important functions have been given to officials appointed by the governor. In many states, the budget director appointed by the governor has a more important role than the elected treasurer or secretary of state. Yet elected officers can often control patronage, attract a following, and thus develop a political base from which to attack the governor's program and administration.

Sometimes progressive and controversial initiatives in state governments come from elected officials. An attorney general in Texas helped design and pass the Texas Open Records Act, one of the broadest and most strictly enforced freedom-of-information statutes in the country. A secretary of state in Massachusetts modernized election laws, helped enact campaign finance laws, and championed conflict-of-interest reforms. A state treasurer in Colorado battled to transfer some of his state's revenue deposits from a few large Denver banks to smaller banks around the state and devised incentives for these banks to lend money to students and small businesses and to support low-income housing and family farms.

THE REWARDS OF BEING A GOVERNOR

No one thinks governors have an easy job. Most governors earn praise for their leadership, and most governors enjoy solid public approval ratings.[46] Recent governors— Zell Miller of Georgia, Marc Racicot of Montana, Thomas J. Vilsack of Iowa, Gary Locke of Washington, Frank O'Bannon of Indiana, Mike Foster Jr. of Louisiana—became popular despite the political "heat" and the need to make tough decisions. "A governor achieves his personal best by being honest and by staying in touch with the people who elected him to serve them," says former Governor Lamar Alexander of Tennessee.[47] Former Governor Tom Kean of New Jersey echoed similar thoughts: "I have tried to show during my political career, and especially my years as governor, that responsible government can meet people's needs and bring them together, that government can make a difference in the way we live."[48]

Ultimately, the best governors are ones who have a keen sense of history and their own circumstance. A popular former governor of Utah, the late Scott Matheson, wrote that they have been the men and women who have the right combination of values "for quality service, the courage to stick to their convictions, even when in the minority, integrity by instinct, compassion by nature, leadership by perception, and the character to admit wrong, and when necessary, to accept defeat."[49]

S U M M A R Y

1. The job of governor is one of the most important and exacting in American political life. Governors are usually white male lawyers in their forties or fifties. At least three out of four governors who run again win reelection.

2. Today, a governor is expected to be the state's chief policy maker, the architect of the state budget, the chief manager of the state administration, and the political and symbolic leader of the state. The governor also plays an increasingly complex role as the crucial link between the national and local governments.

3. Governors have many formal powers. The most important are their appointive and budgetary powers. Governors also have veto and pardon powers and the power to issue executive orders. They are commanders in chief of the National Guard. But a governor's formal powers mean little if he or she is not a persuasive communicator with good judgment and the capacity to focus simultaneously on daily tasks and long-range priorities. Governors who are effective with the media find this an additional source of informal power. Governors help set the policy agenda and frame the debate on important public issues. Yet governors, as a general rule, have more responsibility than power.

4. Over the past generation, reforms in management and organization have strengthened most governorships. Most governors have gained powers that enable them to achieve more of their goals. But constitutional, legal, and political restraints continue to limit their efforts. Thus few governors have an easy tenure, and it is generally agreed that public demands and expectations on governors today are higher than ever.

5. In addition to a governor, the voters in most states also elect other statewide officials such as a lieutenant governor, secretary of state, attorney general, and state treasurer. In about half of the states, the governor and lieutenant governor run as a team ticket, but elsewhere this is not the case, and all other statewide elected officials run separately. Many of the officials play important political and policy roles in their states, and many current governors previously served in some other statewide elected capacity.

F U R T H E R   R E A D I N G

LAMAR ALEXANDER, *Steps Along the Way: A Governor's Scrapbook* (Nelson, 1986).

CECIL ANDRUS AND JOEL CONNELLY, *Cecil Andrus: Politics Western Style* (Sasquatch Books, 1998).

THAD L. BEYLE, ED., *Governors and Hard Times* (CQ Press, 1992).

THOMAS M. CARSEY, *Campaign Dynamics: The Race for Governor* (University of Michigan Press, 2000).

THOMAS E. CRONIN AND ROBERT D. LOEVY, *Colorado Politics and Government* (University of Nebraska Press, 1993).

ROBERT S. ERIKSON ET AL., *Statehouse Democracy: Public Opinion and Policy in the American States* (Cambridge University Press, 1993).

EARL H. FRY, *The Expanding Role of State and Local Governments in U.S. Foreign Affairs* (Council on Foreign Relations Press, 1998).

VIRGINIA GRAY, RUSSELL HANSON, AND HERBERT JACOB, EDS., *Politics in the American States: A Comparative Analysis*, 7th ed. (CQ Press, 1999).

MADELEINE M. KUNIN, *Living a Political Life* (Vintage, 1995).

GERALD C. LUBENOW AND BRUCE E. CAIN, EDS., *Governing California* (Institute of Governmental Studies Press, 1997).

SARAH M. MOREHOUSE, *The Governor as Party Leader* (University of Michigan Press, 1998).

DAVID OSBORNE, *Laboratories of Democracy: A New Breed of Governor Creates Models for National Growth* (Harvard Business School Press, 1988).

GEORGE PATAKI WITH DANIEL PAISNER, *Pataki: An Autobiography* (Viking, 1998).

ALAN ROSENTHAL, *Governors and Legislatures: Contending Powers* (CQ Press, 1990).

SUE THOMAS AND CLYDE WILCOX, *Women and Elective Office* (Oxford University Press, 1998).

TOMMY G. THOMPSON, *Power to the People: An American State at Work* (HarperCollins, 1996).

JESSE VENTURA, *Do I Stand Alone?* (Pocket Books, 2000).

JESSE VENTURA, *I Ain't Got Time to Bleed* (Signet, 2000).

See also the quarterly *Spectrum: The Journal of State Government; Governing; State Policy Reports;* and *State Government News;* see also the valuable University of Nebraska Press series on state politics in the individual states, each of which has a chapter on governors.

The National Governors' Association publishes a variety of surveys, reports, and studies, including the weekly *Governors' Bulletin* and the *Proceedings of the National Governors' Association* annual meetings. These and related documents can be purchased by writing to the National Governors' Association, 444 N. Capitol Street NW, Washington, D.C., 20001.

JUDGES AND JUSTICE IN THE STATES

7

Although we hear more about federal judges than about their state counterparts, most of the nation's judicial business is conducted by the 29,000 state and municipal judges. Put into perspective: federal courts have almost 2 million annual criminal, civil, and bankruptcy filings, whereas state courts confront over 92 million cases, most of which are traffic related (over 55 million).[1] Most state judges are white males, but this imbalance is changing rapidly. Nationwide there are about 5,000 female state court judges, about one in five, and they are now represented on all but one state supreme court (Indiana).[2] State judges preside over most criminal trials, settle most lawsuits between individuals, and administer most estates. They have a vital role in determining who gets what, where, when, and how. Thus they have a crucial role in making public policy.

State judges have the final say—most of the time. Through **writs of habeas corpus**—petitions to federal courts alleging that petitioners are being held by a state as the result of a proceeding that denies them due process of law in violation of the U.S. Constitution—criminal defendants may occasionally get federal district judges to review the actions of state courts. Or if state judges have to interpret the meaning of the U.S. Constitution, a national law, or a national treaty—that is, if the case raises a *federal question*—the losing party may request that the U.S. Supreme Court review the decision of the highest state court to which it may be taken under state law. Of the hundreds of thousands of decisions by state judges each year, very few are reviewed by the U.S. Supreme Court.

In recent decades, state courts have become more prominent in the political life of their state. In many states, a **new judicial federalism** has emerged, with judges interpreting the bill of rights in their state constitutions more broadly than the U.S. Supreme Court has in applying the national Bill of Rights, in such areas as the right of privacy, public school financing, and equal protection of the law.[3] There has also been a revolution in **tort law**—law relating to compensation for injuries to person, reputation, or property. This "tort revolution" has flooded state courts as more people sue more often about more disputes. For example, *product liability suits* are brought by people who believe they have been injured as the result of faulty products, and *malpractice suits* are brought by people who believe they have been injured as the result of mistakes by doctors, hospitals, lawyers, and other professionals. And there have been notable increases in cases relating to property rights and breaches of contract. However, this has triggered a backlash against the explosion of tort filings, and many states have instituted legislative tort reforms making it more difficult to bring lawsuits.

There has also been a significant increase in criminal cases as people press for tougher action against criminals. About half of the states have passed so-called three-strikes-and-you're-out laws, which prescribe a mandatory life sentence after three felony convictions.[4] These felony cases are threatening to overwhelm our courts and our prisons.

As state courts have become more active in our political life, state judges have become embroiled in controversial issues. And as the public has grown more sophisticated about the importance of judges as policy makers, judicial politics in the states is becoming a significant feature of the political landscape.

THE STRUCTURE OF STATE COURTS

Each state has its own court system. Because the 50 systems vary, it is difficult to generalize about them. For convenience, we categorize and discuss state courts as (1) minor courts of limited jurisdiction, (2) trial courts of general jurisdiction, and (3) appellate courts (see Figure 7–1).

Minor Courts

In most states, minor courts handle **misdemeanors**—relatively minor violations of state and local laws—as well as traffic cases and civil suits involving small amounts of money. In some places, they also hold preliminary hearings and set bail for more serious charges. **Felonies** are serious crimes tried in trial courts; the penalty for which can range from imprisonment in a penitentiary for more than a year to death. Decisions of the minor courts may be appealed and in most instances tried *de novo*—that is, tried all over again without reference to what happened in the minor courts. In most places, these courts are financed and administered by the local unit of government—the township, city, or county. In cities, these minor courts are known as *municipal courts* and are often divided into traffic courts, family courts, small claims courts, and police courts. Paid *magistrates* trained in the law preside over most of these courts.

Although traditional justice of peace courts are being phased out, the *justice of the peace* system survives in some states (Arizona, Arkansas, Delaware, Louisiana, Montana,

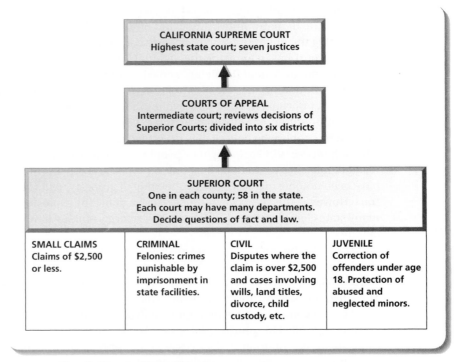

FIGURE 7–1 The California State Courts.
SOURCE: Guide to California Courts, at www.courtinfo.ca.gov/reference/guide.

Texas, and Wyoming) and in rural areas; in New York, these civil authorities are called *town justices.* Justices of the peace are elected for short terms, usually two to six years. They need not be trained in the law, and their authority is limited to performing marriages, notarizing papers, handling traffic violations, and hearing misdemeanors, usually those involving fines of less than $200. They also hear minor civil disputes. Because plaintiffs can often choose among several justices of the peace in a county, they may pick the one most likely to decide in their favor. Thus it has been said that the initials for *justice of the peace,* JP, stand for "judgment for the plaintiff."

Courts handling minor crimes are often so crowded that cases are "processed" with little time for individual attention. While many critics of the legal system contend that judges are too lenient and criminals are back on the streets too quickly, others charge that poor and ignorant defendants often spend days in jail waiting for their cases to go to trial. A new and apparently effective reform is the establishment of *court-watching groups.* In some cities, these groups are sponsored by organizations concerned with seeing that the courts treat fairly those charged with crimes. In other cities, groups are sponsored by organizations concerned that judges are too easy on defendants. Prosecutors, public defenders, and judges, it is alleged, become a comfortable work group, with little or no public scrutiny. Court watchers make these professionals more sensitive to the views of the general public.

Trial Courts of General Jurisdiction

Trial courts where cases first appear (**original jurisdiction**) are called county courts, circuit courts, superior courts, district courts, and common pleas courts. They administer common, criminal, equity, and statutory law. Some states maintain separate courts for criminal and civil matters. States generally also have special *probate courts* to administer estates and handle related matters. These courts are all *courts of record* in which trials take place, witnesses are heard, and juries render verdicts, although most cases are heard and decided by a judge. *Appellate courts* may review decisions of trial courts; however, most decisions of trial judges are not reviewed and are final. There is a growing recognition that these courts do more than apply the law; they also participate in the never-ending process of shaping the law and public policy.[5]

Appellate Courts

In a few states—Delaware, Montana, New Hampshire, Nevada, North Dakota, Rhode Island, West Virginia, and Vermont—trial court decisions are appealed directly to the state supreme court. (In North Dakota, the supreme court can assign cases to a court of appeals composed of three judges chosen from among the trial judges.) Most states, however, have intermediate appeals courts that fit into the system in much the same way that the United States courts of appeals fit into the federal structure.

All states have a *court of last resort*, usually called the supreme court. In Maine and Massachusetts, the court of last resort is called the supreme judicial court; in Maryland and New York, this court is called the court of appeals; in West Virginia, it is the supreme court of appeals. And if that is not confusing enough, in New York, the trial courts are called supreme courts. Texas and Oklahoma have two courts of last resort—a supreme court that handles civil matters and a court of criminal appeals.

Unless a federal question is involved, state supreme courts are the highest tribunal to which a case may be appealed. State courts of last resort have five to nine judges; most have seven. Each state court has developed its own method of operating, with the pattern and practices varying widely among the states. Of the more than 60,000 decisions by state supreme courts, only 2 percent are appealed to the U.S. Supreme Court, which reviews less than 1 percent of all appeals.[6]

All state judges of all state courts take an oath to uphold the supremacy of the U.S. Constitution, and all state judges have the power of **judicial review.** That is, they may refuse to enforce, and may restrain state and local officials from enforcing, state laws or regulations or actions if they conclude that these conflict with the state constitution or the U.S. Constitution. State judges may also declare actions of federal officials or federal laws or regulations to be in conflict with the U.S. Constitution, subject to final review by the U.S. Supreme Court.

State supreme courts have also led the way in making judicial decisions available on the Internet. All have Web sites, and about 98 percent provide access to written opinions and decisions, along with other information, and 10 percent make oral arguments available.[7] The Web site of the National Center for State Courts (www.ncsconline.org) provides links to state court Web sites.

State Courts and State Politics

Judges are a much more prominent part of the American political scene, at both the national and state levels, than in other countries. But state courts differ from federal courts in several ways:

1. State judges are more likely to decide cases involving their legislative and executive branches than the U.S. Supreme Court is with respect to congressional and presidential matters.[8] State judges are likely to be part of the state's legal culture, since most of them have been educated in the state's law schools.[9]

2. State judges are unconstrained by the doctrine of federalism in dealing with local units of government.

3. State judges are much less constrained than federal courts from hearing cases brought by taxpayers. In federal courts, persons lack *standing to sue*—the legal right to sue—unless they show some immediate personal injury. Furthermore, in nine states, the state supreme court can give advisory opinions at the request of the governor or state legislature. An **advisory opinion** is an opinion unrelated to a particular case that gives a court's view about a constitutional or legal issue.

4. Unlike federal judges, most state judges serve for limited terms and stand for election, so they can claim to be representatives of the people. "As elected representatives, like legislators, they feel less hesitant to offer their policy views than do appointed judges."[10] In addition, if there is dissatisfaction with a decision of a state supreme court, it can be more readily set aside than a decision of the U.S. Supreme Court can.[11]

HOW JUDGES ARE CHOSEN

Judges are selected in four different ways (see Figure 7–2): appointment by the governor, election by the legislature, popular election, or a modified appointment plan known as the Missouri Plan.

Appointment by the Governor and Election by the Legislature

In Delaware, Hawaii, Maine, New Jersey, New York, and Vermont, judges are appointed by the governor and confirmed by the state senate. In Delaware and Massachusetts, governors select appointees from names submitted by judicial nominating commissions. Election by the legislature is the constitutional practice in Connecticut, Rhode Island, South Carolina, and Virginia. However, we need to look beyond the formal election procedures. "A majority of the judges serving in states utilizing an elective judiciary . . . are in fact initially appointed by the governor to fill mid-term vacancies, usually occasioned by the retirement or death of sitting judges . . . and these appointed judges are overwhelmingly favored in their first electoral bids following appointment."[12]

In addition to the formal process of nomination and selection, there are several informal processes. Lawyers interested in becoming judges may make their interest known either directly or indirectly to party officials; leaders of the local bar associations may promote favored members; various members of the bar may seek out candidates

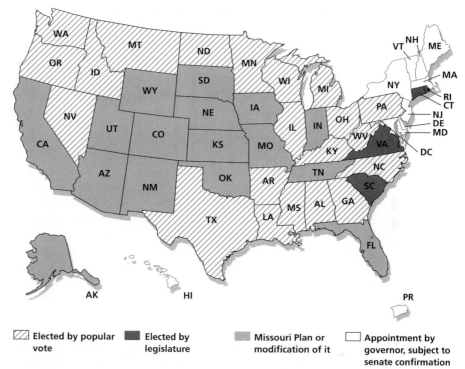

FIGURE 7–2 **Method for Selection of Judges of the Court of Last Resort.**

Legend:

- Elected by popular vote
- Elected by legislature
- Missouri Plan or modification of it
- Appointment by governor, subject to senate confirmation

and recruit them. Political leaders and interest groups also participate. Following such suggestions, the names go through the formal appointment process.[13]

Popular Election

In nearly half the states, judges are chosen in elections. Over 85 percent of all state and local judges face elections, far more than the number of elected state legislators and executive officials. Appellate court judges in eight states face partisan elections, 13 states hold nonpartisan elections, and another 19 states have retention elections for state judges.[14]

Some states, mostly in the West and upper Midwest, hold *nonpartisan* primaries for nominating judicial candidates and elect them on nonpartisan ballots. But nonpartisan judicial elections do not necessarily mean that political parties are not involved. In at least half of the states with nonpartisan judicial elections, parties actively campaign on behalf of candidates. Some states try to isolate judicial elections from partisanship by holding them separately from other elections.

In 1986, California amended its constitution to forbid political parties from endorsing candidates for judicial office. However, federal courts declared the proposition unconstitutional, and California political parties are once again endorsing judicial candidates. Apparently the prevailing view, as Justice Thurgood Marshall observed, is that "the prospect that voters might be persuaded by party endorsements is not a *corruption* of the democratic political process; it *is* the democratic political process."[15]

In recent years, most states have adopted provisions similar to the American Bar Association's code of judicial conduct that bar judicial candidates from telling the electorate anything about their views on legal and political matters—whether they are in favor, for example, of punishing criminals harshly or of expanding privacy rights. A "chief justices' summit" was convened in 2000 by the chief justices of the 17 most populous states with judicial elections and recommended reforms, including public funding for judicial elections and closer monitoring of judicial campaigns. Some states have gone further; the Minnesota Supreme Court, for instance, prohibited judicial candidates from soliciting campaign contributions, declaring their party affiliation, or publicly voicing their positions on controversial issues. But the U.S. Supreme Court struck down Minnesota's ban on judicial candidates' announcing their position on controversial legal and political matters as a violation of the First Amendment guarantee of free speech.[16] State and federal courts in Alabama, Georgia, Michigan, Ohio, and other states have also handed down decisions that are "a roadblock for efforts to curb the increasingly raucous nature of judicial politics."[17]

Until recently, there was little interest in judicial elections, and voter turnout tended to be low. But judicial elections are becoming increasingly costly and spirited. In the 2000 elections, candidates for state supreme courts raised an unprecedented $45 million, over 60 percent more than in 1998 and double that spent in 1994. Interest groups in five states with the most hotly contested judicial races raised an additional $16 million.[18] Special-interest groups focus attention on judges whose decisions they find objectionable. The issues vary from election to election and from state to state. In some states, the issue has been the death penalty. In Texas and California, efforts to limit liability lawsuits and damage awards have led to campaign clashes over judicial candidates, with trial lawyers, consumers, and union groups on one side and business interests on the other. In Idaho, one candidate for the supreme court campaigned on a platform that the theory of evolution could not be true—and won. In Wisconsin, the chief justice won reelection, although she had to fight for her seat and felt compelled to explain why she had once allowed an aerobics class in the court's hearing room. An Illinois judge was unseated because of his decisions in abortion cases. Judges now have to act like politicians and "feel they are under increasing pressure to be accountable to public opinion."[19] The image of impartial courts may well become a casualty of the increasingly heated politics of judicial campaigns and elections.

The costs of judicial elections are escalating. Critics charge that the need to raise large sums for their campaigns compromises the impartiality of judges and judicial candidates. Judicial campaigns have been especially expensive in Alabama, Illinois, Michigan, Mississippi, and Ohio, in which almost $35 million was spent on state supreme court candidates in those five states alone.[20] In many states that elect judges, it is increasingly clear that judicial candidates are dependent on a small number of law firms, businesses, or special-interest groups, such as the U.S. Chamber of Commerce and the Business Roundtable, for their campaign funds.[21]

In response to the growing cost of state judicial elections, the American Bar Association, the American Judicature Society, and other organizations are promoting the public financing of state judicial campaigns and elections.[22] Two states, Wisconsin and North Carolina, provide public financing for some judicial elections. Wisconsin has had publicly financed elections for state supreme court justices since the 1970s; candidates are eligible for $97,000 in state money if they agree to a $215,000 spending limit. The system is paid for through a one dollar check-off contribution on income tax returns, and has been historically underfinanced. In 2004, North Carolina's Judicial Campaign Reform Act went into effect. Under it, all appellate-level judicial races are nonpartisan, and candidates who agree to fund-raising and spending limits receive public financing in the general election. The public financing of judicial elections is also under consideration in a number of other states, including Idaho, Illinois, New York, and Texas.

MINORITY REPRESENTATION The one-person, one-vote rule that applies to legislative elections does not apply to judicial elections.[23] States may create judicial districts so that one judge "represents" many more voters than another judge. However, although there is no requirement that states elect judges, if they choose to do so, the federal Voting Rights Act of 1965 applies to these judicial elections.[24]

Because the Voting Rights Act of 1965 forbids any practice or procedure that dilutes the voting power of minorities, it raises a question about the constitutionality of at-large judicial elections. When judges are elected at large for a city or a state, African American and Hispanic candidates sometimes find it difficult to get elected. African American and Hispanic voters tend to be concentrated in the inner cities or in certain geographical areas; thus their impact is diluted in citywide or statewide elections. For example, in a state in which the population consists of 20 percent African American voters, 20 percent Hispanic voters, and 60 percent Anglo voters, with five judges to be elected on a statewide basis, few if any African American judges or Hispanic judges will be elected. Some Hispanics and African Americans argue that the solution is to divide such a state into five districts, with one judge elected in each district, and draw district lines in such a way that African Americans and Hispanics make up a majority of voters in as many districts as possible, giving them a chance to elect at least one of their own.

Merit Selection: The Missouri Plan

Many lawyers and political scientists have argued in favor of some kind of selection procedure in which there is a screening process before judges are appointed or elected to ensure that only candidates of merit will be considered. Merit systems are used in 16 states.

One of the oldest merit plans is the Missouri Plan.[25] The **Missouri Plan,** as used in most states, provides that when a judicial vacancy occurs, a special *nominating commission* (usually composed of three lawyers elected by the bar, three citizens appointed by the governor, and the chief justice) nominates three candidates.[26] The governor selects one, who then serves as a judge for at least a year. At the next general election, the voters are asked, "Shall Judge X be retained in office?" If a majority of the voters agree, the judge serves a new full term (typically six to 12 years); if not, another person is selected by the same procedure. At the end of his or her term, the judge may ask to have his or her name placed on the ballot, and the voters are again asked whether they want to retain that judge in office.[27] These uncontested elections, in which judges run against their own record, are called *retention elections,* and some require a supermajority vote.

California has a slightly different form of merit selection. The governor appoints judges to the supreme court and the appellate court for 12-year terms, with the approval

CHANGING FACE OF AMERICAN POLITICS

WOMEN AND MINORITIES ON STATE SUPREME COURTS

State supreme courts were once composed overwhelmingly of white males. But women and minorities now constitute over 30 percent of the judges on state supreme courts. In 2003–2004, there were 92 women on state courts of highest resort, and in two states—New York and Washington—they made up over 50 percent of the bench. The New Mexico state supreme court has the largest number of Hispanic judges (60 percent of the bench). African American judges now sit in more than 20 percent of state high courts in Florida, Georgia, Indiana, Tennessee, and Texas. Asian and Pacific Islander judges sit on two state supreme courts, in California and Hawaii.

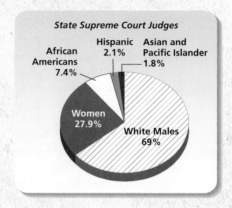

State Supreme Court Judges

Hispanic 2.1%
Asian and Pacific Islander 1.8%
African Americans 7.4%
Women 27.9%
White Males 69%

SOURCE: American Judicature Society at www.ajs.org/js/ select.htm; American Bar Association, *The Directory of Minority Judges of the United States,* 3d ed. (American Bar Association, 2001).

of the Commission on Judicial Appointments. The commission consists of the attorney general, chief justice, and senior appellate presiding justice for supreme court appointments or the senior presiding justice in the appellate district for appellate court appointments. In the next statewide election, the judge runs against his or her own record. The governor appoints trial judges to six-year terms; they may be challenged when seeking reelection, but their names do not appear on the ballot if they are running unopposed.

Even more of a hybrid is the system used in New Mexico, where a judicial nominating commission sends names to the governor, who selects a judge. At the next general election, an opponent nominated in the other party's primary may challenge the judge in a partisan election. If no opponent is nominated, the incumbent gets a "free ride." Whoever wins that election then serves one term and thereafter runs against his or her own record in a retention election.

Until recently, retention elections generated little interest and low voter turnout.[28] In all, of the almost 4,600 judicial retention elections since 1960, fewer than 60 judges have been removed by voters, although a few judges have decided not to run when they realized they might fail to be retained.[29] Recently, some state supreme court justices have been vigorously challenged in retention elections, especially when their decisions differed appreciably from the mainstream of public opinion and aroused the hostility of significant special interests. Frequently, the charge was that the judge was "soft on crime." Interest groups have learned that it is relatively easy to target incumbents, but because of constraints on the way judicial candidates are expected to campaign, it is "difficult for targeted judges to defend themselves."[30]

Most voters know little about judges, and what information they get comes from interested parties and persons, especially those who dislike what the judges have done. To provide a more balanced picture, a few states—Alaska, Utah, Colorado, Arizona, Tennessee—have tried to supply more neutral information about judicial performance. In Colorado, an *evaluation committee* in each judicial district—jointly appointed by the chief justice, governor, president of the senate, and speaker of the house—disseminates information through newspaper supplements, including a final recommendation of "retain" or "do not retain."[31] In Alaska, a judicial council composed of three lawyers, three nonlawyers, and the chief justice provides evaluations that are widely publicized.[32] In Utah, the Judicial Council—consisting of the chief justice, another justice, an appellate court judge, five district court judges, two juvenile court judges, three other lower court judges, a state bar representative, and the state court administration—certifies incumbents, and this certification, or lack of it, is indicated on the ballot.

Even though contested retention elections are the exception, sitting judges are aware that if they make decisions that offend organized interest groups, they may face opposition the next time their names are placed on the ballot. Whether these pressures threaten the independence of the courts or are necessary to ensuring judicial accountability within our political system in which judges play such an important role remains a matter of the political debate.[33]

The Appointive Versus the Elective System

For more than 200 years, people have debated the merits of an appointive versus an elective system for the selection of judges. Those who favor the appointive method contend that voters are generally uninformed about candidates and are not competent to assess legal learning and judicial abilities. Popular election, they claim, puts a premium on personality, requires judges to enter the political arena, and discourages many able lawyers from running for office. They also contend that the elective process conceals what is really going on. Absent name recognition, voters go for party labels, which are increasingly less significant as indicators of ideology.[34] In addition, because retirement and death create many vacancies, it is often the governor who selects the judges. The governor makes an interim appointment until the next election, and the temporary appointee usually wins the election.

Those who favor judicial elections counter that judges should be directly accountable to the people. When judges are appointed, they may lose touch with the general currents of opinion of the electorate. Moreover, the appointive process gives governors too much power over judges. And even if judicial elections do not result in the defeat of many sitting judges, elections serve to foster accountability because judges do not want to be defeated and will try to maintain popular support. In general, bar associations, corporate law firms, and judges themselves tend to favor some kind of merit selection system; plaintiffs, attorneys, women's associations, minority associations, and labor groups are skeptical or opposed.

How Judges Are Judged

Unlike federal judges who hold office during "good behavior"—essentially for life—most state judges are selected for fixed terms, typically six to 12 years. In Massachusetts, New Hampshire, and Puerto Rico, judges serve to age 70; in Rhode Island, they serve for life. Thirty-seven states and the District of Columbia mandate the retirement of judges at a certain age, usually 70.[35]

The states, rather than the national government, have taken the lead in establishing procedures to judge judges. Because impeachment has proved to be an ineffective means to remove judges, today each of the 50 states has a board, commission, or court to handle allegations of judicial misbehavior. Despite the objections of many judges, these commissions are most often composed of both nonlawyers and lawyers. They investigate complaints and hold hearings for judges who have been charged with improper performance of their duties or unethical or unfair conduct. Establishment of these commissions appears to have helped restore public confidence in the state judicial systems.[36]

For developments in the states and efforts to establish standards of conduct for judicial candidates, go to www.constitutionproject.org, the Web site of a nonpartisan group dedicated to protecting the independence of courts from partisan political attacks. See also the site of the Brennan Center's Project on Judicial Independence at the New York University Law School, www.brennancenter.org. You can also subscribe to its biweekly e-mail list to get summaries of news stories relating to judicial independence, judicial elections, and judicial appointments. Another valuable site for information about courts is that of the American Judicature Society, at www.ajs.org.

THE JUDICIAL REFORM MOVEMENT

Many reforms—court unification, centralized management, state financing, and merit selection—have been adopted, but waste and delay continue to plague our courts. We are, many charge, a "litigious society." Dockets are crowded, relief is costly, and inordinate delays are common.[37]

Proposed reforms for improving the administration of justice include the following:

- Judges should be selected by some kind of merit system that screens candidates in terms of their qualifications.

- Judges should be paid adequately so that they have the financial independence to concentrate on their work and so that successful lawyers will be willing to serve on the bench. In most states, judges' salaries are considerably less than the average incomes of practicing attorneys of the same age and experience. Judges are unable to earn anything beyond their salaries, and they must be cautious about investments in order to avoid conflicts of interest.

- Judges should serve for long terms so that they can make decisions without fear of losing their jobs.

- Rule-making powers should be given to the state supreme court or its chief justice. States are permitting judges to adopt procedural rules and codes of professional conduct. Most require lawyers to continue their education by taking refresher courses.

- Although no person should be appointed or elected to a court solely because of race, sex, or ethnic background, our courts need to become more representative of the communities they serve.[38]

- States should provide for alternative dispute resolution.

Alternative dispute resolution (ADR) refers to procedures that serve as alternatives to formal trials. These procedures include mediation, arbitration, conciliation, private judging, and advisory settlement conferences. From time to time, Congress has made grants to encourage states and localities to develop alternative dispute resolution mechanisms, especially for domestic relations issues. ADRs can be part of the established court system or separate from it in neighborhood justice centers or arbitration and mediation forums. Half the states operate arbitration programs as part of their court system.

Despite the trendy nickname "rent-a-judge," the rather old practice of hiring private decision makers has been revived. These decision makers, often retired judges and lawyers, are paid by the parties to the dispute, who agree in advance to abide by the outcome. In some states, appeals courts can review these decisions. There is some concern that these alternative practices are drawing the best lawyers into the private system, resulting perhaps in one system for the rich, a private one, and one for the poor, a public one.

The judicial reform movement has been successful, but like most reform movements, it has its critics and skeptics. Some observers maintain that court delay is not as serious a problem as has been charged and that the remedies may undercut our system of checks and balances. Delay, for example, often works to the advantage of defendants and their attorneys, who wish to postpone trials. At other times, prosecutors want delays in order to put pressure on defendants to accept guilty pleas. Lawyers may seek delays so that they can accept more clients.

No matter how "modernized" the management of court business, the flow of legal business grows continuously. Some people have proposed that traffic violations, automobile injury cases, and so-called victimless crimes be handled by some procedure other than a court trial. New York has led the way in removing from the courts minor traffic offenses that do not involve serious moving violations; other states are following its lead. No-fault insurance programs could reduce the large number of cases stemming from automobile accidents. Because half the people in prison, as well as half the trials that are held, involve victimless crimes such as using marijuana, *decriminalization* could substantially reduce the load on the courts. Six states, for example, have already repealed statutes on public drunkenness and now consider alcoholism a disease rather than a crime.

The reform of state judicial systems is enmeshed in partisan, ideological, and issue politics. Judges are but one part of the total justice system, and their operations are best studied in the context of the entire justice system.

THE JUSTICE SYSTEM

Justice is handled in the United States by a series of institutions that are only loosely connected to each other. In addition to judges, there are juries, prosecutors, defense counsels, public defenders, victims, and defendants. Parole, probation, and prison officials are also part of the justice system.

The Jury

Although most of us will never be judges or serve as professionals in the administration of justice, all adult citizens have an opportunity—even an obligation—to be jurors. Trial by jury in civil disputes is used less often these days; people make settlements prior to trial, elect to have their cases decided by a judge alone, or have their cases referred to a mediator or arbitrator. Furthermore, only a small fraction of criminal cases are actually disposed of by a trial before a jury. Still, jury trials, or the threat of them, remain a key feature of our justice system.

We have moved from a jury system in which service was restricted to white male property owners to one in which jury duty is the responsibility of *all* adult citizens. Today more time and energy are spent in trying to persuade (or coerce) people to serve on juries than in trying to exclude them. Because jury service may be time-consuming and burdensome, many busy people do their best to avoid serving. In the past, judges were often willing to excuse doctors, nurses, teachers, executives, and other highly skilled persons who pleaded that their services were essential outside the jury room. As a result, juries were often selected from panels consisting in large part of older people, those who were unemployed or employed in relatively low-paying jobs, single people, and others who were unable to be excused from jury service. Most states have reacted to these problems by making it more difficult to be excused. In addition, many states have adopted a "one-day, one-trial" policy, which makes jury service less frequent and less onerous. Because jury trials take more time than bench trials (trials before judges) and cost more, some states use juries of fewer than 12 people for some criminal trials. A few states also permit verdicts by less than a unanimous vote. The U.S. Supreme Court has approved these practices, provided the juries consist of at least six persons.[39]

Only a handful of those accused of committing a crime actually stand trial, and only 10 to 15 percent of those who are convicted are declared guilty as the result of a formal trial before either a judge or a jury. Most people who go to prison or who have to pay a criminal fine do so because they plead guilty.

The Prosecutor

The prosecutor is largely an American invention, one of the few governmental positions we did not inherit from England. The 18,000 prosecutors in the United States are usually county officials; most are locally elected and subject to little supervision by state authorities. In Connecticut, however, they are appointed by judges, in the Virgin Islands by the attorney general, and in New Jersey by the governor with the consent of the state senate. A prosecutor has "more control over life, liberty, and reputation than any other person in America."[40]

When presented with a case by the police, the prosecutor must decide first whether to file formal charges. He or she may (1) divert the matter out of the criminal justice system and turn it over to a social welfare agency; (2) dismiss the charges; (3) take the matter before a grand jury, which almost always follows the prosecutor's recommendation; or (4) in most jurisdictions, file an **information affidavit,** which serves the same function as a grand jury **indictment.**

A prosecutor who decides not to charge a person accused of some notorious crime is often subject to political pressure and public criticism. But for routine crimes, the prosecutor is politically in a better position to dismiss a charge than the police are.

Police are supposed to enforce every law all the time. Of course, it is impossible for them to do so, and they must exercise discretion.[41] But officers who fail to arrest a person alleged to have committed a crime could well be charged with failing in their duty. The prosecutor, however, has more leeway. In fact, the prosecutor is less likely to be criticized for dropping a case because of insufficient evidence than for filing a charge and failing to get a conviction.

Defense Counsel, Public Defenders, and Others

Many defendants cannot afford the legal counsel to which they are constitutionally entitled. The **assigned counsel system** is the oldest system to provide such defendants with an attorney, and it continues to be used, especially in rural areas. Judges appoint attorneys to represent defendants who cannot afford them. Most such attorneys are paid from the public treasury, but sometimes they are expected to do the work *pro bono*— for the public good. Seldom are they given funds to do any investigatory work on behalf of their clients. Often judges pick young lawyers just beginning their careers or old ones about to retire. Some less scrupulous lawyers make their living as assigned counsel; because it is often to their financial advantage to do so, they are quick to plead their clients guilty. They are known contemptuously as members of the "cop-out bar."[42]

Dissatisfaction with the assigned counsel system led to the creation of the **public defender system,** first started in Los Angeles in 1914 and now used in most big cities. Under this system, the government provides a staff of lawyers whose full-time job is to defend individuals who cannot pay. This system provides experienced counsel and relieves the bar of an onerous duty. Critics—including some defendants—protest that because public defenders are paid employees of the state, they are not likely to work as diligently on behalf of their clients as they would if they were specifically assigned to those clients. But most observers consider the defender system superior to the assigned counsel system. Steps are being taken to increase the pay of public defenders, protect their independence, and see that they win the confidence of the defendants they represent.

Victims and Defendants

When we talk about our criminal justice system, we sometimes forget the two most important parties in any criminal case—the victim of the crime and the person accused of it.

> The rights of victims or potential victims are not of the same order as the rights of the accused; the rights of the accused are constitutional rights spelled out in amendments, but nowhere in the Constitution is there any mention of the rights of victims or the public. The framers of the Constitution apparently were much more worried about protecting citizens against the government than about protecting citizens from each other.[43]

In general terms, defendants are likely to be "younger, predominantly male, disproportionately black, less educated, seldom fully employed, and typically unmarried. By the time the sorting process has ended, those sent to prison will consist of an even higher proportion of young, illiterate, black males."[44] Victims too—compared to the rest of the population—tend to be young, black or another minority, and uneducated. A substantial number of victims—either because of lack of knowledge of what to do or fear of doing it, or because, as in the case of rape victims, they believe they have little chance of proving their attackers to be guilty—never report crimes to police and prosecutors.

Our system puts the responsibility for prosecuting criminals on the government. In most instances, victims have no role other than as witnesses. They are not consulted about what the charge should be or asked what they think might be an appropriate penalty. The matter is strictly between the state, represented by the prosecutor, and the accused, represented by an attorney.

As a result, in recent decades a victims' rights movement has emerged. The movement originated with liberals (chiefly feminists concerned about the difficulty of winning prosecutions for rape and about the harsh treatment of female witnesses), but has gained the support of conservatives who consider the judicial system unfair to victims. In the 1984 Victims of Crime Act, Congress authorized federal funds, which are distributed by the Office of Crime Victims in the Department of Justice, to support state programs compensating victims and providing funds to some victims of federal crimes as well.

About 30 states have amended their constitutions to provide for a "victims' bill of rights," which makes it easier for victims to recover stolen property held in police custody, among other things. Many also give victims a chance to be heard when prosecutors file formal charges, when judges set bail and impose sentences, and when parole boards consider releasing prisoners. These victims' bills of rights are not without constitutional problems. The introduction of "victim-impact statements" by prosecutors seeking the death penalty, for instance, has been controversial. The U.S. Supreme Court, after first holding to the contrary, has upheld the right of prosecutors to make "victim-impact statements" to a jury in murder trials about the personal qualities of the victim and to allow the jury to consider evidence relating to the murder victim's personal characteristics and the emotional impact of the crime on the victim's family.[45]

Plea Bargaining

Although most criminal cases end with a guilty plea, common practice is for the prosecution to offer to reduce the seriousness of the charge and sentence if a defendant will enter a plea of guilty to a lesser crime. This practice is called a **plea bargain.** At one time, this practice was universally condemned. Many people still consider there is something improper about it, like bartering away justice.

Critics say that plea bargaining forces people to give up their rights; moreover, defendants often do not get off much more leniently by pleading guilty to lesser offenses than if they stood trial.[46] Defenders of plea bargaining contend it works, producing "a result approximating closely, but informally and more swiftly, the results which ought to ensue from a trial, while avoiding most of the undesirable aspects of that ordeal."[47] Many experts and investigators who have looked into the matter have endorsed plea bargaining.

Plea bargaining offers something to all involved. Prosecutors are able to dispose of cases quickly, avoid long and drawn-out trials, eliminate the risk of losing cases, and build up better "election-worthy" conviction records. The accused avoid the danger of being sentenced for more serious charges by pleading guilty to lesser offenses. Defense attorneys avoid "the dilemma of either incurring the expense of going to trial with a losing case or appearing to provide no service whatever to their clients."[48] By being able to handle more clients, they can also make more money. Judges are able to dispose of cases on their dockets more rapidly. In fact, were every case tried, it would overwhelm the judicial system.

Once the bargain between the prosecutor and the defendant's attorney has been accepted, the matter is taken before a judge. The judge goes through a series of questions to the defendant: "Are you pleading guilty because you are guilty? Are you aware of the maximum sentence for the crime to which you are entering a guilty plea? Were you coerced into pleading guilty or offered anything in return for it? Are you satisfied with the representation afforded by your attorney?" Following appropriate responses, the plea is accepted.[49] As long as defendants know what they are doing and enter into the bargain intelligently, they waive their constitutional rights to trial by pleading guilty and may not subsequently back out of the arrangement. Prosecutors must also live up to their side of the bargain.[50]

Sentencing

Due process must be observed in sentencing, which takes place in open court. The prisoner must be present and represented by counsel. In many places, social workers are assigned to help the judge determine the proper sentence. The judge also receives recommendations from the prosecution (and in some jurisdictions from the victim as well), hears the arguments of the defense, and then sets the sentence within the limits prescribed by the state.

The judge sets the sentence, but concerns about sentencing permeate the judicial system. One writer has put it this way:

> Because police and prosecutors screen out a large proportion of the doubtful cases, most left to be dealt with by the courts are those in which there is no serious dispute over the guilt or innocence of the defendant. . . . This fact sets the tone for the process. . . . Everyone concerned—the defense lawyers, the prosecutor, the judge, the probation officer—becomes aware of the fact that he or she is involved in a process where the primary focus is on deciding what to do with the people who are in fact guilty.[51]

Early in our national history, retribution, deterrence, and protection of society were the primary purposes of sentencing. Then rehabilitation became the major goal, and many people thought it was a more humane approach. The indefinite sentence became popular, motivated by the idea that each prisoner should be considered an individual suffering from an "illness." Each prisoner should be diagnosed, a course of treatment should be prescribed, and if and when such experts as psychologists and social workers could certify a "cure," the prisoner should be released.

Most political leaders and many scholars have become disillusioned about our ability to bring about "cures."[52] Others are disillusioned about the deterrent effect of imprisonment. A comprehensive study of rehabilitative efforts inside prisons, although rejecting the conclusion that "nothing works," nonetheless stated: "We do not know of any program or method of rehabilitation that could be guaranteed to reduce the criminal activity of released offenders.[53]

Moreover, judges may enjoy considerable discretion in sentencing, and they frequently give different sentences to defendants convicted of the same crime.[54] To reduce such disparities in sentencing, several reforms have been suggested, including establishing more precise legislative standards, creating advisory sentencing councils, and adopting the British practice of allowing appellate courts to modify sentences.

Disillusionment with rehabilitation and disparate sentencing by judges, combined with growing concerns about crime in the streets and mounting criticism about alleged judicial leniency, has fueled legislative action for mandatory minimum sentencing requirement and for narrowing judicial discretion.[55] State after state has adopted mandatory prison terms—also known as *determinate sentencing*—for more and more crimes. As noted earlier, a three-strikes-and-you're-out requirement has been adopted by many states.

Probation and Prisons

Prison populations in the United States are skyrocketing. Including juvenile facilities, the United States has over 2 million people behind bars, over 1.3 million in state and federal prisons, 621,000 in local jails, and more than 100,000 in juvenile facilities[56] (see Table 7–1). (*Prisons* are for committed criminals serving long sentences; *jails* are for short-term stays for persons awaiting trial and those with sentences of a year or less.) More people are imprisoned in the United States than in any other country. "The American inmate population has grown so large that it is difficult to fathom: imagine the combined population of Atlanta, St. Louis, Pittsburgh, Des Moines, and Miami behind bars."[57]

In addition to those in prison or jails, there are almost 4.5 million adult men and women on probation or parole. (*Probationers* are offenders courts have placed in community supervision rather than putting them in prison; *parolees* are people released after serving a prison term who are under supervision and are subject to being returned to prison for rule violations or other offenses.)

State and federal prison populations in the United States actually declined during the 1960s, but public demands for tougher sentences caused them to climb after 1969. The prison population has more than tripled since 1980 (see Figure 7–3), though declining slightly for the first time in 30 years in 2000.

TABLE 7–1   PRISONERS UNDER THE JURISDICTION OF STATE AND FEDERAL CORRECTIONAL AUTHORITIES

State and federal prisons	1,312,354
Local jails	621,149
Juvenile facilities	108,965
Territorial prisons	16,130
Immigration and Naturalization Service facilities	8,894
Military facilities	2,420
Indian country jails	1,775

SOURCE: U.S. Department of Justice, Bureau of Justice Statistics, "Nation's State Prison Population Falls in Second Half of 2000—First Such Decline Since 1972," press release, August 12, 2001.

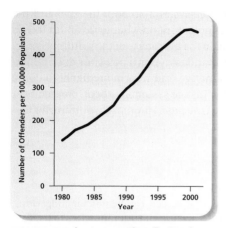

FIGURE 7–3 Incarceration Rates in Federal and State Jurisdictions.
SOURCE: U.S. Department of Justice, Bureau of Justice Statistics, "The Incarceration Rate Has More than Tripled Since 1980," at www.ojp.usdoj.gov/bjs/glance/incrt.htm.

The increase in prison population has resulted in serious overcrowding. In some states, conditions are so bad that in recent years federal judges have issued orders calling for either immediate improvement or the release of persons being held in conditions that violate the Eighth Amendment prohibition against cruel and unusual punishment. Most states are responding to judicial intervention by spending millions to build new prisons and renovate old ones. It costs over $60,000 to build each cell, and an average of $20,000 a year must be spent to guard and feed each prisoner.

Relatively few people commit most violent crimes. One out of every three persons let out of prison returns in three years. If we could identify these "career criminals" (**recidivists**) and keep them in prison, while at the same time releasing offenders who are not likely to commit other crimes, we might be able to cut down on the overcrowding in the prisons and better protect the public. The trouble with this idea is that it is not easy to determine in advance who is a career criminal and who is not. For this reason, some people argue that requiring every criminal convicted of a second offense to stay in prison for five years would cut the crime rate significantly.

Some cities and counties have even resorted to **privatization,** turning over the responsibility for operating jails to private firms on a contractual basis. Prison facilities have been privatized in New Jersey, Wisconsin, and the District of Columbia, as well as in many southern and western states, with Texas and California having the largest number. Correctional peace officers strongly oppose privatization and have become a potent interest group making major contributions to gubernatorial elections.

The high cost of correction is leading some states to rethink the wisdom of mandatory sentencing and to reconsider the need to create such alternatives for nonviolent offenders as halfway houses, intensive probation, work release programs, and other community corrections facilities, even home confinement, first pioneered in New Mexico in 1983, whereby prisoners are observed by a variety of monitoring devices.[58] The problem is that these alternative solutions are subject to political attack for being "soft on criminals." Even so, pressure to find places to hold prisoners is so great that correction officials believe that these alternatives, including home confinement, will become an increasingly important part of the criminal justice system.[59]

COURTS IN CRISIS

Crime is a national issue, confronting everyone. The public's attention has been focused on terrorist attacks, drive-by shootings, random killings—especially in schools—and other forms of violence. Yet courts are already overwhelmed by a huge volume of cases. As the American Bar Association observed, "Justice in the United States takes too long, costs too much and is virtually inaccessible and unaffordable for too many Americans. . . . Our courts are grossly overburdened . . . and woefully underfunded. . . . The justice system is no longer a 'court of last resort' . . . but is becoming an emergency room for every social trauma."[60]

There is widespread agreement that our justice system, on both the civil and the criminal side, is in recurring crisis. There is less agreement on what to do about it. The problems are complex, and the issues are political in the best sense of the word: each suggested reform—alternative dispute resolution, mandatory sentencing, or decriminalization, for instance—has costs and benefits. Change and reform are likely to come slowly, and perhaps this is as it should be, for our justice system has been created over the centuries, built on the accumulated wisdom of the past. How best to administer justice is likely to remain on our political agenda.

S U M M A R Y

1. State and local courts are important forums for the making and carrying out of public policy. As they have become more active in political life, state judges have become embroiled in controversial issues, and the public has recognized their importance as policy makers. A new judicial federalism has emerged with state courts interpreting their state bills of rights more broadly than the U.S. Supreme Court applies the national Bill of Rights.

2. Each state has its own court system. Although the systems vary, they generally include minor courts of limited jurisdiction, trial courts of general jurisdiction, and appellate courts.

3. Judges are selected in four different ways: through appointment by the governor, election by the legislatures, popular election, or a merit system modeled along the lines of the modified appointment plan known as the Missouri Plan. Most legal reformers and political scientists appear to favor either the Missouri Plan or some merit selection system over judicial elections.

4. Judicial reforms are aimed at eliminating the waste and delay that plague courts. Among those suggested are alternative dispute resolution mechanisms, mandatory sentencing, and the decriminalization of some nonviolent crimes. Other reforms include merit systems that screen candidates for judgeships, higher pay and longer terms for judges to increase their judicial independence, rule-making powers for state supreme courts, and the appointment of judges more representative of the communities they serve.

5. Judges, together with jurors, prosecutors, defense counsel, public defenders, and correction officials, make up a loosely interrelated justice system. Many observers believe that this system is not properly dispensing justice to individual defendants or protecting the public from career criminals.

6. In recent years, more attention has been paid to the rights of victims at both the national and state levels, including amendments to state constitutions giving victims and their families the right to participate in the trial and providing for compensation to victims and their families.

7. There are over 2 million persons in our prisons. Prisons are overcrowded. Imprisonment has been justified as retribution, deterrence, protection of society, and rehabilitation. Disillusionment with rehabilitation and the disparate sentencing by judges has led to the enactment of mandatory minimum sentencing requirements, including three-strikes-and-you're-out legislation.

F U R T H E R   R E A D I N G

STEPHEN J. ADLER, *The Jury: Trial and Error in the American Courtroom* (Times Books, 1994).

LAURENCE BAUM, *American Courts: Process and Policy*, 5th ed. (Houghton Mifflin, 1998).

MATTHEW BOSWORTH, *Courts as Catalysts: State Supreme Courts and Public School Finance Equity* (State University of New York Press, 2001).

DAVID COLE, *No Equal Justice: Race and Class in the American Criminal Justice System* (New Press, 1999).

GEORGE F. COLE AND CHRISTOPHER SMITH, *Criminal Justice in America*, 3d ed. (Wadsworth, 2001).

NORMAN J. FINKEL, *Commonsense Justice: Jurors' Notions of the Law* (Harvard University Press, 1995).

SUSAN P. FINO, *The Role of State Supreme Courts in the New Judicial Federalism* (Greenwood Press, 1987).

JULIA FIONDA, *Public Prosecutors and Discretion* (Oxford University Press, 1995).

JOHN B. GATES AND CHARLES A. JOHNSON, *The American Courts: A Critical Assessment* (CQ Press, 1991).

JOSEPH R. GRODIN, *In Pursuit of Justice: Reflections of a State Supreme Court Justice* (University of California Press, 1989).

DAVID HEILBRONE, *Rough Justice: Days and Nights of a Young D.A.* (Pantheon Books, 1990).

RANDOLPH JONAKAIT, *The American Jury System* (Yale University Press, 2003).

LAURA LANGER, *Judicial Review in State Supreme Courts: A Comparative Study* (State University of New York Press, 2002).

CHARLES LOPEMAN, *The Activist Advocate: Policymaking in State Supreme Courts* (Praeger, 1999).

MARILYN D. McSHANE AND FRANK P. WILLIAMS III, EDS., *Encyclopedia of American Prisons* (Garland Press, 1996).

DAVID W. NEUBAUER, *America's Courts and Criminal Justice System,* 7th ed. (Wadsworth, 2001).

DAVID M. O'BRIEN, ED., *Judges on Judging: Views from the Bench* (CQ Press, 2004).

ELLIOT E. SLOTNICK, ED., *Judicial Politics: Readings from Judicature,* 3d ed. (American Judicature Society, 2005).

MICHAEL SOLIMINE AND JAMES WALKER, *Respecting State Courts: The Inevitability of Judicial Federalism* (Greenwood Press, 2000).

HARRY P. STUMPF AND JOHN H. CULVER, *The Politics of State Courts* (Longman, 1992).

G. ALAN TARR AND MARY CORNELIA ALDIS PORTER, *State Supreme Courts in State and Nation* (Yale University Press, 1988).

PAUL B. WICE, *Court Reform and Judicial Leadership* (Praeger, 1995).

See also Judicature, *The Journal of the American Judicature Society,* published bimonthly, and its Web site at www.ajs.org. The National Center for State Courts does not publish a regular journal but is an independent, nonprofit organization dedicated to the improvement of justice. Its materials can be obtained from its headquarters at 300 Newport Avenue, Williamsburg, VA 23185; its home page is www.ncsconline.org.

LOCAL GOVERNMENTS AND METROPOLITICS

L ocal government is big, costly, and overlapping, and it affects every one of us every day. Counties, cities, suburban communities, school districts, townships, metropolitan planning agencies, water control districts—all are crowded together and piled on top of one another. We typically live under several layers of government, pay taxes to nearly all of them, and also elect most of their leaders. The complex and fragmented arrangements of metropolises also exacerbate the ills of inner cities and limit the options for addressing urban problems. In short, "where we live has a powerful effect on the choices we have and our capacity to achieve a high quality life."[1]

Local governments in the United States employ about 11.5 million people in almost 88,000 different jurisdictions (see Table 8–1). North Carolina, for example, has 960 units of local government, including 102 counties, 541 municipalities, and 319 special districts.[2] Illinois has 6,903 units of local government, made up of 102 counties, 1,291 municipalities, 1,433 townships, 3,145 special districts, and 934 school districts.

Why is there such a labyrinth of government in this country? The basic pattern was imported from England, as were many of our governmental forms. Over time, new governments were created to take on new jobs when existing units proved either too small or unequal to the task. Also, people kept moving into, or at least near, the large cities. The past three generations have seen millions of Americans moving from the cities to the suburbs, and a steady migration to urban and suburban areas continues from rural areas as well. Decades of compromise and struggle among conflicting groups have given us

146

TABLE 8–1   **GROWTH OF GOVERNMENTS IN THE UNITED STATES**

Type of Government	1972	1982	1992	2002
U.S. government	1	1	1	1
State governments	50	50	50	50
Local governments	78,218	81,780	84,955	87,849
County	3,044	3,041	3,043	3,034
Municipal	18,517	19,076	19,297	19,431
Township	16,991	16,734	16,656	16,506
School district	15,781	14,851	14,422	13,522
Special district	23,885	25,078	33,555	35,356
Total	**78,269**	**81,831**	**85,006**	**87,900**

Source: U.S. Bureau of the Census, *Statistical Abstract of the United States: 2002*, available at www.census.gov/prod/2003pubs/02statab/stlocgov.pdf.

our present system. It creaks and groans. It costs a lot of money. People claim it is inefficient. But these local governments are democratically accountable and encourage experimentation in making public policy.

THE NATURE OF STATE AND LOCAL RELATIONS

Local governments vary in structure, size, power, and relation to one another. But in a *constitutional* sense, they all rely on power "borrowed" from the state. Most state constitutions create a **unitary system** in which power is vested in the *state* government, and local units exist only as agents of the state.[3] Local government is not mentioned in the U.S. Constitution. Local units exercise only those powers expressly given to them by their respective state governments. Most local units of government, unlike states, do not have constitutional status. State-local relations are generally unitary in nature, in contrast to the federal nature of nation-state relations.

Because local governments are typically created by the state legislatures and usually have no constitutional authority in their own right, there are fewer obstacles to state interference in local matters than there are to national interference in state matters. State officers participate in local government to a much greater extent than federal officers do in state politics. When doubts arise about the authority of local governments, courts generally decide against them.

Initially, state legislatures had almost unlimited authority over their local governments and ran them pretty much at will. They granted, amended, and repealed city charters; established counties; determined city and county structure; set debt limits; and passed laws for the local units.

But by the end of the nineteenth century, voters amended or adopted state constitutions that curtailed the power of state legislatures. Many state constitutions forbade state legislatures from passing laws dealing with local governments, and constitutional provisions determined the structure, and in some cases even the process, of local governments.

Constitutional home rule granted constitutional independence to some local units, primarily larger cities, giving them constitutional authority over their form of government and a wide range of other matters. With the protection of constitutional home rule, state legislatures no longer determined the structure and powers of local units.

The extent of state control over local units today varies from state to state and also among the different kinds of local government within each state. At one extreme, local officials merely have to file reports with specified state officials. At the other extreme, state officials have the authority to appoint and remove some local officials, thus exerting considerable control over local affairs. When local governments prove ineffective, state officials may offer local governments financial assistance with certain strings attached or may even take over responsibilities previously handled by local people. In an unusual move in 2002, for instance, a Pennsylvania school reform commission, created to improve Philadelphia's public school system, decided to take over responsibility from the city and privatize 42 of the city's failing schools, the largest experiment yet in the privatization of public schools.[4] By contrast, after the September 11, 2001, terrorist attacks, governments took responsibility from private companies for screening airline passengers.

State officials are genuinely conscious of local problems. That is in part because problems once thought to be local have come to be viewed as involving the entire state, especially problems relating to law enforcement, the environment, finance, and welfare. This heightened concern is acknowledged by mayors and city managers, who regularly work with both state and federal officials. In recent years, the direct ties between national and local officials, especially in the larger urban areas—ties that used to ally them against state officials—have weakened as federal assistance has been cut back. Municipalities have also become more outspoken in opposing policies of the national government. New York City and over 240 other municipalities and counties, for instance, have enacted resolutions formally opposing the expanded investigatory powers granted to law enforcement agencies under the USA Patriot Act.[5]

COUNTIES IN THE UNITED STATES

Counties are the largest jurisdiction within a state. Yet they get a lot less attention from citizens and the media than do cities or school districts. There are two major types of counties: large urban ones and rural ones. Urban counties have many of the same structures as their rural counterparts, but they are more intertwined with their urban centers. A few counties are better known than the cities or local municipalities within them: for example, Westchester County, New York; Montgomery County, Maryland; Marin and Orange Counties, California; and Cook County, Illinois (which includes Chicago). Some cities, such as Boston, Denver, Baltimore, Philadelphia, San Francisco, and Honolulu, are simultaneously cities and counties; New York consists of five counties—New York, Kings, Queens, the Bronx, and Richmond.

States are divided into counties (in Louisiana they are called *parishes,* and in Alaska they are known as *boroughs*). With a few exceptions (such as Connecticut and Rhode Island, where counties have lost their governmental function), county governments

TABLE 8–2   THE 15 LARGEST U.S. COUNTIES BY POPULATION
1. Los Angeles Co., Calif.
2. Cook Co., Ill.
3. Harris Co., Tex.
4. Maricopa Co., Ariz.
5. Orange Co., Calif.
6. San Diego Co., Calif.
7. Kings Co., N.Y.
8. Miami-Dade Co., Fla.
9. Queens Co., N.Y.
10. Dallas Co., Tex.
11. Wayne Co., Mich.
12. King Co., Wash.
13. San Bernardino Co., Calif.
14. Santa Clara Co., Calif.
15. Broward Co., Fla.

SOURCE: U.S. Bureau of the Census, *Statistical Abstract of the United States, 2001* (U.S. Government Printing Office, 2001).

exist everywhere in the United States. There are 3,034 of them, and they vary in size, population, and functions. Loving County, Texas, for example, has fewer than 150 inhabitants; Los Angeles County, California, has nearly 10 million. Besides Los Angeles County, the most populated counties are Cook County, Illinois; Harris County, Texas; Maricopa County, Arizona; and Orange County, California.[6] (Table 8–2 lists the 15 largest counties.)

Counties were originally organized on the idea that a county seat would be no more than a day's journey for anyone within the county's borders. Farm families could pile into their wagons and head for the county seat, and while farmers were attending to business, their families could shop and pick up the local gossip. Then they could all get home in time to do the evening chores. Today, of course, we can drive across a whole state or several states in a day.

The traditional functions of counties are law enforcement, highway construction and maintenance, tax collection and property assessment, recording of legal papers, and welfare. Until recently, counties were convenient subdivisions that largely carried out policies established elsewhere. Over the past generation, however, counties have taken on more tasks than they have lost. Counties in a few states have given up some of their responsibilities, but in most other states, especially in the South, they are taking over from the states such urban functions as transportation, water and sewer operation, and land use planning.[7] Elsewhere, cities are contracting with counties to provide such joint services as personnel training, law enforcement, and correctional facilities. County governments are least active in the New England states, where the county is little more than a judicial and law-enforcement district; county officials do some road building but not much else.

County Government

Most counties have little legislative power. The typical county has a central governing body, variously titled but most frequently called the *county commission* or *board of supervisors*. Most boards have from three to seven members, with a median size of six. They administer state laws, levy taxes, appropriate money, issue bonds, sign contracts on behalf of the county, and handle whatever jobs the state laws and constitution assign to them (see Figure 8–1).

County boards are of two types. The larger boards are usually composed of township supervisors or other township officials. The smaller boards are usually, though not always, elected in at-large elections. At-large elections make it difficult for minorities to be elected to office, especially when they are concentrated in a few areas. Minorities usually win more seats in a district election than in an at-large system.

The county board shares its powers with a number of other officials, most commonly the sheriff, the county prosecutor or district attorney, the county clerk, the coroner,

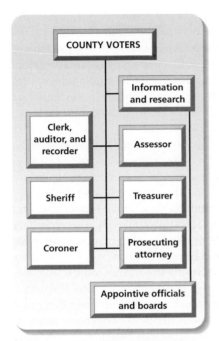

FIGURE 8–1 The Commission Form of County Government.

and the auditor, who are generally elected rather than appointed. Sometimes county treasurers, health officers, and surveyors are also found on the ballot.

In general, counties are administered by an unwieldy collection of relatively independent agencies, and until recently, there was seldom a single executive responsible for coordinating such activities. However, today about 800 counties appoint a chief administrative officer who serves at the pleasure of the county commissioners. Approximately 400 counties now elect a *county executive* who is responsible for most administrative functions (see Figure 8–2).

County Performance

How well do counties perform? The picture is mixed. The existence of counties adds to the fragmentation of authority and responsibility among a variety of elected officials, often producing needless jurisdictional conflicts, inefficiencies in purchasing, duplication of costs, and resistance to developing modern personnel systems.

Although counties have often been the forgotten government within the states, this is changing. Their jurisdictional boundaries give them great potential for solving complex problems that are difficult to solve at the city level or have been decentralized to local levels of government by the states. The growing professionalization of county workforces and the trend of electing or appointing professional county executives are improving efficiency. "City-county functional consolidation in areas such as emergency medical services and natural-disaster planning is growing throughout the United States. . . . Increasing cooperation is likely to occur in the future as cities and counties struggle to provide more services to a tax-resistant public."[8]

TOWNS, CITIES, SUBURBS

The number of towns has been declining (see Table 8–1). But, the New England town meeting remains a celebrated institution. The traditional picture of independent citizens coming together to settle public affairs and speak their minds is a stirring one. The New England town is sometimes pointed to as the one place in the United States where there is no elite and where participatory democracy really exists. The town meeting is our most obvious example of *direct democracy;* voters participate directly in making rules, passing new laws, levying taxes, and appropriating money. At least 1,000 New England towns, especially those with populations under 20,000, still hold annual town meetings. Maine has nearly 400 towns that use the town meeting system of democracy, and Vermont has about 200.

Despite this idealized picture, it is generally a veteran group of activists that provides political and policy-making leadership. The assemblies at town meetings usually

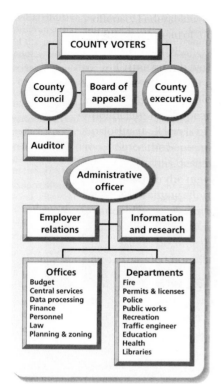

FIGURE 8–2 The Council with Elected Executive Form of County Government.

choose a board of executive officers, historically called *selectmen*. These boards, which generally have three to five members, carry on the business of the town between meetings. The selectmen are in charge of town property; they also grant licenses, supervise other town officials, and call special town meetings. A town treasurer, assessor, constable, and the school board, as well as others, are elected by the voters or appointed by the selectmen. A town administrator often functions as a city manager and reports to the board of selectmen.

Some state and local officials in New England say the town meeting is on the decline. Derry, New Hampshire, for example, held its last town meeting in 1985; then it switched to a mayor-council system. The town meeting had served Derry well for most of its 158-year history, but it proved unable to deal with rapid growth and an influx of people who commute long distances to work. In the 1990s, nearly 60 communities or school districts in New Hampshire modified their town meeting process so that meetings are for discussion purposes only, with final decisions made by the voters at the polls one week later. In Rhode Island, 13 towns abandoned the town meeting, and 18 towns use the meeting only to adopt the town budget.

Many larger communities in New England with populations of more than 25,000 have modified the town meeting by moving to a *representative* town meeting. At representative town meetings, between 50 and 300 local residents from various town precincts are elected to serve three-year terms representing their neighborhoods at their annual town meetings. This is a popular format in many suburbs of Boston with 25,000 to 50,000 residents. Yet the open town meeting, at least in small towns in New England, still proves to be a vital way for people to participate in the policy making of their communities.

During the last half century, the areas around the cities have been the fastest-growing places in the United States (see Figure 8–3). At least 50 percent of Americans now live in suburban communities. Suburbs have grown up at the expense of towns and cities for a variety of reasons: inexpensive land, lower taxes, cleaner air, more open space for recreational purposes, less crime, better highways, and the changing character of the inner cities. There is no one explanation for the exodus to the suburbs. In part it was because people wanted to escape the deteriorating central cities. Resistance to mandatory busing to achieve integrated schools in the 1960s and 1970s also contributed to so-called white flight. But it was just as much a matter of class as of race, with middle- and upper-middle-income-level whites, Asians, and African Americans moving to the suburbs to escape urban crime and to seek more attractive environments in terms of class, religion, race, and lifestyle.[9]

In addition, suburbs have grown because industries have moved from the central cities in search of cheaper land, lower taxes, and less restrictive building and

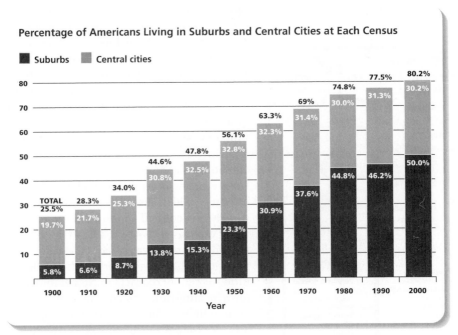

FIGURE 8–3 **Moving to the Suburbs.**

health codes. Other businesses followed the people and the industries, and a myriad of shopping centers grew in outlying communities. Much of this exodus was accelerated by federal policies promoting interstate highways and mortgages insured by the Federal Housing Administration. Most of the new jobs created in the United States continue to be located in the suburbs or newer cities on the fringes of the central cities.

The major tasks of suburban government are often bound together with those of the metropolis.[10] Larger cities usually maintain an elaborate police department with detective bureaus, crime detection laboratories, and communications networks, but its jurisdiction stops at the city line. Criminals, however, seldom stop at the city line. Suburbs have fewer police, and they are often untrained in criminology, so they call on urban police expertise. Cities and suburbs are also tied together by highways, all of which have local access roads. In matters of health, too, there are often wide differences in services between city and suburb, but germs, pollution, and smog do not notice city signposts.

Older suburbs from Long Island to the San Francisco Bay Area are now experiencing some of the problems long associated with disinvestment and population decline. Some suburbs, too, are challenged by sprawling growth that creates crowded schools, traffic congestion, loss of open spaces, and a lack of affordable housing. Many people believe there is a need for collaborative city-suburb strategies to address sprawl and the structural challenges facing older suburbs and inner cities. We'll return to this topic later in this chapter.

The Rise of "Edge Cities"

In recent decades, cities have been built on the edges of older cities. Writer Joel Garreau calls these "edge cities" and suggests that virtually every expanding American city grows in the fashion of Los Angeles, with multiple urban cores.[11] Thus we have Tysons Corner, Virginia, outside Washington, D.C.; the Perimeter Center at the northern tip of Atlanta's Beltway; the Galleria area west of downtown Houston; and the Schaumburg area northwest of Chicago.

Edge cities are defined as places with 5 million or more square feet of office space, 600,000 or more square feet of retail space, and more jobs than bedrooms. More often than not, these edge cities were empty spaces or farmland just 30 years ago. New freeways appeared first, then a shopping mall or two, and then industrial parks.

Some of the problems of the inner city have caught up with edge cities, just as they have with suburbs: traffic congestion, parking problems, crime, pollution, and urban blight. Political problems have cropped up as well. Most edge cities are in unincorporated areas of counties and are subject in varying degrees to control by county governments. These edge cities are sometimes run by "shadow governments"—private owners who set the fees for policing, transportation, and various other services that are normally financed by taxes. There is not much room for government by the people in a community that is essentially a business.

CITY GOVERNMENT TODAY

What does the word "city" call to mind? Bright lights and crowded streets? A city is not merely improved real estate; it is also people—men and women living and working together. Aristotle observed that people came together in the cities for security, but they stayed there for the good life.

The "good life" is defined differently by different people, yet it often includes these attractions:

- Employment opportunities
- Cultural centers, museums, performing arts centers, theaters
- Diverse educational institutions
- Entertainment and night life
- Professional sports teams
- Wide variety of stores and specialty shops
- Good restaurants
- Diversity of people, architecture, and lifestyles

Although a few cities existed when the U.S. Constitution was written, the nation was overwhelmingly rural in 1787, and seven out of ten people worked on farms. People clustered mainly in the villages and small towns scattered throughout the 13 states and adjacent territories. The villages and towns were the indispensable workshops of democracy, the places where democratic skills were developed, where grand issues were debated, and above all, where the people resolved to fight the British to secure their fundamental rights.

The United States is now a nation of about 19,429 cities, and although some cities have just a few hundred people, others have millions. Three American supercities and their suburbs (New York, Los Angeles, and Chicago) have populations larger than the total population of the Republic in the 1780s.

Every municipality has two major purposes. One is to provide government within its boundaries: to maintain law and order, keep streets clean, educate children, purify water, create and maintain parks, and make the area a good place in which to live.[12] As an instrument of the state, the city has a second major purpose: to carry out state functions.

A **charter** is to a city what a constitution is to a national or state government. It outlines the structure of the government, defines the authority of the various officials, and provides for their selection. Although charters are good sources of information on how the people in our cities are governed, they can be misleading. Different structures are not neutral in their impact, for different forms encourage different kinds of participation and responsiveness. In short, power and clout and who gets what, where, and how can definitely be shaped by a city's structural arrangements.

The Mayor-Council Charter

The **mayor-council charter** is the oldest and most popular charter (see Figure 8–4). Under this type of charter, the city council is usually a single chamber. The size of the council varies from as few as two members to as many as fifty, though seven is the median size in cities with more than 5,000 people.

Many methods are used to select council members: nonpartisan and partisan elections, elections by large and small wards, or elections from the city at large. Large cities that elect members affiliated with political parties generally choose them by small districts or wards rather than at large. This arrangement tends to support strong party organizations. Nonpartisan at-large elections make party influence difficult. The larger the election districts, the more likely citywide considerations will affect the selection of council members, and the greater the influence of citywide institutions such as local newspapers.

The difference between at-large citywide elections and elections based on small, single-member districts within a city can be significant for racial and ethnic representation on the city council. The at-large system tends to produce councils made up of the city's elite and middle classes. The small district gives minorities and the less advantaged a somewhat better chance for representation where neighborhoods may have high concentrations of one minority.

The Voting Rights Act of 1965 forbids states and cities with a past history of discrimination against minority voters from adopting the at-large system for electing council members if the effect would be to dilute the voting strength of these minorities. In fact, no local government in regions spelled out in this act can make a change in its voting system without the approval of the U.S. attorney general. But what of cities or counties that have long had at-large elections? Can they be forced to give them up because at-large elections virtually

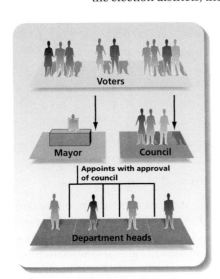

FIGURE 8–4 The Mayor-Council Form of City Government.

ensure that minorities will never be elected? The mere fact that no African American is elected under a certain system does not by itself constitute a violation of the Fourteenth or Fifteenth Amendment. The Constitution forbids only practices adopted or maintained *with the intent to discriminate.*

When Congress debated the extension of the Voting Rights Act in 1982, civil rights advocates urged it to outlaw at-large systems. They contended that city officials are not so foolish as to admit that they want to keep minorities from being elected. Others argued that cities should be free to adopt whatever election system they wished; after all, the Constitution guarantees that no person will be denied the right to vote because of race, not that candidates of the voter's own race will win an election.

The Voting Rights Act as interpreted by the Supreme Court has made it easier to prove that at-large systems violate civil rights. Discriminatory intent need not be proved by direct evidence; it may be inferred if a city or county has a past history of discrimination designed to keep minorities from voting, minorities make up a large majority of the population, and no member of a minority has ever been elected to office under an at-large system.[13]

Weak Mayor Councils and Strong Mayor Councils

The powers of the mayor-council form of government vary from charter to charter and even more widely from city to city and mayor to mayor. There are, however, two basic variations of the mayor-council form: the weak mayor council and the strong mayor council.

In cities with the **weak mayor-council form,** mayors are often chosen from members of the elected city council rather than elected directly by the people. The mayor's appointive powers are usually restricted, and the city council as a whole generally possesses both legislative and executive authority. The mayor must usually obtain the council's consent for all major decisions. Often weak mayor-council cities permit direct election by the voters of a number of department heads, such as police chief or controller. In weak mayor-council cities, there is no single administrative head for the city, and power is fragmented. The weak mayor-council plan was designed for an earlier era, when cities were smaller and government was simpler. It is ill-suited to large cities, where political and administrative leadership is vital.

Under the **strong mayor-council form,** the mayor is elected directly by the people and given fairly broad appointment powers. The mayor, often with the help of his or her staff, prepares and administers the budget, enjoys almost total administrative authority, and has the power to appoint and dismiss department heads. This system obviously calls for a mayor to be both a good political leader and an effective administrator— qualities not always found in the same person.

Many people believe the strong mayor-council system is the best form of government for large cities because it gives the cities strong political leaders and makes responsive administration possible. Further, by centering authority in the hands of a few individuals, it makes less likely the growth of "invisible government" by people who have power but are not publicly accountable for its use.

The Council-Manager Charter

Reformers in the early 1900s acclaimed the **council-manager plan** (also known as the *city-manager plan*), in which the city council hires a professional administrator to manage city

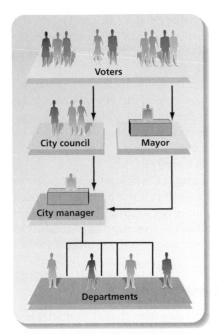

FIGURE 8–5 The Council-Manager Form of City Government.

affairs. It was indeed a significant governmental innovation. In 1908, the small city of Staunton, Virginia, appointed a general manager to oversee the city's work. Little note was taken of the step, but the council-manager plan soon became the darling of both reformers and the business elite. They liked the idea that the council would serve as a sort of "board of directors" in the business sense of setting broad policies, while a professional executive would see that these policies were carried out with businesslike efficiency (see Figure 8–5).

Under the council-manager charter, the council is usually elected in nonpartisan primaries and elections, either on a citywide basis or by election districts much larger than the wards in mayor-council cities. The council appoints a city manager and supervises the manager's activities. The council still makes the laws and approves the budget, and although it is not supposed to interfere in administration, the council often supervises city government through the manager. The mayor is expected to preside over the council and represent the city on ceremonial occasions, but many mayors in fact do a good deal more than this. Contrary to what some textbooks imply, the mayor in council-manager cities can sometimes be a strong policy and political leader as well as a dominant influence in exercising political power.[14] This has surely been the case in cities as different as Cambridge, Massachusetts; San Antonio, Texas; and Colorado Springs, Colorado.

The city manager advises the council on policy and supervises the administration of city business. Because council-manager cities try to attract the best available persons, few of their charters require the councils to select managers from among local citizens, nor do they prescribe detailed qualifications. Although city-manager charters seem to call for a nonpolitical city manager who merely carries out policies adopted by the council and for council members who refrain from interfering with the administration of city affairs, it is often difficult to distinguish clearly between making and applying policy.

Today more than 2,700 cities, located in virtually every state, operate under a council-manager charter. It has, in fact, become the most popular form of local government in medium-sized cities of more than 10,000 citizens. It is especially popular in California, where about 98 percent of the cities use it, as well as in other western and Sun Belt cities. The largest cities operating under a city manager are Dallas, San Antonio, San Diego, Phoenix, Kansas City, Cincinnati, Oakland, and Fort Worth.

How has the city-manager plan worked? In cities characterized by low social diversity and high consensus about community goals, the council-manager form has met with success. Such cities have generally enjoyed improved standards of public employment, reduced costs, and better services. But some observers say this plan has also weakened political leadership in these cities and has confused citizens as to who really provides policy leadership.

In an effort to become more responsive, some council-manager cities have expanded the size of their councils and have abandoned at-large elections for district elections. More than 60 percent of the city-manager cities now also directly elect their mayors in an effort to provide greater political accountability and leadership.[15]

CHANGING FACE OF AMERICAN POLITICS

CITY COUNCILS ARE BECOMING MORE DIVERSE

America's city councils are becoming more racially and ethnically diverse, with the number of people of color serving almost doubling in the last two decades, in all categories of cities (small, medium, and large), from 7 percent to 13 percent.

Over the last decade, Hispanic council membership has increased the most in medium cities, with populations of 70,000 to 199,999—jumping from zero to six percent—and in large cities, with populations over 200,000, growing from 1 percent to 11 percent. During the same time, the percentage of Asian Americans declined from 3 percent to 1 percent.

The representation of women on city councils increased as well. The proportion of women grew from 21 percent to 25 percent in small cities, from 25 percent to 36 percent in medium-sized cities, and from 33 percent to 36 percent in large cities.

SOURCE: National League of Cities, *Research Brief on America's Cities: The Faces of America's City Councils* (September 2003), available at www. nlc.org.

Percentage of Council Members

Year	White	African American	Hispanic	Asian	Native American	Other
1979	92	5	1			
1989	86	10	1	3		1
2001	87	8	3	1	1	1

THE ROLE OF THE MAYOR

Two hundred years ago, the notion of a strong mayor providing vigorous leadership was nonexistent. The need for strong mayoral leadership developed in the late nineteenth century as a means to deal with the social revolution brought on by urbanization, massive waves of immigration, and mounting economic problems of growing cities. In the larger cities, gradually and often grudgingly, the office of mayor became a key position for political leadership.

The typical mayor is a college graduate, an experienced grassroots politician, a business or legal professional, and between 40 and 50 years old. Mayors in the largest cities earn $90,000 to $170,000 and in middle-sized cities between $40,000 and $80,000. City managers, chief city administrators, and top appointees sometimes make more than the mayors.

Although most mayors are male, several of the nation's largest cities have had female mayors, including Pittsburgh; Houston; Dallas; San Diego; San Antonio; and Portland, Oregon. In fact, about 20 percent of municipal governments in the United States with a population of 30,000 or more are headed by women, and the number is growing. Many of them worked their way up through service on school boards and city councils and in the League of Women Voters. An increasing number of African Americans also serve as mayors. More than 300 cities have had African American mayors, including Atlanta, Philadelphia, Denver, Detroit, Houston, San Francisco, Newark, Richmond, and Washington, D.C.

The main job of the mayor is administrative in the broadest sense of the term. Mayors supervise the line agencies—police, fire, public safety, traffic, health, sanitation—as well as a host of special agencies, such as the board of elections, the city planning agency, and commissions that regulate particular occupations and professions. Big-city mayors usually have staffs that carry out typical executive office functions such as personnel, management, budgeting, scheduling, and public relations. In this respect, mayors face the same tasks as corporate executives: coordinating a variety of activities, assigning responsibilities, checking that projects are carried out, finding the ablest people to take charge, and allocating money through control of the budget.

Usually mayors become involved with the private sector in an effort to promote economic opportunities. They try to secure additional jobs, increase the tax base, make the city more attractive to certain kinds of businesses, and coordinate public service expansion with private sector requirements. The private sector becomes involved in economic development because its success depends on having an educated labor base with appropriate skills, a constant consumer population, stable communities, and increasing property values.

Many mayors, such as those in New York, San Francisco, Seattle, Atlanta, Chicago, and Miami, have their own "foreign policies." That is, they play host to foreign dignitaries and business delegations and travel abroad seeking foreign investments as they sing the praises of local exportable goods.[16]

Sometimes a mayor must depend on the party organization to ensure support in the council, as in Chicago, where the huge city council consists of 50 members. Other mayors may have to deal with smaller councils, but they are likely to be weak unless they have enough political support to win cooperation.

Although partisan politics is waning as a feature of city government, mayors as party leaders still often dominate the party's city organizations. Mayors help recruit candidates for office, deal with revolts and opposition within their parties, and represent their parties in Washington or the state capitals. As chief legislator, mayors draw up proposed legislation and also make many specific policies. As chief fund-raisers, mayors bargain for more money for their cities before state and national legislatures. Mayors often climb the political ladder to run for governor or sometimes even president. For example, Ohio's former governor and now U.S. senator, George Voinovich, had previously been mayor of Cleveland, and former California governor Pete Wilson had been mayor of San Diego. U.S. Senator Richard Lugar of Indiana had been mayor of Indianapolis.

Mayors are expected to help revitalize the economy and attract investors, sports teams, tourists, and conventions. It takes courage and missionary zeal to overcome the pessimism and decay that beset most inner cities. But several recent mayors—including Rudolph Giuliani in New York City and both Richard J. Daley and his son Richard M. Daley in Chicago—succeeded in reducing crime, increasing economic opportunities, and revitalizing downtown businesses and residential areas.

In recent decades, mayors, like presidents and governors, have grown in power and importance. Most cities have altered their charters to give their mayors power to appoint and remove heads of departments, investigate departmental activities, send legislative messages to the city councils, prepare budgets, and veto council ordinances. In other words, mayors have been given a share in policy making, and city administration has been centralized under the mayor's direction.

WHO INFLUENCES LOCAL POLICY MAKING?

Most Americans, most of the time, leave the responsibility of running the cities and counties to local officials and people willing to serve on boards and in local civic organizations. This does not mean that Americans rave about the quality of services received from local governments. Although they generally respond favorably to the services they get from city government and local public transportation agencies, they often rate them less favorably than they do the services provided by commercial organizations.

But if most people do not choose to be leaders in their communities, that does not mean they do not care about tax rates, the quality of schools in the community, and the availability of services. Hundreds of local people can be mobilized quickly if city hall mishandles local affairs or makes unpopular decisions. Indeed, activism has increased in recent years. It is now common for people to form groups to protect their communities from landfills, toxic dumps, shopping malls, and highways. With dogged perseverance and shoestring budgets, grassroots protest groups have often successfully taken on city hall or won victories for their neighborhoods in the courts.

A sure way to involve people in city government is to propose a policy that threatens the value or safety of the homes of middle- or upper-middle-class taxpayers. The slightest hint that a correctional facility, a freeway, a garbage dump, or a toxic disposal site is coming to their neighborhood will swiftly mobilize citizens who are otherwise happy to be passive spectators in local government. Similarly, the firing of a popular school principal, the closing of a neighborhood school, or a major increase in the property tax will produce a volley of citizen protests that can change the policy-making process at city hall.

Elected and appointed officials try to sense the mood of the local citizenry. They want to avert marches on city hall, recall elections, and citizen dissatisfaction. Their desire to be reelected and respected keeps them reasonably accountable.[17]

Interest Groups in Cities

The stakes and prizes in city politics are considerable: city jobs and commissioner posts, tax breaks, city contracts, regulations, licenses, and much more. Local politicians must deal with the kinds of interest groups found in any industrial society: organized workers, business leaders, neighborhood associations, professional associations, good government associations, home builders and developers, consumers, taxpayers, environmentalists, and various racial and ethnic groups.

The most powerful groups in most cities are typically business groups. Employers provide the economic base for taxes and for jobs, and mayors know they will win or lose the next election in large part on how well they promote the local economy.

Investors and businesses are free to locate wherever they please. Thus they may move from a central city to a nearby suburb or from one city to another. City policy makers, therefore, must follow an "economic logic" that requires them to adopt policies that persuade businesses and investors to remain as participants in the local economy, either by keeping tax rates relatively low or by increasing the quality of service and amenities. If successful, this kind of growth politics enhances the prospects of city officials for reelection because economic growth, especially business investment, boosts the tax base and increases economic opportunities.[18]

But business groups have to share political power and influence with unions, environmentalists, ethnic groups, and many others. Most business officials learn that they can influence city political decision making by cultivating allies.[19] City politics generally involves informal alliances of public officials working together with private sector individuals and institutions.[20]

Police, firefighters, street cleaners, teachers, and other public employees are organized into unions, many of which are affiliated with national unions. Such unions are often a major influence in larger cities. They fight for improved pay, better working conditions, and job security. Although strikes by city employees providing vital services are prohibited by law in most states, enforcement is difficult. Teachers and municipal workers use the strike, or the threat of a strike, to force cities to increase wages and provide better benefits. Mayors complain that public employee unions are sometimes so powerful that they make the old-fashioned political machine look tame.

In addition, nonprofit groups such as the League of Women Voters, cultural foundations, local nonpartisan civic city clubs, independent local planning groups, and arts leagues exist in most urban areas, and they, too, want to be heard in the policy-making discussions of their cities.

Americans would like to believe that every citizen has a say in local government. Prominent families and local business leaders, however, often have more influence than the rest of us. Nursing home residents, the unemployed, migratory workers, young drifters, and the homeless are unlikely to have much influence. Participation in community affairs is often a middle-class and upper-middle-class practice. Low-income residents and the homeless are often ignored when mayors and business elites pursue aggressive economic development policies. "For renters and low-income residents, . . . a booming economy with rising land values may put affordable housing out of reach."[21] This is true in New York City as well as in places like Aspen, Colorado. There are costs as well as benefits to urban growth. Economic development can destroy neighborhoods and drive cities into debt.

THE CENTRAL CITY AND ITS POLITICS

Today most Americans live in *metropolitan areas,* which include large cities and their suburbs, rather than in the small towns so beloved in American fact and fiction. A metropolitan area is, in the minds of most people, a big city and its suburbs. But the Census Bureau, which counts 280 metro areas, down from 284 in 1990, uses a more formal definition:

> A metro area is built around one or more central counties containing an urban area of at least 50,000 people. It also includes outlying counties with close ties—economic and social—to the central counties. To be considered part of the metro area, the outlying counties must meet certain criteria, including numbers of commuters, population density and growth, and urban population.[22]

About 80 percent of Americans (226 million) live in metropolitan areas, 55 percent live within 60 miles of a coastal shoreline (Atlantic, Pacific, Gulf of Mexico, Great Lakes, or St. Lawrence River), and 30 percent live in central cities. The five fastest-growing metropolitan areas are in the South and the West: Las Vegas, Nevada; Naples, Florida; Yuma, Arizona; McAllen–Edinburg–Misson, Texas; and Austin–San Marcos, Texas.[23]

In the nineteenth century, masses of new immigrants arrived in the cities from Europe. In the twentieth century, migrants came from the rural areas, especially from the South. More recently, this country experienced waves of newcomers from Cuba, Korea, Vietnam, the Philippines, Nicaragua, Haiti, Mexico, and other Latin American countries. The majority of newcomers settled first in the inner cities—usually in the poorest and most decayed sections—which inevitably put great stress on the schools and sometimes on community safety as well. Overcrowding and substandard housing in these areas increased health and fire hazards.

The picture of central cities as composed exclusively of huddled, starving, homeless youth gangs and unemployed masses, however, is misleading. Nor is it fair to say simply that central cities have all the problems and suburbs have all the resources. Central cities do have more "high-cost citizens" (truly needy, handicapped, and senior citizens), and most aging cities have been losing population. They have lost businesses, too, because land, rents, utilities, and taxes are often less expensive in the outer suburbs, and businesses move to lower their operating costs. But their departure means that cities have smaller tax bases. Higher operating costs in the cities also result from aging public works.

As the income gap between city and suburban residents widens, central cities find it hard to raise new revenues or to force suburbanites to pay a larger share of the bill for the city services they use. This is the economic problem. The legal problem is that most of the states have not permitted their cities to raise funds in any meaningful way with a local income tax.[24]

In an effort to recapture part of the tax base that escapes to the suburbs in the evenings, some cities have imposed local payroll or other types of *commuter taxes* to obtain revenue from people who work in the central cities and make frequent use of city facilities yet live in the suburbs. Some city officials say the payroll or commuter tax is an effective way to shift some of the burden to those who benefit from the city but live beyond its borders. But others say it is unlikely to provide significant long-term revenue growth, and they think it encourages even more businesses to leave the city.

Recently, though, many of the once down-and-out central cities have shown signs of rejuvenation and gentrification. Cities such as Boston, Cleveland, Newark, and Washington, D.C., which were losing population a decade or two ago, are now gaining new residents. Gentrification and "yuppie" development have attracted some suburbanites to come back to central cities. The reasons for the rebound of many central cities varies from city to city, yet the sustained economic boom in the 1990s increased local tax revenues, which were then invested heavily in local infrastructure to make cities more appealing. The boom and investment in cities also helped create more jobs.[25]

However, there has also been a growing sentiment against trying to strengthen metropolitan structures and instead to move in the opposite direction. Perhaps the strongest movement in that direction is in Los Angeles, where there are serious attempts to have the San Fernando Valley withdraw from Los Angeles and create its own city. The issue is extremely controversial, especially among the large Hispanic populations in the area, and even though the vote on secession failed in 2002, the matter will continue to be debated.

MEETING THE CHALLENGES OF GROWTH AND ECONOMIC DEVELOPMENT

Until recently, almost everybody wanted to see his or her city grow. Everybody was a city booster. The local newspaper, television stations, radio stations, Chamber of Commerce, union leaders, business community, developers, teachers, and proud citizens worked together to attract new industries. Such industries would bring, they hoped, new jobs, more amenities, increased land values, and more opportunities for the young. The consensus was that a city with a growing population was a healthy one; one with a decreasing population was a sick one.

Local politicians found it risky to oppose economic development and economic growth; those who did feared that they would not be reelected. However, beginning two decades ago, an *antigrowth* movement developed in many cities. There had always been restraints in the wealthy suburbs outside of the central cities; in fact, many suburbs were created to escape the growth taking place in central cities. These suburbs adopted building and zoning codes and land use regulations to make it difficult, if not impossible, for industries to be located there and to keep out people who could not afford large houses on large lots. New suburbs were carefully planned to ensure that they would not become too crowded. These zoning regulations were attacked in the courts as strategies to keep the poor and minorities out, but as long as they were racially neutral on their face, the courts left them undisturbed.

In the last two decades, environmental awareness spread, and coalitions formed to fight unregulated growth. Disturbed by noise, pollution, and traffic jams and fearful that developers would build too many houses too close together and overload the infrastructure of roads, sewage disposal, and schools in the community, opponents of growth joined together.

Strategies to Govern Metro Regions

Divided executive authority, fragmented legislative power, splintered and noncompetitive political parties, the absence of strong central governments, and the necessity to bargain with national, state, and local officials—all these factors suggest that metro regions, where about 80 percent of Americans now live, are shapeless giants with nobody in charge. Metro regions, of course, typically encompass many cities, counties, towns, and suburbs, so they too are complicated and often splintered.

At the turn of the twentieth century, reformers were afraid of domination by political bosses. But in the modern metropolis, political machines do not run the central city. Urban bureaucracies may wield a lot of power, but they do not offer metropolitan leadership. Special interests seldom really control the metropolis, nor does a business elite. Who, then, governs the metropolis? It's typically a "nobody's in charge" arrangement.

Growing fragmentation of government in large metropolitan areas has brought about a variety of reform movements and structural innovations aimed at improving efficiency, effectiveness, and performance. Political scientists and public administration specialists have never been bashful about proposing remedies. Here are the better-known ideas, all of which have been tried somewhere, yet none of which has been adopted nationwide.

ANNEXATION In the South, West, and Southwest, large central cities have absorbed adjacent territories. Oklahoma City, for example, added almost 600 square miles. Houston; Phoenix; San Antonio; El Paso; Colorado Springs; and Kansas City, Missouri, also expanded their boundaries. The now-extended cities serve almost as regional governments.[26]

But annexation has not proved helpful to cities in the Northeast and Midwest because these cities are ringed by entrenched suburban communities that seldom want to be annexed, and state laws make it difficult for the central city to do so against the wishes of the suburbs. Even in such places as the Houston metropolitan area, the annexation option is plagued by legal obstacles and political jealousies.

AGREEMENTS TO FURNISH SERVICES The most common solution to the problems of overlapping and duplicating jurisdictions is for the units of government to contract for services. This reform is applauded by many economists, who say it comes close to providing a market that operates according to laws of supply and demand. Most of these agreements involve a few cities sharing a single activity. For example, a city may provide hospital services to its neighbors or contract with the county for law enforcement. Especially popular in the Los Angeles area, the contract system is used with increasing success in many parts of the country.

PUBLIC AUTHORITIES Public authorities such as the Port Authority in the New York City area or the Tennessee Valley Authority in the South were established to undertake specialized functions in their regions. They have a legal mandate granted to them by the state (or states) to raise money, hire experts, and take over some city services, such as transportation, water, and housing. The Port Authority of New York and New Jersey built the Twin Towers of the World Trade Center, which were destroyed by the terrorist attacks. It is now responsible for redeveloping the area and for overseeing the operation and security of the bridges and tunnels connecting New York and New Jersey. For more information, go to the Web site at www.panynj.gov.

Why public authorities? In part because state legislatures are sometimes hostile to mayors and prefer to place important functions outside the reach of mayors and political machines and in part because such authorities have financial flexibility (for example, they might be able to incur debt outside the limits imposed on the city by the state). But most important, many problems are simply too big or cover too wide a geographical area to be handled properly by a city or a group of cities.

Public authorities pose a special problem for mayors. Not only are many of the vital functions of metropolitan government removed from the mayors' direct control, but even worse, public authorities and special districts constantly come into conflict with local agencies dealing with the same problems in the city.

But if public authorities are a problem for mayors, they are also a temptation. By sponsoring these independent agencies, mayors can sometimes cut down on their administrative load. They can tap other sources of funds and keep city tax rates lower than they would otherwise be. If things go wrong, mayors can say they did not have authority over a certain function and hence cannot be held responsible.

SPECIAL DISTRICTS   Special districts are units of government typically established to provide one or more specific services, such as sewage disposal, fire protection, water supply, or pollution control for a local or regional area. They are often created to enable an existing unit of government to evade tax and debt limits and to spread the tax burden over a wider area than individual municipalities or counties. Many smaller special districts are formed in suburban areas to obtain urban services without having to create a city government or be annexed by one.

Special districts usually have governing boards appointed by officials of other governments or elected by the general public. Special districts are useful for dealing with urgent problems that overlap boundaries of existing governmental units. Many urban and regional problems defy city and county boundaries, and special districts offer economies of scale that make sense. But critics charge that the rapid increase in the number of special districts over the last 30 years has prevented comprehensive planning. They also lament that few citizens know who runs these special districts, and even fewer know how these officials make decisions.

REGIONAL COORDINATING AND PLANNING COUNCILS   Almost all metro regions have some kind of *council of government* (COG). COGs began in the 1950s and were encouraged by the national government. Congress, in fact, mandated that certain federal grants be reviewed by regional planning groups. In essence, these councils bring locally elected officials together. They devote most of their time and resources to physical planning; rarely do they tackle problems of race, poverty, and financial inequities in metro regions. Councils are set up, moreover, in such a way as to give suburbs a veto over virtually any project that would threaten their autonomy. In a few regions, the councils assume operating responsibilities over such regional activities as garbage collection, transportation, and water supply. Critics say these councils rarely provide for creative areawide governance, yet they serve as an important common ground for elected officials to talk about mutual problems, and they help solve some problems in many of the regions.

CITY-COUNTY CONSOLIDATIONS   One traditional means of overcoming the fragmentation of metro regions is to merge the city with the county. This is a pet reform of business elites, the League of Women Voters, and Chambers of Commerce. It is viewed as a rational, efficient way to simplify administration, cut costs for taxpayers, and eliminate duplication.

About 30 city-county mergers have taken place. Occasionally, one city joins with another, as Sacramento and North Sacramento did in the 1960s. Such mergers can usually be brought about only by a referendum approved by the citizens of the region. Although efforts have been made to consolidate cities with counties, few have been successful in recent decades. Other than St. Louis, Nashville, Jacksonville, and Indianapolis, most consolidations have occurred in a handful of smaller urban areas. One recent success of a regional coalition, after decades of failure, is the consolidation of the City of Louisville and Jefferson County, Kentucky.[27]

What happened in Indianapolis is typical of these consolidations, most of which are in the South and West. In 1970, Indianapolis combined with Marion County to create UNIGOV. This merger required special permission by the legislature. UNIGOV provides many services, but the school systems remain separate, as do the police and sheriff departments.

The era of city-county consolidation appears over. Only about ten consolidations have taken place since 1970, and only one—Athens and Clark Counties in Nevada—occurred in the 1990s. Proposed mergers are usually defeated by county voters. But it is no longer unusual to find counties running what used to be city jails, zoos, libraries, and similar services. Formal and informal agreements abound as cities and counties remedy overlap and fragmentation by shifting responsibilities for providing specific services among themselves.

FEDERATED GOVERNMENT   This strategy attempts to take political realities into account by building on existing governments but assigning some crucial functions to an areawide metro government.[28] One of the few attempts—and there have been only a few—to create a federated government is the Twin Cities Metropolitan Council for the Minneapolis–St. Paul region. This regional organization, established by the legislature in 1967, consists of a 17-member council. Sixteen members are appointed by the governor to represent equal-population districts, and the seventeenth is a full-time executive who serves at the pleasure of the governor.

Today the Metropolitan Council, in essence a new layer of government superimposed on top of existing units, serves as a metropolitan planning and policy-making as well as policy-coordinating agency. It reviews applications for federal funds from the region. It guides regional planning and development and opposes local actions that would endanger the overall welfare of the region. It also has taxing authority for the region. The Twin Cities model appears to be a ready candidate for transfer elsewhere, yet this has happened only in Portland, Oregon.

Portland adopted a bold new charter for the Portland Metropolitan Services District. It is a directly elected regional government serving three counties and 24 cities. Its nonpartisan commission members and elected executive officer have an impressive budget and more than 1,200 employees. They oversee waste collection, a zoo, recycling, waste disposal, transportation planning, and regional air and water quality programs, and they constructed Portland's new Convention Center. They have also created a greenbelt around the metro area that preserves extensive open areas.

COMMUNITY SELF-HELP   The problems of governing urban and metro regions have also been addressed by community self-help organizations. Countless people are coming together in their own neighborhood to tackle common problems or to form neighborhood cooperatives. Some of these self-help groups simply handle baby-sitting arrangements or organize charity events or golf tournaments; others are involved in neighborhood crime watches or Little League field construction. Local nonprofit groups in New York have built award-winning apartment complexes amid burned-out inner-city tenements. Other groups have mobilized to bring about storefront revitalization, street improvement, and area beautification programs by initiating farmers' markets, miniparks, and gardens.[29]

The contemporary self-help movement is rooted in an American past that has long been marked by volunteerism and local associations. In former times, the whole community often rallied when a neighbor's barn burned down; volunteer fire departments emerged out of this tradition. But as the nation has become more mobile and impersonal, we have drifted away from these traditions. Today, most Americans shop at shopping malls rather than on Main Street or in the old downtown area. At the same time, they resent the fact that public institutions have become remote and overly professional-ized. Thus people across the country are joining together to do in an informal and de-centralized way what extended families or small villages of the past used to do. Simply, they come together to lend a hand.

Many local groups seeking help from city hall or from county officialdom give up after running into a maze of building codes, zoning rules, and countless regulations that inhibit innovation in local government. The alternative to despair is to do it yourself. And this is exactly what is happening at the grassroots level right now. The more suc-cessful experiments are watched carefully by the professionals at city hall, and some of the innovations are copied by those in office.

Sometimes progress or justice comes about because some activists take issues to court. Such was the case in bringing in alternative housing for lower-income residents in Mount Laurel, New Jersey. And it was also the case in addressing the fatal effects of toxic dumping by businesses in Woburn, Massachusetts.[30]

THE POLITICS OF METROPOLITAN REORGANIZATION

In most metropolitan regions, to combine city and suburbs would be to shift political power to the suburbs. In most northern centers, this would give suburban Republicans more control of city affairs. In other cases, it would enable Democrats to threaten the one-party Republican systems in the suburbs. Under these circumstances, neither De-mocratic leaders in the central cities nor Republicans in the suburbs show much en-thusiasm for metropolitan schemes. African Americans and Hispanics often oppose area consolidation or similar reform proposals that would invariably dilute their polit-ical power, often severely.

Some people believe that solutions to metropolitan problems are beyond the ca-pacity of the metropolis itself. They favor a strengthened role for the national govern-ment, with special emphasis on ensuring "equity" or on relating services directly to needs. Some advocate reviving federal revenue sharing. Others believe that the job must be done by the states, which hold the fundamental constitutional power. Still others put forward bold proposals to establish regional planning and governance arrangements that would embrace "citistate" areas that include two or more metropolitan clusters, like Baltimore and Washington, D.C.[31]

Today's aging central cities unquestionably face problems: congestion, smog, ten-sion, loss of community, drugs, unsafe streets, neglected children, and visual pollution. They live with racial and ethnic tensions, not just white–black rivalry but rivalry among Latinos, Koreans, and a host of other racial and ethnic groups. Gangs, poverty, broken families, drive-by shootings, and drug-related crimes make life miserable for many who live in the inner cities. Yet is this new? Writers and critics since Thomas Jefferson have projected an unflattering image of the city as a cold, impersonal, and often brutal envi-ronment in which crime flourishes and people lose their dignity.

Supporters contend, however, that the big city is not just a place of smog and sprawl; it is the center of innovation, excitement, and vitality. In the last couple of decades, many major cities, including Boston; New York; and Washington, D.C., have promoted the gentrification of run-down areas. The city offers social diversity and puts less commu-nity pressure on the individual to conform. The large community is a meeting place for talent from all over the nation and the world: dancers, musicians, writers, scholars, actors, and business leaders.

Some observers dismiss the notion of an "urban crisis." They contend that most city dwellers live more comfortably than ever before, with more and better housing, schools, and transportation. By any conceivable measure of material welfare, the present generation of urban Americans is better off than other large groups of people anywhere at any time. Most cities, especially in the West and South, are thriving, and older cities such as Boston, Pittsburgh, and Indianapolis are generally viewed as revived and vital, not decaying.

Throughout history, cities have been threatened by political, social, and environmental catastrophes. Urban decay, in one form or another, has always been with us.[32] Cities thrive because over time they respond to crises and because they are an economic necessity. The economy, transportation systems, past investments, and cultural contributions all make cities inevitable. How well cities survive, and with what mix of people, will depend on the tides of the national economy, the way our regions are organized, the way our social and economic policies are designed, the vision and leadership individual cities muster to build their future, and the degree to which our national leaders promote policies that can help our central cities.[33]

S U M M A R Y

1. Local government is big, costly, and overlapping. Local governments in the United States come in a variety of shapes and structures and perform various functions. However, since constitutional power is vested in the states, most counties, cities, towns, and special districts are agents of the state.

2. The most common governmental form at the county level is a board of county commissioners, although larger urban counties are moving to council-administrator or council-elected executive plans.

3. There is no typical suburb. Although many suburbs are homogeneous, the suburban United States is highly heterogeneous. Suburbs are confronting the same problems as the urban areas they surround. In fact, big cities and their suburbs are now referred to as metropolitan areas and are growing fastest in the South and West.

4. The most common governmental forms at the city level are the mayor-council and the council-manager (city-manager) plans. Mayor-council governments generally have a strong mayor elected by voters, though some plans have a weak mayor elected by the council. Council-manager plans appoint a professional administrator. In general, council-manager plans are found in medium-sized to large cities and in cities in the West, especially in the Sun Belt. Mayors and managers are key political leaders.

5. Although local governments are run by officials, business interests and interest group activism also influence policy.

6. The standard of living in the central cities of the United States may be much better than it was 50 years ago, but the inequalities between many central cities and their middle and outer rings of affluent suburbs are increasing. Central cities often face economic hardships, intense racism, and drug-related gangs and criminals. Fragmentation and dispersal of political authority in the metropolitan areas and even in many of the central cities themselves often make it difficult not only to govern the big cities but also to respond with adequate policies and funds to treat the problems of the metropolis.

7. Cities, suburbs, and metro areas all face problems related to growth, uneven tax bases, environmental concerns, and fragmented authority. A variety of strategies have been used in an effort to solve these problems—annexation, agreements to furnish services, public authorities, special districts, regional coordinating and planning councils, city-county consolidations, federated government, and community self-help programs. Almost all of the strategies for meeting the challenges of growth and economic development involve shifts in political power.

F U R T H E R   R E A D I N G

BARBARA ACKERMANN, *"You the Mayor?" The Education of a City Politician* (Auburn House, 1989).

ROGER BILES, *Richard J. Daley: Politics, Race, and the Governing of Chicago* (Northern Illinois University Press, 1996).

BUZZ BISSINGER, *A Prayer for the City* (Random House, 1997).

MICHAEL BRIAND, *Practiced Politics: Five Principles for a Community That Works* (University of Illinois Press, 1999).

FRANK M. BYRAN, *Real Democracy: The New England Town Meeting and How It Works* (Cambridge University Press, 2004).

PETER DREIER, JOHN MOLLENKOPF, AND TODD SWANSTROM, *Place Matters: Metropolitics for the Twenty-first Century* (University Press of Kansas, 2001).

ALAN EHRENHALT, *The Lost City: Discovering the Forgotten Virtues of Community in the Chicago of the 1950s* (Basic Books, 1995).

JOEL GARREAU, *Edge City* (Doubleday, 1991).

STEPHEN GOLDSMITH, *The Twenty-First Century City: Resurrecting Urban America* (University Press of America, 1999).

JOHN J. HARRIGAN AND ROGER VOGEL, *Political Change in the Metropolis,* 7th ed. (Longman, 2000).

DENNIS R. JUDD AND TODD SWANSTROM, *City Politics: Private Power and Public Policy,* 4th ed. (Longman, 2003).

DAVID L. KIRP ET AL., *Our Town: Race, Housing, and the Soul of Suburbia* (Rutgers University Press, 1997).

SUZANNE M. LELAND AND KURT THURMAIER, EDS., *Case Studies of City-County Consolidation* (M. E. Sharpe, 2004).

PAUL G. LEWIS, *Shaping Suburbia: How Political Institutions Organize Urban Development* (University of Pittsburgh Press, 1996).

DONALD C. MENZEL, ED., *The American County: Frontiers of Knowledge* (University of Alabama Press, 1996).

JOHN O. NORQUEST, *The Wealth of Cities: Revitalizing the Centers of American Life* (Addison-Wesley, 1998).

MYRON ORFIELD, *Metropolitics: A Regional Agenda for Community and Stability* (Brookings Institution Press, 1997).

DAVID RUSK, *Inside Game/Outside Game: Winning Strategies for Saving Urban America* (Brookings Institution Press, 1999).

MICHAEL H. SHUMAN, *Going Local: Creating Self-Reliant Communities in a Gobal Age* (Routledge, 2000).

CLARENCE N. STONE, *Regime Politics: Governing Atlanta, 1946–1988* (University Press of Kansas, 1989).

JON C. TEAFORD, *Post-Suburbia: Government and Politics in the Edge Cities* (Johns Hopkins University Press, 1996).

HEATHER ANN THOMPSON, *Whose Detroit? Politics, Labor, and Race in a Modern American City* (Cornell University Press, 2002).

ROBERT J. WASTE, *Independent Cities: Rethinking U.S. Urban Policy* (Oxford University Press, 1998).

WILLIAM JULIUS WILSON, *When Work Disappears: The World of the New Urban Poor* (Harvard University Press, 1996).

See also *Governing: The Magazine of States and Localities,* published monthly by Congressional Quarterly, Inc.; *The National Civic Review,* published by the National Civic League; *The Municipal Yearbook,* published annually by the International City Management Association; and the Web site of the U.S. Conference of Mayors at www.usmayors.org/uscm/home.asp.

MAKING STATE AND LOCAL POLICY

State and local officials constantly wrestle with policy decisions and controversies. What is the best way to attract business and increase the number of jobs yet encourage environmental quality? How should our state deal with the soaring costs of providing Medicaid? What can be done about frustrating peak-hour gridlock on our highways? Should a community close one of its hospitals? Will voters approve a bond issue to construct a needed new high school? Should states approve or ban marriage licensing or civil unions for same-sex couples? And what role should the states play in helping to reduce CO_2 emissions that are increasing global warming? State and local authorities also puzzle about how much they can do about terrorism threats.

Mayors, governors, state legislators, county commissioners, judges, union officials, developers, Chambers of Commerce, political party leaders, and many others strive to come up with public policy compromises to such dilemmas. These deliberations receive little media attention compared to the attention paid to decisions made in Washington, D.C., yet the effect of these choices on our day-to-day lives is often equally or perhaps even more important.

This chapter will examine some of the policy areas that consume much of the attention of state and local officials and the budgets of state and local governments. State and local governments spend most of their budgets on educating people, on welfare and health-related matters, on highway and transportation systems, and on safety and law enforcement issues. We will discuss them as well as the issues of planning and regulation.

PUBLIC EDUCATION

In ancient Greece, Plato and Aristotle saw education as a vital task of government. Thomas Jefferson, too, was convinced that an educated citizenry was essential to democratic government. But only in the twentieth century did the idea that government should provide tax-supported education for everyone become generally accepted.

For a long time, many people opposed "free" education. They feared it would lead to social unrest, undermine the family, give government control over the minds of the young, require huge bureaucracies, and result in a fatal mixture of education and politics. And was it fair, they asked, to make people who could afford to educate their own children in private schools pay taxes to educate other people's children? Despite these objections, today free public education for grades 1 through 12 is an established practice in the United States.

Education is now the number one policy priority for most states. State and local governments have the primary responsibility for education and put up most of the funds. In recent years, there has been a decline in the federal contribution to education; however, this has not deterred the federal government from pushing federal goals for education. An excellent example of this was the George W. Bush–sponsored and congressionally approved No Child Left Behind Act of 2001, a reauthorization of an earlier law that required greater school district accountability, more testing, and increased emphasis on reading, especially for younger children. One of the most intriguing educational reforms in decades, this national legislation used a combination of national standards and comprehensive testing to measure students' progress. If too many children in a public school fail to meet the desired standard, then parents there have the right to move them elsewhere.

Approximately one-third of all state and local government expenditures are for education—more than for any other function of government (see Figure 9–1). The federal government's contribution to education is fairly constant across states, but since 1979, overall state funding has surpassed that of local governments, with the exception of a few states in which revenues for education continue to come primarily from local government. The state role in financing education has increased over the last generation as a result, at least in part, of pressure from the courts to equalize expenditures on education across local school districts. There is also wide variation between states in the total amount of state and local spending per student, from a high of over $11,000 in New York and Connecticut to a low of about $5,000 in Utah, with an average of almost $8,000.[1]

Administration

Unlike most other democracies, which typically administer and fund education at the national level, the basic unit responsible for public elementary and secondary education in the United States is the local school district, and there are nearly 15,000 of them. In almost all districts, voters elect a board of education that sets the school tax rate, appoints a superintendent of schools and other personnel, hires teachers, and runs the schools from kindergarten or grade 1

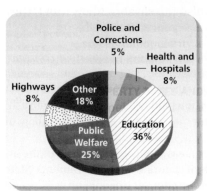

FIGURE 9–1 Typical State Government Expenditures.

through grade 12. Each state has a state superintendent of public instruction or commissioner of education. In about a third of the states, this official is popularly elected; in almost all states, he or she shares authority with a state board of education.

Although actual operation of the public schools is the responsibility of the local community, state officers have important supervisory powers and distribute financial assistance to the communities. State money is distributed according to many formulas, but as noted, the trend is toward giving more money to poorer communities to equalize education spending. Many policies are established at the state level, and it is up to local authorities to enforce them. Local authorities must ensure that new school buildings meet the minimum specifications set by the state. In some states, officials have the authority to set the course of study in schools—that is, to determine what must be taught and what may not be taught. In several states, especially in the South and Southwest, state authorities determine which textbooks will be used as well.

The Role of the National Government

After the former Soviet Union's successful launch of *Sputnik,* the first satellite put into orbit, in 1957, Congress responded by increasing federal funding for education to strengthen math and science education. The national government's share in financing local education rose from about 2 percent in 1940 to about 9 percent in 1980. Since then, however, the trend has reversed, and the federal share of spending on local education declined and has stabilized at 6 percent.

Through the national Department of Education, created in 1979, and other agencies, the federal government makes grants to the states for facilities, equipment, scholarships, loans, research, model programs, and general aid at the elementary, secondary, and higher education levels. But federal control over how the money may be spent comes with these federal dollars. Today federal regulations cover school lunch programs, employment practices, admissions, record keeping, care of experimental animals, and many other matters. Indeed, local school authorities regularly complain that there are more regulations than dollars.

Educational Issues

What shall be taught and who shall teach it are hotly contested matters. Schools are favorite targets for groups eager to have children taught the "right" things. Religious groups want family values and morality emphasized, and some want constraints imposed on the teaching of evolution. Others want the schools to teach facts only, without regard for values, especially in areas like sex education. Labor leaders want students to get the right impression about labor and its role in society. Business leaders are eager for children to see the free enterprise system in a favorable light and want high school graduates who will be well prepared for increasingly technical jobs. Minorities and women's groups want textbooks to present issues from the perspective they consider correct. Professional educators and civil libertarians try to isolate schools from the pressures of all outside groups—or at least the ones with which they disagree. They say decisions regarding what textbooks should be assigned, what books should be placed in school libraries, and how curricula should be designed are best left to professionals.

It has long been an American tradition that education should be kept free from partisan political influences. The separation of schools from politics is strongly supported.

Local school boards are usually nonpartisan and are often elected when no partisan races are on the ballot. Elaborate attempts have been made to isolate educational agencies from the rest of government. This separation is strongly supported by parent–teacher associations, the National Education Association, the American Federation of Teachers, and other educational groups. Most citizens also believe education should be kept out of the hands of mayors and city councils. However, education is of such concern to so many people, and there are so many different ideas about how schools should be run, that it cannot be divorced from politics.

PUBLIC SCHOOL INTEGRATION   During the 1970s and 1980s, battles were fought in many cities over how to overcome racial segregation in the public schools. One method, which became contentious, was to bus students from one neighborhood to another to achieve racial balance in the schools and overcome the effects of past segregation. By the 1990s, battles over school busing were ending, but despite the efforts of the federal courts, racial segregation is still the pattern for the inner-city schools of most large cities in parts of the North, South, and West. Indeed, over the last 15 years there has been a substantial slippage toward segregation in most of the states that had experienced solid desegregation.[2]

EDUCATIONAL REFORM   Over the past two decades, a series of reports on education helped focus national attention on educational reform.[3] A 1990 meeting between President George H. W. Bush and many of the nation's governors laid the foundation for the Goals 2000: Educate America Act, which sought to achieve many of the goals identified as important since the 1960s. With the aid of federal money, states were encouraged to set educational standards in order to achieve a number of goals, including these:

- All children will start school ready to learn.
- The high school graduation rate will be at least 90 percent.
- Students will have mastered a challenging curriculum by grades 4, 8, and 12.
- Teachers will have access to professional development opportunities.
- U.S. students will rank first in the world in science and math achievement.
- All adults will be literate.
- Schools will be free of drugs, violence, and firearms.
- Every school will promote parental involvement in education.[4]

Several states initially objected to Washington's setting goals and standards for public education, which had traditionally been a local function. Further, some observers thought it unfair to "hold students to nationwide standards if they have not had the equal opportunity to learn" due to unequal resources among communities.[5] These concerns, however, did not deter states from setting goals and standards. The autonomy of local and state authorities is also protected, with the federal government's role defined in terms of general goals.

Education has been a key theme in recent elections, with candidates from both major parties and all ideologies insisting that we must improve the quality of public education. However, there are differences about how that should be done. Proposed reforms debated are vouchers, charter schools, national student testing, and more emphasis on reading. Some of these found their way into the Elementary and Secondary

Education Act of 2001 (also called the "No Child Left Behind Act"). And all of them were debated in the 2004 elections at various levels.

VOUCHERS   Some reformers contend we will not see real progress in public education until we inject competition into the system by permitting parents to shop for schools the way they shop for goods and services in the economy. One way to do this would be to provide parents with a set amount of money—**vouchers**—that they could use to pay for part or all of their children's education in a public or private school of their choice. This reform has been labeled "choice in education" because it would give parents the freedom to choose where to send their children to school.[6]

This reform has proved divisive. Voucher advocates say it could help the neediest students escape failed schools and get the valuable academic preparation at private or religious schools. Yet opponents contend it will badly injure financially struggling public schools by diverting much needed money.

Voucher programs have been tried since the mid-1980s in New York, Indianapolis, San Antonio, and Milwaukee. Some programs were directed at low-income students, a plan that, according to one observer, meant some poor families formed political alliances with conservative Republicans, not their more natural liberal Democratic allies. Political scientist and voucher advocate Terry Moe argues:

> In the new politics of education, the conservatives have become the progressives, pushing for major change, promoting the causes of the disadvantaged, and allying themselves with the poor. The progressives of yesteryear, meantime, have become the conservatives of today, resisting change, defending the status quo against threats from without, and opposing the poor constituents they claim to represent.[7]

Among the vigorous opponents of vouchers are teachers' unions, including the National Education Association (NEA) and the American Federation of Teachers (AFT), which, understandably, see vouchers as a threat to jobs and benefits because the use of vouchers could drain off financial support from the public schools.

Some proponents have proposed that voucher programs should include religious schools. Well over 80 percent of the students receiving vouchers in places like Milwaukee and San Antonio attend religious schools, most of them Catholic schools. Opponents of vouchers for religious schools argue that such an arrangement violates the constitutional separation of church and state. They fear too that in some parts of the country, vouchers would be used for schools that practice racial segregation.

Other people oppose the voucher system, even for public schools, on the grounds that such a system would have a negative impact on efforts to reform the public schools. Some argue that it would promote "skimming," meaning that the higher-achieving students would opt out of public schools, leaving behind the underachievers and the discipline problems and creating an increasingly negative atmosphere in public schools. In rural areas, where few private schools exist, some people fear that vouchers might encourage parents to keep the money under the guise of providing "private" home schooling.

Proposals for school vouchers that have been put before the voters have been defeated in Oregon, Colorado, and Washington. In recent years, California and Michigan voters have turned down initiatives that would have established vouchers, in spite of well-financed campaigns supporting their adoption. The political movement pushing vouchers lost some of its steam because of these defeats, the opposition of the teachers'

CHARTER SCHOOLS

In East Los Angeles sits Vaughn Street School, California's first charter school, established in 1992. Most of the children at this elementary school speak English as their second language and live in dangerous neighborhoods. Once the children had to step around a dead body as they approached the school's entryway. It was not a healthy learning environment.

In 1992, Vaughn Street's pupils ranked in the 9th percentile in reading (91 percent of public school students in America could read better than they) and the 14th percentile in math. Now their reading and math scores rank in the 47th and 59th percentile, respectively. Today these students experience hands-on learning about computers in the $1.6 million learning center, and parents from more wealthy neighborhoods want to send their kids to Vaughn. Principal Yvonne Chan attributes these changes to freedom from bureaucracy.

During the past decade, the number of charter schools has grown steadily because of concerns about students' poor academic performance and high dropout rate. About a fifth of all high school students do not graduate. For more state-by-state information, visit the Web site of the Center for Education at www.edreform.com/pubs/chglance.htm.

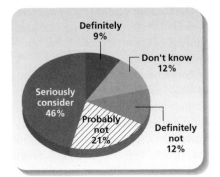

Would Parents Choose Charter Schools?

Source: Public Agenda, reported in "Issues 2000: Education," *The Economist,* September 30, 2000, p. 20. © 2000 The Economist Newspaper Ltd. All rights reserved. Reprinted with permission. Further reproduction prohibited. www.economist.com

unions, and court rulings that said poor families do not have the right to demand vouchers from state and local governments to allow their children to attend better schools.

In 2002, a divided U.S. Supreme Court ruled that poor children could be granted public money (vouchers) to attend religious schools without violating the separation of church and state provisions in the Bill of Rights. Chief Justice William Rehnquist wrote that his majority opinion was "not an endorsement of religious schooling" but merely a means "to assist poor children in failed schools."[8]

Colorado enacted a law in 2003 that provides for students in certain "low" or "unsatisfactory" performance schools to get out of public schools at the request of the parents. "Students qualify if they do badly on state tests and come from poor families living within one of the 11 desegregated districts."[9] A lawsuit was almost immediately filed to block this new Colorado law. The lawsuit claims this voucher program would force taxpayers in many instances to support religion, takes away funding from public schools, undermines our tradition of "full" public schools, and removes local control from school boards.

In 2004, a Florida appeals court ruled that a voucher program in that state violated Florida's constitution because it sent public money to religious institutions.[10]

CHARTER SCHOOLS   One educational reform that does not go as far as vouchers yet still provides publicly funded alternatives to standard public schools is the **charter school.** Some states now grant charters to individuals or groups to start schools and receive public funds if they can meet standards specified by law. Unlike vouchers, which provide funds to the parents, charter schools are under the direct authority of local school boards. There are a few thousand charter schools, with more than 700,000 students. "The vast majority of the schools are operated by local nonprofit organizations, and the educational theories that guide them are as various as the communities they serve."[11]

As with privatization in other government services, charter schools are intended to interject the competition of the marketplace into elementary and secondary education. Charter schools generally have more flexibility to hire and fire teachers and are not subject to the collective bargaining arrangements that prevail in many public school systems. Proponents of charter schools want to remove these schools from state and local regulation as much as possible. Some of their teachers may not have extensive training as education majors, yet proponents of charter schools maintain that classroom performance is more important than the undergraduate major of the teacher.

Teacher unions are concerned about the charter movement, because they might lose their collective bargaining position with school boards if charter schools multiply. Other opponents contend that in school systems already strapped for money, it does not make sense to divert funds to such untested experiments. Concerns about what will be taught in charter schools and the level of teacher competence are often expressed. Also at issue is whether religious schools should qualify for public funds as charter schools.

Charter schools are the fastest form of choice in K–12 education, and they got a big boost from the federally enacted "No Child Left Behind" law that holds out conversion to charter schools as a possible solution for ineffective traditional public schools.

There is much to admire in the charter school movement. Two "Teach For America" alumni launched a series of charter schools under the name of Knowledge Is Power Programs or KIPP. With elementary schools in Houston, New York City, North Carolina, and elsewhere, they have demonstrated effective results. The key to their success is a strict and strong initial commitment by parents and pupils to a philosophy of hard work, longer hours of class time and homework, and no short cuts. That coupled with carefully recruited, dedicated teachers has proven successful.[12]

Yet charter schools vary widely in quality across the country. Indeed, initial test results run in California and by the U.S. Department of Education find that economically disadvantaged students are making more rapid progress in traditional public schools rather than in the new charter schools.[13] This leads critics of the charter movement to say there is no credible evidence that deregulating public education leads to higher student achievement. Supporters contend that the vast majority of charter schools serve students with academic and family problems who are poorly served by traditional public schools. Plainly, there are some excellent and some below average charter schools. Opponents and supporters alike agree that quality schools must be constructed—one at a time.

NATIONAL STUDENT TESTING   Standardized testing is neither new nor controversial. What is new and controversial is *statewide* standardized testing. In 1990, only 14 states had standards for their core curriculum, but 49 states have now adopted standards. After adopting standardized testing for students, Oregon rejected a ballot initiative that would have amended the state constitution to require annual testing of math and verbal skills of public school students in grades 4 through 12.

Even more controversial are *national* tests and *national* norms or goals. Such tests would be administered to students periodically to permit parents, administrators, and legislators to assess how individual students, classes, schools, school districts, and states compare with one another. Moreover, once such testing is established, it could be expanded to include year-to-year measurement of individual students as they progress through the public schools.

Some critics of standardized national tests contend it is unfair and misleading to use such tests to measure learning. Minority students and students in districts in impoverished areas may not do well on these tests, and their low scores will reinforce cultural bias. Other critics worry that the use of such tests will force teachers to "teach to the test." Sensitive to the fact that their students will be compared with students in other classes, teachers will attempt to "beat the test" by emphasizing certain topics and ignoring others. This strategy might work for some students but would limit the learning of others. The main contention of the opponents of national testing, however, is that such measurement will not produce positive changes in education.

State and local policymakers continue to wrestle with how best to fund and implement the standardized testing that is mandated by the federal "No Child Left Behind" Act. While the general goals have been embraced, policymakers and educators hate to have their local schools labeled as "in need of improvement." And local authorities complain that state and national standards often measure factors that are beyond the control of a particular school and its staff. "It's really not fair to judge a school whose kids come without having ever read a book, and compare it to a school where kids go to the library and have libraries in their home," says Lynn Stockleg, a middle school teacher in Tulsa, Oklahoma. "It's rather discouraging when you're one of those schools. You know you're working very, very hard and yet your scores are consistently low."[14]

State and local officials have certainly discovered as well that complying with the "No Child Left Behind" Act is proving far more expensive than anyone had expected.

HIGHER EDUCATION

Until the 1950s, most local school districts provided only elementary and secondary education, although some larger cities also supported junior colleges and universities. Since the end of World War II, however, there has been a major expansion of *community colleges*. Now students may attend the first two years of college or receive a technical education right in their own communities. The trend is to create separate college districts to operate and raise funds for these local colleges.

Administration

States support many kinds of universities and colleges, including land-grant universities such as Michigan State University, created by the Morrill Act of 1862. State colleges and universities are governed by boards appointed by the governor in some states and elected by the voters in others. These boards are designed to give public institutions of higher education some independence, even though they greatly depend on their state legislature and governor for funding.

With about 80 percent of our more than 15 million college students now attending publicly supported institutions, the control and support of higher education have become significant political issues. States spend between 8 and 15 percent of their budgets on higher education, thus making it the third largest allocation of state funds after K–12 spending and Medicaid. States have created boards with varying degrees of control over operations and budgets. In addition, governors have tried to impose controls on universities and colleges that many university administrators insist are inappropriate. Yet institutions of higher education have greater independence from political oversight than other tax-supported institutions. Publicly funded colleges and universities usually can control teaching loads, internal procedures, areas of teaching emphasis, hiring and promotion, and the allocation of funds among internal units.

Funding Higher Education

In the twenty-first century, we face questions of access and funding for our colleges and universities due to increasing enrollments. Who should go? Only those who can afford it? What about minorities who are underrepresented in our colleges and universities? Access to colleges and universities for all students who wish to go has long been the declared goal in many states, but is this goal realistic? Should students be required to pay higher tuition to cover the cost of their education?

Tuition at state universities has gone up, often at two or three times the rate of inflation. Professors' salaries have not kept pace with tuition increases and have grown only slightly more than the rate of inflation. Although many people agree we need an infusion of new money to update college laboratories, improve libraries, and recruit and keep first-rate college professors, there is little consensus about who should pay for these efforts. The federal government is the chief supplier of student financial aid, and many states are now making major efforts to expand their programs of student aid. Many states, such as Georgia, California, Washington, and Alaska, are investing in programs aimed at keeping top students in their states at state-run as well as independent colleges.

Most institutions of higher education—both independent and state-run—receive some kind of government subsidy, through a variety of devices, so that students do not pay the full cost of their education. The national government and most states provide need-based financial assistance in the form of loans and grants, with students in the greatest financial need at the higher-cost institutions eligible for the most aid. Thus higher education has what is in effect a limited voucher system; students receive funds and can choose the kind of college or university that best serves their needs. It also means that in the United States, we have avoided a *two-track system*—one set of colleges and universities for the poor and another for the rich. Poor students can be found in most high-cost independent colleges and universities along with students from higher-income families. Funding for the public universities must compete with the rising costs of other state services, notably Medicaid, transportation, the criminal justice system, and prisons.

Many states are currently experimenting with new ways to fund higher education. As state funds for higher education have gone down in many states, public colleges and universities have been given the okay to raise tuition levels. Gradually the burden of paying for college is being shifted from the state to students and their parents.[15]

Colorado passed a law in 2004 that creates a voucher system for paying for higher education. If this plan survives current court challenges, Colorado will become the first state to fund undergraduate education primarily through grants to individual students. The state's three independent colleges are also entitled to these funds as the law currently stands. Other states will watch whether Colorado has found a better way to fund higher education or whether this mainly masks continued state investments in its higher education institutions.[16]

SOCIAL SERVICES

What role should state and local governments play in making sure all citizens have basic housing, health, and nutritional needs met? How important are these social services compared to government's obligation to provide police and fire protection, education, parks and recreation, and other services? For much of our history, human service needs were left to private charities that ran orphanages, old-age homes, hospitals, and other institutions. Philosophically, this reliance on private charity fit well with the American notions of limited government and self-reliance. That view changed dramatically during the Great Depression of the 1930s, when poverty, unemployment, and homelessness affected such large numbers of people that the government could no longer act as if these were private matters. Then in the mid-1960s, with President Lyndon Johnson's Great Society agenda, the nation embarked on a second major wave of social service programs, which Johnson called the War on Poverty. Today we continue to debate whether such programs accomplish their goals and whether alternatives would prove more successful.

Welfare

Pressure to reform the welfare system increased among both Democrats and Republicans in the last decades of the twentieth century. The number of Americans on welfare soared from about 2 million households in 1950 to close to 6 million in the early 1990s.[17] Why such growth? Some said that this country had finally recognized its obligation to care for the truly poor. Others charged that "government handouts" robbed recipients of the self-confidence they need to go to work and succeed; in this sense, dependence on welfare becomes a curse.

Welfare policy has been a complex web of federal, state, and local programs that shared or matched financial responsibilities. Until recently, the federal government picked up the lion's share of welfare costs. Most of the administrative burden, however, fell on state and local governments. Every state had a department of human services or welfare that either administered welfare programs directly or supervised local officials who administered these programs. County welfare departments determined who was entitled to assistance and dealt directly with recipients.

In 1996, fundamental changes were made in the role of the federal government in providing welfare. Most of the responsibility for welfare was shifted to the states, with national guidelines for administration. The landmark legislation that ended the Aid to Families with Dependent Children (AFDC) program was named Temporary Assistance for Needy Families (TANF).[18] States now receive federal block grants that require state matching funds. Each state files a plan with the secretary of health and human services every two years that (1) explains how it will ensure that recipients engage in work activities within two months of receiving benefits, (2) establishes goals to prevent and reduce out-of-wedlock pregnancies, (3) describes treatment of families moving into the state, and (4) explains whether it intends to provide aid to noncitizens. Money is distributed to states based on the highest amount of federal funding they received in the previous three fiscal years. To continue receiving federal funds, states must spend at least 75 percent of the amount they spent in 1994. Federal money is disbursed through state legislatures, not controlled by the governors. Additional federal funds are available to states as incentives for high performance and as loans in times of financial hardship for the state.

States are encouraged to experiment with welfare programs. Their experiments are evaluated by the federal government in order to ensure that they meet policy goals. Some states had previously started to cut back on welfare payments. For example, Wisconsin's governor, Tommy Thompson (who later served as George W. Bush's Secretary of Health and Human Services), proposed capping welfare payments for unwed teenage mothers, regardless of the number of children they have. Larger grants were paid to those who were married.[19] This provision is now included in national law. Previously, federal laws had unintentionally encouraged fathers to leave the family by making it easier for single-parent families to receive benefits. Current law seeks to overcome this disincentive by offering higher benefits to two-parent families.

Other states have developed **responsibility contracts,** requiring recipients to sign a written agreement specifying their responsibilities and outlining a plan for them to obtain work and achieve self-sufficiency. Some states provide child care and Medicaid benefits beyond the federal one-year extension for families who lose benefits due to unemployment.

About half of the states, including Massachusetts, New York, Wisconsin, and California, have experimented with **workfare** programs designed to help welfare recipients develop the self-confidence, skills, and habits necessary for regular employment. Workfare gives able-bodied adults who do not have preschool-aged children the opportunity to learn job skills that can lead to employment. Another government program creates **enterprise zones** in large cities that give tax incentives to companies that provide job training for the unemployed in depressed neighborhoods.[20]

As a result of the 1996 welfare reform, the percentage of people on welfare was reduced by more than half—from close to 6 million families in the early 1990s to less than half that in recent years. Initially, federal and state welfare expenditures declined significantly, though the booming economy of the late 1990s doubtless helped create a lot of jobs and thus contributed to this decline.

At first glance, the 1996 welfare reform seemed a successful policy; however, the program has had its shortcomings. One critic who worked closely with the bill, Georgetown University Law Center's Peter Edelman, says: "The main lesson of the 1996 law is that having a job and earning a livable income are two different things."[21] It is true that many of the recipients who found jobs through the 1996 law found low-income or part-time jobs. While these jobs technically removed names from the poverty list, they did not decrease the very real difficulty of finding grocery money each week. A survey conducted by the National Governors' Association found that most governors believe the plan requires more contrived community service jobs and costs far more money than allotted.[22] In times of recession, and because many of those left on welfare after the 1996 law are the hard cases—people with little education, no work experience, and tenuous personal backgrounds—creating even more stringent work requirements does not even begin to address the individual needs of those on welfare.

States are now the prime laboratories for making and implementing social policy. The federal government originally became involved in welfare programs because states had been unwilling or unable to tackle these problems on their own. When confronted with competing demands in other policy areas, will states give the needs of poor people a lower priority? And what happens when good economic times turn bad? How will the states cope with larger numbers of needy people?

State welfare expenditures fell again because the recession of 2001 and 2002 forced just about every state to lower payments, tighten eligibility requirements, and shorten the time limits on recipients. Yet several states continue to experiment, sometimes successfully, with reducing poverty, promoting work, and encouraging marital stability.[23]

Health

During the hot summer of 1794, a yellow fever epidemic ravaged Philadelphia. The streets were deserted. All who could afford to do so had fled with their families to the country. Every night, the sounds of the death cart echoed through the nearly empty city. Most families that remained behind lost a child, a father, or a mother. Only when cool weather returned did the city resume normal activity.

Yellow fever, dysentery, malaria, and other diseases periodically swept American cities in the eighteenth and nineteenth centuries. As late as 1879, yellow fever struck hard in the South. Memphis was nearly depopulated. Following the lead of Louisiana and Massachusetts, state after state established a board of health to deal with such epidemics. Spurred by the medical discoveries of Louis Pasteur and other scientists, authorities undertook additional efforts to protect public health. Open sewers were covered, and hygienic measures were instituted.

Prevention and disease control are still major public health activities today. Doctors are required to report cases of communicable disease. Health department officials then investigate to discover the source of the infection, isolate the afflicted, and take whatever action is called for. Most state health departments give doctors free vaccine and serum, and many local departments give free vaccinations to those who cannot afford private physicians. Mobile units take free x-rays of schoolchildren, teachers, and the general public; county health departments provide free or low-cost inoculations, vision tests, and hearing tests. Public health officials also try to protect water supplies and ensure the safe disposal of waste and sewage. They protect the community's food supply by inspecting hotels, restaurants, and food markets.

Today the overwhelming public health issues are pollution, AIDS, smoking, drug abuse, depression, and obesity. Issues such as "mad cow" disease and the West Nile virus also demand state as well as national attention. Like the contagious and infectious disease issues of prior times, they require concerted efforts and public health policies. Thousands of local governments—counties, cities, townships, and special health districts—have some kind of public health program. Every state has an agency, usually called a department of health, that administers the state program and supervises local health officials. At the national level, the U.S. Public Health Service conducts research, assists state and local authorities, and administers federal grants to encourage local agencies to expand their programs. Every state also administers various federally funded medical benefit programs for the needy, such as Medicaid, not to be confused with Medicare—the Social Security health care program for people over 65. Medicaid is the second largest item in overall state budgets.

The current health care crisis in the United States involves access and cost. Wealthy people can afford the costs and gain access; poor people on welfare have somewhat less access to health care, and the quality of their care is often lower. Also, the people in the middle regularly worry about whether their personal insurance will be adequate to cover their health care needs. Programs such as Medicaid seek to fill the health insurance gaps for low-income persons. The larger goal of Medicaid is to improve the health of those who might otherwise go without health care.

Medicaid continues to be a huge concern for state governments nationwide. The increasing number of Medicaid-eligible citizens, coupled with the rising cost of prescription drugs, long-term health care, and HMOs—all far beyond the rate of inflation—add up to a Medicaid program in need of help. Further, the program was expanded during strong financial times, often to include low-income children as well as parents, but when state fiscal conditions are less than perfect, Medicaid is in danger.[24] "That's the irony of Medicaid: The program has a difficult time doing its job when its services are most needed. A sour economy increases demand for coverage and spending, at the same time revenues are eroding and putting heavy pressure on state budgets," notes Trinity Tomsie, who covers Medicaid issues for the National Conference on State Legislator's Fiscal Affairs Program.[25]

State policy makers now face tough questions about whether or not to maintain coverage and if so, how: Should reforms limiting the number of people eligible be implemented to cut costs? Can drug manufacturers be leaned on for rebates? Should a preferred-drug list, based on cost and efficacy, be established? The program is enormous, covering the health care needs for over 40 million Americans and taking an average of at least 13 percent of annual state funds.

Governors around the country pressed President George W. Bush and Congress to increase the federal share of Medicaid's costs, to no avail. Many were frustrated when the president advocated a large farm bill appropriating money for farm subsidies, seemingly ignoring what many think a more pressing financial issue, Medicaid funding. State officials acknowledge nowadays that soaring Medicaid spending threatens recent state goals such as reducing public school class size, increasing public transportation infrastructure, and funding innovative environmental programs. Some states "have reached into the funds received in settling their suits with tobacco companies, or tapped public employee pension funds, or drained their rainy day reserves in order to meet the requirement in state constitutions that they balance their budgets."[26] Other state officials proposed imposing premiums, copayments, and enrollment caps on Medicaid clients as a way to cut costs and raise revenues.

LAW ENFORCEMENT

Many state and local government powers stem from their **police powers,** the inherent power of states to use physical force if necessary to protect the health, safety, and welfare of their citizens. This power is among those not delegated to the federal government by the Constitution and reserved to the states. It is on this basis that mayors or governors impose curfews, as they have in some urban riots. But the police power extends to other activities of government, such as regulating public health, safety, and morals.

The State Police

In 1835, the famous Texas Rangers were organized as a small border patrol. In 1865, Massachusetts appointed a few state constables to suppress gambling, a job the local police had proved unable or, more probably, unwilling to do. But not until 1905, with the organization of the Pennsylvania State Constabulary, did a state police system come into being. It was so successful that other states soon followed.

The establishment of the Pennsylvania State Constabulary marked a sharp break with traditional police methods. This was a mounted and uniformed body organized on a military basis; centralized control was given to a superintendent directly responsible to the governor. The Pennsylvania pattern was followed by other states.

RACIAL PROFILING

Racial profiling—state police stopping and arresting minorities—made news in New Jersey but was also found to occur in other states as well. An extensive review based on interviews with troopers, state officials, and victims revealed a pattern of selective enforcement that had gone on for more than a decade.

The story begins in the mid-1980s, when the federal Drug Enforcement Administration (DEA) responded to the street violence of the crack epidemic by enlisting local police forces to catch smugglers who were importing drugs from Latin America, often to Florida, and moving them to major American cities by car.

By 1989, the New Jersey State Police had become such a successful part of "Operation Pipeline" that DEA officials hailed the troopers as exemplary models for most other states.

But on New Jersey roadways, black and Hispanic drivers were subjected to such frequent and unjustified traffic stops and searches that they complained of a new violation in the state's traffic code: "DWB—driving while black." In state police barracks, some black and Hispanic troopers bitterly acknowledged that even though the state officially prohibited racial profiling, senior troopers trained them to single out drivers on the basis of their ethnicity or race.

On April 22, 1998, troopers shot and wounded three unarmed black and Hispanic men during a traffic stop on the New Jersey Turnpike, propelling the controversy to the center of the state's political stage. State officials, including Governor Christine Todd Whitman, at first clung to their insistence that there was no pattern of profiling. But under pressure from civil rights leaders and the federal Justice Department's Civil Rights Division, the Whitman administration ultimately acknowledged racial profiling, revamped its narcotics strategy, and agreed to let a federal judge monitor the force.

A 2001 court decision wiped out most of these arrests and paid compensation to the victims.

State police became a part of our law enforcement system for a variety of reasons. The growth of urban and metropolitan areas, the coming of the automobile (and the resulting demand for greater protection on the highways and the creation of a mobile force for catching fleeing criminals), and the need for a trained force to maintain order during strikes, fires, floods, and other emergencies all promoted the creation of state police.

Other Police Forces

State police are not the only law enforcement agencies maintained by state governments. There are liquor law enforcement officials, fish and game wardens, fire wardens, detective bureaus, and special motor vehicle police. This dispersion of functions has been criticized, yet each department insists it needs its own law enforcement agency to handle its special problems.

At the local level, almost every municipality maintains its own police force; the county has a sheriff and deputies, and some townships have their own police officers. In fact, there are more than 40,000 separate law enforcement agencies in the United States, employing more than 600,000 men and women.

With crime continuing to be an important issue to many voters, crime control is always on the minds of elected officials. State and local governments spend more than $50 billion on police protection and correctional or prison institutions. Local governments pay for over 70 percent of all law enforcement costs, including such routine activities as controlling traffic and patrolling neighborhoods but also maintaining court security and preventing juvenile crime. The number of police officers increased by 10 percent during the 1990s and may increase even more with recent state and federal homeland security legislation. The federal government in the 1990s provided grants for recruiting and temporarily paying for nearly 100,000 new local police officers throughout the country. But when these grants later expired, many local governments experienced fiscal budget shortfalls. Local governments now struggle to pay for these recently added police officers.

Federal–State Action

The national government has gradually moved into law enforcement, a field traditionally reserved for state and local governments, although the main cost of local law enforcement is still borne by local governments. Today, for example, it is a federal offense to transport kidnapped individuals or stolen goods across state lines. Taking firearms, explosives, or even information across state lines for illegal purposes is also a federal offense. Federal law enforcement agencies include the Federal Bureau of Investigation (FBI), the Bureau of Alcohol, Tobacco, and Firearms (ATF), and the Drug Enforcement Administration (DEA).

Crime rates have been declining. Despite positive trends, politicians in both parties continue to press for government to do more about crime. Some advocate stricter laws regulating guns, while others favor more police on the street or more prisons. Because politicians fear appearing "soft on crime," taking action on crime is almost always a high priority at all levels of government.

Since the September 11, 2001, terrorist attacks on New York City and the Pentagon, every state has designated a homeland security coordinator. These state officials are working with the new federal Department of Homeland Security to beef up preparedness and training efforts aimed at preventing and dealing with future terrorist attacks. The national government approved federal funds in 2002 that were to be used to train and equip "so-called first responders, along with grants to prevent bioterrorism, which have increasingly become the focus of many state officers."[27] While there is a clear need for new and expanded homeland security efforts, few states have the resources to do so. Many local and state officials have complained that most new federal funds are being redirected toward new homeland security concerns such as bioterrorism preparedness while ignoring many of the traditional and basic public safety systems. This has added to budget shortfalls in most states and has led state and local officials to insist on greater federal funds and greater flexibility in how states and localities decide what their priorities are.[28]

PLANNING THE URBAN COMMUNITY

Are our cities good places in which to live and work? Crime, pollution, garbage, crowded shopping areas, dented fenders, slums and blighted areas, inadequate parks, challenging traffic patterns, and shattered nerves—are these the inevitable costs of urban life?

For at least the first century of the United States' existence, American cities were allowed to grow unchecked. Industrialists were permitted to erect factories wherever they wished; developers were allowed to construct towering buildings that prevented sunlight from reaching the streets below; commuters, bicyclists, and pedestrians ended up with transportation systems that rarely met their needs.

Zoning Laws

The most common method of ensuring orderly growth is *zoning*—creating specific areas and limiting property usage in each area. A community may be divided into designated areas for single-family, two-family, or multifamily dwellings; for commercial purposes; and for light or heavy industry. Regulations restrict the height of buildings or require that buildings be located a certain distance apart or a certain distance from the boundaries of the lot.

Zoning regulations attempt to enable the city or county government to coordinate services with land use and to stabilize property values by preventing, for example, garbage dumps from being located next to residential areas. Day-to-day enforcement is usually the responsibility of a building inspector, who ensures that a projected construction project is consistent with building, zoning, fire, and sanitary regulations before granting a building permit. A zoning ordinance, however, is no better than its enforcement. In most cases, a zoning or planning commission or the city council can amend ordinances and make exceptions to regulations, and these officials are often under tremendous pressure to grant exceptions. But if they go too far in permitting special cases, the whole purpose of zoning is defeated.

Zoning is only one kind of community planning. Until recently, city planners were primarily concerned with streets and buildings. Today most are also concerned with the quality of life. Consequently, planning covers a broad range of activities, including methods to avoid air pollution, improve water quality, and provide for better parks. Planners collect all the information they can about a city and then prepare long-range plans. Can smaller-scale communities be devised within urban centers? Can downtown areas be revitalized, and if so, how? Where should main highways or mass-transit facilities be constructed to meet future needs? Will the water supply be adequate for the population 10, 20, or 50 years from now? Are hospitals and parks accessible to all? Does the design of public buildings encourage crime or energy waste?

Controlling Growth

Critics of urban and state planning are skeptical whether governors, mayors, or state and local legislators can prevent what they sometimes call the "Los Angelization" of the United States, by which they mean urban growth without much planning for transportation, environmental protection, or management of water and other resources. Unregulated market forces can cause severe harm to residents, and "politics as usual" does not ensure sensible growth patterns or protect the air, water, and beauty of most states and communities.

Seattle and San Francisco residents voted to limit the height and bulk of downtown buildings in an effort to protect these cities from excessive growth. Maryland and many other states have passed "smart growth" laws aimed at preserving large blocks of contiguous land and ensuring that the necessary roads, sewers, and schools are in place before development proceeds. This legislation is implemented in two ways. The state gives priority funding to development in areas designated by counties as having the proper infrastructure and meeting other guidelines; state funds are also allocated to local governments and private land trusts to purchase the development rights to land "rich in agricultural, forestry, natural, and cultural resources."[29]

The population of the United States will soar by 50 to 60 million by 2025. A few urban planners recommend looking at European cities such as Paris, where choice neighborhoods in the heart of the city combine elegant six- and seven-story apartment buildings above neighborhood retail stores. Most Americans would reject this dense, crowded lifestyle devoid of driveways, grassy front lawns, and backyard pools. But a closer look at European cities often finds a great number of interior gardens within apartments and meticulously groomed neighborhood parks. Columnist Neal Peirce writes that "density and mixed use aren't bad; they're just different—and sometimes better" and notes the discussion and advocacy of a U.S. version of Parisian greenery in a group called Community Greens: Shared Parks in Urban Blocks (www. communitygreens.org).[30]

Obviously, planning and sensible growth depend on public support. They also depend on market forces. No plan will be effective, however, unless it reflects the interests and values of major groups within the community. Planning is clearly a political activity. Different groups view the ends and means of planning differently, and agreements on tough policy options are often hard to reach. Moreover, one of the barriers to successful planning is the general fear of government power. Effective planning therefore requires imaginative collaboration among planners, community leaders, and the popularly elected officials who must bear the responsibility for implementing the plans.[31]

Environmental Regulation

State and local governments have long been concerned about managing land use and protecting the environment. In such heavily polluted places as Pittsburgh, smoke abatement ordinances were enacted as early as 1860, but aggressive action on air pollution did not come until after World War II.[32] By the 1950s, states had established agencies to deal with resource management issues, but it was the federal legislation of the early 1970s that pushed environmental protection onto their agendas.[33] One important reason for the expanded federal role is the reality that pollution does not recognize state boundaries. Air and water pollution are particular examples of the interstate nature of environmental problems.

In the 1950s and 1960s, the federal government provided grants to state and local governments for research and assistance in developing and implementing their own environmental standards. The key piece of legislation in the transition to a greater role for the federal government was the Federal Environmental Protection Act, passed in 1970, which created the Environmental Protection Agency (EPA). Other acts dealing with specific environmental problems followed: the Clean Air Act of 1970, the Clean Water Act of 1972, the Safe Drinking Water Act of 1974, the Toxic Substances Control Act of 1976, and Superfund (the federal Comprehensive Environmental Response, Compensation and Liability Act) of 1980. Most of these acts have been amended one or more times. Subsequent to the passage of the Superfund Act in 1980, which was created in response to public outcry regarding the most contaminated toxic dump sites across the United States, several state and local policies have been established to cover the toxic sites that do not qualify as Superfund sites but still warrant cleanup action.[34]

As states became more involved in toxic waste regulation and air pollution in the 1960s and 1970s, pressure on the national government to develop national environmental standards increased. Part of the pressure for federal legislation was due to the inconsistent state policies being considered and enacted. Not surprisingly, states tend to have different environmental concerns. For example, swine and poultry regulations are more important in the Midwest and Plains states, whereas nuclear cleanup is important in the West and Southwest, and timber regulation is of concern to the Pacific Northwest. Not only did environmental activists want a single national approach to the overarching problems of air and water pollution, but so did many of those who were being regulated. Automobile manufacturers, for instance, preferred one national standard for automobile emissions rather than dozens of differing state standards. Businesses operating in several states also pressed for uniform federal environmental standards.[35]

The basic model of environmental regulation has been for the federal government to set national standards for water and air quality. State and local governments are typically put in charge of both implementing standards and monitoring compliance. Typically, too, states complain that federal regulations and unfunded mandates impose a heavy financial burden on them.

Another area in which states are increasingly responsible for environmental policy is waste management. Not unexpectedly, states where the economy is growing have regulated waste management more aggressively than states where this is not the case. Economically hard-pressed states fear driving industries away. Fears about nuclear waste, acid rain, and hazardous wastes have sparked extensive efforts at regulation within states, as well as court battles with nearby states over the export of unwanted byproducts of energy development.

Although the EPA gets lots of headlines, state and local governments have more people working to control pollution. States can and do experiment with ways to improve air quality. California, for instance, has been a leader in testing automobile emissions. One innovation being considered is *remote sensing*, which uses roadside devices that shoot an infrared beam across a road to detect the emissions of passing cars. This device also has a video camera that records the license plates of vehicles in violation of emission standards. Such a system could replace the periodic state inspections now required for all vehicles.

Many states have been using alternative renewable energy both to cut down on energy costs and to rejuvenate dwindling rural economies. Large-scale wind-energy projects, for example, have been started in New York, Pennsylvania, Colorado, Iowa, Kansas, Texas, and Washington, among other states. Most of these were begun in the 1990s or more recently. As fossil fuel costs became increasingly unpredictable, states started to diversify their approach by investing in biomass, wind, hydroelectric, solar, and geothermal projects. Some states have even implemented innovative tax incentives and "net metering" programs (a practice allowing customers who have solar panels or other personal energy-generating capital to sell their energy back to the overall grid) in order to encourage more individual responsibility. Although none of these tactics have yet become widely accepted, nor is renewable energy expected to soon replace traditional energy sources, they are evidence of active state and local environmental efforts (Figure 9–2). Many states have also taken the lead in regulating cold-fired power plants, unsafe mercury pollution levels and greenhouse gas emissions.[36]

Environmental interest groups continue to press for stronger state and local environmental regulation, cars that go more miles on a gallon of gas and "smart" hybrid cars, and continue to demand that stiff penalties be imposed for violations of environmental laws. Further, some of the effort has shifted to individual action—recycling, conservation, saving and planting trees, and using public transportation. As the need for environmental regulation becomes more and more pressing, many state and local governments continue to react by expanding existing legislation and appropriating money for research and regulatory agency staff.[37]

Transportation

Before the automobile, long-distance commercial travel was mainly by canal and railroad. Local roads were built and repaired under the direction of city, township, and county officials. Able-bodied male citizens were required either to put in a certain number of days working on the public roads or to pay taxes for that purpose. By the 1890s,

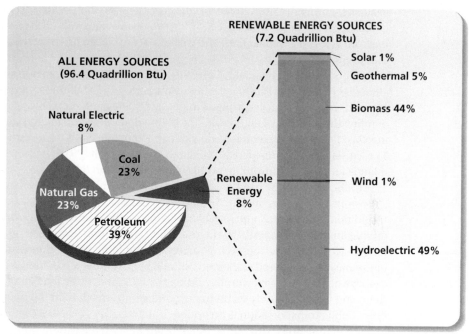

FIGURE 9–2 U.S. Energy Consumption by Source, 1999.
From 1998 to 1999, electricity generated from wind power increased 50 percent and geothermal use increased 14 percent.
SOURCE: Energy Information Administration.

bicycle clubs began to urge the building of hard-surfaced roads, but it was not until the early 1900s and the growing popularity of the automobile that road building became a major industry. This function was gradually transferred from the township to larger units of government, but counties and townships still have important building and maintenance functions.

Although much of the money comes from the federal government, it is the state and local governments that build the highways, public buildings, airports, parks, and recreational facilities. State and local governments, in fact, spend more money on transportation than on anything else except education and welfare. Because highways and bridges around the nation are aging, a federal tax on gasoline was levied to help rebuild these public facilities.

The national government has supported state highway construction since 1916, and through various federal highway laws passed since then, federal aid has increased. States do the planning, estimate the costs, and arrange for the construction work, even when they receive federal assistance. In order to receive support, however, states must submit their plans to, and have their work inspected by, the U.S. Department of Transportation (DOT). All federally funded highways must meet DOT standards governing the engineering of the roadbed, employment conditions for construction workers, and weight and load conditions for trucks.

Under the Federal Highway Act of 1956, states planned and built the National System of Interstate and Defense Highways. The interstate system consists of 43,000 miles of superhighways linking almost all cities with a population of 50,000 or more. The federal government paid 90 percent of the cost of this system, with most of the money coming from taxes on gasoline, tires, and trucks that are placed in a trust fund designated for that purpose.

In 1998, Congress passed a $216 billion, six-year surface transportation bill that included $173 billion in funding for highways as well as $2 billion for highway safety. The bill funds repairing cracked asphalt, increasing safety reinforcements on bridges, and expanding the network of highways. One billion dollars is dedicated to state programs to increase the percentage of drivers who use safety belts and to prevent drunk driving. The legislation also provided $41 billion for mass transit.[38] This massive federal investment is funded by continuing the 18.3 cents-per-gallon tax on gas.

Traffic has become a major problem in recent years—especially in older cities such as Boston; Denver; Los Angeles; Seattle; San Francisco; Washington, D.C.; and New York. In addition to a growing population and an increasing number of car owners, drivers are driving more each year. As a result, traffic and congestion have become pressing issues for state governments. Increasing road space, building public transportation systems, or establishing staggered work hours should help; however, transportation policy makers have not found it that simple. Adding roads or lanes often leads more people to use them and may ultimately result in new traffic patterns that are no better than the old ones. Public transportation is an option, but Americans love their vehicles, illustrated by the fact that cities with public transportation often have more traffic problems than those without. Staggering work hours is also difficult because businesses work most effectively through collaboration—both with other businesses and within a firm—and so, it is most efficient for workers to be on the job at the same time each day. Consequently, as population and car ownership continue to rise and the traffic solution remains elusive, automobile congestion will continue to be a pressing state public policy issue.[39]

Economic Development

Another central priority for governors and mayors, as well as other state and local officials, is providing jobs for their citizens. Governors commonly spend a significant amount of time encouraging companies to relocate within their borders, courting corporate officials, going on trade missions to other countries to promote their state's products, and negotiating favorable tax and other incentives with new businesses. This interest is not new. What is new is the international scope of these activities. Former Utah Governor Norman Bangerter was fond of saying, "The one thing you will always see on an economic development trip to Tokyo is another governor."

States compete with one another because economic development is the key to increasing the tax base that funds government services. But states face a dilemma, because satisfying the demands of new businesses can be expensive, and tax incentives can reduce the tax return the new companies will generate. Competition among states has intensified to the point that localities are worried about keeping the jobs they have, not just persuading new companies to move to their area. New York City has offered billions of dollars in incentives to influence several companies not to leave. Critics of these "bidding wars" believe that states should spend tax money on rebuilding infrastructure and strengthening education rather than offering public funds to selected large private companies.

REGULATION

States and local communities adopt safety regulations on the assumption (sometimes mistaken) that the benefits to the general public will outweigh the costs to the individuals and groups being regulated. Thus laws requiring drivers' licenses, compelling motorists to stop at red lights, mandating seat-belt use, or imposing severe penalties on people caught driving under the influence of alcohol or drugs are intended to protect the safety and freedom of innocent pedestrians or occupants of other motor vehicles. Most such laws are accepted as both necessary and legitimate. States have raised the drinking age and stiffened the punishments for drunk driving, in most cases because the federal government tied federal funds to the passage of such legislation. An interest group, Mothers Against Drunk Driving (MADD), also lobbied effectively to force the issue.

Public Utilities

Corporations receive their charters from the states. Banks, insurance companies, securities dealers, doctors, lawyers, teachers, barbers, and various other businesses and professions are licensed by the states, and their activities are supervised by state officials. Farmers and industrial and service workers are also regulated. But of all businesses, public utilities are the most closely monitored.

It is easier to list than to define public utilities. They include water plants, electric power and natural gas distribution companies, telephone companies, railroads, and bus lines. Public utilities are distinguished from other businesses because government gives them special privileges, such as the power of **eminent domain** (the right to take private property for public use), the right to use public streets, and a certain amount of protection from competition (monopoly). In return, utilities are required to give the public adequate service at reasonable rates.

Public utilities supply essential services in fields in which market competition may be counterproductive. In the United States, private enterprise—subject to public regulation rather than public ownership—has been the usual method of providing essential services. Nevertheless, more than two-thirds of our cities own their own waterworks, about 100 operate their own gas utilities, and many are taking over the operation of their transit systems. But other services—intercity transportation, airlines, telephone, and the supply of natural gas—are almost everywhere provided by private enterprises subject to government regulation.

Every state has a utilities commission (usually called the Public Utilities Commission, or PUC) to ensure that utilities operate in the interest of the public. In 36 states, utility commissioners are appointed by the governor with the consent of the state senate. In Virginia and South Carolina, they are chosen by the legislature, and in eleven other states, they are elected by the voters.[40] PUC posts were once considered political plums, and commissioners used them as stepping-stones to higher elective office. This is less true these days.

PUCs must strike a balance between fair rates for consumers and adequate profits for the utility companies. "The tremendous work load on these commissions," writes one observer, "finds commissioners constantly walking a tightrope between helping a regulated industry get a decent return on investment, and making sure consumers get good service at a fair price."[41] Utility commissioners raise or lower utility rates—perhaps the most visible part of their job—but they are also involved in toxic waste disposal, nuclear power, and truck regulation, as well as telephone, cable television, and other energy-related disputes. The average tenure for commissioners is only about three and a half years, a statistic that suggests the burnout involved in the job.

Utility commissioners operate under the assumption that their decisions are not political, yet nearly every decision they make comes under political attack or stirs political reaction. Several states have enacted laws prohibiting conflicts of interest, limiting commissioners' affiliations with the utilities they regulate and, for at least a year after they resign from the PUC, prohibiting them from accepting employment with any company that was under their regulation. Other states have established a separate office of consumer advocate to encourage even greater responsiveness to consumer needs.

Technology and innovation are driving the deregulation of utilities across the nation. The deregulation of utilities is a controversial topic in virtually every state legislature, as telephone and power companies seek to influence the new rules for competition. Telephone communication is no longer limited to transmissions over telephone lines but now includes cellular and satellite communications. Gas turbines now make it possible for some consumers to generate their own electricity rather than depend on power from public utility companies. Much of the political pressure for deregulation of utilities comes from businesses as well as from consumers.[42]

State legislatures and utility regulators are adopting a marketplace model in which competition between providers is encouraged rather than restricted. In the past, state utility regulators structured rate systems to provide a subsidy to rural and low-income consumers of telephone and electricity services. It is likely that these subsidies will continue, but it is more difficult to identify who pays the subsidy with so many firms now providing telephone and electricity services.

The politics of regulation, especially regulation of public utilities, is of growing interest to citizens and consumers. In many areas, citizens' groups make presentations to the PUC and regularly monitor PUC operations. There has been an increasing interest in PUC activity all across the country, especially in regulating nuclear power and monitoring the cost of energy. For example, after many years of citizen concern over the environmental impact of the San Onofre Nuclear Generating Station, the California Coastal Commission adopted a plan that would mitigate, but not prevent, the destruction of fish and kelp.[43] In Virginia, the water in Chesapeake Bay was found to contain high levels of pollutants that cause an increased risk of cancer, and that discovery led the public utilities director to impose a strict monitoring program and stiff fines for violations.

Employers and Employees

Despite the expanded regulations of the national government, state and local governments still have much to say about working conditions.

- ■ *Health and Safety Legislation:* States require proper heating, lighting, ventilation, fire escapes, and sanitary facilities in work areas. Machinery must be equipped with safety guards. Some standards have also been established to reduce occupation-related diseases. Health, building, and labor inspectors tour industrial plants to ensure compliance with the laws.

- *Workers' Compensation:* Today all states have workers' compensation programs based on the belief that employees should not have to bear the cost of accidents or illnesses incurred because of their jobs. The costs of accidents and occupational diseases are borne by employers and passed on to consumers in the form of higher prices. In the past, employees had to prove that their employers were at fault if they suffered an accident on the job. Today if people are injured or contract a disease in the ordinary course of employment, they are entitled to compensation set by a prearranged schedule. Workers' compensation is a controversial issue, with employers arguing that employee claims of workplace stress are excessive and will make American firms uncompetitive.

- *Child labor:* All states forbid child labor, yet state laws vary widely in their coverage and in their definition of child labor. Many states set the minimum age for employment at 14. Higher age requirements are normal for employment in hazardous occupations and during school hours. Many of these regulations have been superseded by stricter federal laws.

- *Consumer Protection:* This movement, which became prominent in the 1960s and 1970s, believes that consumers should be provided with adequate safety information and should have their complaints heard. Most states have offices to hear consumer complaints, including lawyers working in the offices of the state attorney general. State governments often establish professional standards and handle complaints about legal and medical services or insurance practices.

Recent state activity to protect consumers has focused on fraud, especially "guaranteed prize schemes," which are mailed to more than 50 million Americans and to which millions respond. When the prize is not exactly what was promised or the method for selecting winners is deceptive, people often complain to their state government. Other areas in which state governments have been active in attempting to protect consumers include charitable solicitations by telephone, long-distance phone service promotions, credit and promotions, and auditing irregularities and fraud in corporations.

THE IMPORTANCE OF STATE AND LOCAL POLICY

All 50 state governments and more than 86,000 local governments are on the front lines of trying to solve community and regional social problems. They must often work closely with one another and the national government, and this is a frequent source of frustration.[44]

Divided government in Washington in recent years has meant neither political party could have its way with domestic policy. Bill Clinton and George W. Bush had different priorities, and the generally divided U.S. Senate in recent years has usually taken a cautious approach on such issues as health care and environmental regulation.

State officials continue to be frustrated with national legislation such as the "No Child Left Behind" and homeland security legislation in recent years that mandate extensive federal requirements into core areas of state and local policy responsibilities yet provide inadequate federal funds to assist in the achievement of these goals.

Innovative governors and state legislators have sponsored important changes in welfare reform, educational testing, transportation, urban planning, and insurance regulation. But the challenges facing state and local officials never let up.

S U M M A R Y

1. We ask our state and local governments to do many things for us, and what we request in the areas of education, public welfare, health and hospitals, public safety, and transportation are the most costly, accounting for most state and local expenditures.

2. In addition, we ask states and communities to keep our streets safe, protect our natural resources, provide parks and recreation, encourage job opportunities, and protect consumers. There are, of course, great differences in how states and communities set their priorities in these areas. Some communities are so concerned about environmental quality that they are settling for selective growth at the expense of job opportunities. Other communities favor attracting jobs and industry despite environmental costs.

3. Education has been a major area of state and local government activity and concern. It moved to center stage because of a growing concern that our system was not keeping pace with our needs or our global competitors. Several reform efforts have sought to improve our system.

4. Concern about the U.S. system of higher education has also grown as states attempt to balance budgets and meet pressing demands in corrections, health, welfare, and other areas. Few people question the need for a major investment in laboratories, computer instruction, and libraries at colleges and universities, yet the federal government has not offered to pay for these things, and most states do not have the resources to do more than stay afloat in this policy area.

5. The huge national welfare overhaul legislation in 1996 eliminated any federal implementation of programs, transferring all responsibility to the states, supported with block grants of federal money. It was prompted by a desire to trim the federal budget and to eliminate disincentives for self-sufficiency and responsibility that the former welfare system seemed to create. Before the national legislation was passed, many states had experimented with limiting their caseload, placing time limits on welfare, implementing a work requirement, and placing special requirements on teenage mothers. Most of these ideas were then included in the 1996 federal law.

6. States play an important role in setting policies relating to public health. States have long sought to eradicate disease and foster practices conducive to a healthy population. The challenges for states today include the administration of federal outlay programs such as Medicaid, reforming health care services, and controlling the AIDS epidemic. Soaring Medicaid costs have posed an additional challenge to state governments.

7. Law enforcement is a traditional responsibility of state and local governments. After several decades of rising crime rates, that trend has recently been reversed, in part because of increased national and state expenditures.

8. Some state and local governments have taken the lead in protecting the environment, but more generally it has been the federal government that sets the policy standard in environmental matters. Businesses operating in several states are often most involved in pressing for national standards of air and water quality and policies on toxic wastes. The federal government typically sets environmental standards; the states enforce them.

9. Transportation is a major area of state and local government activity. Although the federal government provides some financial assistance with the construction of roads and highways as well as urban mass transit, the responsibility of planning, building, and maintaining these transportation systems lies with the states. Federal and local fuel taxes have been used to help pay for transportation.

10. States openly compete with one another in the area of economic development by offering tax incentives, waiving environmental regulations, and giving other enticements to businesses to locate or stay within their boundaries.

11. The primary purpose of regulation is to protect the health and safety of individuals and to promote fairness in the marketplace. Among the most regulated industries are public utilities because they enjoy a monopoly. Government usually gives these companies special privileges, specifically eminent domain—the power to take private property for public use. Public utilities, like other industries, are being deregulated as state and federal governments permit competition in these areas. States regulate other economic activities by conducting inspections, granting licenses, and limiting land uses.

F U R T H E R R E A D I N G

BURT S. BARNOW, THOMAS KAPLAN, AND ROBERT A. MOFFITT, EDS., *Evaluating Comprehensive State Welfare Reforms* (Brookings Institution Press, 2000).

JOHN D. DONAHUE, *Disunited States* (Basic Books, 1997).

DENNIS DRESANG AND JAMES GOSLING, *Politics and Policy in American States and Communities,* 2d ed. (Prentice Hall, 1998).

R. KENNETH GODWIN AND FRANK KEMERER, *School Choice and Tradeoffs: Liberty, Equity, and Diversity* (University of Texas Press, 2002).

VIRGINIA GRAY AND RUSSELL HANSON, *Politics in the American States: A Comparative Analysis,* 8th ed. (CQ Press, 2003).

DAVID HAGE, *Reforming Welfare By Rewarding Work: One State's Successful Experiment* (University of Minnesota Press, 2004).

JOHN J. HARRIGAN, *Politics and Policy in States and Communities,* 6th ed. (HarperCollins, 1997).

NORMAN R. LUTTBEG, *The Grassroots of Democracy: A Comparative Study of Competition and Its Impact in American Cities in the 1990s* (Lexington Books, 1999).

DAVID C. NICE, *Policy Innovation in State Government* (Iowa State University Press, 1994).

GARY ORFIELD AND CHUNGMEI LEE, *Brown at 50: King's Dream or Plessy's Nightmare* (Harvard Civil Rights Project, 2004).

MICHAEL A. PAGANO AND ANN O. M. BOWMAN, *Cityscape and Capital: The Politics of Urban Development* (Johns Hopkins University Press, 1997).

DENISE SCHEBERLE, *Federalism and Environmental Policy,* 2d ed. (Georgetown University Press, 2004).

MARK SCHNEIDER, PAUL TESKE, AND MELISSA MARSHALL, *Choosing Schools: Consumer Choice and the Quality of American Schools* (Princeton University Press, 2002).

C. EUGENE STEUERLE, VAN DOORN OOMS, GEORGE PETERSON, AND ROBERT D. REISCHAUER, EDS., *Vouchers and the Provision of Public Services* (Brookings Institution Press, 2000).

SANDRA VERGARI, ED., *The Charter School Landscape* (University of Pittsburg Press, 2002).

R. KENT WEAVER, *Ending Welfare as We Know It* (Brookings Institution Press, 2000).

JOHN F. WITTE, *The Market Approach to Education: An Analysis of America's First Voucher Program* (Princeton University Press, 1999).

See also *Governing: The Magazine of States and Localities,* published monthly by Congressional Quarterly, Inc., and the series of excellent books on state government public policy making published by the University of Nebraska Press.

STAFFING AND FINANCING STATE AND LOCAL GOVERNMENTS

S tate and local government workers are American government's first responders. New York City police and firefighters were the first to arrive at the World Trade Center on September 11, 2001; city paramedics were the first to treat the victims; city social workers were on the scene almost immediately to deal with the grief and shock; and virtually every city worker was involved in some way in the recovery.

The nation's state and local employees are more than first responders to disaster, however. Six million are public school teachers; 1.2 million work as police and firefighters; 700,000 work as prison guards and correction officers; 600,000 work in social welfare; 450,000 work in state, county, and city hospitals; and 200,000 work in parks and recreation.

State and local employees have some of the most challenging jobs in the nation. They help families move from welfare to work; provide shelter for the homeless; keep the streets and sidewalks clean; drive the subways and buses; provide vaccinations for poor children; pave the streets and purify the water; build and run affordable housing; enroll families and children for Medicaid coverage; provide unemployment insurance and counseling; and even take the tickets at National League Baseball games. The federal government may design the economic regulation and social policy, but state and local government employees are the ones who often deliver on the promises.

This chapter will examine the role of state and local employees in more detail, while asking how states and localities raise the money to pay for such a large workforce. The chapter will also review the increasing financial pressure states and local governments face as needs increase and funding gets tighter.

THE ROLE OF PUBLIC EMPLOYEES

State and local governments are responsible for many policy goals, including greater accountability in public education, greater access to health care for uninsured children, and economic development for poor communities; but they do most of that work by hiring state and local government employees to actually deliver the goods and services. Unlike the federal government workforce, which actually has relatively few employees who work directly with citizens, almost all state and local employees have contact with the citizens.

As of 2002, roughly 19 million people worked for state and local governments, roughly ten times the number that worked for the federal government. And according to the U.S. Bureau of Labor Statistics, state and local governments will continue growing well into the next decade—by 2012, over 21 million Americans will work in the nation's roughly 87,000 state and local governments, a growth rate of almost 20 percent. During the same period, the federal government is expected to stay the same size.[1]

Merit Systems

More than one-third of the cost of state and local government is for people. How are these people chosen? A few of them are elected. The rest are generally hired through some kind of **merit system** in which selection and promotion depend on demonstrated performance (merit) rather than on political patronage. Although in many jurisdictions it still helps to know the right people and belong to the right party, patronage is not as prevalent as it once was. Affirmative action requirements call for recruitment through open procedures. The fact that many public employees now belong to unions has also reduced patronage.

Throughout much of the nineteenth century, governments at all levels were dominated by political patronage, a political **spoils system** in which employment was a reward for partisan loyalty and active political support in campaigns and elections. However, in 1939, Democratic Senator Carl Hatch of Arizona pushed through Congress the first Hatch Act, which promoted the merit principle and limited the political activities of federal, state, and local employees whose salaries were supported with federal funds. Subsequently, state and local governments enacted "little Hatch Acts" that enforced merit principles and restricted the political activities of their employees. Merit testing is now used in 30 states for hiring or promoting employees.[2] Moreover, under a 1976 Supreme Court decision, states cannot dismiss civil servants for political reasons.[3]

Merit systems are generally administered by an office of state personnel, which prepares and administers examinations, provides lists of job openings, establishes job classifications, and determines salary schedules. It also serves as a board of appeal for employees who are discharged. State personnel offices are concerned with training the already employed, bargaining with labor unions, administering affirmative action programs, and filling top-level executive positions.

Critics complain that state personnel offices take too much time to fill job vacancies, in part because they are hampered by red tape and clumsy rules, and in part because job lists are not kept up-to-date. Some critics also complain that hiring and firing rules deprive responsible officials of authority over their subordinates. It is argued that there is so much

CHANGING FACE OF AMERICAN POLITICS

THE STATE AND LOCAL WORKFORCE

Like the federal government, state and local governments have become more diverse over the past two decades and will become even more diverse as they add new jobs. Excluding school teachers, who are overwhelmingly white and female, the U.S. Census Bureau reports that the state and local workforce is becoming an employer of choice for both women and minorities. The increasing percentage of Hispanics is largely due to population growth in states such as California, Florida, and Texas, where Hispanic workers are moving into state and local government jobs at high rates.*

Although the percentages of women and minority workers have increased over the past two decades, both groups remain underpaid relative to males and whites. In 2001, males made an average of $39,800 a year, compared with $32,100 for females, $31,500 for African Americans, and $33,500 for Hispanics. Among high-paid professional jobs, men made almost $9,000 a year more than females, in part because men tend to concentrate in the higher-paying professions such as law, finance, and health administration, while women tend to concentrate in historically underpaid professions in human services such as child welfare.

	1981	2001
Male	59%	55%
Female	41	45
White	79%	69%
African American	16	19
Hispanic	4	8

*See U.S. Census Bureau, *Statistical Abstract of the United States, 2003* (U.S. Census Bureau, 2004), table no. 470.

emphasis on insulating public employees from political coercion that employees enjoy too much job security. Administrators cannot get rid of incompetents; sometimes it takes months and several elaborate hearings to dismiss public employees unwilling or unable to do their jobs. Although merit systems are supposed to emphasize ability and minimize political favoritism, they sometimes discourage able people from seeking public sector jobs.

Public Employee Unions

Public employee unions grew rapidly over the past generation as government workers organized to demand better wages, hours, working conditions, and pensions. These unions now wield considerable political clout in most states and cities. In places such as New York City, they are viewed as one of the most powerful forces in political life. In dealing with unions, state and local governments participate in **collective bargaining**—negotiating disputes between unions and management—and **binding arbitration**—settling disputes by agreeing to adhere to the decision of an arbitrator.

Thirty-five percent of state employees and 46 percent of local employees are represented by unions, compared with less than 10 percent of private-sector employees.[4] Indeed, national employee unions see state and local government as a significant growth area.

The American Federation of State, County, and Municipal Employees (AFSCME), is the largest state and local government union, representing over 1.4 million members, followed by the Service Employees International Union (SEIU), with more than 600,000 state and local government members. In addition, National Education Association (NEA) represents roughly 2.5 million of the nation's 6 million public-school teachers, followed by the American Federation of Teachers (AFT), which represents another 1 million.

Many police officers and firefighters are also union members. The firefighters' union is often considered one of the most effective political organizations among public employee unions, and the union sometimes engages in door-to-door and telephone campaigning to elect city officials. Unions often raise funds for candidates and sponsor letter-writing campaigns to influence local and national elections. Union pressure in the 1970s and 1980s was a major reason the average pay of public employees, including benefits, rose faster than that of workers in private industry. However, since 1995, employees in private businesses have done better than public employees.

The failure of the merit system to meet many of the needs of public employees encouraged the growth of public sector unions. Growth was also spurred by the example of the success of collective bargaining in the private sector (see Table 10–1). But much

---

TABLE 10–1   COMPARISON OF MERIT AND COLLECTIVE BARGAINING SYSTEMS

	Merit System	*Collective Bargaining*
Management rights	Extensive	Minimal
Employee participation and rights	Union membership not required	Union membership required
Recruitment and selection	Open competitive exam; open at any level	Union membership and/or occupational license
Promotion	Competitive on basis of merit (often including seniority)	On basis of seniority
Classification of position	Based on objective analysis	Classification negotiable
Pay	Based on balanced pay plan or subject to prevailing rates	Negotiable and subject to bargaining power of union
Hours, leave, conditions of work	Based on public interest as determined by legislature and management	Negotiable
Grievances	Appeal through management with recourse to civil service agency	Appeal by union representation to impartial arbitrators

SOURCE: From *Democracy and the Public Service*, 2d ed., by Frederick C. Mosher, © 1982 by Oxford University Press, Inc. Used by permission of Oxford University Press, Inc.

of the success of public employee unions has come about because government workers learned how to become a political force in government. Most public employees are educated, intelligent people who can deliver two of the most valuable components of campaigns: money and labor (not to mention the votes of their members, members' families, and friends).

Many people think that public workers have more job security and better wages and fringe benefits than people working in the private sector. Critics point out that public employees seem to have the best of both worlds: job protection coupled with the bargaining power of a labor union. Although collective bargaining and unionization have been generally accepted in the private sector, these rights were not as widely accepted in the public sector.

Because the public sector provides services almost everyone wants and perceives as necessities, demand is relatively constant. Also, public employee unions are an effective political force, so they can influence crucial decisions that affect taxation and the allocation of revenue. Some analysts believe these two factors may result in policies that favor public employees. Awareness of this political clout of the unions has stiffened the spines of some city and state officials. Today it is not uncommon for mayors in large cities to fight the unions and win support from taxpayers and business groups who think the unions have overstepped their bounds.

Should Public Services Make a Profit?

To make government more efficient and curb the growing influence of public employee unions, many communities have "contracted out" certain public services to the private sector. This practice, called **outsourcing,** can mean that governments save money while the private sector providers still make a profit.[5] Because state and local governments retain the power to raise the revenue for outsourced activities, they maintain control of how the private firms perform through very precise contracts. Today virtually every community service is contracted out somewhere in the United States, and this trend is expected to continue.[6]

In Texas, for example, any citizen who seeks public assistance can call a toll-free help number answered by private employees who have instant computer access to an array of state and local government benefits, as well as the caller's own financial information. Using the information, these telephone operators can tell each caller whether he or she qualifies for a variety of programs, from food stamps to health insurance for their children.

Texas is also poised to outsource its entire human service bureaucracy. In 2004, the state consolidated twelve separate human services agencies into four, then asked private contractors to run the entire operation. Although state employees will still make the final decision about who actually gets the benefits, private firms will actually run the administrative side of the new departments, from hiring employees to buying computers.[7]

Many state and local governments have also given private companies complete control of certain activities such as garbage collection through full **privatization.** Privatization involves the complete severance of a function from government—private firms are responsible for both performing a service and also for collecting the revenues through regular billing. Although states and localities vary widely in the extent to which they privatize, public–private partnerships have grown during the past two decades in order to reduce the costs of government services and to improve economic development.

One frequently cited example of privatization is Indianapolis; under the leadership of former Mayor Stephen Goldsmith, the city claimed to have saved $230 million over a decade through outsourcing and full privatization.[8]

As cities and states have become pressed for cash, efforts to encourage entrepreneurs to provide public services at a profit have increased. Delegation of emergency and police powers to profit-making corporations, however, raises questions of liability and protection of individual rights. It also raises fears that private contractors will hire transient help at less pay, undermining merit systems and public employee morale.

For successful privatization to occur, the contract between the government and the private company providing the service must define that service to the satisfaction of both parties. On one hand, because of the wide range of services provided by local police departments or health departments, it may be difficult to word such a contract. On the other hand, garbage collection and snow removal can easily be defined and specified in a contract, making these services attractive for privatization, so the trend toward outsourcing municipal services like these will continue.[9]

PAYING FOR STATE AND LOCAL GOVERNMENT

John Shannon, an authority in the field of public finance, has written that there were three "R's" that shocked state and local governments in the recent past. The first "R" was the *revolt* of the taxpayers, which started with California's Proposition 13 and quickly became a national phenomenon. The second "R" was the *recession* of the late 1980s and early 1990s, which placed demands on state and local governments to care for the unemployed and needy. And the third "R" was the *reduction* in federal grants, which meant state and local governments were on their own.[10] States had to search for ways to make ends meet and to live within their revenue projections.

The three "R's" returned with a vengeance in the late 1990s and early 2000s. Taxpayers continue to protest against tax increases, especially property and income taxes; recession returned in 2001 with a devastating impact on state budget revenues; and the federal government continued to tighten grants. Although federal grants to the states did go up from $285 billion in 2000 to nearly $400 billion in 2004, three-quarters of the increase was due to increased spending for health care under the Medicaid program for poor citizens and for food stamps. With unemployment payments surging with the recession, most states found themselves with little or no leeway to meet their budget needs. As of 2003, the 50 states found themselves with a combined $21.5 billion budget shortage, which they closed through budget cuts. By 2005, however, the economy had started to recover, and state revenues rose as a result. According to the National Conference of State Legislatures, the total budget gap in 2004 was just $720 million total. Although 20 states still faced budget deficits, 30 actually reported surpluses. Florida, Nevada, Oklahoma, South Dakota, and Wyoming actually reported surpluses larger than 5 percent of their total spending. "But this breathing room comes after three consecutive years of fiscal crisis, when states had to cut funding in such core areas as education, health care and corrections," writes the National Conference of State Legislatures.[11]

States are far from healthy, however. Most had to cut spending or raise taxes to balance their budgets for 2005. Most also faced increased spending pressure as the federal government continued to trim its own spending.

Sources of Revenue

State and local governments get most of their money from taxes.[12] Yet unlike the federal government, they are more likely to share control of the process of raising taxes with the voters through referendums, which are sometimes required before they can levy new or higher taxes. In addition, state and local governments frequently have to meet responsibilities mandated by higher levels of government, which do not always provide the funding for those mandates.

The politics of reducing the federal budget deficit and the antitax mood of the public in recent decades have meant that Congress and the president often enacted policies and expected state and local governments to pick up the tab. At the same time, citizens had high expectations for services provided by their state and local governments—and wanted even more services. This combination of increasing demand and decreasing federal funding made state and local governments the fiscal "stress joints" of American government. When the economy is thriving, states often have surplus revenue and enact tax cuts, but when times are not as good, they have to raise taxes and cut spending. Because most states are constitutionally forbidden to use deficit spending for general government programs, they have to balance their budgets and respond to shortfalls by strengthening and diversifying their revenue bases.[13]

The overlapping layers of government in the United States complicate the tax picture. Tax policies at different levels of government often conflict. While the federal government is reducing taxes, states may be raising them. Indeed, when the federal government cuts both taxes and federal grants, state and local governments have little choice but to raise taxes or cut spending. This is precisely what happened in the late 1970s and early 1980s, and in the economic slow-down of 2002.[14] But the ability of states to respond to changing economic circumstances has been hampered by the tax revolt of the late 1970s, which lowered taxes and brought forth constitutional amendments that make it harder to raise them. Many states also enacted spending limits, which reduced the discretion of state and local elected officials.

The ability of different levels and units of government to make their own tax policy has made tax collection more complicated and expensive. For example, national officials, state officials, and some local officials collect taxes on gasoline, and each level of government maintains its own tax-collecting office. Taxpayers are allowed to deduct certain business expenses and state income taxes from their federal income tax. Texas, Florida, South Dakota, New Hampshire, Nevada, Washington, and Wyoming have no personal income tax and rely primarily on sales taxes. In those states, taxpayers lose the deduction for state income taxes on their federal tax returns. By contrast, in Alabama, Iowa, Louisiana, Missouri, Montana, North Dakota, Oklahoma, Oregon, and Utah, taxpayers may deduct their federal income tax from their state taxes.[15] Thus changes in state laws can affect the amount of federal and state taxes a person must pay. Although there is little coordination in setting tax policy, there is cooperation between state and federal tax administrators.

No matter who collects the taxes, all the money comes out of a single economy. Although each level of government has a different tax base and each tax hits some groups rather than others, all taxes ultimately depend on the productivity of the American people. And that productivity is affected by many of the activities of government.

Who Pays the Taxes?

Who bears the cost of state and local services is decided in the United States by politics. State and local governments are free to extract whatever taxes they wish from whomever they wish, as long as their taxing practices meet the stipulations of the U.S. Constitution and, in most cases, unless the tax is in conflict with federal laws. The Constitution has been interpreted to prohibit states from taking the following actions:

1. Taxing exports or imports or levying tonnage duties without the consent of Congress

2. Using their taxing power to interfere with federal operations

3. Discriminating against interstate commerce, unduly burdening it, or taxing it directly

4. Using their taxing power to deprive persons of equal protection of the law

5. Depriving individuals of their property without due process

Constitutional lawyers and judges spend much of their time applying these principles to concrete situations. Out of hundreds of disputes, courts have decided that states may collect sales taxes from interstate sales and income taxes from persons and corporations within the states, even if the income was earned from interstate business. However, states may not tax the privilege of engaging in interstate commerce or the profits made through interstate transactions that cannot be apportioned to a single state. Congress has placed a moratorium on state sales taxes on Internet sales, to the anguish of most state officials and traditional firms competing with Internet commerce.

State constitutions also restrict state legislatures' taxing power. Certain kinds of property, such as that used for educational, charitable, and religious purposes, are exempt from taxation. State constitutions frequently list the kinds of taxes that may be collected and stipulate the amount of tax that may be collected from various sources.[16]

General Property Tax

Widely criticized as "one of the worst taxes known to the civilized world," the **general property tax** is a chief revenue source for local governments. The property tax is difficult to administer, leads to favoritism and inequities, and takes little account of ability to pay.[17] Forty years ago, it provided 45 percent of the revenues for state governments and an even higher percentage of the revenues for local governments. But during the past two decades, reliance on property taxes has declined. Today they provide less than one-third of total state and local government revenues. But some states remain acutely dependent on property taxes. New Hampshire, for instance, raises nearly two-thirds of its state and local revenues from the property tax. At the other end of the scale, Alabama and New Mexico raise only about one-tenth of their state and local tax dollars from the property tax.[18]

ADMINISTRATION OF THE PROPERTY TAX   A hundred years ago, wealth was primarily *real property*—land and buildings—that was relatively easy to value. Assessors could guess the value of the property a person owned, and that assessment was a good indicator of his or her ability to pay taxes. Today wealth takes many forms. People own varying amounts of personal property—both *tangible* (furniture, jewels, washing machines, rugs, paintings) and *intangible* (stocks, bonds, money in the bank). It is possible to concentrate a large amount of wealth in a small rented apartment. The nature of real property has also changed. It no longer consists mainly of barns, houses, and land but rather of large industrial plants, huge retail stores, and office buildings whose values are hard to measure. In addition, property ownership is less likely these days to reflect ability to pay taxes. An elderly couple with a large house valued at $300,000 may be living on Social Security payments and a small allowance provided by their children. But they have to pay higher property taxes than a young couple with two healthy incomes who live in a rented apartment.

Although many communities stipulate that the general property tax be imposed on all property, this is not what actually happens. Significant amounts of real property are exempted from property taxes because they are owned by tax-exempt groups, such as churches and charitable organizations. Local governments often waive the tax as an economic development inducement or for other reasons. As a result, two taxpayers may own similar property, but one is assessed at a higher rate, and the principle of horizontal equity is violated. Intangible personal property is also seldom taxed. Some communities deliberately impose a lower rate on intangible property to induce owners to declare ownership. In addition, tangible personal property such as watches, rings, and other jewelry often escapes taxation or is grossly undervalued.

The general property tax is hard to adjust to changing circumstances. This tax is typically administered by an assessor, who attempts to place a value on property—an **assessment.** The assessment may or may not reflect the real market value of the property. In some states, the assessment is legally required to be a percentage of market value—say, 25 percent. The property tax rate is usually a tax per $100 or $1,000 of assessed valuation or some other such measure. Local and state governments can do very little to change the assessment, but they can raise or lower the tax rates.

During times of rising prices, assessed values increase much more slowly than the general price level does. So when governments need more money, the lagging tax bases fail to provide it. When prices fall, valuations do not drop at the same rate. When people cannot pay taxes, property may be sold on the market to cover tax delinquency, but such occurrences are rare. In some areas, property taxes are already so high that to increase them may discourage businesses and lower-income families from moving into the locality.

A property tax bill typically includes fees or taxes charged by three, four, or more governmental units, such as the city, county, school board, water utility, and other special districts. The lump-sum payment aspect of the property tax is one reason for its widespread unpopularity and has prompted some places to permit taxpayers to pay their taxes in installments, often collected with their mortgage payments.

PROPERTY TAXES AND PUBLIC EDUCATION   Local reliance on the property tax to support public schools has generated increasing controversy in recent years. The amount of money available to finance education varies tremendously from area to area; rich suburban areas with a high property valuation per pupil are able to spend much more than poor areas like the central cities, which need the money most. Reformers have urged the states to take over the financing of public education, or at least to assume a greater share of the burden, in order to equalize differences from community to community. Although this is not a popular idea, most states do distribute funds to local districts in an attempt to ensure more equitable expenditures.

Those hoping for greater state support for the public schools have often turned to the courts. Several state courts have ruled that wide differences between school districts in per-pupil expenditures are inconsistent with the equal protection clause of the Fourteenth Amendment.[19] The California Supreme Court, for example, saw such differences as violating the California constitution.[20] However, in 1973, the U.S. Supreme Court held that there is no federal constitutional requirement that the amount spent per pupil in each school district must be the same.[21] The Court's 1973 decision temporarily slowed the push toward equalization of school expenditures, but the controversy and the issues remain. Several state courts have now handed down rulings similar to that of the California Supreme Court. Kentucky, New Hampshire, New Jersey, New York, Ohio, Texas, and Wyoming courts, for example, have held that their state constitutions require that education be financed in a way that avoids differences in funding due to differences in wealth among local school districts.[22]

Despite its weaknesses, the general property tax remains an important source of revenue for local government. Supporters of the tax say it is a practical and suitable tax because real rather than personal property is the chief beneficiary of many local services, such as fire protection. Alternatives are few, and each has disadvantages. Moreover, some of the bad features of the general property tax can be corrected by improving assessment and administration methods.

One effort to reform the general property tax is the *circuit-breaker exemption* (sometimes called a *negative income tax*) by which most states and certain cities give a form of tax relief to lower-income families and the elderly. The idea is to protect family income from property tax overload in the same way an electrical circuit breaker protects a family home from an electrical current overload: "When the property tax burden of an individual exceeds a predetermined percentage of personal income, the circuit breaker goes into effect to relieve the excess financial pressure."[23] The circuit-breaker property tax exemption seems to be most popular in the Great Lakes and Plains states and least popular in the Southeast, where property tax burdens are low.

TAX REFORM AND REVOLT   Hostility to the property tax spawned the tax revolts of the last three decades of the twentieth century. The watershed event in the politics of tax cutting was the passage in 1978 of California's Proposition 13, which limits increases in property taxes to a maximum 2 percent each year. Throughout the 1970s, California property taxes had risen dramatically, spurring voters to pass this initiative to cut them.

Such direct citizen involvement in making fiscal policy is not uncommon in the United States, and there has been a resurgence of initiative and referendum activity in recent decades.[24] Passage of Proposition 13 made tax reduction an important issue nationwide. Heralded as the start of a modern tax revolt, it triggered taxing and spending limits in more than a dozen states and helped launch movements for constitutional amendments setting federal spending limits, requiring a balanced federal budget, and **indexing** income tax brackets (automatically adjusting income tax rates to rise with inflation so that, in effect, they remain constant). Tax reduction was not limited to ballot initiatives but spread to state legislatures, most of which reduced income, sales, or property taxes.

State and local tax cuts are only one way of attempting to limit government spending. States and localities have also adopted various limits on government spending. In

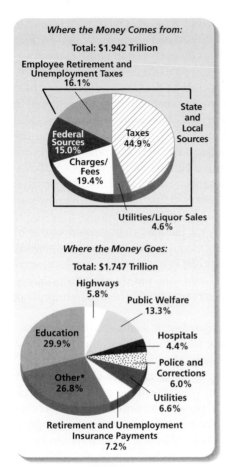

Where the Money Comes from:

Total: $1.942 Trillion

Employee Retirement and Unemployment Taxes 16.1%

Federal Sources 15.0%

Taxes 44.9%

State and Local Sources

Charges/Fees 19.4%

Utilities/Liquor Sales 4.6%

Where the Money Goes:

Total: $1.747 Trillion

Highways 5.8%

Public Welfare 13.3%

Education 29.9%

Hospitals 4.4%

Police and Corrections 6.0%

Other* 26.8%

Utilities 6.6%

Retirement and Unemployment Insurance Payments 7.2%

FIGURE 10–1 State and Local Revenues and Expenditures, 2003.
*Includes administration, parks and recreation, housing, transportation, etc.
SOURCE: U.S. Bureau of the Census, *Statistical Abstract of the United States, 2003* (U.S. Census Bureau, 2004), table no. 443.

their simplest form, such limitations restrict future spending to current levels; more typically, they provide for an annual increase in spending that is either limited to a fixed percentage or tied to increases in personal income or inflation. Spending limitations can be enacted without tax cuts and, unlike tax cuts, can incur few political costs since no services are being reduced in the short run. New Jersey was the first state to enact spending limits that applied to both state and local governments. Passed in 1976, the New Jersey law limited the growth in state expenditures to the annual percentage increase in per capita personal income and restricted localities to increases of no more than 5 percent without voter approval. Nearly half of the states have followed New Jersey's example and imposed limits on state expenditures.[25]

One consequence of the tax revolt is that the property tax has become a less significant part of the tax base of local governments. As a result, local governments have had to develop other sources of funding.

Other Taxes

State and local governments also raise revenues through a wide range of other taxes that have become increasingly popular since the property tax revolts of the 1970s and 1980s (see Figure 10–1). States and localities seek to diversify their taxes to "spread the pain" of taxes as much as possible.

SALES TAXES   Born during the Great Depression, the **sales tax** is the most important source of revenue for states, which annually collect over $170 billion. Almost all states impose some kind of general sales tax, normally on retail sales, with Washington State (64 percent of all revenues comes from the sales tax), Florida (59 percent), Tennessee (57 percent), Nevada (54 percent), and South Dakota (53 percent) all well above the national average of 32 percent.

Local sales taxes were uncommon until after World War II, but now 34 states also allow cities to impose sales taxes. Sales taxes are unpopular with local merchants, who fear they drive business away. In most cases, this is a minor issue that arises only along state borders where consumers can drive into another state with a lower sales tax to make purchases. Most consumers do not pay that much attention to the sales tax on most items.

Sales taxes are easy to administer and produce large amounts of revenue. Many consumers consider sales taxes relatively painless because paying a small amount every day avoids having to pay a large tax bill all at one time. But labor groups and low-income consumers remain opposed to sales taxes, favoring wider use of the income tax instead. They argue that people with small incomes spend a larger percentage of their budgets on food and clothing than the wealthy do, so sales taxes fall heaviest on those least able to pay. That is why many states exempt necessities—primarily food and drugs—from the sales tax.

States continue to search for ways to tax services, both because the states are under acute pressure to find new revenues and because the service sector of the economy continues to expand. All states tax some services, but none has a broad-based tax on services. Among the kinds of services taxed are cable television, landscaping, income tax preparation, pest control, videotape rental, laundry and dry cleaning, and photocopying.

State and local officials listen with concern to talk about the federal government's imposing a **value-added tax (VAT)** like that used in many western European countries. This tax is imposed on the value added to a product at *each stage* of production and distribution. Should the federal government impose such a tax, state and local officials fear that their ability to use the sales tax will be reduced.

There is a running battle about whether states can tax mail-order catalog and Internet sales. Opponents contend that taxing such sales violates the constitutional provisions governing interstate commerce. The Supreme Court has generally left the issue to Congress, and Congress has imposed a moratorium on all Internet taxes until 2007 while it sorts out the pros and cons. Under the moratorium, nine states are allowed to tax Internet sales, while another six allow local governments to tax Internet sales as well.[26]

Although Internet taxes only account for $80 to 120 million today, the future stakes are high. Online retail sales are estimated to reach $130 billion by 2006.[27] By 2005, 10 to 12 percent of apparel, accessory, and toy sales and 20 to 25 percent of book, music, software, video, and consumer electronics sales could be by Internet.[28] Billions in revenues could go to states and localities if they taxed these purchases at the same rate they tax merchants operating within their states.

But there is a question of fairness. Local merchants who have to collect sales taxes are at a disadvantage if mail-order and Internet firms can escape these taxes. Mail-order merchants and their lobbyists claim it would be an administrative nightmare to collect and reimburse all the sales taxes, and they argue that they should not be obligated to collect taxes for a state in which they do not have a physical presence. But this position does not reduce complexity. It means if there is an Eddie Bauer store in your state and you buy a shirt from the Eddie Bauer catalog, you are charged sales tax, while a similar shirt from a Lands' End catalog would escape the tax in every state where it has no stores.

The large volume of commerce now conducted electronically suggests that some more sensible and consistent policy will have to be developed. Congress enacted the Internet Tax Freedom Act of 1998, creating the Advisory Commission on Electronic Commerce to study the matter. In the meantime, the federal government imposed a moratorium on state and local taxes on e-commerce. State and local governments contend that the moratorium unfairly preempts their authority and will erode the tax base of many governments. The issue of taxation of e-commerce is becoming more controversial and significant as the size of e-commerce grows. On one hand, how can retailers avoid multiple taxation, overregulation, and conflicting state regulations? On the other hand, is it fair to require bricks-and-mortar firms to collect sales taxes but not their electronic competitors? And as e-commerce grows and is exempted from state taxes, state sales tax revenues will decline, and schools and other institutions supported by such taxes will suffer, or other taxes will have to be increased.

INCOME TAXES   The state income tax has been one of the fastest-growing revenue sources for most states, with Oregon (income taxes account for 74 percent of its revenues), New York (59 percent), Massachusetts (58 percent), Virginia (55 percent), and Colorado (52 percent) well above the national average of 37 percent.

Several states impose a tax on personal income, and income tax revenue is higher than general sales tax revenue in more than 20 states. Personal income taxes are generally mildly **progressive taxes;** that is, the rate goes up with the size of the income. State income tax rates, however, do not rise as sharply as the federal income tax and seldom go above 8 percent of taxable income. Corporation incomes are frequently taxed by states at a flat rate. In some states, exemptions are generous.

States generally do not allow local governments to levy income taxes. However, some cities—following the lead of Philadelphia and Toledo—now collect a *wage tax,* and most cities in Ohio and cities, towns, and school districts in Pennsylvania levy a similar *payroll tax* on all persons. For instance, visiting professional athletes who compete in Philadelphia are subject to the city's earned-income tax. The Toledo tax also applies to corporate profits. A municipal income tax enables hard-pressed cities to collect money from citizens who use city facilities but live in the suburbs. Similar taxes are collected by New York City, Detroit, and Louisville.

EXCISE TAXES   Almost all states tax gasoline, alcohol, and cigarettes; taxes on specific items are known as **excise taxes.** Because many cities also tax these items, the combined local, state, and federal levies often double the cost of these "luxury" items to the consumer. Gasoline taxes are sometimes combined with the funds collected for automobile and driver's licenses and are earmarked for highway construction and maintenance. Liquor taxes often consist of both license fees to manufacture or sell alcoholic beverages and levies on their sale or consumption; they are often used for general government spending.

Some states own liquor stores, with the profits going to the state treasury. High taxation of liquor is justified on the grounds that it reduces the amount of alcohol consumed, falls on an item that is not a necessity of life, and eases the task of law enforcement. Some states, like North Carolina, set aside part of their alcohol taxes for mental health programs and the rehabilitation of alcoholics. If the tax is raised too high, however, liquor purchases tend to be diverted into illegal channels, and tax revenues fall off.

The rationale for taxing cigarettes is similar. High tobacco taxes in states like Alaska, New Jersey, and Hawaii, which do not grow tobacco, and low tobacco taxes in tobacco-growing states like Virginia and the Carolinas, have led to interstate smuggling. Some states levy a general sales tax on top of the excise tax, especially on tobacco products.

SEVERANCE TAXES   In several states, **severance taxes** have been a key source of revenue. These are taxes on the privilege of "severing" or removing such natural resources as coal, oil, timber, and gas from the land. In recent years, severance taxes accounted for more than 20 percent of tax collections in eight states: Alaska, Louisiana, Montana, New Mexico, North Dakota, Oklahoma, Texas, and Wyoming. Although more than 30 states rely on some type of severance tax, significant revenues from this tax are not available to most states. Tax revenues from severance taxes go up and down with the price of oil, gas, and coal.

The state and local taxes described here do not begin to exhaust the kinds of taxes collected by state and local governments. Admission taxes, stock transfer taxes, inheritance taxes, parimutuel taxes, corporate franchise taxes, and taxes on utilities and insurance are common.

Other Revenues

In addition to taxation, states derive revenue from fees and special service charges. At least 10 percent of the money collected by state and local governments comes from inspecting buildings, recording titles, operating courts, licensing professions, disposing of garbage, and other services. Parking meters have become an important revenue source for some cities. Municipal governments frequently operate water supply and local transit systems. City-operated liquor stores are administered by, and turn a profit in, certain cities in Alaska, Minnesota, North Carolina, and South Dakota. The city of Dallas owns and operates an FM radio station (WRR), which plays classical music. Some states and cities run other business enterprises, such as cable television services, from which they make money (and sometimes lose it, too). North Dakota, for example, operates a state-owned bank. Municipally owned gas and power companies often contribute to city treasuries. In some cases, utility profits are large enough to make other city taxes unnecessary.

LEGALIZED GAMBLING Recent years have seen a dramatic increase in legalized gambling in the United States. Only Hawaii and Utah do not permit some form of legalized gambling. For many years, only Nevada permitted legalized casino gambling, but now 37 states, the District of Columbia, and Puerto Rico have legalized gambling, including lotteries, and 20 states allow casinos. This increase occurred because Native American tribes asserted their right to self-rule on reservations and brought casinos to states like California, Michigan, Connecticut, and South Dakota. In addition, gambling companies asserted that prohibitions against land-based casinos did not apply to floating ones, and they promoted gambling on riverboats and dockside casinos. A casino is estimated to be within a four-hour drive for 95 percent of all Americans. "The Bible Belt might as well be renamed the Blackjack Belt, with floating and land-based casinos."[29]

Over time, states have become some of the largest sponsors of gambling, most notably through state lotteries, which are used in states as well as Canadian provinces and generate net profits in excess of $37.8 billion. Many of the state lotteries were adopted as a result of statewide referendums, which sometimes promised to provide funding for education or other important state services. New York State provides an explanation of how the lottery benefits public education at www.nylottery.org. Not surprisingly, there is now a North American Association of State and Provincial Lotteries, and its Web site (www.naspl.org) provides a broad range of information on gambling in the United States.

More recently, video poker and other forms of gambling have been spreading to more states. As improvements have been made in data encryption, it is now technologically possible for people to engage in virtual gambling in the privacy of their homes. What does this technology do to state laws limiting or banning gambling? The possibility of betting online also raises the issue of whether those who take bets can be prosecuted for permitting underage gambling.

The federal government has tried to play a role in restricting gambling in various forms, such as betting on college or high school sports and underage gambling. Many coaches of college sports have requested that limitations be placed on betting on their games. The American Gaming Association (www.americangaming.org) provides media updates on government efforts to restrict gambling. Or you can refer to the links and resources provided by the North American Gaming Regulators Association at www.nagra.org.[30]

LOTTERIES   Lotteries are a special form of state-sponsored and state-administered gambling that are used to raise money for public purposes. Along with the District of Columbia and Puerto Rico, 37 states operate lotteries to generate revenue without raising taxes. Lotteries are not entirely new; the Continental Congress ran a lottery to help finance the Revolutionary War. Indeed, all 13 original states used lotteries as a form of voluntary taxation in the 1780s. Lotteries also helped establish some of the nation's earliest colleges, notably Princeton, Harvard, and Yale. In 1964, New Hampshire was the first state to revive the practice in modern times to help balance its budget.

In recent decades, state lotteries have increased in popularity, in part because they increase revenues without raising taxes. Although state-run lotteries provide less than 3 percent of all state revenues, they provide essential revenues that would have to be replaced by other sources, all of which are less politically popular. States pay out between 50 and 70 percent of their gross receipts from lotteries in prizes and roughly 6 percent to cover administration costs. The remaining revenues are used for public purposes.

Revenues from lotteries are used for a variety of purposes. About half of the states with lotteries earmark most or all of their proceeds for education; a significant number of the remaining states commit their proceeds to the state general fund. Some states, like Kansas and Oregon, designate lottery profits for economic development; Minnesota commits part of what it makes through the lottery to the environment; Pennsylvania and West Virginia designate senior citizens' programs to receive lottery profits.

Proponents of lotteries identify a popular cause like education, the environment, or senior citizens as the beneficiaries of lottery profits in hopes of getting popular support for passage of the lottery. Opposition to the lottery often comes from church groups, which contend that state lotteries are immoral because they are a form of legalized gambling. Proponents counter that churches often raise funds through raffles, bingo, and other games of chance. Opponents also argue that lotteries are a bad investment because they yield a poor rate of return. Proponents respond that tickets are purchased more for their entertainment value than as an investment.

GRANTS   Grants from states to local governments have become increasingly important during the past several decades. The national government once allocated large sums to cities, but has largely stopped providing such direct support. Local governments now go to the states to get more than $300 billion in assistance. State officials return revenues collected from certain taxes to local governments, often without specifying the purposes for which the money should be used. Local governments receive state and federal grants in a wide range of areas, including education, transportation, corrections, law enforcement, housing, welfare, community development, and health care. One reason local governments receive so much money in the form of grants is that they are the unit of government closest to the people and most experienced at providing services.

Local governments often see state and federal grants as enhancing the services they provide. In return for a modest investment of local tax revenue, local governments can get grant money from state or federal governments. But grant money may not be available for some pressing local priorities, or the strings attached to the money may permit state and federal governments to set local priorities. In such cases, are local governments wise to pursue the grants, or should they put their money into their most pressing priorities? Local governments also worry about depending on grant money if state or federal money should dry up in the future.

Borrowing Money

State and local governments collect large sums of money to pay for current operating expenses—garbage collection, police protection, and social services. To fund long-term projects—so-called *capital expenditures*—cities and states often have to borrow money. This long-term borrowing is necessary for building schools, constructing roads, and clearing slums—projects whose costs are so large that it is not feasible to pay for them out of current revenue. Moreover, because these improvements have long lives and add to the wealth of the community, it is reasonable to pay for them over time. For this purpose, governments issue bonds, most often with voter approval.

During the early years of the nineteenth century, states and cities subsidized railroad and canal builders. The money for these and other public improvements came from bonds issued by the cities or states and purchased by investors. Provision for payment of these debts was inadequate, and citizens were burdened with debts long after the improvements had lost their value. As a result, default on obligations was frequent. Aroused by the legislatures' abuse of their authority, voters insisted on constitutional amendments restricting legislative discretion to borrow money. The power to borrow money for the long term now routinely requires voter approval.

Increasingly important since the passage of the National Tax Reform Act are special-purpose governments or special districts: airport authorities, bridge and highway authorities, water and wastewater districts, public transit authorities, and community college districts. Their creation has resulted in turning more and more to *revenue bonds* to help finance their operations. The repayment and dividends due investors come from tolls and fees charged by the facility. In most cases, revenue bonds do not require voter approval, making it much easier to issue this kind of debt and also to spend more on services like public transportation.[31]

State and local bonds are attractive to investors because the interest is exempt from federal income tax. State and local governments can borrow money at a lower interest rate than private businesses can, and although credit ratings differ sharply according to economic health, the credit of most cities and states is good. Hence they can easily find buyers for their bonds. Because governments are often permitted to issue bonds beyond the limitations on their general indebtedness, they use them whenever possible. However, as New York City learned in the 1970s, excessive reliance on bonds can be detrimental to the fiscal health of a state or city.

INTERGOVERNMENTAL COMPETITION

State and local governments exist in a competitive environment in which they seek to enhance their own economy and overall reputation. They have become more competitive in courting business and economic growth because of the increasing mobility of business and the stagnant growth in some sectors of the economy and in some regions of the country. One way governments compete in this marketplace is through the use of *tax incentives* that offer reduced tax rates to promote business investment in the local community. Government officials assume that a progrowth policy is good politics because voter confidence increases when new jobs and businesses move into a community or state.

Local governments that are successful in luring businesses to locate within their boundaries also assume that in the long run these new businesses will add to the tax base by stimulating sales taxes and property taxes. In the case of large shopping malls that attract shoppers from surrounding communities, the revenues from the sales tax may actually lower the tax burden for residents of the city because of sales taxes paid by nonresidents.

Developers of shopping malls or office complexes who are thinking about relocating often play one local government against another in an effort to drive down their tax burden. Established businesses in the community then cry foul about the tax incentives offered to attract new businesses or keep those who threaten to leave. Economists are skeptical about how important these incentives really are. Some believe that such factors as space availability, cost of land, cost of labor, and quality of life are at least as important in decisions about where businesses locate.[32]

Sports teams, stadiums, and arenas provide another example of intergovernmental competition for tax incentives. In recent years, competition between cities, especially larger cities, has drawn them into funding the construction of major sports facilities for professional football, basketball, hockey, or baseball teams. Because the teams are identified with the city or state and are perceived to enhance the community's reputation, local and state governments have been responsive to the demands of team owners. Some cities have offered team owners "sweetheart deals" to keep the team or build them a new stadium.[33] The New York Yankees threatened to leave their historic location in the Bronx for New Jersey's Meadowlands but agreed to stay put after winning concessions from local government. Often the building of new facilities requires a referendum, but other arrangements, such as the proceeds from parking and vendors, are open to negotiations between the owners and government officials.[34]

Finally, local governments are also competing to build prisons and other correctional facilities. As the number of people in prison has soared from 218,000 in 1974 to 1.3 million in 2000, the number of prisons has grown from from 600 to more than 1,000. In small counties and poor areas of the country, a new prison can provide a variety of economic benefits, from jobs to construction income. In Texas, which has the largest number of state prisons in the country, the number of counties with a prison increased from just 3 percent in 1979 to 28 percent in 2000; in Florida, which has the second largest number, the number surged from 45 percent to 78 percent.[35]

Competing for businesses, baseball teams, and prisons can have negative impacts on a state or local government, not the least of which is the uneven distribution of income on the basis of bidding wars. A dollar spent on prison construction and employment in one county means a dollar not spent in another—some experts estimate that Cook County, Illinois, will lose $88 million in federal benefits from 2000 to 2010 because thousands of its residents were counted in the county in which they were imprisoned rather than the county in which they originally lived.

ASSESSING STATE AND LOCAL PERFORMANCE

As the old saying goes, states and localities are where the rubber meets the road. They are often responsible for delivering on the promises that the federal government makes, whether in health care, homeland security, economic development, or welfare reform. As the federal budget deficit continues to grow, and Social Security and Medicare spending grows, states can expect even greater pressure to fill the gap created by dwindling federal spending for discretionary programs.

Unfortunately, state and local governments vary greatly in their administrative capabilities. According to *Governing* magazine, which rates states, counties, and cities, on overall management, only 10 states won an A or A− grade for their financial management in 2001, just three got an A or A− for managing their employees effectively, five received an A or A− for their ability to measure and manage the results of their programs, and six earned an A or A− for information technology. Alabama got the worst report card in 2001, with a C+ in financial management, a D+ in employee management, a D+ in managing for results, a C− in information technology, and a C− overall; while Michigan, Utah, and Washington came out on top with enough A's and B's to earn an A− overall.[36]

Although many state and local governments are getting better every year, they still have a long way to go to meet public expectations. They also tend to cut budgets for management improvement during the lean years, which contributes to future performance problems.

S U M M A R Y

1. Wages for public employees constitute more than one-third the cost of state and local government. These public employees, who are the first point of contact for many Americans, are hired through merit systems.

2. One of the most controversial aspects of state and local government in recent years has been the unionization of over 50 percent of public employees at the state and local levels. Public employee unions have been increasingly successful in recruiting new members and bargaining for better wages, hours, working conditions, and pensions. Their success has caused some public backlash.

3. One response to growing costs has been the outsourcing of public services to the private sector. Garbage collection, recreation, and even emergency services are now contracted out in some cities. Arguments in favor of privatization include lower cost and better services. But others argue that this movement reduces government accountability and may lead to corruption in the awarding of contracts.

4. State and local governments get most of their money from taxes. Decreasing federal funding has made state and local governments the "stress joints" of American government.

5. The general property tax, despite its unpopularity, remains the most important source of revenue for many local governments. Property is generally thought of as real estate but can include other personal property like automobiles or boats. Administration of the tax is generally handled at the local level, but several states provide oversight. The property tax is a major revenue source for public schools.

6. Tax revolts in the 1970s and 1980s resulted in limits on property taxes in several states and often made it more difficult to raise property taxes. The property tax is now a less significant part of the tax base of local governments.

7. State and local governments have traditionally received revenues primarily from property taxes but also from sales taxes, income taxes, excise taxes, and severance taxes. Recently, they have diversified

their revenue sources by turning to such devices as lotteries, legalized gambling, user fees, other fees and special service charges, and taxes not previously used at the state and local levels. This diversification was made necessary by economic downturns and by cutbacks in federal support. Intergovernmental grants from states to cities and school districts have increased in importance as local governments have had to deal with rising

costs and expectations but limited revenues. In addition, the growth in special-district governments has led to greater reliance on revenue bonds to finance local services.

8. States and local governments have also become more competitive in courting business and economic growth, especially through tax incentives and subsidies.

F U R T H E R   R E A D I N G

J. RICHARD ARONSON, ELI SCHWARTZ, AND DAVID S. ARNOLD, *Management Policies in Local Government Finance,* 4th ed. (International City/County Management Association, 1996).

DAVID BRUNORI, ED., *The Future of State Taxation* (University Press of America, 1998).

TERRY N. CLARK AND LORNA C. FERGUSON, *City Money: Political Processes, Fiscal Strain, and Retrenchment* (Columbia University Press, 1983).

RONALD C. FISHER, *Intergovernmental Fiscal Relations* (Kluwer, 1997).

KATHRYN A. FOSTER, *The Political Economy of Special-Purpose Government* (Georgetown University Press, 1997).

M. DAVID GELFAND, ED., *State and Local Taxation and Finance in a Nutshell,* 2d ed. (West, 2000).

STEVEN D. GOLD, ED., *The Fiscal Crisis of the States: Lessons for the Future* (Georgetown University Press, 1995).

CHARLES T. GOODSELL, *The Case for Bureaucracy,* 3d ed. (Chatham House, 1994).

ROY T. MEYERS, ED., *Handbook of Government Budgeting* (Jossey-Bass, 1999).

National Conference of State Legislatures, Legislative Budget Procedures in the 50 States (National Conference of State Legislatures, 1998).

DAVID ALAN NIBERT, *Hitting the Lottery Jackpot: State Governments and the Taxing of Dreams* (Monthly Review Press, 2000).

MICHAEL PAGANO AND RICHARD MOORE, *Cities and Fiscal Choices* (Duke University Press, 1985).

B. GUY PETERS, *The Politics of Taxation: A Comparative Perspective* (Blackwell, 1991).

JOHN E. PETERSEN AND DENNIS R. STRACHOTA, EDS., *Local Government Finance: Concepts and Practices* (Government Finance Officers Association, 1991).

HENRY J. RAIMONDO, *Economics of State and Local Government* (Praeger, 1992).

HARVEY S. ROSEN, *Public Finance,* 6th ed. (McGraw-Hill, 2002).

E. S. SAVAS, *Privatization: The Key to Better Government,* 2d ed. (Chatham House, 1998).

RONALD SNELL, ED., *Financing State Government in the 1990s* (National Conference of State Legislatures and National Governors' Association, 1993).

THOMAS R. SWARTZ AND JOHN E. PECK, EDS., *The Changing Face of Fiscal Federalism* (Sharpe, 1990).

Also, the U.S. Bureau of the Census regularly publishes reports on state and municipal finances.

GLOSSARY

advisory opinion   An opinion unrelated to a particular case that gives a court's view about a constitutional or legal issue.

amendatory veto   The power of governors in a few states to return a bill to the legislature with suggested language changes, conditions, or amendments. Legislators then decide either to accept the governor's recommendations or to pass the bill in its original form over the veto.

assessment   The valuation a government places on property for the purposes of taxation.

assigned counsel system   Arrangement whereby attorneys are provided for persons accused of crimes who are unable to hire their own attorneys. The judge assigns a member of the bar to provide counsel to a particular defendant.

bicameral legislature   A two-house legislature.

binding arbitration   A collective bargaining agreement in which both parties agree, in case of dispute over the terms of the union contract, to adhere to the decision of an arbitrator.

blanket primary   Primary election open to all voters, who may vote for a candidate from any party for each office.

caucus   A meeting of local party members to choose party officials or candidates for public office and to decide the platform.

centralists   People who favor national action over action at the state and local levels.

charter school   A publicly funded alternative to standard public schools in some states, initiated when individuals or groups receive charters; charter schools must meet state standards.

charter   City "constitution" that outlines the structure of city government, defines the authority of the various officials, and provides for their selection.

closed primary   Primary election in which only persons registered in the party holding the primary may vote.

collective bargaining   Method whereby representatives of the union and employer determine wages, hours, and other conditions of employment through direct negotiation.

commerce clause   The clause of the Constitution (Article 1, Section 8, Clause 3) that gives Congress the power to regulate all business activities that cross state lines or affect more than one state or other nations.

concurrent powers   Powers that the Constitution gives to both the national and state governments, such as the power to levy taxes.

confederation   Constitutional arrangement in which sovereign nations or states, by compact, create a central government but carefully limit its power and do not give it direct authority over individuals.

constitutional home rule   State constitutional authorization for local governments to conduct their own affairs.

constitutional initiative petition   A device that permits voters to place specific amendments to a state constitution on the ballot by petition.

council-manager plan   Form of local government in which the city council hires a professional administrator to manage city affairs; also known as the "city-manager plan."

crossover voting   Voting by a member of one party for a candidate of another party.

decentralists   People who favor state or local action rather than national action.

delegate   An official who is expected to represent the views of his or her constituents even when personally holding different views; one interpretation of the role of the legislator.

devolution revolution   The effort to slow the growth of the federal government by returning many functions to the states.

disclosure   A requirement that candidates specify where the money came from to finance their campaign.

eminent domain   Power of a government to take private property for public use; the U.S. Constitution gives national and state governments this power and requires them to provide just compensation for property so taken.

enterprise zone   Inner-city area designated as offering tax incentives to companies that invest in plants there and provide job training for the unemployed.

excise tax   Consumer tax on a specific kind of merchandise, such as tobacco.

executive order   Directive issued by a president or governor that has the force of law.

express powers   Powers specifically granted to one of the branches of the national government by the Constitution.

extradition   Legal process whereby an alleged criminal offender is surrendered by the officials of one state to officials of the state in which the crime is alleged to have been committed.

federal mandate   A requirement imposed by the federal government as a condition for the receipt of federal funds.

federalism   Constitutional arrangement whereby power is distributed between a central government and subdivisional governments, called *states* in the United States. The national and the subdivisional governments both exercise direct authority over individuals.

felony   A serious crime, the penalty for which can range from imprisonment in a penitentiary for more than a year to death.

full faith and credit clause   Clause in the Constitution (Article IV, Section 1) requiring each state to recognize the civil judgments rendered by the courts of the other states and to accept their public records and acts as valid.

general property tax   Tax levied by local and some state governments on real property or personal, tangible property, the major portion of which is on the estimated value of one's home and land.

gerrymandering   The drawing of legislative district boundaries to benefit a party, group, or incumbent.

implied powers   Powers inferred from the express powers that allow Congress to carry out its functions.

indexing   Providing automatic increases to compensate for inflation.

indictment   A formal written statement from a grand jury charging an individual with an offense; also called a *true bill.*

information affidavit   Certification by a public prosecutor that there is evidence to justify bringing named individuals to trial.

inherent powers   The powers of the national government in the field of foreign affairs that the Supreme Court has declared do not depend on constitutional grants but rather grow out of the very existence of the national government.

initiative   Procedure whereby a certain number of voters may, by petition, propose a law or constitutional amendment and have it submitted to the voters.

interstate compact   An agreement among two or more states. The Constitution requires that most such agreements be approved by Congress.

issue advocacy   Promoting a particular position on an issue paid for by interest groups or individuals but not candidates. Much issue advocacy is often electioneering for or against a candidate and until 2004 had not been subject to any regulation.

item veto   Right of an executive to veto parts of a bill approved by a legislature without having to veto the entire bill.

judicial interpretation   A method by which judges modify the force of a constitutional provision by reinterpreting its meaning.

judicial review   The power of a court to refuse to enforce a law or a government regulation that in the opinion of the judges conflicts with the U.S. Constitution or, in a state court, the state constitution.

lobbying   Engaging in activities aimed at influencing public officials, especially legislators, and the policies they enact.

lobbyist   A person who is employed by and acts for an organized interest group or corporation to influence policy decisions and positions in the executive and legislative branches.

majority-minority district   A congressional district created to include a majority of minority voters; ruled constitutional so long as race is not the main factor in redistricting.

malapportionment   Having legislative districts with unequal populations.

mayor-council charter   The oldest and most common form of city government, consisting of either a weak mayor and a city council or a strong mayor elected by voters and council.

merit system   A system of public employment in which selection and promotion depend on demonstrated performance rather than political patronage.

misdemeanor   A minor crime; the penalty is a fine or imprisonment for a short time, usually less than a year, in a local jail.

Missouri Plan   A system for selecting judges that combines features of the appointive and elective methods. The governor selects judges from lists presented by panels of lawyers and laypersons, and at the end of their term, the judges may run against their own record in retention elections.

national supremacy   Constitutional doctrine that whenever conflict occurs between the constitutionally authorized actions of the national government and those of a state or local government, the actions of the federal government prevail.

necessary and proper clause   Clause of the Constitution (Article I, Section 8, Clause 3) setting forth the implied powers of Congress. It states that Congress, in addition to its express powers, has the right to make all laws necessary and proper for carrying out all powers vested by the Constitution in the national government.

new judicial federalism   The practice of some state courts using the bill of rights in their state constitutions to provide more protection for some rights than is provided by the Supreme Court's interpretation of the Bill of Rights in the U.S. Constitution.

office block ballot   Ballot on which all candidates are listed under the office for which they are running, making split-ticket voting easier.

one party state   A state in which one party wins all or nearly all the offices and the other party receives only a small proportion of the popular vote.

open primary   Primary election in which any voter, regardless of party, may vote.

original jurisdiction   The authority of a court to hear a case "in the first instance."

party caucus   A meeting of the members of a party in a legislative chamber to select party leaders and develop party policy. Called a *conference* by the Republicans.

party column ballot   Type of ballot that encourages party-line voting by listing all of a party's candidates in a column under the party name.

plea bargain   Agreement between a prosecutor and a defendant that the defendant will plead guilty to a lesser offense to avoid having to stand trial for a more serious offense.

police powers   Inherent powers of state governments to pass laws to protect the public health, safety, and welfare; the national government has no directly granted police powers but accomplishes the same goals through other delegated powers.

preemption   Associated with the Bush doctrine, a belief that a nation is justified in attacking another nation to prevent possible attacks on itself. Also, the right of a federal law or regulation to preclude enforcement of a state or local law or regulation.

privatization   Contracting public services to private organizations, including the power to collect revenues.

pro bono   To serve the public good; term used to describe work that lawyers (or other professionals) do for which they receive no fees.

progressive tax   A tax graduated so that people with higher incomes pay a larger fraction of their income than people with lower incomes.

public defender system   Arrangement whereby public officials are hired to provide legal assistance to people accused of crimes who are unable to hire their own attorneys.

recall   Procedure for submitting to popular vote the removal of public officials from office before the end of their term.

recidivist   A repeat offender.

redistributive policies Governmental tax and social programs that shift wealth or benefits from one segment of the population to another, often from the rich to the poor.

redistricting The redrawing of congressional and other legislative district lines following the census, to accommodate population shifts and keep districts as equal as possible in population.

reduction veto The power of governors in a few states to reduce a particular appropriation.

referendum Procedure for submitting to popular vote measures passed by the legislature or proposed amendments to a state constitution.

responsibility contract A welfare strategy adopted by some states in which recipients sign a written agreement specifying their responsibilities and outlining a plan for obtaining work and achieving self-sufficiency.

revision commission A state commission that recommends changes in the state constitution for action by the legislature and vote by the voters.

sales tax General tax on sales transactions, sometimes exempting food and drugs.

severance tax A tax on the privilege of "severing" such natural resources as coal, oil, timber, and gas from the land.

social stratification Divisions in a community among socio-economic groups or classes.

soft money Money raised in unlimited amounts by political parties for party-building purposes. Now largely illegal except for limited contributions to state and local parties for voter registration and get-out-the-vote efforts.

split ticket A vote for some of one party's candidates and some of another party's candidates.

spoils system A system of public employment based on rewarding party loyalists and friends.

states' rights Powers expressly or implicitly reserved to the states and emphasized by decentralists.

straight ticket A vote for all of one party's candidates.

strong mayor-council form Form of local government in which the voters directly elect the city council and the mayor, who enjoys almost total administrative authority and appoints the department heads.

tort law Law relating to injuries to person, reputation, or property.

trustee An official who is expected to vote independently, based on his or her judgment of the circumstances; one interpretation of the role of a legislator.

turnout The proportion of the voting-age public that votes, sometimes defined as the number of registered voters that vote.

two-party state A state in which the two major parties alternate in winning majorities.

unicameral legislature A one-house legislature.

unitary system Constitutional arrangement in which power is concentrated in a central government.

value-added tax (VAT) A tax on increased value of a product at each stage of production and distribution rather than just at the point of sale.

veto Rejection by a president or governor of legislation passed by a legislature.

vouchers Money provided by the government to parents for payment of their children's tuition in a public or private school of their choice.

weak mayor-council form Form of local government in which the members of the city council select the mayor, who then shares power with other elected or appointed boards and commissions.

workfare A welfare strategy adopted by some states that gives able-bodied adults who do not have preschool-age children the opportunity to learn job skills that can lead to employment.

writ of habeas corpus Court order requiring explanation to a judge why a prisoner is being held.

NOTES

Chapter 1

1. Dale Russakoff and Amy Argetsinger, "States Plan Big Tuition Increases," *The Washington Post,* July 22, 2003, p. Al.
2. See Jon M. Broder, "Despite Rebound, States' Budgets Are Still Reeling," *The New York Times,* January 5, 2004, p. Al.
3. For a discussion of what factors improve economic performance and state policy effectiveness, see Paul Brace, *State Government and Economic Performance* (Johns Hopkins University Press, 1993); and Susan E. Clarke and Martin R. Saiz, "Economic Development and Infrastructure Policy," in *Politics in the American States,* eds. Virginia Gray, Russell Hanson, and Herbert Jacob, 7th ed. (CQ Press, 1999), pp. 540–543.
4. U.S. Bureau of the Census, *Statistical Abstract of the United States,* available at www.census.gov/prod/ 2003pubs/02statab/stlocgov.pdf.
5. Robert S. Lynd and Helen M. Lynd, *Middletown* (Harcourt, 1929). See also their analysis of Muncie ten years later in *Middletown in Transition* (Harcourt, 1937).
6. Floyd Hunter, *Community Power Structure* (University of North Carolina Press, 1953). For a reassessment and rebuttal of Hunter's findings, see M. Kent Jennings, *Community Influentials: The Elites of Atlanta* (Free Press, 1964).
7. Robert A. Dahl, *Who Governs? Democracy and Power in an American City* (Yale University Press, 1961).
8. See the interesting study of San Jose, California, by Phillip J. Troustine and Terry Christensen, *Movers and Shakers: The Study of Community Power* (St. Martin's Press, 1982). See also Clarence N. Stone, *Regime Politics: Governing Atlanta, 1946–1988* (University Press of Kansas, 1989).
9. See, for example, Peter Bachrach and Morton S. Baratz, *Power and Poverty: Theory and Practice* (Oxford University Press, 1970); Matthew A. Crenson, *The Unpolitics of Air Pollution: A Study of Non-Decision Making in Two Cities* (Johns Hopkins University Press, 1971); and John Gaventa, *Power and Powerlessness: Quiescence and Rebellion in an Appalachian Valley* (University of Illinois Press, 1980).
10. Bryan D. Jones and Lynn W. Bachelor, *The Sustaining Hand: Community Leadership and Corporate Power,* 2d ed. (University Press of Kansas, 1993), p. 254. See also Stone, *Regime Politics.*
11. U.S. Census, *Statistical Abstract of the United States,* "Federal Government Civilian Employees" (December 31, 2002), at www.census.gov/govs/apes/02federalstate. txt; and "State Government Employment Data" (March 2002), at www.census.gov/govs/apes/02stlus.txt.
12. U.S. Census, *Statistical Abstract of the United States,* at www.census.gov/press-release/www/release/archives/ governments/001531.html.
13. Stone, *Regime Politics,* p. 232.
14. For a detailed analysis of how the W. R. Grace Company and Beatrice Foods Company had to rely on law firms to fight legal actions surrounding their operations in Woburn, Massachusetts, see Jonathan Harr, *A Civil Action* (Vintage Books, 1996). See also Alan Rosenthal, *The Third House: Lobbyists and Lobbying in the States,* 2d ed. (CQ Press, 2001).
15. See Clive S. Thomas and Ronald J. Hrebenar, "Interest Groups in the States," in *Politics in the American States,* ed. Gray et al., pp. 122–158.
16. For a general discussion of ethics reform and enforcement efforts, see *Spectrum: The Journal of State Government* (Winter 1993).
17. On various efforts to improve ethical practices and professionalism in the state legislatures and the limits of these efforts, see Alan Rosenthal, *Drawing the Line: Legislative Ethics in the States* (University of Nebraska Press, 1996).
18. Jimmy Carter, *Why Not the Best?* (Bantam Books, 1976), p. 101. See also the memoir by Tom Loftus, a former speaker of the Wisconsin State Assembly, *The Art of Legislative Politics* (CQ Press, 1994), chap. 3.
19. Diane D. Blair, *Arkansas Politics and Government* (University of Nebraska Press, 1988), p. 118.
20. William P. Browne and Kenneth VerBurg, *Michigan Politics and Government* (University of Nebraska Press, 1995), pp. 241–245.
21. Paul Peterson, *City Limits* (University of Chicago Press, 1981); p. 124. See also the useful discussion of the challenge of covering state legislative politics in Browne and VerBurg, *Michigan Politics and Government,* pp. 242–245.
22. Joseph F. Zimmerman, *The New England Town Meeting: Democracy in Action* (Praeger, 1999).
23. See for example, Daniel Kemmis, *The Good City and the Good Life* (Houghton Mifflin, 1995); and David L. Kirp, John P. Dwyer, and Larry A. Rosenthal, *Our Town: Race, Housing, and the Soul of Suburbia* (Rutgers University Press, 1997).
24. Eugene F. Rivers III, "High-Octane Faith," in *Community Works: The Revival of Civil Society in America,* ed. E. J. Dionne Jr. (Brookings Institution Press, 1998), p. 61.
25. For the efforts of a big-city mayor and his team of advisers, see Buzz Bissinger, *A Prayer for the City* (Random House, 1997). See also the example of Milwaukee's mayor, John O. Norquist, *Wealth of Cities* (Addison-Wesley, 1998).

Chapter 2

1. Quoted in Elisabeth Bumiller, "Marriage Amendment Backed," *The New York Times,* December 17, 2003, p. A30.
2. See Nicol C. Rae, "A Right Too Far? The Congressional Politics of DOMA and ENDA," in Colton C. Campbell and John F. Stack, Jr., eds., *Congress and the Politics of Emerging Rights* 65 (Rowman & Littlefield, 2002).
3. John P. Feldmeier, "Federalism and Full Faith and Credit: Must States Recognize Out-of-State Same-Sex Marriages?" *Publius* 25 (Fall 1995), p. 126.

4. See Jeremy D. Mayer and Louis-Philippe Rochon, "Gay Rights in the USA: The States Lead the Way," *Federations* 2 (November 2001).
5. *Lawrence* v. *Texas,* 539 U.S. 558 (2003).
6. For background, see Samuel H. Beer, *To Make a Nation: The Rediscovery of American Federalism* (Harvard University Press, 1993).
7. The term "devolution revolution" was coined by Richard P. Nathan in testimony before the Senate Finance Committee; quoted in Daniel Patrick Moynihan, "The Devolution Revolution," *The New York Times,* August 6, 1995, p. B15.
8. See Michael Burgess, *Federalism and the European Union: The Building of Europe, 1950–2000* (Routledge, 2000), and Kalypso Nicolaidis and Robert Howse, eds., *The Federal Vision: Legitimacy and Levels of Governance in the United States and the European Union* (Oxford University Press, 2001).
9. *United States* v. *Lopez,* 514 U.S. 549 (1995).
10. *Alden* v. *Maine,* 527 U.S. 706 (1999); *Kimel* v. *Florida Board of Regents,* 528 U.S. 62 (2000); *Vermont Agency of Natural Resources* v. *United States ex rel. Stevens,* 529 U.S. 765 (2000).
11. *Saenz* v. *Roe,* 526 U.S. 489 (1999).
12. *Reno* v. *Condon,* 528 U.S. 141 (2000).
13. Martha Derthick, "American Federalism: Half-Full or Half-Empty?" *Brookings Review* (Winter 2000), pp. 24–27.
14. William H. Stewart, *Concepts of Federalism* (Center for the Study of Federalism/University Press of America, 1984). See also Preston King, *Federalism and Federation,* 2d ed. (Cass, 2001).
15. Morton Grodzins, "The Federal System," in *Goals for Americans: The Report of the President's Commission on National Goals* (Columbia University Press, 1960).
16. Thomas R. Dye, *American Federalism: Competition Among Governments* (Lexington Books, 1990), pp. 13–17.
17. Michael D. Reagan and John G. Sanzone, *The New Federalism* (Oxford University Press, 1981), p. 175.
18. Gregory S. Mahler, *Comparative Politics: An Institutional and Cross-National Approach* (Prentice Hall, 2000), p. 31.
19. Frederick K. Lister, *The European Union, the United Nations, and the Revival of Confederal Governance* (Greenwood Press, 1996); Daniel J. Elazar, "The United States and the European Union: Models for their Epochs," in Nicolaidis and Howse, *The Federal Vision,* pp. 31–52.
20. William H. Riker, *The Development of American Federalism* (Academic, 1987), pp. 14–15. Riker contends not only that federalism does not guarantee freedom but also that the framers of our federal system, as well as those of other nations, were animated not by considerations of safe-guarding freedom but by practical considerations of preserving unity.
21. The Court, however, ruled in several recent cases that Congress exceeded its power to regulate interstate commerce. See *Printz* v. *United States,* 521 U.S. 898 (1997); *United States* v. *Lopez,* 514 U.S. 549 (1995); *New York* v. *United States,* 505 U.S. 144 (1992); and *United States* v. *Morrison,* 529 U.S. 598 (2000).
22. *Gibbons* v. *Ogden,* 9 Wheaton (22 U.S.) 1 (1824).
23. *Champion* v. *Ames,* 188 U.S. 321 (1907).
24. *Caminetti* v. *United States,* 242 U.S. 470 (1917).
25. *Federal Radio Commission* v. *Nelson Brothers,* 289 U.S. 266 (1933).
26. *Heart of Atlanta Motel* v. *United States,* 379 U.S. 241 (1964).
27. See *United States* v. *Morrison,* 529 U.S. 598 (2000), striking down the Violence Against Women Act.
28. See *New York* v. *United States,* 505 U.S. 144 (1992), and *Printz* v. *United States,* 521 U.S. 898 (1997).
29. Ibid.
30. *Seminole Tribe of Florida* v. *Florida,* 517 U.S. 44 (1996); *Alden* v. *Maine,* 527 U.S. 706 (1999); *Kimel* v. *Florida Board of Regents,* 528 U.S. 62 (2000).
31. See *Franchise Tax Board of California* v. *Hyatt,* 538 U.S. 488 (2003).
32. *California* v. *Superior Courts of California,* 482 U.S. 400 (1987).
33. David C. Nice, "State Participation in Interstate Compacts," *Publius* 17 (Spring 1987), p. 70. See also Council of State Governments, *Interstate Compacts and Agencies* (1995), for a list of compacts by subject and by state with brief descriptions.
34. *McCulloch* v. *Maryland,* 4 Wheaton 316 (1819).
35. Joseph F. Zimmerman, "Federal Preemption Under Reagan's New Federalism," *Publius* 21 (Winter 1991), pp. 7–28.
36. Oliver Wendell Holmes Jr., *Collected Legal Papers* (Harcourt, 1920), pp. 295–296.
37. *U.S. Term Limits, Inc.* v. *Thornton,* 514 U.S. 779 (1995).
38. *Garcia* v. *San Antonio Metro,* 469 U.S. 528 (1985).
39. See, for example, *United States* v. *Lopez,* 514 U.S. 549 (1995).
40. *U.S. Term Limits, Inc.* v. *Thornton,* 514 U.S. 779 (1995).
41. *Seminole Tribe of Florida* v. *Florida,* 517 U.S. 44 (1996).
42. *Alden* v. *Maine,* 527 U.S. 706 (1999); *Kimel* v. *Florida Board of Regents,* 528 U.S. 62 (2000); *Vermont Agency of Natural Resources* v. *United States ex rel. Stevens,* 529 U.S. 765 (2000).
43. George Will, "A Revival of Federalism?" *Newsweek,* May 29, 2000, p. 78.
44. *United States* v. *Morrison,* 529 U.S. 598 (2000).
45. John E. Chubb, "The Political Economy of Federalism," *American Political Science Review* 79 (December 1985), p. 1005.
46. Paul E. Peterson, *The Price of Federalism* (Brookings Institution Press, 1995), p. 127.
47. Donald F. Kettl, *The Regulation of American Federalism* (Johns Hopkins University Press, 1987), pp. 154–155.
48. See Paul J. Posner, *The Politics of Unfunded Mandates: Whither Federalism?* (Georgetown University Press, 1998).
49. Joseph Zimmerman, "Congressional Regulation of Subnational Governments," *PS: Political Science and Politics* 26 (June 1993), p. 179.
50. See Jerome J. Hanus, ed., *The Nationalization of State Government* (Heath, 1981).
51. Advisory Commission on Intergovernmental Relations, *Restoring Confidence and Competence* (Advisory Commission on Intergovernmental Relations, 1981), p. 30.

52. Cynthia Cates Colella, "The Creation, Care and Feeding of the Leviathan: Who and What Makes Government Grow," *Intergovernmental Perspective* (Fall 1979), p. 9.

53. Aaron Wildavsky, "Bare Bones: Putting Flesh on the Skeleton of American Federalism," in *The Future of Federalism in the 1980s* (Advisory Commission on Intergovernmental Relations, 1981), p. 79.

54. Peterson, *Price of Federalism*, p. 182.

55. John Kinkaid, "Devolution in the United States: Rhetoric and Reality," in Nicolaidis and Howse, *The Federal Vision*, p. 144.

56. Eliza Newlin Carney, "Power Grab," *National Journal*, April 11, 1998, p. 798.

57. Luther Gulick, "Reorganization of the States," *Civil Engineering* (August 1933), pp. 420–421.

58. David E. Osborne, *Laboratories of Democracy* (Harvard Business School Press, 1988), p. 363.

59. Dye, *American Federalism*, p. 199.

60. Richard A. Oppel and Christopher Drew, "States Planning Their Own Suits on Power Plants: Battle that E.P.A. Quit," *The New York Times*, November 9, 2003, p. Al; and Scott Richards and Yvette Hurt, "States Sue the Federal Environmental Agency," *Federations* 11 (November, 2003).

61. Edward Felsenthal, "Firms Ask Congress to Pass Uniform Rules," *Wall Street Journal*, May 10, 1993, p. B4.

62. John J. Dilulio Jr. and Donald F. Kettl, *Fine Print: The Contract with America, Devolution, and the Administrative Realities of American Federalism* (Brookings Institution Press, 1995), p. 60.

63. Kincaid, "Devolution in the United States," p. 148.

Chapter 3

1. Kavan Peterson, "50-State Rundown on Gay Marriage Laws," *Stateline* (February 25, 2004), available at www.stateline.org.

2. Temporary New York State Commission on Constitutional Revision, Effective Government Now for the New Century (Nelson A. Rockefeller Institute of Government, 1995).

3. Mario M. Cuomo, "Real Reform: It's Time for a People's State Constitutional Convention," *Rockefeller Institute Bulletin* (1993), pp. 41–46.

4. Richard Perez-Pena, "Voters Reject Constitutional Convention: Last-Minute Campaign Appears to Sway Ballot," *The New York Times*, November 5, 1997, p. Bl.

5. Michigan Department of State, Bureau of Elections, at www.sos.state.mi.us/law; and Arkansas Government Relations, at www.uark.edu/~govinfo/PAGES/History/del.html.

6. Gerald Benjamin, "The Functions of State Constitutions in a Federal System," papar presented at the American Political Science Association Round Table, Washington, D.C., 1984.

7. John Adams, quoted in Judith S. Kaye, "Federalism's Other Tier," *Constitution* 3 (Winter 1991), p. 50.

8. *Providence Journal*, July 7, 2000, as reported at www.projo.com.

9. G. Alan Tarr, *Understanding State Constitutions* (Princeton University Press, 2000), p. 47.

10. Donald S. Lutz, "Toward a Theory of Constitutional Amendment," in *Responding to Imperfection: The Theory and Practice of Constitutional Amendment*, ed. Sanford Levinson (Princeton University Press, 1995), pp. 237–274.

11. *The Book of the States, 2002–2003* (Council of State Governments, 2002), p. 3; John Kincaid, "State Constitutions in the Federal System," *Annals of the American Academy of Political and Social Science* 496 (March 1988), p. 14.

12. See Richard J. Ellis, *Democratic Delusions: The Initiative Process in America* (University Press of Kansas, 2003).

13. *Book of the States, 2002–2003*, p. 14.

14. Steve Geissinger, "Changing the Constitution Is a Powerful Government-Reform Tool Avoided by Officials," *Alameda Times-Star*, November 9, 2003, p. Cl.

15. Jack W. Strain, *An Outline of Oklahoma Government*, ed. Leroy Crozier and Carl F. Reherman (Bureau of Local Government Services, Department of Political Science, Central State University, 1984), p. 21.

16. South Dakota Constitution, Article XI, Section 8.

17. Alabama Constitution, Amendment 383 (1901).

18. Christopher W. Hammons, "State Constitutional Reform: Is It Necessary?" *Albany Law Review* 64 (2001), pp. 1328–1334.

19. Christopher W. Hammons, "Was James Madison Wrong? Rethinking the American Preference for Short, Framework-Oriented Constitutions," *American Political Science Review* 93 (December 1999), p. 838. See also ibid.

20. *Indiana* v. *Gerschoffer*, 763 N.E. 2d 960 (Ind., 2002).

21. *Anchorage Police Department Employees Association* v. *Anchorage*, 24 P.3d 547 (Alaska, 2001).

22. *American Academy of Pediatrics* v. *Lungren*, 490 P.2d 797 (Calif. 1997).

23. Kaye, "Federalism's Other Tier," p. 54.

24. See, e.g., Matthew Bosworth, *Courts as Catalysts: State Supreme Courts and Public School Finances Equity* (State University of New York Press, 2001); and Charles Lopeman, *The Activist Advocate: Policy Making in State Supreme Courts* (Praeger, 1999).

25. *Michigan* v. *Long*, 463 U.S. 1032 (1983); "Our Judicial Federalism," *Intergovernmental Perspective* 15 (Summer 1989), pp. 8–15; and William M. Wiecek, Some Protection of Personal Liberty: Remembering the Future, and Kermit L. Hall, "Mostly Anchor and Little Sail: The Evolution of American State Constitutions," in *Toward a Usable Past: Liberty Under State Constitutions*, eds. Paul Finkelman and Stephen E. Gottlieb (University of Georgia Press, 1991), pp. 371–417.

26. Deborah Baker, "Canvassing Board Certifies Amendment Election," *Santa Fe New Mexican* (October 14, 2003), at Al.

27. According to the *Book of the States, 2002–2003*, p. 11, in 1998–1999, of the 266 legislative proposed amendments in the 49 states that require submission to the voters for ratification, 210, or 78.8 percent, were adopted.

28. Tip H. Allen Jr., "The Enduring Traditions of the State Constitutions," in Dale Krane and Stephen D. Shaffer, *Mississippi Government and Politics: Modernizers Versus Traditionalists* (University of Nebraska Press, 1992), pp. XX–XXV.

29. *Book of the States, 2002–2003*, p. 14.

30. David B. Magleby, "Direct Legislation in the American States," in *Referendums Around the World: The Growing Use of Direct Democracy*, eds. David Butler and Austin Ranney (American Enterprise Institute Press, 1994), p. 225.

31. California Commission on Campaign Financing, *Democray by Initiative: A Summary of the Report and Recommendations of the California Commission on Campaign Financing* (Center for Responsive Government, 1992), p. 25.

32. *Amador Valley Joint Union High School District* v. *State Board of Equalization*, 22 Cal. 3d 208 (1978), quoted in Eugene C. Lee, "The Revision of California's Constitution," *CPS Brief: A Publication of the California Policy Seminar* 3 (April 1991), p. 1.

33. *Book of the States, 2002–2003*, p. 11. See also Magleby, "Direct Legislation," p. 251.

34. Tarr, *Understanding State Constitutions*, p. 158.

35. Ibid., pp. 160–61.

36. Gerald Benjamin and Thomas Gais, "Constitutional Conventionphobia," in *State Constitutions: Competing Perspectives*, eds. Burton C. Agata and Eric Lane (Hofstra Law and Policy Symposium, 1996), vol. 1, p. 69; and Tarr, *Understanding State Constitutions*, p. 25.

37. Caleb Nelson, "Majorities, Minorities, and the Meaning of Liberty: A Reevaluation of Scholarly Explanations for the Rise of the Elective Judiciary in Antebellum America," Yale Law School (1991), p. 51, elaborating the thesis of Gordon Wood, *The Creation of the American Republic, 1776–1787* (University of North Carolina Press, 1969), pp. 306–325.

38. Elder Witt, "State Supreme Courts: Tilting the Balance Toward Change," *Governing*, August 1988, p. 33.

39. G. Alan Tarr, Keynote Address, conference on State Constitutional Reform, May 4, 2000, at www. camlaw. rutgers.edu/statecon/keynote.html.

40. Lee, "Revision of California's Constitution," p. 7. See also Lutz, "Toward a Theory of Constitutional Amendment," pp. 355–370.

41. Re Jan Ruggiero, Director of Elections, Elections Division, Office of the Secretary of State, Providence, R.I., at www.state.ri.us.

42. Common Cause of Rhode Island, "Separation of Powers," at www.commoncauseri.org/news.

43. Cecil Morgan, "A New Constitution for Louisiana," *National Civic Review*, July 1974, pp. 343–356.

44. Tarr, *Understanding State Constitutions*, p. 143.

45. Beryl E. Pettus and Randall W. Bland, *Texas Government Today* (Dorsey Press, 1979), pp. 34–36. See also Janice C. May, "Texas Constitutional Revision and Laments," *National Civic Review*, February 1977, pp. 64–69.

46. Andre Henderson, "Selling a Constitution: California Desperately Needs a New Charter, That Doesn't Mean It Will Get One," *Governance*, December 1995, pp. 30–31.

47. B. Drummond Ayres Jr., "Alabama Governor Set for Tough Race," *The New York Times*, February 27, 2002, - p. A16.

48. Albert E. McKinley, "Two New Southern Constitutions," *Political Science Quarterly*, 18 (September 1903), pp. 480–511.

49. For more information, go to the Web site of the Alabama Citizens for Constitutional Reform at www.constitutionalreform.org.

50. *Montgomery Advertiser*, December 11, 2002, the Associated Press, "Constitution Work May Come in 2003," at www.montgomeryadvertiser.com.

51. Editorial, "Constitutional Count, House Sending Clear Message: People Can't Be Trusted," *The Birmingham News*, March 21, 2002, p. A20.

52. David White, "Constitution Could Lose Segregation Provisions," *The Birmingham News*, April 16, 2003, p. A1.

Chapter 4

1. John Mintz, "It's Not as Easy as 1-2-3; Problems Exist with Both Hands, Machine Counts," *The Washington Post*, November 19, 2000, p. A1.

2. See electionline.org. The Electionline project started in the wake of the election administration problems in the 2000 presidential election. Funded by the Pew Charitable Trusts, the project is a nonpartisan clearinghouse on election reform.

3. Katharine Q. Seelye, "Panel Suggests Election Changes That Let States Keep Control," *The New York Times*, February 5, 2001, p. A16.

4. John F. Bibby, *Politics, Parties, and Elections in America*, 5th ed. (Wadsworth, 2003).

5. Florida Department of State, at election.dos.state.fl.us.

6. www.electionline.org.

7. According to Todd Taylor, executive director, Utah Democratic party, these requirements are intended to promote gender equity; personal communication, November 18, 1998.

8. See Cornelius P. Cotter, James L. Gibson, John F. Bibby, and Robert J. Huckshorn, *Party Organizations in America* (Praeger, 1984).

9. Ronald E. Weber, ed., *American State and Local Politics: Directions for the 21st Century* (Chatham House, 1999), p. 174.

10. Federal Election Commission, "National Voter Registration Act Report, 2002" at www.fec.gov.

11. Benjamin Highton and Raymond E. Wolfinger, *Political Behavior*, vol. 20, no. 2. (June, 1998), pp. 94–97.

12. California Secretary of State, at www.ss.ca.gov/elections/ror_021902.htm.

13. Mary Clare Jalonick, "Utah GOP Floats a Salt Lake Split-Up," *Congressional Quarterly Weekly*, May 5, 2001, p. 1032.

14. Federal Election Commission, at www.fec.gov/pages/2000turnout/reg&to00.htm.

15. For a discussion of coordinated campaigns, see Paul Herrnson, "National Party Organizations and the Postreform Congress," in *The Postreform Congress*, ed. Roger Davidson (St. Martin's Press, 1992), pp. 65–67.

16. See Cotter et al., *Party Organizations in America*.

17. Richard Perez-Pena, "A Federal Soft-Money Ban Could Benefit State Parties," *The New York Times*, March 22, 2002, p. B6.

18. Richard A. Oppel Jr., "Election Panel Rebuffs Effort to Weaken 'Issue Ad' Limits," *The New York Times*, June 20, 2002, p. A1.

19. David B. Magleby, ed., *Financing the 2000 Elections* (Washington, D.C.: Brookings Institution Press), p. 223.
20. Ibid., p. 203.
21. David B. Magleby and J. Quin Monson., *The Last Hurrah* (Washington, D.C.: Brookings Institution Press), p. 5.
22. See Bruce E. Keith, David B. Magleby, Candice J. Nelson, Elizabeth Orr, Mark C. Westlye, and Raymond E. Wolfinger, *The Myth of the Independent Voter* (University of California Press, 1992), p. 52.
23. The Field Poll, "Voters Very Dissatisfied with State Budget Negotiations. Blame Davis and Both Parties in the Legislature. Three in Four Fear the State Is Seriously Off on the Wrong Track," at www.field.com/fieldpollonline/subscribers/RLS2074.pdf. 15 July 2003.
24. The Field Poll, "How Schwarzenegger's History and Characteristics Helps and Hurts Him in His Bid to Become Governor," at www.field.com/fieldpollonline/subscribers/RLS2083.pdf, 17 August 2003.
25. Jodi Wilgoren, "Gov. Ventura Says He Won't Seek Reelection," *The New York Times,* June 19, 2002, p. A14.
26. Lawrence McQuillan, "Democrat Wins Republican State," *USA Today,* January 7, 2002, at www.usatoday.com/news/politicselections/2002-11-06-sebelius_x.htm.
27. William H. Flanigan and Nancy H. Zingale, *Political Behavior of the American Electorate,* 8th ed. (CQ Press, 1994), p. 171.
28. See BetterCampaigns.org at www.bettercampaigns.org/standard/display.php?StoryID=10.
29. William Glaberson, "Fierce Campaigns Signal a New Era for State Courts," *The New York Times,* June 5, 2000, p. A1.
30. Willis D. Hawley, *Nonpartisan Elections and the Case for Party Politics* (Wiley, 1973), pp. 81–82. See also Brian F. Schaffner, Matthew Streb, and Gerald Wright, "Teams Without Uniforms: The Nonpartisan Ballot in State and Local Elections," *Political Research Quarterly* 54 (March 2001), pp. 7–30.
31. Susan Welch and Timothy Bledsoe, "The Partisan Consequences of Non-Partisan Elections and the Changing Nature of Urban Politics," *American Journal of Political Science,* vol. 30, no. 1 (February, 1986), pp. 128–139.
32. Election Data Services, at www.electiondataservices.com/home.htm.
33. Terrel L. Rhodes, *Republicans in the South: Voting for the State House, Voting for the White House* (Praeger, 2000), p. 88.
34. Harvey L. Schantz, "Sectionalism in Presidential Elections," in *American Presidential Elections: Process, Policy, and Political Change,* ed. Harvey L. Schantz (SUNY Press, 1996), pp. 106–107. See also Zell Miller, "The Democratic Party's Southern Problem," *The New York Times,* June 4, 2001, p. A17.
35. U.S. Bureau of the Census, *Statistical Abstract of the United States, 2001* (U.S. Government Printing Office, 2001), p. 26.
36. Raymond E. Wolfinger and Steven J. Rosenstone, *Who Votes?* (Yale University Press, 1980), p. 130.
37. Election Data Service, at www.electiondataservices.com/home.htm.
38. Ibid.
39. Ibid.
40. David B. Magleby, "Participation in Mail Ballot Elections," *Western Political Quarterly* 40 (March 1987), pp. 79–91.
41. Absentee ballots for all states are available from www.justvote.org.
42. Diane Morgan, Office of the Washington Secretary of State, personal communication, March 22, 1999.
43. Bruce E. Cain and Elisabeth R. Gerber, eds., *Voting at the Political Fault Line: California's Experiment with the Blanket Primary* (University of California Press, 2002), p. 341.
44. *California Democratic Party et al. v. Jones, Secretary of State of California, et al.,* 530 U.S. 567 (2000); and Linda Greenhouse, "Split Decisions: The Court Rules, America Changes," *The New York Times,* July 2, 2000, sec. 4, p. 1.
45. Malcolm E. Jewell and David M. Olson, *Political Parties and Elections in American States,* 3d ed. (Dorsey Press, 1988), p. 121; and Flanigan and Zingale, *Political Behavior of the American Electorate,* p. 195.
46. James I. Lengle, *Representation and Presidential Primaries: The Democratic Party in the Postreform Era* (Greenwood Press, 1981). For more on primary elections, see Larry M. Bartels, *Presidential Primaries and the Dynamics of Public Choice* (Princeton University Press, 1988); Jeane J. Kirkpatrick, *The New Presidential Elite: Men and Women in National Politics* (Basic Books, 1976); and Barbara Norander, "Ideological Representativeness of Presidential Primary Voters," *Journal of Politics* 51 (November 1989), pp. 977–992.
47. Federal Election Commission, at www.fec.gov.
48. Other "clean money" states are Vermont, Arizona, and Massachusetts. Edward Zuckerman, "Maine Campaign Reform: Were Voters 'Hoodwinked' by Outside Groups?" *Political Finance and Lobby Reporter,* December 24, 1996, pp. 1–4.
49. David B. Magleby, "Campaign Spending and Referendum Voting," paper presented at the annual meeting of the Western Political Science Association, Albuquerque, N.M., March 1994.
50. *Financing California's Statewide Ballot Measures: Receipts and Expenditures Through December 31, 1998* (California Secretary of State, 1998), p. 2.
51. David B. Magleby, *Direct Legislation: Voting on Ballot Propositions in the United States* (Johns Hopkins University Press, 1984), chaps. 7–9.
52. California Secretary of State Kevin Shelly, at www.ss.ca.gov/elections/elections_recall_faqs.htm#20.
53. U.S. Department of State, "Schwarzenegger Wins California Gubernatorial Vote," at www.usinfo.state.gov/dhr/Archive/2003/Oct/09-562246.html.
54. See Larry Gerston and Terry Christensen, *Recall: California's Political Earthquake* (M. E. Sharpe, 2004).
55. California Voter Foundation, at www.calvoter.org/voter/elections/archive/recall/index.html.

Chapter 5

1. For a useful look at Nebraska's unique legislature, see Jack Rodgers, Robert Sittig, and Susan Welch, "The Legislature," in *Nebraska Government and Politics,* ed. Robert D. Miewald (University of Nebraska Press, 1984), pp. 57–86.

2. Tom Birmingham, quoted in Karen Hansen, "Legislator Pay: Baseball It Ain't, *State Legislatures* (July–August 1997), p. 20.

3. Richard A. Clucas, "Exercising Control: The Power of State House Speakers," paper presented at the annual meeting of the Western Political Science Association, Los Angeles, March 1998. See also Malcolm E. Jewell and Marcia Lynn Whicker, *Legislative Leadership in the American States* (University of Michigan Press, 1997).

4. *The Book of the States, 2000–2001* (Council of State Governments, 2000), p. 46.

5. See James D. King, "Changes in Professionalism in U.S. State Legislatures," *Legislative Studies Quarterly* 15 (May 2000); pp. 327–343.

6. Alan Rosenthal, *Legislative Life: People, Process, and Performance in the States* (Harper & Row, 1981), pp. 112–113.

7. See Peverill Squire, "Uncontested Seats in State Legislative Elections," *Legislative Studies Quarterly* 35 (February 2000), pp. 131–146.

8. Alan Rosenthal, "The Legislative Unraveling of Institutional Fabric," in *The State of the States*, 3d ed., ed. Carl E. Van Horn (CQ Press, 1996), p. 118.

9. Gary F. Moncrief, Peverill Squire, and Malcolm E. Jewell, *Who Runs for the Legislature?* (Prentice Hall, 2000).

10. Frank Smallwood, *Free and Independent: The Initiation of a College Professor into State Politics* (Stephen Greene Press, 1976), p. 223.

11. *Book of the States, 2000–2001*, p. 70.

12. See Sue Thomas, *How Women Legislate* (Oxford University Press, 1994). See also Lesley Dahlkemper, "Growing Accustomed to Her Face," *State Legislatures*, July–August 1996, pp. 37–45, and Kathleen Dolan and Lynne Ford, "Change and Continuity Among Women State Legislators," *Political Research Quarterly*, vol. 50 (March 1997), pp. 137–151.

13. For fascinating comparative data, see *Inside the Legislative Process: A Comprehensive Survey by the American Society of Legislative Clerks and Secretaries* (National Council of State Legislatures, 1998).

14. Keith E. Hamm and Gary F. Moncrief, "Legislative Politics in the States," in Virginia Gray et al., *Politics in the American States*, 7th ed. (CQ Press, 1999), p. 184.

15. Lobbying strategies are outlined in Jay Michael and Dan Walters, *The Third House: Lobbyists, Power, and Money in Sacramento*, (Berkeley Public Policy Press, 2001). Other lobbying realities are discussed in Loftus, *Art of Legislative Politics*, chap. 10, and Alan Rosenthal, *Drawing the Line: Legislative Ethics in the States* (University of Nebraska Press, 1996).

16. Thomas Frank, "Ex-Legislators Use Contacts," *The Denver Post*, July 5, 1996, p. 16A. See also Loftus, *Art of Legislative Politics*.

17. Samuel K. Gove and James D. Nowlan, *Illinois Politics and Government* (University of Nebraska Press, 1996), p. 53.

18. Joel A. Thompson and Gary F. Moncrief, eds., *Campaign Finance in State Legislative Elections* (CQ Press, 1998).

19. Frank Smallwood, *Free and Independent* (S. Greene Press, 1976) p. 165. See also Alan Rosenthal, *The Third House: Lobbyists and Lobbying in the States*, 2d ed. (CQ Press, 2001); but also "State Legislators Mix Public and Private Business, Study Says," *The New York Times*, May 21, 2000, p. 26.

20. Winnie Hu, "Lobbying Code Puts an End to Lawmakers' Gravy Train," *The New York Times*, April 11, 2000, pp. A1, A27. See also Christopher Swope, "Winning Without Food and Cigars," *Governing*, November 2000, pp. 40–46.

21. Charles Mahtesian, "The Ethics Backlash," *Governing*, October 1999, pp. 39–41.

22. John E. Brandl, *Money and Good Intentions Are Not Enough: Or, Why a Liberal Democrat Thinks States Need Both Competition and Community* (Brookings Institution Press, 1998), p. 58.

23. Quoted in David Ray, "The Sources of Voting Cues in Three State Legislatures," *Journal of Politics*, Vol. 44 (November 1982), p. 1081. See also John J. Kennedy, *The Contemporary Pennsylvania Legislature* (University Press of America, 1999).

24. Karl T. Kurtz, "The Old Statehouse, She Ain't What She Used to Be," *State Legislatures*, January 1994, pp. 20–23. See also Alan Rosenthal, *The Decline of Representative Democracy* (CQ Press, 1998).

25. Alan Rosenthal, "The Legislative Institution: In Transition and at Risk," in *The State of the States*, 2d ed., ed. Carl E. Van Horn (CQ Press, 1993), pp. 136–137. See also Alan Ehrenhalt, "An Embattled Institution," *Governing*, January 1992, pp. 28–33; and Karen Hansen, "Our Beleaguered Institution," *State Legislatures*, January 1994, pp. 12–17.

26. Rosenthal, "The Legislative Institution," p. 144.

27. See, for example, Christopher Conte, "Laptop Legislatures," *Governing*, November 1999, p. 36.

28. Carrie Koch, "A Room for a View," *State Legislatures*, May 1997, pp. 32–34.

29. Bette H. Dillehay, "E-Government as Virginia's Vision," in *Spectrum: The Journal of State Government* (Winter 2002), pp. 24–25.

30. Rich Jones, "The State Legislatures," in *The Book of the States, 1992–1993* (Council of State Governments, 1992), p. 125.

31. Michael Janofsky, "Idaho Legislature Repeals Term Limit Law, Undoing Voter Approved Measure," *The New York Times*, February 2, 2002, p. A11. See also Wayne Hoffman, "The Battle over Term Limits," *State Legislatures*, May 2002, pp. 25–29.

32. Janofsky, "Idaho Legislature," p. A11.

33. See Daniel B. Wood, "The Term-Limit Movement of the '90s Stalls," *Christian Science Monitor*, April 27, 2004, p. A1.

34. See John M. Carey, Richard G. Niemi, and Lynda W. Powell, *Term Limits in the State Legislatures* (University of Michigan Press, 2000).

35. Jack Quinn et al., "Redrawing the Districts, Changing the Rules," *Washington Post National Weekly Edition*, April 1, 1991, p. 23.

36. Gordon E. Baker, *The Reapportionment Revolution* (Random House, 1966), p. 47.

37. *Baker* v. *Carr*, 369 U.S. 186 (1962).

38. *Wesberry* v. *Sanders*, 376 U.S. 1 (1964).

39. *Reynolds* v. *Sims*, 377 U.S. 533 (1964).

40. *Brown* v. *Thomson*, 103 S.Ct. 2690 (1983).

41. *Shaw* v. *Reno*, 509 U.S. 630 (1993); *Abrams* v. *Johnson*, 138 L.Ed. 2d 285 (1997). For a summary of state and federal judicial cases on drawing legislative district

lines, see *Redistricting Case Summaries from the '90s* (National Conference of State Legislatures, 1998); see also Ronald E. Weber, "Emerging Trends in State Legislative Redistricting," *Spectrum: The Journal of State Government,* Vol. 75 (Winter 2002), pp. 13–15; additional updates can be found at the National Conference of State Legislature Web site, www.ncsl.org.

42. Samuel Issacharoff, "In Real Elections, There Ought to Be Competition," *The New York Times,* February 16, 2002, p. A31.

43. Ibid.

44. See Spencer C. Olin, *California's Prodigal Sons: Hiram Johnson and the Progressives, 1911–1917* (University of California Press, 1968).

45. Alan Greenblatt, "Total Recall," *Governing,* September, 2003, p. 21.

46. Editorial, *The New York Times,* October 29, 1993, p. A16.

47. See National Conference of State Legislatures, "Voters Decide High-Profile Issues on State Ballots," November 3, 2004.

48. See, for example, Eugene C. Lee, "The Initiative Boom: An Excess of Democracy," in *Governing California,* eds. Gerald C. Lubenow and Bruce E. Cain (Institute of Governmental Studies, University of California, 1997), pp. 113–136. See also David S. Broder, *Democracy Derailed: Initiative Campaigns and the Power of Money* (Harcourt, 2000). But see Zolton L. Hajnul, Elisabeth R. Gerber, and Hugh Louch, "Minorities and Direct Legislation: Evidence from California Ballot Proposition Elections," paper presented at the annual meeting of the American Political Science Association, Washington, D.C., September 1–3, 2000. See also Elisabeth Gerber, *The Populist Paradox* (Princeton University Press, 1999).

49. See Peter Schrag, *Paradise Lost: California's Experience, America's Future* (New Press, 1998). See also the decidedly negative appraisal offered by Richard Ellis, *Democratic Delusions: The Initiative Process in America* (University Press of Kansas, 2002).

50. David B. Magleby and Kelly D. Paterson, "Consultants and Direct Democracy," *PS: Political Science and Politics* 31 (June 1998), pp. 160–161. See also Broder, *Democracy Derailed.*

51. David B. Magleby, "Ballot Initiatives and Intergovernmental Relations," paper presented at the annual meeting of the Western Political Science Association, Los Angeles, March 1998, p. 2.

52. Ibid., p. 13.

53. Thomas E. Cronin, *Direct Democracy: The Politics of the Initiative, Referendum, and Recall* (Harvard University Press, 1989).

54. Michael G. Hagen and Edward L. Lascher Jr., "Public Opinion About Ballot Initiatives," paper presented at the annual meeting of the American Political Science Association, Boston, September 3–6, 1998.

Chapter 6

1. See Thad L. Beyle, "Enhancing Executive Leadership in the States," *State and Local Government Review* (Winter 1995), pp. 18–35, and Thad L. Beyle, "The Governors," in *Politics in the American States: A Comparative Analysis,* 7th ed., eds. Virginia Gray, Russell Hanson, and Herbert Jacob (CQ Press, 1999), pp. 191–231.

2. Lamar Alexander, *Steps Along the Way: A Governor's Scrapbook* (Nelson, 1986), p. 112. Similar views can be found in former Vermont Governor Madeleine M. Kunin's memoir, *Living a Political Life* (Vintage, 1995).

3. See Earl H. Fry, *The Expanding Role of State and Local Governments in U.S. Foreign Policy* (Council on Foreign Relations Press, 1998). See also, for example, Alan Johnson, "Taft Shows He's Up to the Job on Foreign Grounds," *Columbia Dispatch,* February 14, 2000.

4. *The Book of the States, 1998–1999* (Council of State Governments, 1998), p. xxiii.

5. Ibid., tab. 2.3, p. 18.

6. This story is adapted from Robert S. McElvaine, *Mario Cuomo: A Biography* (Scribner, 1988), pp. 337–338. See also the assessment of Governor Pete Wilson's turbulent first years as governor of California in Robert Reinhold, "The Curse of the Statehouse," *New York Times Magazine,* May 3, 1992, pp. 27–28, 54, 58–59.

7. Thad L. Beyle, "Governors," *The Book of the States, 2002* (Council of State Governments, 2002), p. 135.

8. Charlie LeDuff, "The California Recall: The Governor-Elect," *The New York Times,* October 9, 2003, p. A33.

9. James M. Perry, "Virginia's New Governor Joins a GOP Trend," *The Wall Street Journal* February 11, 1998, p. A24.

10. Richard F. Winters, "The Politics of Taxing and Spending," in *Politics in the American States,* ed. Gray et al., p. 329.

11. Fred Branfman and Nancy Stefanik, "Who Says Raising Taxes Is Political Suicide?" *Washington Post National Weekly Edition,* February 13, 1989, p. 24. See also the excellent case studies of governors in Michigan, Massachusetts, Pennsylvania, Arizona, and elsewhere who pushed through economic development programs in the 1980s, in David Osborne, *Laboratories of Democracy: A New Breed of Governor Creates Models for National Growth* (Harvard Business School Press, 1988).

12. In some cases, a governor's style and strategy alienate legislators. See, for example, Charles Mahtesian's analysis of Minnesota's Jesse Ventura, "Can He Govern?" *Governing,* May 2000, pp. 36–42. In contrast, Governor Bruce Babbitt worked effectively even with a legislature controlled by the opposition party. See David R. Berman, *Arizona Politics and Government* (University of Nebraska Press, 1998), pp. 116–117.

13. For a lighthearted commentary by a member of Governor Pete Wilson's Electronic Commerce Advisory Council, see Stewart Alsop, "Helping the Governor Figure Out E-Commerce," *Fortune,* June 8, 1998, p. 269.

14. National Conference of State Legislatures, news release, April 7, 2004, www.ncsl.org/programs/press/2004/pr040407.htm, accessed on April 27, 2004.

15. Kathleen Gray, "Granholm Stars in Her Own 'Kill Bill,'" *Detroit Free Press,* April 26, 2004, p. A1.

16. Cited in a profile of New York in *Governing,* February 1999, p. 66.

17. Thad L. Beyle, "Being Governor," in *The State of the States,* 3d ed., ed. Carl E. Van Horn (CQ Press, 1996), p. 89. See also Beyle, "The Governors."

18. But see Governor Tommy Thompson's defense of using frequent vetoes, *Power to the People: An American State at Work* (HarperCollins, 1996), and the view of one of his main critics in the Wisconsin legislature, Tom Loftus, *The Art of Legislative Politics* (CQ Press, 1994), chap. 5. On the varied effectiveness of the line item veto as a tool for fiscal responsibility, see Glenn Abney and Thomas P. Lauth, "The Item Veto and Fiscal Responsibility," *Journal of Politics*, vol. 59 (August 1997), pp. 882–892. On how a governor's rash use of the line item veto can infuriate legislators, see Mahtesian, "Can He Govern?" p. 40.

19. Ronald Smothers, "Mississippi Governor Bans Same-Sex Marriages," *The New York Times*, August 24, 1996, p. A6.

20. Katie Zezima, "Obey Same-Sex Marriage Law, Officials Told," *The New York Times*, April 25, 2004, p. A15.

21. *Perpich et al.* v. *Department of Defense*, 110 L.Ed. 312 (1990).

22. Kathleen Hunter, "Guard Deployments Spark State Security Concerns," Stateline.org, Tuesday, April 27, 2004, p. 1.

23. For background on this controversy, see Jonathan Alter, "The Death Penalty on Trial," *Newsweek*, June 12, 2000, pp. 26–34.

24. "Governor Ryan's Brave Example," *The New York Times*, July 3, 2000, p. A20. See also Judy Keen, "Death Penalty Issue Looms over Bush Campaign," *USA Today*, June 16, 2000, p. 17A.

25. The entire Ryan Commission report is available online at www.idoc.state.il.us/ccp/. See also Francis Clines, "Death Penalty Is Suspended in Maryland," *The New York Times*, May 10, 2002, p. A16.

26. For a scholarly analysis of the role political parties play in nominating and assisting governors, see Sarah McCally, *The Governor as Party Leader: Campaigning and Governing* (University of Michigan Press, 1998).

27. Beyle, "The Governors," p. 230.

28. Sarah F. Liebschutz et al., *New York Politics and Government* (University of Nebraska Press, 1998), p. 93.

29. Thomas Hardy, "The 'Weak' Governor," in *Mississippi Government and Politics*, eds. Dale Krane and Stephen Shaffer (University of Nebraska Press, 1992), p. 152.

30. See, for example, how hard it is for a governor to control the economic fortunes of a state, especially during a recession, in Paul Brace, *State Government and Economic Performance* (Johns Hopkins University Press, 1993).

31. *State Legislatures*, June 2000, p. 7.

32. Kunin, *Living a Political Life*, p. 382.

33. Beyle, "The Governors," pp. 224–226.

34. Thomas H. Kean, quoted in Barbara Salmore and Stephen Salmore, *New Jersey Politics and Government* (University of Nebraska Press, 1998), p. 136.

35. Jesse Ventura, *I Ain't Got Time to Bleed* (Signet Press, 2000), pp. 296–297.

36. Beyle, "The Governors," pp. 224–226.

37. Alan Ehrenhalt, "Reinventing Government in the Unlikeliest Place," *Governing*, August 1993, pp. 7–8.

38. Richard C. Elling, "Bureaucracy: Maligned Yet Essential," in *Politics in the American States: A Comparative Analysis*, 6th ed., eds. Virginia Gray and Herbert Jacob (CQ Press, 1996), p. 308.

39. Jonathan Walters, "Fad Mad," *Governing*, vol. 9, September 1996, p. 49.

40. Beyle, "Being Governor," p. 106.

41. See the discussion of Governor George W. Bush and his relationship with his lieutenant governor in Jonathan Walters, "The Taming of Texas," *Governing*, July 1998, p. 20. See also "The Future of the Texas Lieutenant Governor," *Comparative State Politics*, October 1995, pp. 21–24.

42. But see Charles N. Wheeler III, "Why Illinois Still Needs Lieutenant Governor's Position," *Illinois Issues*, September 1994, pp. 6–7.

43. On the recent fate of attorneys general who have aspired to become governors, see Charles Mahtesian, "Blocked Path to the Big Job," *Governing*, March 1996, p. 47.

44. Attorney General Bob Butterworth, at www.legal.firn.edu.

45. Office of the Attorney General, State of California, at www.caag.state.ca.us.

46. Professor Thad L. Beyle at the University of North Carolina at Chapel Hill tracks state polls on governors' job performances and finds that Democratic, Republican, and Independent governors alike all averaged about 60 percent public approval in the 1990s.

47. Alexander, *Steps Along the Way*, p. 141.

48. Thomas H. Kean, *The Politics of Inclusion* (Free Press, 1988), p. 248.

49. Scott Matheson with James Edwin Kee, *Out of Balance* (Peregrine Smith Books, 1986), p. 186. See also the reflections of another popular western governor in Cecil Andrus and Joel Connelly, *Cecil Andrus: Politics Western Style* (Sasquatch Books, 1998).

Chapter 7

1. National Center for State Courts, *Overview of State Trial Court Caseloads* (National Center for State Courts, 2001), p. 13.

2. See Mark S. Hurwitz and Drew Noble Lanier, "Women and Minorites on State and Federal Appellate Benches," *Judicature* 85 (September–October 2001), p. 84; and Chris W. Bonneau, "The Composition of State Supreme Courts," *Judicature* 85 (July–August 2001), p. 26.

3. See Michael Solimine and James Walker, *Respecting State Courts: The Inevitability of Judicial Federalism* (Greenwood Press, 2000); and Matthew Bosworth, *Courts as Catalysts: State Supreme Courts and Public School Finance Equity* (State University of New York Press, 2001).

4. The Supreme Court upheld these laws in *Ewing* v. *California*, 538 U.S. 11 (2003).

5. Lynn Mather, "Policy Making in State Trial Courts," in *The American Courts: A Critical Assessment*, eds. John B. Gates and Charles A. Johnson (CQ Press, 1991), pp. 119–157.

6. Henry R. Glick, "Policy Making and State Supreme Courts," in ibid., pp. 87–88.

7. Patrick Schmidt and Paul Martin, "To the Internet and Beyond: State Supreme Courts on the World Wide Web," *Judicature* 84 (May–June 2001), pp. 314–325.

8. Robert F. Williams, "In the Supreme Court's Shadow: Legitimacy of State Rejection of Supreme Court

Reasoning and Results," *South Carolina Law Review* 56 (Spring 1984), p. 353.

9. Harry P. Stumpf and John H. Culver, *The Politics of State Courts* (Longman, 1992), pp. 8–11.

10. Hans A. Linde, "Observations of a State Court Judge," in *Judges and Legislators: Toward Institutional Comity*, ed. Robert A. Katzmann (Brookings Institution Press, 1988), p. 118.

11. Peter J. Galie, "The Other Supreme Courts: Judicial Activism Among State Supreme Courts," *Syracuse Law Review* 33 (1982), pp. 731–793.

12. Philip L. Dubois, "State Trial Court Appointments: Does the Governor Make a Difference?" *Judicature* 68 (June–July 1985), pp. 20–21.

13. Charles H. Sheldon and Nicholas P. Lovrich, Jr., "State Judicial Recruitment," in *The American Courts*, pp. 172–173.

14. See American Judicature Society at www.ais.org/is/judicialselectioncharts.pdf.

15. Thurgood Marshall, in *Renne* v. *Geary*, 501 U.S. 312 (1991).

16. *Republican Party of Minnesota* v. *White*, 536 U.S. 765 (2002).

17. William Glaberson, "Court Rulings Curb Efforts to Rein in Judicial Races," *The New York Times*, October 7, 2000, p. A8.

18. Roy A. Schotland, "Financing Judicial Elections," in *Financing the 2000 Elections*, ed. David B. Magleby (Brookings Institution Press, 2002), p. 103.

19. "Judges Say Political Influence Threatens Independence of Judiciary," *Press and Dakotan*, at www.pressandakotan.com/stories/101797/judges.html.

20. Schotland, "Financing Judicial Elections."

21. Michael Scherer, "The Making of the Corporate Judiciary," *Mother Jones*, November 2003, p. 72.

22. See Justice at Stake Campaign, the Brennan Center for Justice at New York University Law School and the National Institute on Money in State Politics, *The New Politics of Judicial Elections* (Justice at Stake Campaign, 2001); and American Bar Association, Standing Committee on Judicial Independence, *Public Financing of Judicial Campaigns: Report of the Commission on Public Financing of Judicial Campaigns* (American Bar Association, 2002).

23. *Wells* v. *Edwards*, 409 U.S. 1095 (1973).

24. *Chisom* v. *Roemer*, 501 U.S. 400 (1991); *Houston Lawyers' Association v. Texas Attorney General*, 501 U.S. 419 (1991). See also Tracy Thompson, "The New Front in the Battle for Civil Rights: Judgeships," *Washington Post National Weekly Edition*, December 18, 1989, p. 34.

25. J. W. Peltason, *The Missouri Plan for the Selection of Judges* (University of Missouri Studies, 1945). The plan was previously known as the Nonpartisan Plan for the Selection of Judges or the Kales Plan until called the Missouri Plan by this monograph.

26. Beth M. Henschen, Robert Moog, and Steven Davis, "Judicial Nominating Commissioners: A National Profile," *Judicature* 73 (April–May 1990), pp. 328–334.

27. Philip L. Dubois, "The Politics of Innovation in State Courts: The Merit Plan of Judicial Selection," *Publius* 20 (Winter 1990), p. 40.

28. Warren K. Hall and Larry T. Aspin, "What Twenty Years of Judicial Retention Elections Have Told Us," *Judicature* 70 (April–May 1987), pp. 340–347; Susan B. Caron and Larry C. Berkson, *Judicial Retention Elections in the United States* (American Judicature Society, 1980).

29. Larry T. Aspin, "Trends in Judicial Retention Elections, 1964–1968," *Judicature* 83 (September–October 1999), p. 79; "Evaluating the Performance of Judges Standing for Retention," *Judicature* 79 (January–February 1996), pp. 190–195.

30. Traciel Reid, "The Politicization of Retention Elections," *Judicature* 83 (September–October 1999), p. 68.

31. Thomas E. Cronin and Robert D. Loevy, *Colorado Politics and Government* (University of Nebraska Press, 1993), pp. 251–253.

32. "The Need for Judicial Performance Evaluations for Retention Elections," *Judicature* 75 (October–November 1991), p. 124.

33. Henry Weinstein, "Forum Airs Questions of Jurist Independence," *The Los Angeles Times*, November 22, 1998, p. A18.

34. Anthony Champagne and Greta Thielemann, "Awareness of Trial Court Judges," *Judicature* 74 (February–March 1991), p. 276.

35. Jeffrey Shaman, Steven Lubet, and James Alfini, *Judicial Conduct and Ethics*, 3d ed. (Lexis, 2000), sec. 15.07.

36. Jolanta Juskiewicz Perlstein and Nathan Goldman, "Judicial Disciplinary Commissions: A New Approach to the Discipline and Removal of State Judges," in *The Analysis of Judicial Reform*, ed. Phil Dubois (Lexington Books, 1982), pp. 93–106.

37. Franklin M. Zweig et al., "Securing the Future for America's State Courts," *Judicature* 73 (April–May 1990), pp. 297–298.

38. Beverly Blair Cook, "Women Judges in the Opportunity Structure," in *Women, the Courts, and Equality*, eds. Laura L. Crites and Winfred L. Hepperle (Sage, 1987), pp. 143–171.

39. *Burch* v. *Louisiana*, 441 U.S. 130 (1979); *Ballew* v. *Georgia*, 435 U.S. 223 (1978). See Reid Hastie, Steven D. Penrod, and Nancy Pennington, *Inside the Jury* (Harvard University Press, 1983), for a study showing that nonunanimous verdicts are more likely to bring convictions than those requiring unanimity. Federal courts often use juries of fewer than 12 for civil cases. For federal criminal trials, the Supreme Court still requires both the common law jury of 12 and unanimous verdicts.

40. Robert H. Jackson, quoted in Jack M. Kress, "Progress and Prosecution," *Annals of the American Academy of Political and Social Science* (January 1976), p. 100.

41. William K. Muir, *Police: Streetcorner Politicians* (University of Chicago Press, 1977).

42. Charles E. Silberman, *Criminal Violence, Criminal Justice* (Random House, 1978), p. 303.

43. Jay Livingston, *Crime and Criminology* (Prentice Hall, 1992), p. 474.

44. Silberman, *Criminal Violence*, p. 218. See also David Cole, *No Equal Justice: Race and Class in the American Criminal Justice System* (New Press, 1999).

45. *South Carolina* v. *Gathers*, 490 U.S. 805 (1989).

46. Thomas M. Uhlman and N. Darlene Walker, "A Plea Is No Bargain: The Impact of Case Disposition on

Sentencing," *Social Science Quarterly* 60 (September 1979), pp. 218–234. See also Malcolm M. Feeley, *The Process Is the Punishment* (Russell Sage, 1979).

47. Thomas Church, Jr., "Plea Bargains, Concessions and the Courts: Analysis of a Quasi-Experiment," *Law and Society Review* 14 (Spring 1976), p. 400. For a contrary view, see National Advisory Commission on Criminal Justice Standards and Goals, *Report of the Task Force* (U.S. Government Printing Office, 1979).

48. Church, "Plea Bargains," p. 400.

49. Jonathan D. Casper, *American Criminal Justice: The Defendant's Perspective* (Prentice Hall, 1972), pp. 52–53. Abraham S. Goldstein, *The Passive Judiciary: Prosecutorial Discretion and the Guilty Plea* (Louisiana State University Press, 1981), is critical of judges for not supervising plea bargains more actively.

50. *Santobello* v. *New York*, 404 U.S. 257 (1971).

51. Edward Barrett, "The Adversary Proceeding and the Judicial Process," lectures to the National College of State Trial Judges, quoted in Lynn M. Mather, "Some Determinants of the Method of Case Disposition: Decision-Making by Public Defenders in Los Angeles," *Law and Society Review* 12 (Winter 1974), pp. 187–188.

52. Henry N. Pontell, *A Capacity to Punish* (Indiana University Press, 1985).

53. Lee Sechrest, Susan O. White, and Elizabeth D. Brown, eds., *The Rehabilitation of Criminal Offenders: Problems and Prospects* (National Academy of Sciences, 1979), pp. 3–6.

54. John Hagan and Kristin Bumiler, "Making Sense of Sentencing: A Review and Critique of Sentencing Research," in *Research on Sentencing*, eds. Alfred Blumstein et al. (National Academy Press, 1983), vol. 2; Susan Welch, Michael Combs, and John Gruhl, "Do Black Judges Make a Difference?" *American Journal of Political Science* 32 (February 1988), pp. 126–135.

55. William B. Eldridge, "Shifting Views of the Sentencing Functions," *Annals of the American Academy of Political and Social Science* (July 1982), pp. 104–111.

56. Bureau of Justice Statistics, "The Nation's Prison Population Growth Rate Slows," press release, August 9, 2000.

57. Eric Schlosser, "The Prison-Industrial Complex," *Atlantic*, December 1998, p. 52.

58. Barbara Fink, "Opening the Door on Community Corrections," *State Legislatures*, September 1984, pp. 24–31.

59. Gary Enos, "Despite New Technology, Home Confinement Faces Risks, Public Opposition," *City and State*, May 21, 1990, p. 14.

60. Quoted in Associated Press, "ABA 'Public Jurist' Considers Reforms in Legal System," December 1993.

Chapter 8

1. Peter Dreier, John Mollenkopf, and Todd Swanstrom, *Place Matters: Metropolitics for the Twenty-first Century* (University Press of Kansas, 2001), p. 21.

2. Jack Fleer, *North Carolina Government and Politics* (University of Nebraska Press, 1994), p. 198.

3. *Hunter* v. *City of Pittsburgh*, 208 U.S. 161 (1907).

4. See Jacques Steinberg, "42 Failing Schools in Philadelphia to Be Privatized," *The New York Times*, April 18, 2002, p. A1.

5. Michelle Garcia, "N.Y. City Council Passes Anti-Patriot Act Measure," *The Washington Post*, February 5, 2004, p. A11.

6. U.S. Bureau of the Census, *Statistical Abstract of the United States, 2001* (U.S. Government Printing Office, 2001).

7. An excellent overview of counties is Donald C. Menzel, ed., *The American County: Frontiers of Knowledge* (University of Alabama Press, 1996).

8. Ellen Perlman, "Polite Tenacity," *Governing*, November 2000, pp. 34, 214.

9. For a history of suburban development, see Rosalyn Baxandall and Elizabeth Ewen, *Picture Windows: How the Suburbs Happened* (Basic Books, 2000).

10. See Paul G. Lewis, *Shaping Suburbia: How Political Institutions Organize Urban Development* (University of Pittsburgh Press, 1996).

11. Joel Garreau, *Edge City* (Doubleday, 1991).

12. For the views of three mayors on the good city, see Stephen Goldsmith, *The Twenty-First Century City* (Regnery, 1997); Daniel Kemmis, *The Good City and the Good Life* (Houghton Mifflin, 1995); and John O. Norquist, *The Wealth of Cities: Revitalizing the Centers of American Life* (Addison-Wesley, 1998).

13. *Rogers* v. *Lodge*, 458 U.S. 613 (1982); *Thornburg* v. *Gingles*, 478 U.S. 30 (1986).

14. For the experience of one mayor in a council-manager city, see the memoir by Cambridge, Massachusetts, Mayor Barbara Ackermann, *"You the Mayor?" The Education of a City Politician* (Auburn House, 1989).

15. See James H. Svara and Associates, *Facilitative Leadership in Local Government. Lessons from Successful Mayors and Chairpersons in the Council-Manager Form* (Jossey-Bass, 1994).

16. See Earl H. Fry, *The Expanding Role of State and Local Governments in U.S. Foreign Affairs* (Council on Foreign Relations, 1998), esp. chap. 4.

17. It is fascinating to examine how mayors of different cities view their roles and responsibilities. Excellent books about important mayors are Roger Biles, *Richard J. Daley: Politics, Race, and the Governing of Chicago* (Northern Illinois University Press, 1995); Adam Cohen and Elizabeth Taylor, *American Pharaoh: Mayor Richard J. Daley: His Battle for Chicago and the Nation* (Little, Brown, 2000); and Robert A. Dahl, *Who Governs? Democracy and Power in an American City* (Yale University Press, 1961), a classic study of Mayor Richard Lee of New Haven. See also two reflective books by mayors in medium-sized or smaller cities: Kemmis, *The Good City and the Good Life*; and Ackermann, *"You the Mayor?"*

18. Dennis R. Judd and Todd Swanstrom, *City Politics: Private Power and Public Policy*, 2d ed. (Longman, 1998), p. 7.

19. See, for example, the analysis of other groups such as the African Americans in Atlanta in Clarence N. Stone, *Regime Politics: Governing Atlanta, 1946–1988* (University Press of Kansas, 1989). See also Bryan D. Jones and Lynn W. Bachelor, *The Sustaining Hand: Community Leadership and Corporate Power*, 2d ed. (University Press of Kansas, 1993).

20. For suggestions on how to form community groups and effective alliances seeking progress in cities, see Michael

Briand, *Practical Politics: Five Principles for a Community That Works* (University of Illinois Press, 1999).

21. Judd and Swanstrom, *City Politics*, p. 7.

22. For greater detail, see U.S. Bureau of the Census, "Standards for Defining Metropolitan Areas," at www.census.gov.

23. U.S. Bureau of the Census, *Statistical Abstract of the United States, 2000* (U.S. Government Printing Office, 2000).

24. The legal constraints on Baltimore, for example, are outlined in David Rusk, *Baltimore Unbound: A Strategy for Regional Renewal* (Abell Foundation/Johns Hopkins University Press, 1996).

25. D'Vera Cohn, "A New Millennium for America's Cities," *Washington Post National Weekly Edition*, October 30, 2000, p. 34.

26. David Rusk, former mayor of Albuquerque, makes this case well in *Baltimore Unbound* and in *Cities Without Suburbs*, 2d ed. (Woodrow Wilson Center Press/Johns Hopkins University Press, 1995).

27. See Suzanne M. Leland and Kurt Thurmaier, eds., *Case Studies of City-County Consolidation* (M. E. Sharpe, 2004); and Jered B. Carr and Richard C. Feiock, eds., *City-County Consolidation and Its Alternatives* (M. E. Sharpe, 2004).

28. See Myron Orfield, *Metropolitics: A Regional Agenda for Community and Stability* (Brookings Institution Press, 1997); and Manuel Pastor, ed., *Regions That Work: How Cities and Suburbs Can Grow Together* (University of Minnesota Press, 2000).

29. See E. J. Dionne, Jr., ed., *Community Works: The Revival of Civil Society in America* (Brookings Institution Press, 1998).

30. See David L. Kirp, et al., *Our Town: Race, Housing, and the Soul of Suburbia* (Rutgers University Press, 1997); and Jonathan Harr, *A Civil Action* (Vintage, 1996).

31. See the recommendation often prescribed by a major proponent of regionalism, Neal R. Peirce, in Charles Mahtesian, "The Civic Therapist," *Governing*, September 1995, pp. 24–27. See also Dreier, Mollenkopf, and Swanstrom, *Place Matters*, ch. 7.

32. "The End of Urban Man? Care to Bet?" *The Economist*, December 31, 1999, pp. 25–26.

33. See the thoughtful recommendations in Robert J. Waste, *Independent Cities: Rethinking U.S. Urban Policy* (Oxford University Press, 1998). But also see Clarissa Rile Hayward, "The Difference States Make: Democracy, Identity, and the American City," *American Political Science Review* 97 (November 2003), p. 501.

Chapter 9

1. *Governing: State and Local Source Book* (Governing Magazine, 2004) p. 15.

2. See Gary Oldfield and Chungmei Lee, *Brown at 50: King's Dream or Plessy's Nightmare,* (The Harvard Civil Rights Project, 2004). Also see Gary Orfield, Susan E. Eaton, and the Harvard Project on School Desegregation, *Dismantling Desegregation: The Quiet Reversal of Brown* v. *Board of Education* (New Press, 1996).

3. National Commission on Excellence in Education, *A Nation at Risk: The Imperative for Educational Reform—An Open Letter to the American People* (U.S. Government Printing Office, 1983). Ernest L. Boyer, *High School: A Report on Secondary Education in America* (Harper & Row, 1983), based on observations of high schools, contains a detailed series of recommendations. See also the National Science Board Commission on Precollege Education, *Mathematics, Science, and Technology: Educating Americans for the 21st Century* (U.S. Government Printing Office, 1983), and Carnegie Forum on Education and the Economy, *A Nation Prepared: Teachers for the 21st Century* (Carnegie Forum, 1986).

4. James B. Steman and Wayne C. Riddle, *Goals 2000: Educate America Act Implementation Status and Issues* (Congressional Research Service, 1996), pp. 2–4.

5. Rochelle L. Stanfield, "Learning Curve," *National Journal*, July 3, 1993, pp. 1688–1691.

6. C. Eugene Steuerle, Van Doorn Ooms, George Peterson, and Robert D. Reischauer, eds., *Vouchers and the Provision of Public Services* (Brookings Institution Press, 2000). See also "Colorado Adopts Statewide School Vouchers," *State Legislatures*, July–August 2003, p. 7.

7. Terry M. Moe, "Private Vouchers," in *Private Vouchers*, ed. Terry M. Moe (Hoover Institution Press, 1996), p. 35. Yet see also John F. Witte, *The Market Approach to Education: An Analysis of America's First Voucher Program* (Princeton University Press, 1999).

8. William H. Rehnquist, quoted in Richard Rothstein, "Failed Schools? The Meaning Is Unclear," *The New York Times*, July 3, 2002, p. A14.

9. Colorado Adopts Statewide School Vouchers," *State Legislatures*, July–August, 2003, p. 7.

10. Greg Winter, "Florida Court Rules Against Religious School Vouchers," *The New York Times*, August 17, 2004, p. A15.

11. Elizabeth Kolbert, "Unchartered Territory," *New Yorker*, October 9, 2000, p. 36. For the example of charter schools being initiated in Rhode Island, see Maureen Moakley and Elmer Cornwell, *Rhode Island Politics and Government* (University of Nebraska Press, 2001), pp. 189–190.

12. See, for example, Lynn Rosellini, "Closing the Gap," *U.S. News*, March 22–29, 2004, pp. 87–88.

13. See Diana Jean Schemo, "Charter Schools Lagging Behind, U.S. Data Reveal," *The New York Times*, August 17, 2004, pp. A1, A16. See also Richard Lee Colvin, "What's Wrong With Our Schools?," *State Legislatures*, September, 2003, pp. 12–15.

14. Quoted in "Statewide Student Tests," *State Legislatures*, February 2004, p. 33. See also Dewayne Matthews, "No Child Left Behind: The Challenge of Implementation," *The Book of States* (Council of State Governments, 2004), pp. 493–496. See also, June Kronholz, "Bush's Education Law Gets an Incomplete," *The Wall Street Journal*, September 1, 2004, p. A6.

15. See Christine Walton and Julie Davis Bell, "New Ways to Fund Higher Ed," *State Legislatures*, December, 2003, pp. 28–31. See also John Buntin, "Setting Colleges Free," *Governing*, September, 2003, pp. 18–22.

16. See Alexander Russo, "Varsity Vouchers," *State Legislatures*, June 2004, p. 27.

17. Ed Lazere, "Welfare Balances After Three Years of TANF Block Grants," report, Center on Budget and Policy Priorities, January 12, 2000, p. 1.
18. R. Kent Weaver, *Ending Welfare as We Know It* (Brookings Institution Press, 2000).
19. See Tommy G. Thompson, *Power to the People: An American State at Work* (HarperCollins, 1996).
20. See Burt S. Barnow, Thomas Kaplan, and Robert Moffitt, eds., *Evaluating Comprehensive State Welfare Reforms* (Brookings Institution Press, 2000); Carol W. Weissert, ed., *Learning from Leaders: Welfare Reform Politics and Policy in Five Midwestern States* (Brookings Institution Press, 2000).
21. Peter Edelman, "The True Purpose of Welfare Reform," *The New York Times*, May 29, 2002, p. A21.
22. Robert Pear, "Study by Governors Calls Bush Welfare Plan Unworkable," *The New York Times*, April 4, 2002, p. A14.
23. See, for example, David Hage, *Reforming Welfare by Rewarding Work, One State's Successful Experiment* (University of Minnesota Press, 2004), and Countney Jarchow and Jack Tweedie, "Welfare and Wedding Vows," *State Legislatures*, April 2003, pp. 24–28.
24. See Katherine Barrett, Richard Greene, and Michele Mariani, "A Case of Neglect: Why Health Care Is Getting Worse, Even Though Medicine Is Getting Better," *Governing*, February, 2004, pp. 22–24. See also other articles in this edition of *Governing*.
25. Trinity D. Tomsie, "Managing Medicaid in Tough Times," *State Legislators*, June 2002, p. 13.
26. David S. Broder, "States in Fiscal Crises," *Washington Post National Weekly Edition*, May 27, 2002, p. 4.
27. Jodi Wilgoren, "New Terror Alert Brings No Change in States' Security," *The New York Times*, May 25, 2002, p. A11.
28. See Amy C. Hughes, "State Emergency Management: New Realities in a Homeland Security World," *The Book of States* (Council of State Governments, 2004), pp. 485–488.
29. Larry Morandi, "Growing Pains," *State Legislatures*, October–November 1998, pp. 24–28.
30. Neal Peirce, "Parisian Green: A Hint for Us," Washington Post Writers Group, at www.npeirce@citistates.com, June 2, 2002, p. 1.
31. See Robert B. Albritton, "Subsidies: Welfare and Transportation," in *Politics in the American States: A Comparative Analysis*, 7th ed., eds. Virginia Gray, Herbert Jacob, and Kenneth Vines (CQ Press, 1999), and E. J. Dionne, Jr., ed., *Community Works: The Revival of Civil Society in America* (Brookings Institution Press, 2000).
32. For a discussion of the evolution of environmental policy in a particularly interesting place, see Charles O. Jones, *Clean Air: The Policies and Politics of Pollution Control* (University of Pittsburgh Press, 1973).
33. Jacqueline Vaughn Switzer and Gary Bryner, *Environmental Politics*, 2d ed. (St. Martin's Press, 1998), pp. 64–66.
34. Jeff Dale, "Realistic Redevelopment," *State Legislatures*, February 1999, pp. 28–31.
35. Bruce A. Williams, "Economic Regulation and Environmental Protection," in *Politics in the American States*, eds. Gray et al. (CQ Press, 1996), pp. 478–515.
36. See Larry Morandi, "Clearing the Air," *State Legislatures*, February, 2004, pp. 30–31. And Jeffrey Ball, "Governors of 3 West Coast States Join to Combat Global Warming," *The Wall Street Journal*, September 22, 2003, p. A4.
37. See Garry Boulard, "The Great Hydrogen Hope," *State Legislatures*, February 2004, pp. 12–15.
38. Alan K. Ota, "Congress Clears Huge Transportation Bill, Restoring Cut-Off Funding to States," *Congressional Quarterly Weekly*, May 23, 1998, pp. 1385–1386.
39. But see Michele Mariani, "Transit's High-Tech Route," *Governing*, May, 2004, pp. 60–67; and Rob Gurwitt, "Connecting the Suburban Dots," *Governing*, October, 2003, pp. 36–40.
40. *The Book of the States, 2003* (Council of State Governments, 2003), p. 466.
41. Nancy M. Davis, "Politics and the Public Utilities Commissioner," *State Legislatures*, May 1985, p. 20. See also William T. Gormley, Jr., "Policy, Politics, and Public Utility Regulation," *American Journal of Political Science* 27 (February 1983), pp. 86–105.
42. See, for example, Rebecca Smith, "States Face Fights as Caps Expire on Electric Rates," *The Wall Street Journal*, August 17, 2004, p. 1 and p. 12.
43. Amy Wallace, "San Onofre Mitigation Plan Wins Approval," *The Los Angeles Times*, July 17, 1991, p. A3.
44. See Donald F. Kettl, "Federalism, Anyone?" *Governing*, February, 2004, p.14.

Chapter 10

1. U.S. Bureau of Labor Statistics, "Table 1: Employment by major industry division, 1992, 2002, and projected 2012 employment," www.bls.gov/news.release/ecopro.to1.htm, accessed on May 2, 2004.
2. Ibid., p. 350.
3. *Elrod* v. *Burns*, 427 U.S. 347 (1976).
4. U.S. Census Bureau, "Table 3: Union Affiliation of Employed Wage and Salary Workers by Occupation," News release, www.bls.gov/news.release/union2.t03.htm, accessed on May 3, 2004.
5. Werner Z. Hirsch, "Factors Important in Local Government's Privatization Decisions," *Urban Affairs Review*, 31 (November 1995), pp. 226–243.
6. Edwin Blackstone and Simon Hakim, "Private Ayes: A Tale of Four Cities: New York, Philadelphia, Indianapolis, and Phoenix," *American City and County* 112 (February 1997), pp. 4–8.
7. See Jonathan Walters, "Going Outside," *Governing*, May, 2004, pp. 7–15.
8. Stephen Goldsmith, *The Twenty-First Century City* (Regnery, 1997), p. 10.
9. See Reason Public Policy Institute, a pro-privatization think tank, at www.privatization.org.
10. John Shannon, "The Deregulation of Fiscal Federalism," in *The Changing Face of Fiscal Federalism*, eds. Thomas R. Swartz and John E. Peck (Sharpe, 1990), p. 31.
11. National Conference of State Legislatures, "State Budget Gaps Shrink, NCSL Survey Finds," news release, April 28, 2004, www.ncsl.org/programs/press/2004/040428.htm, accessed on May 3, 2004.

12. See Henry S. Wulf, "Trends in State Government Finances," in *Book of the States, 2002* (The Council of State Governments, 2002) pp. 269–277.

13. John Shannon, "The Deregulation of the American Federal System, 1789–1989," in *The Changing Face of Fiscal Federalism,* eds. Swartz and Peck, pp. 17–34.

14. Roy W. Bahl, Jr., "Changing Federalism: Trends and Interstate Variations," in ibid., p. 59.

15. *Book of the States, 2002,* p. 290.

16. For a recent discussion of state and local tax issues, see Katherine Barrett, Richard Greene, Michele Mariani, and Anya Sostek, "The Way We Tax: A 50-State Report," *Governing,* February, 2003, pp. 11–40.

17. For a brief history of the property tax, see Dennis Hale, "The Evaluation of the Property Tax: A Study of the Relation Between Public Finance and Political Theory," *Journal of Politics* 47 (May 1985), pp. 382–404. See also C. Lowell Harris, ed., *The Property Tax and Local Finance* (Academy of Political Science, 1983).

18. *Critical Issues in State-Local Fiscal Policy: A Guide to Local Option Taxes* (National Conference of State Legislatures, 1997), p 10. See also *Statistical Abstract of the United States, 2001* (U.S. Government Printing Office, 2001), pp. 278 ff.

19. See Roy Bahl, David L. Sjoquist, and W. Loren Williams, "School Finance Reform and Impact on Property Taxes," *Proceedings of the Eighty-Third Annual National Tax Association Conference, 1990* (National Tax Association, Tax Institute of America, 1991), pp. 163–171.

20. *Serrano v. Priest,* 5 Cal.3d 487, 96 Cal. Rptr. 601 (1971).

21. *San Antonio Independent School District v. Rodriquez,* 411 U.S. 1 (1973).

22. David L. Kirp, "New Hope for Failing Schools: State Courts Are Remedying the Shame of Inadequate Education Funding," *Nation,* June 1, 1998, p. 20. See also *Board of Education, Levittown, Etc. v. Nyquist,* 439 N.E.2d 359 (1982); *Washakie County School District Number One v. Herschler,* 606 Pac.2d 310 (1980); and *Edgewood Independent School District v. Kirby,* 34 Tex. Sup.Ct. J. 386 (1991).

23. J. Richard Aronson and John L. Hilley, *Financing State and Local Governments,* 4th ed. (Brookings Institution, 1986), p. 138. See also U.S. Advisory Commission on Intergovernmental Relations, *Property Tax Circuit-Breakers: Current Status and Policy Issues* (U.S.

Government Printing Office, 1975), and Steven D. Gold, "Circuit Breakers and Other Relief Measures," in *Property Tax and Local Finance,* ed. Harris, pp. 119–132.

24. David B. Magleby, *Direct Legislation: Voting on Ballot Propositions in the United States* (Johns Hopkins University Press, 1984), pp. 61–76.

25. *Survey of Legislative Fiscal Officers* (National Conference of State Legislatures, 1996); Mandy Rafool, NCSL tax specialist, personal communication, September 15, 1998.

26. Carl Hulse, "Senate Extends until 2007 Ban on Internet Access Tax," *The New York Times,* April 30, 2004, p. A-12.

27. Ken Park, *World Almanac and Book of Facts, 2002,* (World Almanac, 2001) p. 630.

28. Ernst & Young, "Global Online Retailing: A Special Report," p. 7, at www.ey.com.

29. James Popkin and Katia Hetter, "America's Gambling Craze," *U.S. News and World Report,* March 14, 1994, p. 43.

30. To find out more about lotteries go on the Web site of the Multi-State Lottery Association at www.musl.com or the North American Association of State and Provincial Lotteries at www.naspl.org. You may find more about the history of lotteries at www.scigames.com.

31. Kathryn A. Foster, *The Political Economy of Special-Purpose Government* (Georgetown University Press, 1997); Robert L. Bland and Wes Clarke, "Budgeting for Capital Improvements," in *Handbook of Government Budgeting,* ed. Roy T. Meyers (Jossey-Bass, 1999), pp. 653–677.

32. For a thorough discussion of issues related to intergovernmental competition in attracting business and related tax issues, see Robert L. Bland, *A Revenue Guide for Local Government* (International City Managers Association, 1989), chap. 9.

33. Charles Mahtesian, "The Stadium Trap," *Governing,* May 1998, p. 22.

34. See Mark Rosentraub, *Major League Losers: The Real Cost of Sports and Who's Paying for It* (Basic Books, 1997).

35. Sarah Lawrence and Jeremy Travis, *The New Landscape of Imprisonment: Mapping America's Prison Expansion* (Urban Institute, 2004), p. 14.

36. See "Grading the States, 2001," *Governing,* February, 2001.

INDEX